Boston's
Banner Years:
1965–2015

Boston's
Banner Years:
1965–2015

A Saga of Black Success

Melvin B. Miller, Editor

Archway Publishing books may be ordered through booksellers or by contacting:

Archway Publishing
1663 Liberty Drive
Bloomington, IN 47403
www.archwaypublishing.com
1 (888) 242-5904

Because of the dynamic nature of the Internet, any web addresses or links contained in this book may have changed since publication and may no longer be valid. The views expressed in this work are solely those of the author and do not necessarily reflect the views of the publisher, and the publisher hereby disclaims any responsibility for them.

Any people depicted in stock imagery provided by Getty Images are models, and such images are being used for illustrative purposes only. Certain stock imagery © Getty Images.

ISBN: 978-1-4808-6252-4 (sc)
ISBN: 978-1-4808-6251-7 (hc)
ISBN: 978-1-4808-6253-1 (e)

Library of Congress Control Number: 2018951114

Print information available on the last page.

Archway Publishing rev. date: 7/19/2018

Contents

Editor's Acknowledgments

Special appreciation to:

The Boston Foundation
Eastern Bank
OneUnited Bank

whose generosity made this book possible

And our gratitude to:
Howard Gotlieb Archival Research Center at Boston
University for maintaining the archives of the *Bay
State Banner* and assisting with this book project

The editor and all the writers and scholars working
on the book also thank Rachel Reardon, and Leslie
Crossley, our project savants, and the *Bay State
Banner* staff for their invaluable assistance

Introduction

Twenty cities in the United States have more African American residents than Boston, and each undoubtedly has an intriguing historic tale to tell. Yet we have chosen Boston as the place to record the efforts of blacks to assert their place in society. Since Boston is the birthplace of the republic, it is appropriate to review how its black population is prospering more than two centuries after the nation's founding. But there is also a personal reason—Boston is my hometown. Both of my parents were born in Boston.

My father, John Miller, was born on the north slope of Beacon Hill in 1896, the same year that the US Supreme Court decided in *Plessy v. Ferguson* that racial segregation was constitutional as long as the accommodations were "separate but equal." Like many Americans in those days, both of my father's parents were immigrants. His father was from Jamaica and his mother was Canadian. My mother's father, Ernest O'Banyoun, was born in 1884 in Allston, a section of Boston, and her mother came from South Carolina as a young girl.

As a longtime resident of Roxbury, a neighborhood of Boston, I have been privy to the significant elements of the community's history. As publisher and editor of the *Bay State Banner* since 1965 I have acquired substantial institutional memory of local events. For more than fifty years the *Bay State Banner* has been the newspaper of record for Boston's black community, and that makes the *Banner* specially qualified to publish the unique history of Boston's African Americans.

Over the years the *Banner* has had to spend substantial journalistic energy to counter flawed accounts of African Americans by the major media. Those stories easiest to rebut were based on alleged facts that are false. It was merely necessary to present the accurate record in order to prevail against them. But other more subtle inaccuracies were more difficult. For example, a common flaw of the mass media is the implication that all blacks adhere to one common point of view. They are all thought to be the same.

Sometimes that seems to be true when blacks present a united front in opposing racial discrimination. One objective of *Boston's Banner Years* is to provide a better awareness of the diverse cultures in what is generally called the black community. Some are ethnically based such as Cape Verdeans, Haitians, Ethiopians, and various other African nationalities. Some have separate languages that are spoken in addition to English. They also have special ethnic diets and various religious practices. In addition to those groups, there are Native Americans; Caribbean immigrants from Jamaica, Trinidad, and elsewhere; and black Yankees with multigenerational New England roots.

Such a diverse group, loosely defined as African American, would normally not be expected to agree on almost any issue. But since they share a genetic abundance of melanin, they are often viewed by the media as a united group. This assumption of cultural homogeneity is inaccurate, but it is not as damaging as other media distortions. Just think how unacceptable it would be for an analyst to assert that the culture of Italians was identical to that of the British and the French to the Germans, or the Iberians to the Scandinavians. They have multiple differences except that they are all white Europeans and have only a moderate amount of melanin.

The diversity of Boston's black residents was not a consideration at all in early years. While there has been a black presence in Boston since colonial times, the size of the population was small. In 1865 at the end of the Civil War, Boston was a relatively large city of 192,318, with only 2,348 black residents. Anthony W. Neal's chapter on the achievements of black residents in those early days is even more impressive when one considers that the population was so small.

Growth of the black population was gradual, and it reached only 23,679 by 1940, the period of my childhood. Blacks were then only 3.1 percent of Boston's population. That is hardly enough to establish a significant political bloc. Blacks had attained political office in earlier times because the Yankee philosophy was that everyone should contribute to public service. Citizens were expected to perform their duty of service and then return to their private professions. This policy is still observed in New Hampshire, where state representatives are paid only $200 for a two-year term. Compensation for public service was more generous in Massachusetts, and various ethnic groups understood the economic value of holding the power of political office.

For decades in the twentieth century, blacks were unable to retain the political involvement they previously enjoyed when their major home base was the north slope of Beacon Hill. When they moved to the South End and Roxbury, adjacent neighborhoods of Boston, blacks became a minority in their new voting districts. Brian O'Connor's chapter on blacks in politics provides a record of their political involvement and how outstanding members of the black community—Edward W. Brooke and Deval Patrick—rose to become US senator and state governor of Massachusetts.

By the time that Senator Ed Brooke emerged as a political power, Boston's black community had grown larger. As is often the case with larger groups, cultural rules of public engagement develop. The rules that define a culture are usually not written down and codified. They are simply common practices of behavior that most of the members of the group have come to accept. They often stem from the house rules of respected members of the community.

Scholars might call these rules of behavior the ethos or norms of the group. Because they are not formally adopted, it is difficult to establish precisely what they are. However, it is important to understand how or why such developments occurred. There is also the problem of determining whether I am describing accurately the aspect of Roxbury culture most familiar to me, which I refer to as middle-class-oriented values. Even so, it is easy to be influenced by nostalgia and the prism of selective memory. People seem to be forever connected to the place of their birth and the incidents of their youth, even more than they realize. It has not surprised me that many blacks have returned to their hometowns down South, although their families have had to flee their homes to escape Jim Crow.

The Family, and Then the Village

The values and practices that constitute the culture are usually acquired informally. One lesson I learned early from my father, a US Post Office administrator, was dignity. My father once took my brother Jack and me to a parade downtown. As we waited along the parade route in front of a hotel, guests in the rooms above began throwing coins out the window to those below. Without a second thought, Jack and I went after the coins. Before we could get too far, my father snatched up Jack in one hand and me in the other. He said sternly, "Millers do not grovel in the gutter for pennies."

That was my first lesson in learning that dignity is not for sale. He also made us understand at a young age that self-discipline is also necessary to maintain dignity. It was never permissible to run wild when dignified behavior was appropriate. He also made us understand that we could not maintain our own dignity by denying the right of dignity to others. It was not uncommon for blacks to be dignified despite the severe circumstances of their lives.

One aspect of this teaching was that among my contemporaries, I have never heard the hated n----- word used. Apparently, scores of others had also concluded that it was undignified to use the n----- word. Not surprisingly, another epithet rarely if ever used was to call someone "poor." We believed at that time that to be poor meant much more than having insufficient funds. It also meant that you were unwilling or incapable of providing for yourself and your family, at least at a modest level. That is certainly a state of mind that is lacking in dignity.

This attitude toward being poor, according to the black community's standard, is not the same as the disdain that creates political conservatives' reluctance to provide "entitlements." Racial discrimination has frequently created hard times for many blacks. It was common in the community for others to step up and help those who were having financial difficulties, but there is also the expectation that those being helped must take heart and do what they can to improve their situation. No one was wealthy, so it was always expensive to help others.

Back in the day, there was also an expectation that everyone, perhaps excluding family members and close friends, would be greeted formally. Men were called by their surname preceded by mister or an appropriate title. Women were always miss or missus and their surname. It was always unacceptable to address an adult, especially a senior citizen, in an informal manner. I used to wonder whether the fixation with such formality resulted from the insulting treatment of blacks by whites in the South.

The mass media seemed to endorse this attitude and have always tried to demean African Americans and rob them of their dignity. In cartoons and films, they have characterized them as stupid, fearful, and lazy, qualities to render them unworthy of respect. But my parents made us understand at a young age that this was a propaganda strategy of a group of whites who failed to understand that we are all members of the same human species. My father often said, "You don't let your opponents define you."

My parents were always opposed to pitting blacks against whites or fair-skinned blacks against their darker brothers. One day when an older neighbor was taking my brother Jack and me to grammar school, we told her with enthusiasm, "Lois, you are really black." She began crying and insisted that she would complain to our mother.

Jack and I were dumbfounded. We both thought that being black was a good thing. But we could not console, or understand, Lois. She rang the doorbell, and as soon as my mother opened the door, Lois blurted out, "Melvin and Jackie called me black." With consummate diplomacy my mother said, "I told you boys many times that it is impolite to comment about peoples' appearance." Lois seemed to be consoled, and that was the end of the incident.

In discussing the matter years later, my mother said that there was no way she would state there was a problem with being black. There was never any discussion in my house on skin color or one shade being preferential. Years later, there was a girl who looked like she was artistically carved from polished mahogany. Her name was Betsy, but we privately referred to her as "Black Beauty." She was definitely admired. In second grade when I refused to participate in reading *The Story of Little Black Sambo,* the teacher required me to bring a parent to school. I would not read when it was my turn because I thought the story was racially demeaning. So did my mother. She had the book withdrawn from public schools.

Back then, Roxbury was a racially mixed neighborhood. While it was rare for open race-based hostilities to arise, it was obvious that whites were moving out and blacks continued to move in. Conflicts often arose, however, in public schools. Sometimes teachers could precipitate problems because of their lack of racial sensitivity.

For example, my sixth-grade teacher, Miss Forsyth, organized a choral performance of students for an audience of parents. Unfortunately, she had included some slave songs on the program. When I refused to participate, she became angry and gave me a failing grade in music. I knew that Miss Forsyth, who was actually my neighbor, was simply insensitive to racial issues. She had no idea that it would be an abnegation of self-respect for an African American to sing "Shortnin' Bread."

There was always an awareness of respect, or its absence. Once some friends and I were playing ball in the street when Roland Hayes left a house where he was visiting a friend. Roland Hayes (1887–1977) was born in Curryville, Georgia, and became a world recognized lyric tenor who ultimately settled in Boston. At the sight of Mr. Hayes the game stopped, and all the boys, almost in unison, greeted him. What struck me at the time was that all my friends knew who Roland Hayes was, and they understood that he was deserving of special respect. They must have learned about him at home.

During my adolescent years there was a general interest in classical music. The Boston Public Schools had a good music program, which featured the classics. We also took pride in black musical achievement. Community residents once lined up to hear a piano concert by Philippa Schuyler, a black child prodigy from New York. As a new Boston Latin School student, I was impressed that Buckner Gamby, a black upperclassman, was the most talented classical pianist in Boston's most prestigious public school. I played cello in the Boston Junior Symphony Orchestra, but Latin School's academic load induced me to hit the books and leave my cello in the closet. However, there was a continuing interest in classical music in the black community. Everyone was proud of Eugene Walcott, the city's best violinist among my contemporaries. He later became better known as Minister Louis Farrakhan of the Nation of Islam.

Young boys are often raucous, but they were nonetheless expected to be respectful of women. While boys could settle disputes with fisticuffs after school, even threatening a girl was prohibited. Vile language or physical abuse of a girl would provoke retaliation from the males in her family. There would be what we called "a visitation," in which the males in the victim's family would call upon the offending boy and settle matters.

A Different Era

But times change. Some years ago I saw robust high school boys sitting in a bus while elderly women had to stand and hold onto the rail. In my day, those boys would be teased as weenies. Now boys of that same age call each other the despised n----- word as though it's a term of endearment. Once while running for public office in 1972, potential voters at several locations castigated me because I refused to indicate in my campaign literature that I grew up poor. There seemed to be no awareness that that term is offensive.

Clearly, the cultural values and norms among some groups that existed in Boston's black community before 1965 have changed somewhat. This induced me to inquire about the epithets that were once unacceptable: n----- and poor. Friends who belonged to the community's middle-class-oriented group indicated that they rarely ever heard the hated n----- word used and that they would never encroach upon anyone's dignity by calling him or her poor.

In the past, several of my contemporaries who have been successful adults have stated to me that they never realized that they were poor until they grew up and were on their own. One said that when he was a schoolboy he thought that putting newspaper in his sneakers was just a cool way of insulating his feet against the snow and cold in winter. He did not understand then that his family could not afford winter overshoes.

Another important value in the culture of the black community was for everyone to be well educated. It was apparent to me, even as a young man, that appropriate employment was not always available for well-educated blacks. Black lawyers had to work as Pullman porters, postmen, or office clerks. A friend who was a Latin School alumnus and a Harvard graduate once had to work for a time as a hospital orderly in order to provide for his family. Nonetheless, there was a great expectation that everyone capable of academic achievement should seek a college education.

During my Boston Latin days, I would often walk over to the Museum of Fine Arts. This once caused a bit of a difficulty with my class V history teacher. The book on ancient history had an illustration of Egyptians that made them appear to come from the heart of Scandinavia. I pointed out that this depiction was contrary to the artistic work by the ancient Egyptians of their own people. The teacher was not pleased with my observation, but perhaps I was a bit too assertive.

I later took a Saturday art course at the Boston Museum of Fine Arts School, in order to determine whether I had any drawing ability. I had an interest in architecture but only if I had the talent to excel with the artistic requirements. It would not have satisfied me to be limited to the engineering side. I concluded after the course that I should find another line of work. However, my father was pleased to see that I was serious about pursuing an education.

My father was a high school dropout. The death of his father imposed on him the responsibility to provide for his widowed mother and younger siblings. The loss of the opportunity for higher education was a disappointment he suffered for the rest of his life. He was absolutely committed that his children would not experience a similar fate. He provided all six of his children with the necessary financial resources for a college education, and four of them received advanced degrees from Ivy League colleges.

Education experts are right with their assertion that academic success starts in the home. For some reason my father expected me to become a doctor, so he thought it would be helpful for me to be motivated by talking with medical doctors. I remember two trips to Canton to visit Dr. William A. Hinton, the outstanding medical professor at Harvard. Also on every trip to Cambridge, my father would always drive to Harvard Square to point out where I would later attend college. There was a constant paternal reminder of the ultimate goal. In addition to Dr. Hinton, there were other blacks who had been professionally recognized and known in the black community, such as Dr. Solomon Carter Fuller, a Framingham resident and the nation's first black psychiatrist.

Another source of inspiration for educational achievement was the academic success of the older brothers of my two closest friends, William Wharton and Jimmy McCree. William's brother Clifton went to Harvard, earned a PhD in agricultural economics from the University of Chicago, and went on to become president of Michigan State University and CEO of TIAA-CREF. When we were in elementary school, William and I looked upon Clif as a hero when he was still just a Harvard student. Jimmy's brother Wade became a judge of the Sixth Federal Circuit Court and solicitor general of the United States. We're all proud of his achievements. He was a neighbor of mine when he was a Harvard Law School student.

A common impediment to progress for blacks is discouragement over racial barriers that have prevented employment or promotion. My father was a constant cheerleader, promoting the sustained academic effort of his children despite the impending hazards of competing in the white world. I later understood that he took me to visit Dr. Hinton so that I could see what success looks like.

While there had been achievements for blacks in medicine and other professions, there was little evidence of much progress in management positions in industry. I remember my surprise as a young boy to learn that my neighbor, Mr. Herbert B. Dowse, was part of the management team of the Boston Linotype Company. In the days of hot type, before the development of computerized typesetting, Boston Linotype provided type for area newspapers and other printers. One day when a Boston Linotype truck pulled up in front of Mr. Dowse's house, I was overcome with curiosity so I later sidled up to Mr. Dowse to learn the whole story.

My father was always supportive of black business. When I was a young boy, my father told me about Henry Owens, a black man from Cambridge who started a moving company with a horse and wagon. His son now runs the business, which is still in operation. Calvin Grimes was also a prominent community businessman with his oil trucks. When I was in high school I was really impressed with two business developments involving black entrepreneurs. Louis Roberts and Richard Walker were two of the four founders of Microwave Associates, which was then a high-tech company. It still operates as MACOM, located in Lowell, Massachusetts. Heny Hill, an MIT chemical engineer, launched a company named National Polychemicals Inc.

There were many reasons for blacks to be encouraged about their prospects for success even though the odds seemed unfavorable. In the 1950s the goal for academic achievement in America was merely a high school diploma. At that time, only about 5 percent of Americans had earned bachelor's degrees, but my gang, the Spartans, had higher aspirations. We jokingly called ourselves a gang, even though there was no violence, and none of the guys ever had difficulties with the police.

We started hanging out together in our junior high school years, and most of us later went to college. Some of the college connections are as follows: Reggie Alleyne went to Tufts and UCLA Law School, Olly Galloway went to Brown, Ted Howe went to Bowdoin, Francis Proctor went to BC, Jimmy Galloway and Frazier Taylor went to Lincoln, Gene Ellis went to BU, my brother Jack went to NYU and Harvard for a master's degree, Richie Roye went to BU, Bill Antoine went to MIT, Jimmy McCree went to Fiske, and Ed Dixon went to Virginia State. More than half of the twenty-eight Spartans went to college. That is ten times greater than the national average.

Not everyone went to college. Some didn't have to. Milton Roye is an acclaimed auto mechanic with an intuitive talent to diagnose arcane motor maladies. Not surprisingly, one of his sons went to MIT and has a career in management in the auto industry. Also, there were other similar gangs for boys from other areas. The Spartans were residents of the Hill, a section of Roxbury near Franklin Park. The Eagles and the Panthers were from "in town," a section of Roxbury next to the South End near Dudley Square, which was once Boston's second largest shopping area. Kresge, Dutton, Woolworth, and Timothy Smith all had department stores there.

A Growing Population Group

The number of black residents of Boston grew to 63,165 by 1960. The dynamic Washington Park Urban Renewal Project removed deteriorated housing in Roxbury, and by 1965 Roxbury had become the center of Boston's black community. By 1970, when the city's population reached 641,071, the number of black residents had grown to 104,707, 16.3 percent of the total.

However, Boston is both a place and a concept. From colonial times blacks also lived in surrounding towns and suburbs. There have always been some black residents in Cambridge, Brookline, Newton, West Medford, Lynn, Milton, and New Bedford. Now the black population is growing in Randolph and Stoughton as the residential expense of

Boston increases. Consequently, all of those towns are still considered to be part of Boston's black community. My brother Jack and I never felt confined to Roxbury. When we were young, we would consistently venture out on our J.C. Higgins bicycles to explore the region. A favorite trip during World War II was to the naval base in Hingham. Once we rode to Worcester to the White City Amusement Park, but we went on a Monday when the park was closed. So we turned around and pedaled back home. It was an all-day trip. The idea of being restricted from visiting any neighborhood was alien to us and our friends.

As the population grew, longtime residents were glad that the significant size of the black population would create greater political clout. Families that had been in Boston for generations made no claims about having greater status because of their longevity in the area. This acceptance made it easy for newcomers to be involved in community affairs. For example, I learned, quite by accident, that my cousins are descendants of Paul Cuffee, an outstanding black businessman and sea captain who was born in 1759. Cuffee was probably the wealthiest black man in America during his life. He had several ships engaging in international trade. He lived in Westport, Massachusetts, but he conducted much of his business in Boston and New Bedford. When there was some resistance to admitting his children and other black students to the public school, Cuffee built his own school, hired the teachers, and invited everyone to enroll.

As Senator Ed Brooke discovered, he suffered no political disadvantage from his birth in Washington, DC, and his later arrival in Boston to attend Boston University Law School following his service in the army. He had grown up in a sophisticated urban black community in the nation's capital that had a culture similar to that of some Boston residents.

Community Diversity

Boston's Banner Years will include accounts of people such as Ed Brooke, who were born elsewhere but came to Boston and established their professional reputation here. Those who were born and raised in Boston will be included even if their greatest work was elsewhere. That is reasonable because the lack of opportunities in Boston forced many to leave.

As one might conclude from the story of blacks in Boston, the community developed over many generations a culture of personal dignity as well as respect and concern for others. There was a commitment to acquire a good education and to work hard to acquire opportunities. As the size of the community grew, some of the old cultural values were gradually superseded. And of course not everyone embraced what I describe as the middle-class-oriented culture.

With growing numbers, it became clear that blacks' opinions were heterogeneous. Supporters for various philosophical positions became more prominent. Some preferred the commitment to universal racial integration as espoused by William Monroe Trotter (1872–1934) as opposed to the subservient acceptance of a lesser role as proposed by Booker T. Washington (1856–1915). Pan-Africanists supported the racial separation encouraged by Marcus Garvey, who died in 1940.

Then there were the various religious groups: Baptists, Episcopalians, Catholics, Methodists, Congregationalists, African Methodist Episcopalians, and also the Nation of Islam. Participation in the civil rights movement required acceptance of the principle of nonviolence. Still others were in favor of revolutionary or violent action. All of this diverse opinion makes it impossible to view African Americans as a homogeneous group, united by their melanin.

The pleasant memories of growing up in Roxbury have been so strong for some old-time residents that for years they have held an annual Roxbury Homecoming in June. Former residents from all over the country return for the festivities. It is much like a family reunion except that we are all neighbors, not just family members. Old Roxbury residents do not want future generations to ignore the fact that we had developed a productive culture with shared "values, norms and beliefs about the world."[1] *The Cultural Matrix* further asserts that "culture is not immutable, as is commonly believed."[2] Today's changes obscure the real nature of the old Roxbury.

Overcoming Discrimination

Missing from this account of Boston's black community in the decades before 1965 is substantial mention of racial discrimination. Indeed, blacks were discriminated against in employment, housing, and even in places of public accommodation. However, there was not the slightest fear from blacks of successful physical assault by whites. Most racial confrontations were handled personally unless the assistance of others was required. The establishment of the Fair Employment Practices Commission (FEPC) in 1946 provided official opposition to racial discrimination but few solutions.

Of greatest concern was the negative and derogatory depiction of blacks in the media or in movies. Purveyors of sophisticated versions of institutional racism would often have elaborate accounts of the factual basis for their statements. There always seemed to be an assertion of the absence of any intention to be racially discriminatory. It was always difficult to rebut such assertions.

Many of the old-time residents of Roxbury, as well as African Americans elsewhere, have had to overcome racially discriminatory resistance to their progress. Many have stories to tell about such impediments, but those are personal stories. It is unlikely that bigoted whites will admit to being unfair. Yet it is generally accepted that there is a national problem with racial discrimination and the absence of diversity. There has to be some mention in the book about the barriers to be overcome by those contributing to black progress.

Research by Professor Martin Gilens, who was then a Yale political scientist, established that over a period of four years the major media had exaggerated the number of blacks as compared with whites who were poverty-stricken. He examined 182 newsmagazine stories and 534 television stories from 1988 through 1992 that focused on poverty or relief of the poor. Although blacks were 29 percent of the poor at that time, "national newsmagazines—including *Time, Newsweek* and *U.S. News & World Report* used images of black people to illustrate stories about the poor 62 percent of the time," and

ABC, NBC, and CBS television networks' stories on the poor showed blacks 65 percent of the time.[3]

Professor Gilens concluded that "this distorted portrait of the American poor cannot help but reinforce negative stereotypes of blacks as mired in poverty and contribute to the belief that poverty is primarily a 'black problem.'" As a political scientist, Gilens was essentially concerned with the reluctance of Americans to support welfare. He published a book at that time entitled *Why Americans Hate Welfare: Race, Media and the Politics of Antipoverty Policy.*

Although Gilens was not focusing on resolving the race problem, it was evident that this research validly established the existence of a negative attitude about blacks. Undoubtedly Roxbury blacks of decades earlier were aware of the problem and determined not to insult others by calling them poor. African Americans were always sensitive to being psychologically branded. The desire to have an authentic and independent voice is what inspired the establishment of the *Banner.* Even many of those purporting to be sympathetic to the efforts of blacks to attain full equality inadvertently issue deprecating remarks about the black community. It was once common to state, though often benignly, that blacks are "culturally deprived."

Theater, music, dance, painting, and sculpture have always been significant elements of black life in Boston. It is grossly inaccurate to assert that the Roxbury community was culturally deprived. Indeed, no matter how great the cultural opportunities, there will always be some who will turn their backs on them. But is that also not the situation elsewhere?

Distinguished Predecessors

The immediate antecedent of the *Bay State Banner* is the *Boston Guardian* that was founded in 1901 by William Monroe Trotter. A member of the Harvard class of 1895, Trotter was Harvard's first black Phi Beta Kappa. He advocated for full racial equality, and protested President Woodrow Wilson's racist policy of discrimination in federal service. Trotter also opposed showing the racist film *Birth of a Nation* in a Boston theater.

Trotter died in 1934, and his sister, Maude Steward, a Wellesley graduate, continued publication of the *Guardian* with her husband, Dr. Charles Steward, the last surviving member of the so-called Boston Radicals. Dr. Steward granted his blessings to the establishment of the *Bay State Banner*, and shortly before his death in 1967, he ordained the *Banner* as the successor to the *Guardian*.

While still students at Harvard University, my classmate Otis Gates and I used to speculate about what we might do to improve opportunities for other blacks. We were aware that as Harvard alumni, we had a head start. This was in the 1950s, before the smartphone and the laptop. It was clear that without an effective means of communication it would be impossible to organize any progressive strategy. So we invested our limited funds and established the *Bay State Banner*. Robin Washington's chapter on Boston's media history will offer greater historical information about the *Banner's* early years.

The goal of Boston's Banner Years

The purpose of *Boston's Banner Years* is to develop an accurate journalistic account of some of the outstanding events and efforts of local organizers and newsmakers that emerged since 1965, the date the *Banner* was launched. With the passage of time, the accuracy of the record on some events needs to be restored and the achievements of some Roxbury people who might otherwise be ignored need to be highlighted so that future generations will have a clear understanding of how famously some of their predecessors performed.

Chapter 1
Quality public education

Mention public education in Boston, and the first thought that comes to mind is the busing controversy. However, the process of attaining an education in Boston for blacks has been arduous for generations even well before the 1974 *Morgan v. Hennigan* case. I have documented some of the major community attitudes toward education from colonial times that influence public policy today.

Chapter 2
Toward political power

When African Americans in the South were struggling even to be registered to vote, blacks in Boston were holding high elective office. Then when Boston politics became aggressively based on ethnicity, the much smaller black population was vanquished. In 1940, Boston's black population was only 3.1 percent of the total. Brian O'Connor, a journalist with broad political experience, has deciphered the numbers and details black strategies to recover.

Chapter 3
Major protests

Roxbury residents stand against policies they perceive to be disruptive, unjust, or inhumane. Such attitudes launched the protest against plans to build I-95 through the community. Another protest was to end apartheid in South Africa. Sandra Larson has reported on those two events and has presented a report to terminate the description of the police attack in Grove Hall in 1967 as a race riot.

Chapter 4
Law enforcement

In 1965 there were few blacks on the Boston police force. That number has increased over the years, to some extent with the aid of anti-discrimination lawsuits. As in other cities, problems developed over police killings of blacks. Also, when urban youth violence erupted, black ministers took credit for solutions, even while programs of the

Nation of Islam seemed to be more effective. Yawu Miller, with considerable experience on the street beat, has separated information on the combatants.

Chapter 5
Building a bank

Although Boston ranks only twenty-one for the size of its black population, it is the home office for OneUnited Bank, the nation's largest black-owned and managed bank. Jule Pattison-Gordon has provided an account of how the tiny Unity Bank survived to become the OneUnited Bank, and how other local commercial banks and financial institutions have attempted to respond to the commercial needs of black Bostonians. She has also included an account of redlining that changed community demographics.

Chapter 6
Real estate successes

The State Street Bank headquarters, Crosstown Center, John Cruz's Harvard Commons, and United Housing Management are all substantial real estate projects with black developers. Yawu Miller and Sandra Larson have provided an account of how each was achieved.

Chapter 7
Employment efforts

The fair employment of African Americans has been a perpetual national problem. There was some hope that with affirmative action the problem would be resolved. However, unemployment rates for blacks remain twice as high as the rate for whites. James Jennings and Anthony Neal have reviewed the pattern of discrimination in Boston and some of the different programs and projects by local residents to make a change.

Chapter 8
Boston's media history

Blacks have struggled to be involved in Boston's media. As expected, there is much to report. The *Say Brother* program on WGBH-TV was a national prize winner. Ken Nash operated WILD radio for many years. Of course, the *Bay State Banner* was launched in 1965. And in an incomparable national event, a racially mixed group challenged the license for Channel 7 and won. In addition, there were a number of TV personalities that became prominent. Robin Washington, a seasoned journalist and former *Banner* managing editor, has reported on those issues.

Chapter 9
The colonial era

Blacks have been in Boston since colonial times. In fact, the assertiveness of Crispus Attucks, a black man from Framingham, helped to ignite the Revolutionary War. While slaves were in chains in the South, blacks in Boston worked with whites for their manumission. Anthony W. Neal has provided a record of the commercial, political, and educational activities of blacks in Boston in those days. This introduction provides a picture of the historical roots of Boston's blacks well before 1965.

1

The Quest for Education

Melvin B. Miller

The Abiel Smith School still stands near the top of Joy Street on Beacon Hill as a proud reminder of the early efforts of black Bostonians to provide an education for their children. The building has been appropriately repurposed as the Museum of African American History. Constructed in 1835 with the proceeds of a bequest made by Abiel Smith, a wealthy and philanthropic member of Boston's merchant class, it was the first public school in America that was built for black students. But the benefits of this historic legacy quickly began to dwindle with the acceleration of disputes over policies governing education. This experience established that the pursuit of quality education is a perpetual preoccupation.

With the founding of the Boston Latin School in 1635, Boston became the first city in the nation to establish free public education. Then as now, Latin School has been an institution for intellectually talented students who are capable of handling an academically demanding curriculum. It was not until 1877 that Latin School graduated its first black student, Parker Bailey. But during the early years, the racial diversity of the Latin School student body was of no major concern.

Photograph by Autumn Cole, 2017. Copyright Museum of African American History, Boston, Massachusetts. Abiel Smith School, 46 Joy Street, Boston, Massachusetts. Established in 1835 as the first school in America built for black students.

The major problem is that there were originally no grammar schools in Boston. Students admitted to Latin School had the benefit of a high level of home schooling or studies supervised by tutors who were paid by their affluent parents. In fact, it was first thought that education was the responsibility of parents and not the city. In a 1642 school law, the state imposed a penalty for parents who were delinquent in the education of their offspring. When that did not improve the academic achievement level, a 1647 state law required larger cities to establish grammar schools.

Boston's seventeenth-century school department cannot be compared to the highly professional bureaucracies that now manage school systems in major cities. A volunteer, elected school committee decided how to disperse Boston's limited funds for education. It was not until

1851 that Boston's first superintendent was appointed. A primary school board operated from 1818 to 1855. While there was no law requiring the schools to be racially segregated, the practice of excluding black children from the schools became common.

For decades, Boston's black citizens petitioned the school board for fair treatment but to no avail. Finally, in 1787, Boston blacks demanded that the state legislature provide alternative education opportunities for blacks—a campaign to establish the concept of racially separate schools. Boston's so-called "free schools" did not benefit black children. As might be expected, the legislature refused their request even though this was 152 years after public schools were established in Boston with the founding of Boston Latin School.

Black boys and girls had endured incessant bullying and harassment in the public schools. So, contrary to the petition for integrated schools in the *Brown v. Board of Education* case that was decided by the US Supreme Court in 1954, Boston blacks sought all-black schools 167 years earlier. This is historically the first time in the nation that blacks tried to separate from whites in schools.

At the same time, there was a group of white citizens who staunchly supported the idea that a public school system should be for everyone. Black Bostonians continued to campaign for separate schools even though the number of immigrant families began to increase.

Prince Hall, an immigrant from Barbados, emerged as a significant black leader at this time. Speaking on June 24, 1797, at the Masonic African Lodge No. 1 in the village of Menotomy (what is now Arlington), he called for patience within the black community. Otherwise, he said, "We could not bear up under the daily insults we meet on the streets of Boston." He also said, "My brethren, let us not be cast down under these and many other abuses we at present labour under, for the darkest hour is before the break of day."[4]

It was clear from Prince Hall's remarks that blacks were no longer willing to tolerate disrespect and abuse from some whites. Within a year, blacks were able to open their own primary school in the home of Prince Hall's son, Primus, at 63 West Cedar Street on the corner of

Revere Street. With most blacks living on the north slope of Beacon Hill, this was a convenient location. Primus Hall's school became the first black school to open in Boston. However, it did not survive for long because of Boston's yellow fever epidemic.

It was quite common in those days for schools to open in the houses or apartments of teachers or of participating parents. The neighborhoods were not dotted with school buildings. Undoubtedly, the intimate nature of each school induced parents who were controlling the school locus to admit only those with whom they felt most comfortable. Black children were often not chosen to attend.

Black parents continued to protest for schools for their children, and the school committee finally agreed to reopen the private school in Primus Hall's house in 1802. A greater number of the members of the school committee began to believe that a separate school for blacks would be a better learning environment.

The African Meeting House was built at 46 Joy Street in 1806, and it is still connected to the Abiel Smith School as part of the Museum of African American History. It is reputed to be the oldest black church in America, built by blacks, that is still standing. Its first purpose was as the Belknap Baptist Church, but the basement was renovated to accommodate the school that had been operating in Primus Hall's house. "The African School was now, in effect, a private school, since the School Board would not officially acknowledge or administer it," wrote Stephen and Paul Kendrick in their book about the efforts of free black Bostonians to achieve political and educational equality at that time. "However, this began to change by 1812, with the School Board beginning to make annual contributions to the school. Noticing the increasing success of the school, the School Board considered extending its control over it."[5]

Once the school committee began making stipends to support the school in the African Meeting House, the loss of local administrative control was inevitable. There was no intention to permit autonomy for any of the other black schools that were established.

Boston's public schools had become completely segregated by

1830, with the school committee assuming all the expenses. Public officials had accepted the arrangement, which was essentially what many blacks had sought.

> Under the aegis of the Committee and the Primary Board three primary schools had functioned to provide elementary instruction for Black youth. Both the Committee and the Board congratulated themselves at having tried to hire the best available teachers for the Black schools under admittedly trying circumstances. If Black parents were not always satisfied with the results, both groups of educators were equally dissatisfied with the slack attendance at the schools. The city, after all, had done all that it could to meet the educational wishes and needs of the Black community—or so the city fathers claimed. In future years, members of the School Committee and the Primary Board recalled with pride their efforts on behalf of the Black citizens of Boston. From a private school for Black children had grown a publicly supported system of segregated schools that attested the educational beneficence of the city.[6]

Even as the segregated school system was developing, black parents and others complained about the educational quality. The complaints fell on an unresponsive school committee. However, growing support among their members for issues raised by black protests urged the school committee to build a school for black students with a $5,000 legacy left by Abiel Smith for the education of black students.

In 1835, the new school opened and was named after Abiel Smith, but it was not long before students' parents complained that the curriculum was unsatisfactory. By 1840, the noted abolitionist William Cooper Nell filed a petition in objection to all segregated schools. Within another four years, a greater number of notable blacks had joined the protest, including Robert Morris, a lawyer, and John Hilton, a businessman, but the official attitude was that black students should continue to stay in all-black schools. [7]

Community response to the protest became charged when the press generated Boston's first school boycott in opposition to school segregation. William Lloyd Garrison's *The Liberator* had become prominent as Boston's journalistic voice of the antislavery movement. His readers were responsive to an extension of their political opposition to slavery to the growing antipathy to the Smith School. *The Liberator* decreed that "all colored parents are to see to it, at whatever inconvenience or expense, that none of the children be sent to the Smith School." Attendance at the Smith School dropped from a maximum of 150 to only fifty-three by 1849.[8]

But as black parental dissatisfaction mounted, it was amplified by abolitionist whites who protested on their behalf. It was anomalous for Boston to be home of the antislavery movement and have racially segregated schools. David Walker, a lawyer who was one of the founders of the New England Anti-Slavery Society and a member of the school committee, confronted squarely the problem of discrimination toward blacks and substandard schools. He argued for remedial action, even if it meant reallocating money for white schools to the African School.[9]

In the meantime, Hilton, Nell, and Morris had decided by 1845 that the Boston School Committee would remain unresponsive, so they created a political action party called the School Abolishing Party in order to take their claim to the Legislature. With the assistance of abolitionist Wendell Phillips (the son of the mayor) and Ellis Gray Loring (a Yankee Brahmin who was Nell's mentor) they submitted a proposed bill to the Joint Standing Committee on Education that would prevent the exclusion of any child from a public school because of race. Any child so victimized could sue and collect damages if the student won the case.

The Legislature was unwilling to confront the issue of school segregation at that time. Their solution was a bill enabling students to sue for being denied "public school instruction." Being denied admission to a particular school because of race did not constitute an offense as long as education was available at another public school.[10] This law did not remedy the racial discrimination confronted by black students.

The quality of the Smith School continued to deteriorate according to an 1845 report of the Annual Visiting Committee of the Public Schools of the City of Boston. The Smith School was declared to be "the poorest of the eighteen grammar schools visited in each of the four required grammar school studies—grammar, definitions, history and geography."[11]

The following year, a group of black parents led by George Putnam petitioned the Primary School Board in 1846 to abolish the segregated system that included two black elementary schools. They objected that "the establishment of exclusive schools for our children is a great injury to us, and deprives us of those equal privileges and advantages in the public schools to which we are entitled as citizens." Putnam further stated:

> These separate schools cost more and do less for the children than other schools, since all experienced teaches that when a small and despised class are shut out from the common benefit of any public institutions of learning, and confined to separate schools, few or none interest themselves about the schools—neglect ensues, abuses creep in, the standard of scholarship degenerates, and the teachers and the scholars are soon considered and of course become an inferior class.
>
> But to say nothing of any other reasons for this change, it is sufficient to say that the establishment of separate schools for our children is believed to be unlawful, and it is felt to be if not in intention, in fact, insulting. If as seems to be admitted, you are violating our rights, we simply ask you to cease doing so.
>
> We therefore earnestly request that such exclusive schools be abolished, and that our children be allowed

to attend the Primary Schools established in the respective Districts in which we live.

(Signed)

George Putnam

And eighty-five others[12]

As expected the Primary Board rejected the petition, but their solid front was cracking. A minority report by their members who were abolitionists established "an essentially moral and psychological argument for integrated schools."[13]

Another petition to the School Committee was submitted in 1849 by 202 blacks led by Jonas W. Clark, calling for the end of segregated schools. Others opposing segregation also submitted petitions around that time.[14] This was just fifty-one years after black residents had campaigned for separate schools.

But not all black Bostonians agreed with the demands in 1849 for racially integrated schools. Some black leaders preferred to have separate schools in which the black community would have influence over the curriculum and the recruitment of teachers.

Protests, petitions, boycotts, and legislation all failed to provide public education without racial discrimination. The only remaining recourse was the courts. In 1849, Benjamin Roberts filed suit to gain admission for his daughter Sarah in a school near their home.

As blacks moved from the north slope of Beacon Hill to the North End, the West End, and the Back Bay, the more remote location of the grammar schools designated for blacks became a problem. Sarah had to walk past a school in her neighborhood that was designated for whites in order to reach the school for black students located at a distance from her home.

Her father, Benjamin Roberts, became antagonistic over the petty injustice, so he brought suit in 1849. His attorneys were Robert Morris, one of the nation's first black lawyers, and Charles Sumner, a Harvard graduate and abolitionist who later became a US senator.

Benjamin Roberts was a prominent citizen. He wrote for *The*

Liberator and was also publisher of the *Anti-Slavery Herald,* a black community newspaper. Roberts's case was heard by Lemuel Shaw, chief justice of the Supreme Judicial Court.

The issues confronting Chief Justice Shaw were whether the refusal to enroll black students in white school classes was a violation of their civil rights, and whether the Boston School Committee had the authority to determine what school assignments are in the best interest of the process of education.

Chief Justice Shaw had to consider the conclusions of a number of respected citizens on both sides of the issue. Some blacks, including the esteemed Frederick Douglass, wanted to retain black schools in order to develop a black consciousness for progressing in America. The retention of black schools was also supported by a majority of the members of the School Committee. Liberals and a minority of the School Committee wanted to end segregation for moral principles. Other blacks wanted to end black schools because they had already experienced the deprivation of educational resources to black schools that led to inferior quality.

Plaintiffs would have been helped by the "equal protection" clause of the Fourteenth Amendment to the US Constitution, but that was not ratified until 1868. That left plaintiffs to depend on Article I of the Declaration of Rights of the Commonwealth of Massachusetts (1780) which states that "all men are free and equal," much like the Declaration of Independence, but the implementation of this philosophical credo is left up to the courts and the legislature.

The court therefore concluded that the School Committee has been empowered by the state legislature to make such decisions. Under the circumstances it was relatively easy for Justice Shaw to determine whether the legislature would agree with the School Committee position. The legislature had just rejected an opportunity to change the law to sanction the disapproval of racially segregated schools.

Chief Justice Shaw stated, "In the absence of special legislation on this subject, the law has vested the power of the committee to regulate the system of distribution and classification; and when the power is reasonably exercised ... the decision of the committee must be deemed conclusive."[15]

Later courts have cited the opinion in the Roberts case as an early expression of the segregation doctrine of "separate but equal." Such a conclusion is not well supported. Chief Justice Shaw stated in his opinion: "It is urged that this maintenance of separate schools tends to deepen and perpetuate the odious distinction of caste, founded in a deep-rooted prejudice in public opinion."[16] Shaw thereby disassociates himself from personal attitudes of racial enmity.

Shaw's more liberal attitude was not unusual in Boston at that time. Within five years of the opinion in the Roberts case, the state legislature voted to make racial segregation in school unlawful. Compare that with the opinion in *Dred Scott* v. *Sandford* only two years later in 1857. In a 7–2 decision, Chief Justice Roger Taney of the US Supreme Court held that "a Negro has no rights which the white man is bound to respect."[17]

With the passage of Chapter 256 of the Laws of 1855, it became illegal in Massachusetts to discriminate for admission to public school on the basis of race.

> An Act in amendment of "An Act concerning Public Schools," passed March twenty-fifth, eighteen hundred and forty-five.
>
> *Be it enacted by the Senate and House of Representatives, in General Court assembled, and by the authority of the same, as follows:*
>
> Sect. 1. In determining the qualifications of scholars to be admitted into any public school or any district school in this Commonwealth, no distinction shall be made on account of the race, color or religious opinions, of the applicant or scholar.

Sect. 2. Any child who, on account of his race, color or religious opinions, shall be excluded from any public or district school in this Commonwealth, for admission to which he may be otherwise qualified, shall recover damages therefor in an action of tort, to be brought in the name of said child by his guardian or next friend, in any court of competent jurisdiction to try the same, against the city or town by which such school is supported.

Sect. 3. In filing interrogatories for discovery in any such action, the plaintiff may examine any number of the school committee, or any other officer of the defendant city or town, in the same manner as if he were a party to the suit.

Sect. 4. Every person belonging to the school committee, under whose rules or directions any child shall be excluded from such school, and every teacher of any such school, shall, on application by the parent or guardian of any such child, state in writing the grounds and reasons of such exclusion.

Sect. 5. This act shall take effect from and after the first day of September next. [*Approved by the Governor, April 28, 1855.*]

As a result, Boston classrooms were racially integrated for at least a century. While younger students attended their local grammar and elementary schools, older students could travel to high schools at more distant locations.

Emergence of Another Issue

While Boston residents were debating the advantages and problems of black, as opposed to integrated, schools as well as the elimination of slavery, major population changes were under way. Between 1845 and 1855 there was an influx of Irish immigrants who were fleeing the potato famine at home. A third of the city's population was foreign born in 1845, and that number rose to 54 percent by 1855. Fewer than half of the descendants of Bostonians who were there in 1820 remained in the city. Boston was transformed from its original dominant colonial population of English Puritans to a more varied citizenry of newcomers.

Horace Mann, who was appointed first state secretary of education in Massachusetts in 1837 and also the first in the nation, claimed that "the public school is the greatest discovery ever made by man," embracing "children of all religious, social, and ethnic backgrounds." Mann believed that universal public education, "beyond all other devices of human origin, is a great equalizer of the conditions of men—the balance wheel of the social machinery."[18] But it was the nonsectarian Puritan ideal that he seemed to envision in a city with the school-age population becoming increasingly Catholic.

The black population at that time was not large enough for them to become effectively embroiled in this conflict over the character of Boston's public schools. While school attendance exceeded twenty-five thousand at the time of the Civil War, the total black population was only 2,572. The Catholics eventually developed the parochial schools, but they had no intention of surrendering political control of the public school committee. That was a wise move since by the late twentieth century an estimated 40 percent of Boston's budget was spent on public education.

Even though after 1855 blacks in Boston attended racially integrated schools, by the 1950s there were few black administrators or black teachers, and there was no racially sensitive curriculum. When the school districts were later redesigned in the 1960s to create all black schools, the black leaders objected. The School Committee denied any intention to discriminate. They claimed it was the result of accidental (de facto) discrimination because of residential neighborhoods that are predominantly black. Allegedly, it also just accidentally happened that the schools for blacks were old and deteriorating and were not well-maintained.

Two of the protesters who emerged to campaign to improve the quality of education for blacks were graduates of the Boston Public Schools. Ruth Batson was an alumna of Girls' Latin School. She hoped to improve conditions from inside the political system, and she ran for a seat on the Boston School Committee in 1951 and lost. Mel King, a graduate of Boston Technical High School, ran for that office three times ('61, '63 and '65) and lost each time.

As chairman of the NAACP education committee, Ruth Batson diplomatically addressed the School Committee several times to report appropriately the objections of black citizens. Mel King became prominent in the front lines of the protests that inevitably followed the Boston School Committee's intransigence.

The problems of the 1960s were not simply a case of history repeating itself from the racial discrimination in Boston of black students in the eighteenth and nineteenth centuries. When such racial discrimination became illegal in 1855, public officials complied, and black and white students were able to attend class together. That state law is still valid. However, the 1855 state statute and the 1954 Supreme Court decision in *Brown* v. *Board of Education* were both insufficient to deter Boston's bigoted School Committee in the mid-twentieth century.

It is also historically important to note that black citizens rose in the 1960s primarily to confront the attack on their rights to a quality education. That was a far more significant issue than racially integrated classrooms. Inexperienced teachers, overcrowded classrooms, and deteriorating schools were the major complaints. Strategists supported integration only in the belief that the School Committee would be less likely to withhold funds from schools with a substantial white student body.

That conclusion has a historical precedent. The black Smith School on Joy Street was rendered deficient as a result of inadequate funding. It was clear to black residents of Boston that the schools that their children normally attended in the 1960s were financially deprived, a status not confronting schools with large white student bodies.

When the School Committee became even more obstinate, the community activists realized it was time to take the protest to the streets. Reverend James P. Breeden, a 1956 graduate of Dartmouth College and a recently ordained Episcopal priest, naturally fell into the role of field marshal. Breeden had an even temperament and was readily available. Many of the others had jobs and professions that from time to time called them away from the fray.

In 1963 the leaders called for black junior and senior high school students to stay out of school and boycott for freedom. About three thousand students joined the protest, which was so successful that another "Stay Out for Freedom" was called for 1964. The civil rights movement was heating up across the country, so this boycott attracted about twenty thousand participants. Mel King, who was the group's leader for the protest, had a confrontation with the police that established his reputation as a stand-up opponent of excessive repression of public opposition to official policies.

Breeden had arranged with Dr. Bernice Miller, an educator from Chicago, to establish "Freedom Schools." The goal was to continue the students' education, particularly if the boycott was to last a long time. The Freedom Schools also provided a secure place for younger students who had left public schools. There was also some talk about establishing black-controlled schools, an idea so unrealistic that it was not enthusiastically pursued.

Paul Parks, a black engineer from Purdue, had come to Boston to establish an engineering firm and became active in the black community. In the process of developing his engineering firm, Parks had established numerous contacts on Beacon Hill. Parks was able to function as a liaison between blacks involved in the education protest and politicians from outside of Boston. It is thought that Parks's involvement with Muriel Snowden of Freedom House and Melnea Cass helped to gain passage of the Racial Imbalance Act of 1965. Parks went on to become the first black state Secretary of Education (1974–79) under Governor Michael Dukakis.

The Racial Imbalance Act requires school committees across Massachusetts to assure that no school enrollment exceeds 50 percent nonwhite students. Failure to comply with that law assured that the Boston School Committee would lose a suit for discrimination. Such litigation was not filed until 1972.

In the meantime, the Boston School Committee failed to comply with its own rules and regulations in order to exclude black students. Residents of a neighborhood had first rights to attend the neighborhood schools. If there were any open seats after all the locals had chosen, then those seats would be available for students from other districts. However, the school system would provide no transportation for those seeking the open seats. Ellen Jackson organized "Operation Exodus" to transport students to those schools.

Ellen Jackson, another Girls' Latin alumna, was able to establish in 1965 a transportation system of volunteers who would show up in the morning and then later in the day to transport students to better schools and back home. Some principals stood by the doors to bar enrollment of black students, much like Governor George Wallace did in Alabama to oppose desegregation.

Operation Exodus was a great success, but most people outside of Roxbury understood only its racial integration aspect. It was not until Jonathan Kozol's 1967 book *Death at an Early Age* recounted the depressing conditions in a Roxbury-North Dorchester school that people in Greater Boston became aware of the disparate standards in public schools for blacks.

METCO (Metropolitan Council for Education Opportunity), a voluntary desegregation program that bused black students to suburban schools, was established during this period, and some supporters of the biased Boston School Committee cynically supported the program to reduce the number of black students in the Boston schools in order to facilitate compliance with the Racial Imbalance Act. Other more fair-minded citizens were pleased that black students would have an opportunity to receive a better education in suburban schools of higher quality. It was also possible for students in the primarily white suburbs to associate with black students for the first time.

After decades of suffering the hostility and discrimination of the Boston School Committee, the Boston Branch of the NAACP decided to file suit in 1972. *Morgan* v. *Hennigan* brought decades of racially infused conflict to be resolved in the federal district court. Judge W. Arthur Garrity Jr., a Worcester native and alumnus of Holy Cross College and Harvard Law School, heard the case and issued an opinion in 1974.

When the NAACP filed suit, blacks were somehow accused of damaging the city with false accusations. However, the NAACP had accurately reported that "six of the city's nine black elementary schools were overcrowded; four of the district's thirteen black schools had been recommended for closure for health and safety reasons, while eight needed repairs to meet city standards; per pupil spending averaged $340 for white students but only $240 for black students; teachers at predominantly black schools were less permanent and often less experienced than those assigned to white schools; the curriculum at many black schools was outdated and often blatantly racist; and the school district overwhelmingly tracked black students into manual arts and trade classes rather than college preparatory ones."[19]

The Boston School Committee refused to acknowledge their deficiencies as the trial began, and once the verdict was issued against them, they refused to cooperate with Judge Garrity to establish a workable remedy. Rather than accede to their disrespect for the authority of the federal district court, Judge Garrity was forced to develop a remedy that did not require the cooperation of the School Committee. Thus the school busing plan was formed.

With its obstinacy, the Boston School Committee had caused Boston to lose $65 million in state and federal funds in 1973 because of its school segregation policy. Then its refusal in 1974 to acknowledge its judicial defeat forced Judge Garrity to impose busing as the remedy. And its hostility to African Americans has brought considerable embarrassment to the city of Boston. One wonders, what was the advantage of such ill-advised policies in the minds of the members of the School Committee?

An Underestimation

One will never know for certain why the Boston School Committee pursued such a losing strategy. However, one issue is clear: the conflict was not a racial hostility equivalent to the white vs. black opposition in Alabama, Georgia, or Mississippi. The political support from whites for David Nelson, an outstanding black Catholic layman, was extraordinary in the 1970 primary race to replace the retiring Speaker John McCormack in the South Boston Ninth Congressional District. Nelson polled only eleven hundred votes less than runner-up Joe Moakley, who lost to Louise Day Hicks. A black candidate in the South at that time would go nowhere.

That is not to say there is no conflict between the races in Boston. The city is still very tribal, a milder form of racism. The Irish are very politically aggressive. They understand that politics is a zero-sum game. In an election there is a winner and a loser. Sometimes the conflict can be a bit hostile, like between the Red Sox and the Yankees, because at the end of the season only one team will hold the American League pennant. The Irish have had to fight for control of the education administration. They won and had no intention of losing that control.

According to reports, Louise Day Hicks, the leader of the School Committee campaign, was very cordial to African American fellow students at Boston University Law School. But she could be quite hostile when in battle mode. She was awarded with a seat in Congress (1971–73) for her early strategies that seemed to be effective. But when the challenges by African Americans gained public support, Hicks's status declined. She lost her reelection to Congress in 1972. She was then left with the leadership of ROAR (Restore our Alienated Rights), a weak antibusing organization that was supported primarily by the working class. This was a major fall from grace for the daughter of a well-respected South Boston Irish judge.

Over the years, the conflict between African Americans and the Boston School Committee led to lawsuits. In 1967, members of the state legislature who were friends of the School Committee tried unsuccessfully in court to have the Racial Imbalance Act declared unconstitutional. In 1971, the Massachusetts Commission against Discrimination (MCAD) and the US Department of Health, Education and Welfare attempted to find the School Committee in violation of Title VI of the 1964 Civil Rights Act, but without success.

The state Board of Education was also named as a defendant in the *Morgan v. Hennigan* class action suit filed by fourteen black parents and their children against the Boston School Committee in the US Federal District Court of Massachusetts. The lawsuit alleged that defendants had denied black children equal protection under the law, as required by the Fourteenth Amendment.

The trial ran from February 4 until March 22, 1973. On June 21, 1974, Judge W. Arthur Garrity Jr. issued an opinion that supported in 152 well-reasoned pages the allegations of the plaintiffs. The opinion stated that the school department had:

> Knowingly carried out a systematic program of segregation affecting all of the city's students, teachers and school facilities and [has] intentionally brought about and maintained a dual school system. Therefore the entire school system of Boston is unconstitutionally segregated.[20]

Judge Garrity had reviewed every aspect of School Committee management and that organization's policies for the Boston school system and found them racially discriminatory. He reviewed facilities utilization, districting, feeder patterns, faculty and staff, open enrollment and controlled transfers, and examination schools. Garrity found the discrimination of the Boston School Committee to be pervasive. However, he found that state agencies that plaintiffs had impleaded were innocent of constitutional violations. His opinion stated: "The evidence established that they did everything within their limited authority under the law to compel the city defendants to obey the state law and the federal constitution."[21]

Having determined that the racial segregation in the schools was intentional and purposeful, Garrity ordered the School Committee defendants:

> To begin forthwith the formulation and implementation of plans which shall eliminate every form of racial segregation in the public schools of Boston, including all consequences and vestiges of segregation previously practiced by the defendants.[22]

School Committee members delayed development of an acceptable desegregation plan, and School Committee members John Kerrigan, John McDonough, and Paul Ellison were ultimately found in contempt and were required to pay monetary fines. However, when confronted with unwavering judicial censure, the defiant School Committee members complied with the court order.

Busing plans found that twenty-one thousand of the city's 72,249 students had to be bused to achieve desegregation. While refusing to term the policy "forced busing," Garrity stated, "The harvest of these years of obstruction and of maintenance of segregated schools is that today, given the locations and capacities of its school buildings and the racial concentrations of its population, Boston is simply not a city that can provide its black school children with a desegregated education absent considerable mandatory transportation."

Garrity became the incessant target of media hostility for ordering busing. At the time of his death from cancer in 1999, the *New York*

Times reported, "He was scorned and snubbed by many; his name appeared in profane city graffiti; he was hanged in effigy, and demonstrators came to his home."

But Judge Arthur Garrity will be remembered by those who knew and respected him as a man who honestly and steadfastly abided by the law regardless of the consequences.

With sustained political effort on the part of Boston's black community, the first black school superintendent, Laval S. Wilson, was appointed in 1985 and served until 1990. In 2007 Dr. Carol R. Johnson became the second black superintendent, until her resignation in 2013. The driving force of the community effort now is to improve academic achievement.

2

Political Highlights of the *Banner* Years

Brian Wright O'Connor and Peter C. Roby

In September 1965, when the *Bay State Banner's* first edition appeared on the streets of Boston, black America was in a state of heightened political consciousness. The Voting Rights Act had become law just a month before, securing access to the ballot box after a century of lethal opposition to black voter power. The Watts riots, sparked by an incident of police brutality, had laid waste to a broad swath of Los Angeles. Liberation movements were sweeping across Africa, removing colonial control by European powers.

Half a world away, America's first combat troops had landed in Vietnam, opening up a new front in the conflict. Tensions between the traditional civil rights leadership and a younger, more militant cadre over the ongoing battle to end disparities in housing, education, employment, and health care between the two Americas, one black and one white, were upsetting the old order.

In Boston, political struggles continued over familiar turf: improving public education for black children consigned to overcrowded classrooms with broken windows, inadequate heat, and outdated supplies; ensuring that urban renewal would preserve neighborhoods and not simply result in "Negro removal"; and winning broader political representation of the black community by ending long-standing practices of gerrymandering districts to dilute African American voting power. When the Reverend Martin Luther King Jr. headlined a rally against school desegregation on the Boston Common in April 1965, electoral power and not just moral suasion was a major concern in the Hub's African American community.

The backdrop was paltry representation in the halls of power: Boston's all-white, nine-member City Council and its all-white school board, and just three African American legislators on Beacon Hill, in spite of a demographic tide that had seen Boston's nonwhite population more than double from 1940 to 1960 and nearly double again by middecade. In 1960, the row houses and tenements of the South End and Lower Roxbury were the center of Boston's black population. By 1965, black families had moved in large numbers into the specious homes, apartment buildings, and triple-deckers of upper Roxbury and Dorchester, leading to the election of new representatives. The 1964 victories of Franklin Holgate and the Reverend Michael Haynes to win seats in the Massachusetts House of Representatives, where they joined two-term Representative Royal L. Bolling Sr., marked progress but fell far short of electoral parity for black Boston.

But there were reasons for hope. Black Bostonians living in the mid-1960s were building a record of negotiating with outside political forces. The 1962 election of the handsome and charismatic Edward William Brooke III as Massachusetts attorney general, the nation's first black chief prosecutor, was a shining example of that skill. Reelected in 1964, Brooke's prospects at winning even higher statewide office were redeemed with his 1966 election to the US Senate.

The political trajectory of black Boston during the *Banner's* first fifty years are bracketed by the rise of Brooke and another adopted son of Massachusetts—Deval Laurdine Patrick, who won election as the state's first black governor in 2006, won reelection in 2010, and left office in 2015 with his good friend President Barack Obama serving a second term in the White House.

Between the ascension of these talented individuals to high office, significant political advances took place that merit mention among the high-water marks of black political progress in Boston. Diligent work to redraw political boundaries succeeded in expanding black political power, including the creation of two state senate districts now represented by people of color. The 1970 campaign by black attorney David Nelson to deny race-baiting antibusing leader Louise Day Hicks a seat in Congress was unsuccessful that year, but set a high standard for black voter mobilization and coalition building.

The landmark election of Thomas I. Atkins to an at-large seat on the Boston City Council in 1967 was followed by expanded representation in the charter change instituted in 1983 that led to district seats and newly empowered black voices on the council and school board. That same year, state Representative Melvin H. King became the first African American to win a spot in the Boston mayoral final election, establishing in the process the remarkable "Rainbow Coalition" model that the Reverend Jesse L. Jackson would emulate in his 1984 run for the White House.

In Boston City Hall, Bruce C. Bolling won election among his colleagues in 1986 to become the first black City Council president. In the *Banner's* fiftieth year, at-large City Councilor Ayanna Pressley became the first black candidate to top the City Council ballot.

At the State House, black representation grew from three members in 1965 to a coalition of thirteen African American and Latino legislators gathered together under the banner of the Massachusetts Black and Latino Caucus. Increased political power in the State House and in city hall have led to policy gains that have made a real difference in the lives of black families seeking their share of the American dream.

Throughout the last five decades, the *Bay State Banner* has served as the paper of record for black Boston's political struggles and triumphs, its aspirations as well as its setbacks. This chapter, by no means an exhaustive chronicle of black politics in the *Banner* years, seeks to capture the efforts of African Americans to successfully control their own political destiny.

Ed Brooke Makes History

Edward W. Brooke III's rise to the US Senate defied expectations because it defied demographics. Black, Republican, and Protestant, he won elections in a state that was 98 percent white, overwhelmingly Democratic, and largely Catholic. His 1966 victory made him the first popularly elected African American to the US Senate and the first black American to take a seat in the chamber since Reconstruction. But Brooke had already made history. In 1962, he bested a millionaire scion of Brahmin Massachusetts in the Republican primary and went on to defeat a former lieutenant governor in the final election to become the nation's first black attorney general. That race prompted no less a political pundit than President John F. Kennedy to call Brooke's victory "the biggest news in the country."

Brooke's ascension to the Senate in the second year of the *Banner's* existence set a high standard of black political accomplishment—a testament to Brooke's charisma, hard work, and political acumen in building a winning coalition that crossed lines of race and geography.

Brooke, born in 1919, grew up in Washington, DC's black middle class, attended the segregated Dunbar High School and entered Howard University. Brooke enlisted in the US Army shortly after the bombing of Pearl Harbor and was assigned as a lieutenant to the segregated 366th Regiment. As a soldier arriving at Fort Devens in Ayer, Massachusetts, Brooke said he "felt racial discrimination more keenly than ever before." The segregated training facility, featuring an all-white officers club, swimming pool, and tennis court, offered black soldiers none of the comforts offered to whites. A series of charges would see him defend fellow black soldiers in military court as a "soldier's lawyer," sparking his eventual legal career.

Deployed to Europe in 1944, Brooke chafed at the unit's menial assignments to protect minor bridges or bases behind the front lines in Italy. When the 366th finally faced combat, it performed heroically. Brooke himself made a mark by crossing enemy lines to communicate with Italian partisan guerrillas harassing retreating German forces.

During the push through Italy, he proposed a daring daylight raid on a German artillery battery entrenched on Mount Faeto. The commanding general agreed to the plan but declined his request to lead the assault. Brooke's combat missions with the 366th, on Mount Faeto in particular, earned him a Bronze Star and a Distinguished Service Award.

At the end of the war, stationed near Pisa, Brooke traveled along the Italian Riviera, where he met and fell in love with Remigia Ferrari-Scacco, with whom he would soon reunite in Boston. Two friends from the regiment, future state Representative Al Brothers and Clarence Elam, convinced him to abandon his plans to return to Washington and instead study law at Boston University. As a law student, Brooke lived in the crowded West End, a largely Italian neighborhood at the time. Married to Remigia, Brooke would gain a fluency in Italian that would pay dividends for him during future campaign stops in Boston's Italian neighborhoods. The two would go on to buy a house with help from the GI Bill at 26 Crawford Street in Roxbury, a formerly Jewish neighborhood, shortly after the birth of their first child and Brooke's completion of law school.

Having passed the bar exam, Brooke built a solo law practice in the neighborhood, housed in Necco Wafer's empty theater on Humboldt Avenue. He talked the owners into renting him space by pledging to bring in tenants to help cover the big building's heating costs. Those tenants included the Freedom House, a civil rights advocacy group founded by Otto and Muriel Snowden, and helped put him in at the heart of a new political hub for Boston's black community. Brooke was also the first post commander of AMVETS Post #128, which Brooke helped to found to encourage veterans to take full advantage of their benefits. His advocacy for veterans would become a hallmark of his campaigns over the next three decades, creating a bridge for Brooke to approach and engage with voters of different backgrounds.

The presence of the handsome young lawyer in the changing neighborhood prompted friends, neighbors, and clients to encourage Brooke to seek office. His first campaign came in the 1950 election for the Massachusetts House of Representatives. With little political background to draw upon, Brooke had yet to settle on a party affiliation, prompting him to run in both the Democratic and Republican primaries. This practice, known as cross-filing, increased Brooke's visibility and odds of ending up on the final ballot.

Brooke would go on to win in the Republican primary while finishing third in the Democratic contest, a result that reinforced Brooke's own political instinct about his opportunities in the Democratic Party. Brooke "always felt politically more like a Democrat" but knew "there wasn't much room for him with the Democrats," said *Banner* publisher Melvin B. Miller, who worked as a teenage volunteer in the first Brooke campaign.

But the question of Brooke's party affiliation was not settled easily, despite his loss in the 1950 general election. His character and skill set drew the attention of party leaders in both camps. As early as 1951, only a year after Brooke's first race for office, then-Congressman John F. Kennedy told Brooke, "You know, Ed, you ought to be a Democrat," as the two men received awards in Boston. Brooke's reply was simply, "Jack, you ought to be a Republican." On the Republican side, Christian Herter—a Brahmin congressman who grew up in Paris and graduated from Harvard—told Brooke at a Roxbury political gathering, "We could certainly enjoy having someone like you in the Republican Party," as Miller recalled. When GOP presidential hopeful Dwight Eisenhower came to Boston on the eve of the 1952 election, Brooke rode next to him through Roxbury's precincts as the party's local nominee.

Brooke would go on to lose in 1952, but only by a surprisingly small three hundred votes. When Herter found himself victorious, he offered Brooke, who had also been moonlighting as Herter's Roxbury campaign coordinator, the position of executive secretary for the Governor's Council, a role that historically served as patronage for blacks and one that Brooke ultimately declined. Instead, Brooke would pause his political career and turn his attention back toward his law practice. It was as much a period of rebuilding and reenergizing as anything else. Though Brooke would find success in the legal field—winning the second-largest award for damages in state history at the time—his political aspirations were never far from his mind. Brooke used the time to nurture his public profile, and he was elected as first vice president of the Boston NAACP, the nation's oldest branch, and was named to the board of the Urban League of Eastern Massachusetts. His veterans' advocacy continued, and he became the first black AMVETS state commander.

Brooke's earlier losses at the ballot box were no deterrent for his ambitions, as he reentered the political arena in 1960, seeking election as secretary of state. The statewide race, though ultimately unsuccessful, would prove to be a launching pad. His campaign was itself historic for the long odds he faced. Massachusetts' black population numbered just 2 percent of the total. "You have got to look at the numbers," Miller said. Running for office in those days "wasn't a very attractive thing to do. We didn't have a significant political base to make it look like a slam dunk." For Edward Brooke, there was little merit to a simplistic demographic calculus—he just expected to win white votes.

At the Republican convention, Brooke's nomination was put forward by the niece of powerful US Senator Leverett Saltonstall, clearing the field of five challengers who each would concede to Brooke. In winning that nomination, Brooke became the first black man in state history to be nominated for statewide office. In his acceptance speech, Brooke nodded toward that milestone as a pledge to prove that Republicans could truly claim to be "the party of Lincoln." His campaign would go on to bring him to every corner of the state, and his charm made him inroads from Boston to Western Massachusetts.

Brooke faced off against then-Boston City Councilor and future Boston Mayor Kevin White. White argued that voters needed to elect a Democrat who could negotiate with the state's Democratic leadership. White's campaign also relied on "Vote White" bumper stickers that drew strong rebuke from Brooke himself. White, of course, insisted the bumper sticker had nothing to do with race, going so far as to remind Brooke that "White" was his last name.

Brooke ended up raking in 1,095,054 votes, falling within 112,000 votes of White. Brooke had earned over a million votes, clearing a symbolic hurdle for black candidates in a largely white state.

As with earlier races, Brooke's narrow loss challenged demographic-based predictions and made him a rising star within the party. John Volpe, a millionaire developer from leafy Winchester, was elected governor in 1960 over the tainted incumbent Foster Furcolo and put Brooke in charge of the Boston Finance Commission in the hopes of reinvigorating the city hall watchdog. As Brooke wrote, "The only appointed office that I have ever accepted was the chairmanship of the Boston Finance Commission, and nobody else wanted that, and Volpe couldn't understand why I did. Volpe thought he was getting off easily—but the Commission had subpoena power. I knew what was going on. The corruption was rampant in Boston, as it was throughout the Commonwealth. So I went in and took the job. It paid only $5,000 a year. I went in, did my thing, worked at it, and we had good results."

As head of the watchdog agency, Brooke was tireless. He quickly kicked off investigations into an $800 Hyde Park land sale to a state representative that cost the city auctioneer his job—winning state Supreme Court victories reaffirming the commission's investigatory powers along the way. He would go on to investigate a series of jail-breaks at the Charles Street Jail and brought about a corruption investigation into the Boston Police Department by the International Police Chiefs Association. Brooke's work at the commission earned him a reputation as an anticorruption crusader and reinforced his independent political bona fides.

By 1962, Brooke was ready to run again, this time for attorney general, and his candidacy pitted him against the rising Yankee star being groomed for leadership, Elliot Richardson, in the Republican primary. From Brooke's perspective, "Elliot had a lot of things going for him. He had been an Assistant Secretary here in Washington. He was US Attorney in Massachusetts, editor in chief of the *Harvard Law Review*, and on and on and on, and besides, he had money. Elliot had great credentials, impeccable credentials, no question about it.

It was a tough, uphill fight. I was an unknown and the media said, 'Well, Brooke is a Protestant in a Catholic state. He's a Republican in a Democratic state. He's a black in a white state, and he's poor.'"

At the state convention, Brooke won the conclave's endorsement by a single vote, and went on to top Richardson in the hotly contested primary.

Years later, Brooke would describe his primary campaign against Elliot Richardson as the "most difficult political fight, certainly within the Republican Party," that he'd ever had. "After the convention, and I got endorsed by the convention—Elliot lacked only one vote on the first ballot. That shows you how important one vote is," wrote Brooke.

He would go on to beat Francis Kelly, a product of Boston Irish Democratic politics, in the general election. Kelly had begun his political career in the Boston City Council, before joining the Democrats' 1936 ticket as lieutenant governor under Charles Hurley. That November, Brooke became the nation's first African American attorney general by a 250,000-vote margin.

As attorney general, Brooke continued to serve as an anticorruption crusader who was willing to take on the entrenched powers. A short four days after taking office, Brooke denied a request to allow a fellow Republican to be honored at a banquet held by the insurance industry—a common way to bring regulators together with the regulated. Brooke also pursued a bribery investigation into former Governor Foster Furcolo and four members of the Governor's Council.

Easily the highest-profile case during Brooke's time in office was the investigation into the Boston Strangler. During a span of twenty months beginning early in Brooke's first term, thirteen women were attacked and killed across eastern Massachusetts. As the state's top cop, Brooke set up a commission to coordinate investigations between the multiple police departments working on the cases, thrusting him into the public eye at a moment of intense scrutiny.

Just a few months after the *Banner's* first issue hit the streets of Boston, Brooke announced his campaign for US Senate. His announcement followed some deft political maneuvering by Brooke once Senator Leverett Saltonstall announced his retirement. Brooke called the next obvious contender, Governor John Volpe, to ask if he planned to run for reelection or for Saltonstall's seat. Brooke told Volpe he planned to run in whichever race Volpe did not and urged him to make a decision on that very call. Volpe pushed back, "Ed, why the rush? Why are you in such a hurry?" But Brooke's pressure ultimately worked, and later that day Volpe confirmed he would only seek reelection. Within twenty-four hours of Saltonstall's announcement, Brooke announced his candidacy for Senate. Brooke's tactics cleared the Republican field for him, giving him a head start into the general election against the state's former governor, Endicott "Chub" Peabody.

Chub Peabody presented a formidable challenge for Brooke. He was a polished Harvard alumnus and All-American football star. Brooke tells of Peabody riding a large white horse in an East Boston parade, a contrast that Brooke thought he got the better of among the working-class citizens lining the parade route. Peabody had lost previous races for attorney general in 1956 and 1958 before he edged out the incumbent John Volpe for governor in 1962 by a mere fifty-four hundred votes. His campaign would draw the support from Democratic political powerhouses like the Kennedy family and sitting President Lyndon B. Johnson.

In Brooke, a stately man himself, Peabody would find his match. Brooke was "born to be a senator," said Miller, and he was "made to be a politician" with his genuine love for people, which was returned in kind. But Brooke took little for granted in this campaign, and followed the same playbook of personal outreach that was a hallmark of his previous races. His campaign offices drew a diverse cast of foot soldiers in which black volunteers were well represented, Miller remembers. Brooke's campaign again took him well beyond the black community, still largely confined to a handful of neighborhoods in Boston and Cambridge after decades of redlining.

Brooke's support from white voters was something that "everybody understood was essential to winning," said Miller, "and I don't think that people saw him as a candidate for blacks. There was something universal about Ed Brooke right from the beginning. He wasn't into the kind of black militancy that was either faked or real with some people who ran for political office."

Brooke was a staunch supporter of civil rights, the defining battle of black politics in that era. As attorney general he led efforts to uphold the constitutionality of the Voting Rights Act, and in the Senate he would lead efforts to establish fair housing and affordable housing programs across the nation. For all of Brooke's commitment to civil rights, he refused to limit himself. He saw the race for Senate as an opportunity to branch out. In his autobiography, *Bridging the Divide,* Brooke wrote,

> I wanted to prove an African American in the U.S. Senate could impartially represent people of all races. That was the message I wanted to send to African American candidates across the county and to young African Americans who aspired to elective office. I never doubted that the vast majority of Massachusetts voters, black and white, were proud of my role in championing civil rights.

Throughout the campaign, Brooke took repeated questions about the role of race in politics. Brooke's instinct was to seek a middle ground for the diverse electorate he represented at the time of heightened sensitivity. Brooke sought to distance himself from the nationalist politics of Black Panther leader Huey Newton, insisting that he was no "Negro politician." Brooke would go so far as to tell the *Boston Globe* that he was "Attorney General first, Negro second." Unrelenting, Boston's mainstream press continued to speculate about an impending "white backlash" to the civil rights movement. In Brooke's words, "Insofar as race was an issue, it was largely unspoken. Because our state's African American population was so small, perhaps 2 percent of the voters, I shook mostly white hands, looked into mostly white faces, and with very few exceptions, saw no anger in their eyes. But the press kept writing about a white backlash. I must have said a thousand times, 'Judge me on my qualifications. The racial issue has been beaten, beaten, beaten. Take me for what I am and what I stand for.'"

Brooke would go on to win the race in a landslide, with some 450,000 votes over Peabody. The *Bay State Banner* proudly proclaimed Brooke the "First Negro Senator Since Reconstruction" in its headline. His election came just one year after the adoption of the Voting Rights Act even as the *Bay State Banner* noted that Brooke won 72 percent of the vote in overwhelmingly white Western Massachusetts.

During his twelve years in the Senate, Brooke became known as a champion of the underserved and opened up new directions for the civil rights movement. He successfully pushed for housing protections in the Civil Rights Act of 1968, ground-breaking legislation that took on the lived inequalities remaining after the earlier victory of the Voting Rights Act. When Congress took up housing again in 1969, Brooke won an amendment to cap the percentage of rent paid to live in public housing at 25 percent of a tenant's income.

In January 1968, Brooke paid a formal visit to Africa with his army buddy and longtime friend and aide Clarence Elam. His stated goal was to assess the effectiveness of social development programs on the continent. But his criticism of recent cuts in aid to African nations signaled his true intentions. Brooke's trip helped expose a Massachusetts audience to the African continent, as reporters published stories from his travels back home. For one journalist covering the trip, Anne Chamberlin, "The Africans seemed more anxious to ask him as an American senator about economic aid and Vietnam than as a Negro about black power." Along the way, Brooke met the British-educated military ruler of Nigeria, Yaku Gowon, with whom Brooke would correspond whenever he heard about escalations of violence in Nigeria's prolonged civil war. Upon returning to Washington, Brooke pushed the administration of Lyndon B. Johnson to cut trade with South Africa's apartheid regime. A speech to that effect on the floor of the Senate elicited the ire of the *Washington Post*, which published letters that suggestively wondered why Brooke wanted to cut trade with South Africa even as he promoted trade with some communist countries.

Brooke served on the 1968 Kerner Commission following a violent race riot in Detroit the previous year that sparked similar clashes in other cities. The commission's landmark report famously found that the country was "moving towards two societies, one black and one white—separate and unequal." That report, which sold millions of copies, placed the blame for America's racial inequalities squarely at the feet of white racism, housing patterns that ghettoized black communities, and complicit media outlets it charged with basking "in a white world looking out of it, if at all, with white men's eyes and white perspective."

Brooke, who became an opponent of the Vietnam War, was one of the first to push for a holiday on Dr. Martin Luther King Jr.'s birthday, raising the issue shortly after Dr. King's assassination. But for black communities across the nation, many of the most important political battles were playing out at a local level. In Boston's busing crisis, for example, Brooke avoided taking a side, instead trying to promote reconciliation. Nonetheless, Brooke's national leadership played a critical role for local political efforts when it counted. As local activists were engaged in pitched battles with the Boston Redevelopment Authority—now the Planning and Development Agency—over urban renewal plans for black neighborhoods, Brooke weighed in with pressure on the US Department of Housing and Urban Development to show more sensitivity to neighborhood concerns. Brooke's criticism of HUD empowered activists' efforts to counter Urban Renewal plans. And when the attention of Boston's black community was riveted on the Southwest Corridor, where a planned highway would have cut black neighborhoods in Roxbury off from white communities on the other side of the route, Brooke got the federal gas tax rules changed to include mass transit projects just in time for the MBTA to seek funding for the new Orange Line. It was Brooke who announced $40 million in federal funding to spur development along the line. The progressive activist, historian, and legislator Byron Rushing calls Brooke's role in the gas tax the "most significant thing" that he ever did for Boston's black community.

Brooke would live out his reputation as an independent never more so than under President Nixon. The two were never close, particularly once Nixon adopted the "southern strategy" to attract racist southern voters who were unnerved by the civil rights movement. Barry Goldwater's 1964 race had demonstrated a limited but loyal constituency for explicit racism. When Nixon oversaw a campaign of racial dog-whistles, Brooke kept his distance. And Nixon's troubled presidency gave Brooke ample opportunity to demonstrate his renowned independence. Brooke led colleagues in the Senate to block two of Nixon's picks to the high court for their poor records on race, and rebelled against a third.

By October 1973, Nixon's presidency was mired in the Watergate scandal. Brooke was invited to the White House with other senators to advise the president. But Brooke's advice was unexpectedly blunt: "Mr. President," said Brooke, "I think you have lost the confidence and respect of the American people. I think if you continue on, you're going to get impeached, and I think you should not subject yourself, the party, your family, and most importantly the country, to an impeachment process. So for the good of the country and for the good of the American people and your family and yourself, I think you should step down."

Nixon, of course, declined. And when Brooke publicly called on Nixon to resign shortly after, Nixon would emphatically tell four hundred Associated Press editors, "I'm not a crook." His eventual downfall left Brooke vindicated in his impartiality and healthy skepticism of party loyalty.

But Brooke would soon face his own crisis. Brooke's May 1977 divorce settlement from Remigia made the front page of the *Boston Globe*, beginning a steady trickle of damaging news stories as the 1978 election approached. That year, Brooke was facing a serious challenge to his Senate seat from Lowell Congressman Paul Tsongas, who had the backing of the state's Democratic senator, Ted Kennedy. Seeing the forces aligned against him, Brooke sought to get out in front of the most damaging headlines, disclosing to the press six months before the election that there were problems with his ethics paperwork. But, that June, Brooke's divorce was being relitigated, and covered on the front page of the *Globe*. And through September and October, new details about damaging personal loans taken by Brooke hit the newsstands. That November, Brooke lost to Tsongas by 200,000 votes. After leaving office, Brooke settled into life as a Washington lawyer, living on a Virginia farm with his second wife and continuing to speak out as a moderate Republican, even endorsing Barack Obama for president in 2008.

Older black Bostonians will always remember Ed Brooke's classic smile, his brilliant oratory, and cool leadership. But for a younger generation, his memory lives on in the institutions dedicated in his name: the shining Edward W. Brooke Courthouse located in the old West End where the young law student once resided with his Italian bride, and in the Edward Brooke charter schools that have produced the highest academic achievements in math and science of any public schools in the commonwealth. His legacy will endure through the elected officials of color that follow in his footsteps to higher office, and through the generations of families whose lives were touched, one way or another, by the achievements of Edward W. Brooke.

Fighting to Redraw Political Power

Over the course of the *Bay State Banner's* first fifty years, Boston's black population more than doubled. Ideally, that growth would have led to steady gains in representation at all levels of elected government. And while a growing number of legislators would be elected at the city and state level, numerical gains were typically preceded by hard-won changes to district lines to unlock the electoral clout portended by raw population numbers.

The first redistricting fight of the late 1960s was a battle over a black state senate seat. Boston's black community, centered in Roxbury and the South End, had grown large enough to form the majority of a senate seat. But the way legislative lines were drawn split the community into the districts of four different senators, making blacks a small minority in each. This was the tried-and-true practice of gerrymandering. For centuries, state legislatures have been accused of disenfranchising voters by dividing communities with a similar interest into districts of voters with contrary interests. The practice, and the challenge of combating it, continues today.

In 1967, Franklin Holgate, one of the "most active, and imaginative, hard-working state reps we had up to that era," according to *Banner* Publisher Mel Miller, led the charge for a black senate seat. Holgate circulated a map to create a district with 75 percent black residents to demonstrate the impact of the existing lines. "Due to the present make-up of the senatorial districts," Holgate argued in the *Banner*, "we do not stand a chance of ever electing a Negro to the senate." Terming the existing lines "discriminatory in the extreme," Holgate—noting that three of the community's four senators voted against the major 1965 Racial Imbalance Act—argued that Roxbury was being "tacked on to larger and larger districts and [becoming] less and less significant." Holgate called for the legislature "to tie these wards together and have someone who will be responsible to them." Holgate's advocacy—five years before the state's political leadership got on board—set the stage for the successful push a few years later.

That push gained momentum in 1970 in the midst of a national flurry of activity on redistricting. A ballot initiative that year backed by the League of Women Voters reduced the number of seats in the House, whose districts were redrawn in accordance with the ballot initiative in time for the 1972 election, paving the way for the expansion of black power on Beacon Hill.

In that election, the number of African Americans in the legislature grew from three to five. The Massachusetts Black Legislative Caucus was inaugurated on New Year's Day of 1973 at the Elma

Lewis School. Roxbury Realtor Royal Bolling Sr. was joined by public housing resident Doris Bunte, Mel King, Bill Owens, and Royal Bolling Jr. One of the caucus's major priorities was to create the new Senate seat.

The caucus's push was buoyed by state court rulings in their favor. Following a charge by a *Bay State Banner* editorial that the Senate districts amounted to an unconstitutional "ethnic dilution," Massachusetts' highest court ruled against the existing districts, forcing the legislature to draw new districts from scratch. Former Representative Royal Bolling Jr. recalled that court case helped "legitimize and elevate the fight" and validate the arguments of the black caucus. "It was kind of a perfect storm of the national movement, availability of resources to do the research and mount a court offensive, and our political push to create the district, all that came together," he said. Legislators drew significant support from organizations such as the NAACP Legal Defense Fund and the Lawyers' Committee for Civil Rights under Law—formed in 1968—that pushed redistricting to the national forefront. Just as Franklin Holgate had in the decade before, the NAACP circulated a sample map with a black Senate seat to draw attention to the arbitrary and damaging decisions made by the legislature. The litigious national climate allowed the caucus to threaten lawsuits to bring public pressure to bear on decision-makers. *Banner* publisher Mel Miller filed a lawsuit with Jean McGuire—who later became the first black woman to serve on Boston's school committee—in the early stages of the process, giving credence to each subsequent threat.

Nonetheless, early plans that fell short of the caucus's goals were publicly dismissed, prompting the caucus to float a request for a Department of Justice investigation. The members even held a televised press conference where Mel King ruminated on switching parties thanks to the support they received from Republicans, leveling accusations at the Democratic leadership as having "no regard for or understanding of the aspirations of or the issues besetting the black and Spanish-speaking citizens of Massachusetts." Other maps that fell short were met with public criticism by members of the caucus. Royal Bolling Sr. memorably named one after the notoriously racist television character Archie Bunker, since it added Bunker Hill to the district.

Senate leadership's obvious loyalties to incumbent members pitted the two chambers against each other. But for Bill Owens, the conflict played out along ethnic lines as well. "You had a lot of Irish people in the house and senate and they were not interested in creating a district," said Owens. On the House side, a coalition formed to block maps that didn't contain a majority black Senate district. Mel King wrote in "Chain of Change" about the unexpected support of Representative John Loring (R-Acton), who was persuaded by a constituent to join the effort. But by and large, the coalition was formed between "the black caucus, the Republican caucus, and the liberal white community in the House," said Owens. Republicans joined the effort tactically, said Royal Bolling Jr.:

> The redistricting issue became a political pawn between the Republican party and the Democratic party. So that's why [Governor Frank] Sargent latched on to it, because it was a way of getting back at the Democrats and we sought out his support at the time because we didn't like the plan and he saw an opportunity to further his agenda.

Redistricting was a deeply partisan issue, particularly after the state's Democratic leadership offered in 1968 to form a black Senate district at the expense of Boston's only Republican senator, Oliver Ames, even drawing strong rebuke from Royal Bolling Sr. Unable to vote down a map outright, the increase in black representation in 1973 proved definitive, as the coalition sustained multiple vetoes with only one vote to spare. Between June and August, the Senate formally advanced three plans through both chambers before one could pass without a veto being sustained by the group.

Despite the tense negotiations, the caucus prevailed in August 1973 as Chairwoman Bunte announced their support for the latest plan. The caucus had won itself the Second Suffolk Senate seat, which incidentally created new fronts for conflict between members. The next year, the race was on. Representative Royal Bolling Sr., a Roxbury Realtor known for a courtly Virginia demeanor, lost to Representative Bill Owens, who had moved from Alabama to Boston as a teenager and started a dry cleaning business. The bitter contest wore down much of the unanimity that the caucus and black community had known a few years before. The seat went back and forth between Bolling Sr. and Owens for eighteen years, until Dianne Wilkerson was elected in 1992. That initial redistricting fight for the Senate seat had a ripple effect, according to Bolling Jr., on the later push for redrawn City Council district lines.

At the city level, redistricting battles affected both the City Council and School Committee. In both cases, the use of an at-large election format marginalized black voters. Just as Senate gerrymandering had made black voters a minority within a broader electoral district, the at-large seats grouped all of the city's voters together. But, in a district format—as it had been for decades earlier that century—the city's segregated black neighborhoods could form the majority of multiple seats, allowing both bodies' membership to better reflect the demographics of the city. As this movement gained steam throughout the late-1970s, Boston Mayor Kevin White sought to broker his own compromise through a home-rule petition that White crafted with the sitting City Council. White's proposal was a half-measure at best. In exchange for a district-based school committee, White would have stripped the body of most of its spending power, doubled term lengths and the number of seats on both bodies, and rescheduled partisan municipal elections to coincide with the governor's race.

White's measure drew criticism from state Representative Mel King—the tireless advocate for Boston's poor and elderly from the South End—and Councilor Tom Atkins. Atkins, who in 1967 became the first African American to win under the at-large system, denied that the bill amounted to real charter reform, asking, "What good will it do the people of Roxbury, East Boston and Allston-Brighton to have School Committee representation when the School Committee has been reduced to a toothless pussycat?" White's proposal lost a House vote in early 1977 over his refusal to let the measure go before the voters in a referendum, opening the door for alternative measures on the ballot that year. That summer, the campaigns for the ballot initiatives failed, but John O'Bryant succeeded in winning election to the School Committee. The municipal redistricting fight finally won approval from the voters in 1981, creating a council and school board composed of four at-large members and nine district members. Two of the district seats in each body were carved from majority black population bases.

The next major redistricting battle came just after Dianne Wilkerson's 1992 election to the Second Suffolk Senate seat. As the legislature began preparing the redrawing of state Senate district lines after the 1990 census for the 1994 election, the new senator began plotting to unpack the district—now surpassing 80 percent black and Latino—whose lines had once been drawn to maximize the percentage of minority voters. Over time, demographic trends had continued in Boston, and once-Jewish neighborhoods became increasingly black. A new wave of immigrants came to those same neighborhoods of Boston from diverse Spanish-speaking countries, Haiti, and Cape Verde. Boston's minority neighborhoods stretched from Roxbury to Mattapan and had more than enough voters for two Senate seats, yet were represented by only one senator. Wilkerson recalls the pressure, and frustrations, of being responsible for so many of the state's minority residents, many suffering from disproportionate rates of poverty and single-mother households with limited access to social services. But power in the legislature stemmed from the numbers within the chamber, not the convictions of any one member.

Wilkerson's efforts began to gain traction in the press and with Republicans who were already pushing back on maps drawn by the heavily Democratic legislature. Even Republican Governor Bill Weld came out in favor of a second majority-minority Senate district to the chagrin of his sometimes-ally Senate President William "Billy" Bulger, just weeks before such a map was finalized. Bulger's district, rooted in South Boston, was a prime candidate to host a majority-minority district with Roxbury and the South End. As Byron Rushing recalls,

> You know when we did the first cut at getting the two senatorial districts, Bulger was still in office. So we look at the stuff, and I go to Bulger and I say, "You should do this, you should put all these people in your district," and said, "You are never going to lose! Right? You will never lose, but your successor will be black." He couldn't do it, he couldn't do it.

Within the Senate chamber, this advocacy fell on deaf ears. "Needless to say, that was a battle, a lonely battle, because I did not have the support, at all, from leadership," Wilkerson said. Her move to unpack the district in 1993 unsettled many who deemed it "crazy" given Wilkerson's strong support from the neighborhoods that would be divided. She was even told to be "grateful" for the "protection" that the status quo offered her.

At the same time, community advocates, including Joyce Ferriabough and Tony Van Der Meer, were focused on Congress. A shuffle was necessary after Massachusetts lost a congressional seat in the 1990 census. For Rushing there were "two parallel things going on with redistricting: One was to get the first senatorial district, then the second senatorial district. But the other was to get all the black people in one congressional district." While the black community in Boston and Cambridge was not large enough for a majority-minority district, the goal was just to draw district lines where blacks were the largest minority.

The caucus succeeded by combining the minority populations of the districts represented by Congressmen Joe Moakley and Joe Kennedy into Kennedy's Eighth Congressional District. "When we worked out the numbers … it was clear that we had to be in the Congressional District that Cambridge was in," said Rushing. "Moakley had to give it up. He had to give up all his black people. And that got worked out when Barney Frank and Moakley had a meeting and Barney convinced him to do it. And I can still remember, at the last minute, I get a call from Moakley in the morning, I hardly ever got a call from Moakley in the morning, and Moakley says, 'I didn't realize I was giving up this many black people, I'm not going to have any! I'm going to have only white people.' I mean he was really concerned, just he was really concerned." And while the Eighth Congressional District has still not yet been represented by a person of color, the demographics trend in that direction.

A decade later, the big news following the 2000 census was that Boston had become a majority-minority city. In that context, Senator Wilkerson had a conversation with the new Senate president, Tom Birmingham, about creating a second minority state senate district. "I want you to serve on the redistricting committee," Birmingham told her.

Wilkerson responded, "Mr. President you do know that I have very strong opinions about this, right?"

"Oh yeah, I know, I'm very well aware, and I expect that you will share those opinions with the members of the committee," he said.

This time around, the legislature tried to be more receptive, organizing hearings across the state to solicit input on redistricting lines. The black caucus successfully turned the First Suffolk District into a majority-minority district in time for the 2002 elections. However, in 2001, after the death of South Boston Congressman Joe Moakley, the incumbent state senator, Stephen Lynch, succeeded Moakley in a special election and was replaced in the Senate by fellow son of Southie Jack Hart. There had been expectations that state Representative Marie St. Fleur would win the newly redrawn First Suffolk seat, but she declined to challenge Hart. It was not until Hart's resignation in 2013 that a second senator of color joined the legislature. In the special election to replace Hart in the majority-minority district, Haitian

American activist Linda Dorcena-Forry, a state representative from Dorchester, emerged victorious over South Boston's state representative, Nick Collins.

Meanwhile House Speaker Thomas Finneran was on the defensive. Yawu Miller, managing editor at the *Banner*, cites Finneran as "the biggest challenge" during the 2000 cycle. Finneran's Milton district, which bordered the increasingly black neighborhoods of Mattapan Square and north Milton, wound up at the very center of the House redistricting process. As Yawu recalled, "Finneran's district was still majority-minority, but he was working to make it more white. And so when the first draft of the redistricting [was released], people saw that and called him out." And "called out" he was, as multiple lawsuits were filed over the House process. Boston Vote, led by Maria Lazu, organized a federal suit under the Boston Voting Rights Redistricting Coalition and a Latino advocacy group, ¿Oisté?, sued separately over district lines dividing the heavily Latino neighborhoods of East Boston and Chelsea. The most significant case was a 2003 suit by the Black Political Task Force and ¿Oisté? alleging broad "racial gerrymandering" in the creation of House districts. It was this latter lawsuit that led to Speaker Finneran's downfall, as he was indicted in 2005 for perjury and obstruction of justice when he said under oath that he had not spoken to the committee chairman about the lines of his district. In the end, the district lines were ordered redrawn and Linda Dorcena-Forry took Finneran's place.

Given the political mess that was the 2000 redistricting process, as well as the election of the progressive Deval Patrick to the corner office in 2006, the legislature was determined to get the 2010 process right. The committee chair, Representative Michael Moran of Brighton, continued the statewide hearings on redistricting while systematically soliciting input from advocacy groups. As Yawu Miller recalled, "2010 was just like an alternate universe; the legislative leadership was just like really amenable ... the redistricting committee went above and beyond what anybody expected them to do."

On the congressional front, Massachusetts was in for a shuffle.

The 2010 census results ensured the state would lose one congressional seat, going down to ten members. John Olver announced his retirement, and then Barney Frank did as well. This gave the legislature the political flexibility to make sweeping changes without directly confronting the interests of incumbent members. The Eighth Congressional District was renumbered the Seventh and became the state's first majority-minority seat. Minor changes were also made to Boston's two majority-minority Senate seats. The First Suffolk District lost Chinatown neighborhoods to the seat anchored in East Boston while both seats picked up neighborhoods in Hyde Park, where communities of Haitian and Caribbean immigrants were on the rise.

Perhaps the biggest changes came far outside of Boston. Over time, large Latino populations had settled in places such as Springfield, Lawrence, East Boston, and Holyoke. Boston, Cambridge, and Lawrence had elected multiple Latino representatives over the years, including Nelson Merced, Jeffrey Sanchez, and Jarrett Barrios—also the first Latino state senator. But Latino candidates started winning across the state after the latest maps took effect. Lawrence, where Latinos make up a supermajority of the residents, accounting for twice the number of blacks, whites, and Asians combined, elected Frank Moran in 2013 to join fellow Lawrence resident Marcos Devers in the chamber. Holyoke elected Aaron Vega the same year as well. The next election cycle saw two Latino candidates—Carlos Gonzalez and Jose Tosado—win in Springfield. By then, legislators had combined their forces into the Black and Latino Caucus.

Legislators of color have come to number thirteen between the two chambers of the General Court. The growing clout of the caucus has helped achieve important priorities, such as maintaining the independence of Roxbury Community College, building the Reggie Lewis Center, pushing for minority executive appointments, naming black and Latino justices to the bench, funding community development corporations, cracking down on predatory lending, and passing criminal justice reform. While the growing clout of minority legislators helps ensure a fair hearing for minority concerns, the ascension of state Representative Byron Rushing to assistant majority leader is a testament not only to his personal clout but also to the power of the caucus, secured with the help of fair redistricting.

David Nelson Takes on Louise "You Know Where I Stand" Day Hicks

The 1970 resignation of House Speaker John McCormack after forty-two years in Congress unleashed a scramble for his seat. McCormack's Ninth Congressional District contained most of Boston with the exception of the Back Bay, Allston-Brighton, and East Boston. The district lines gathered the majority of the city's white working class triple-decker neighborhoods together, attracting the polarizing stalwart of Southie politics, Louise Day Hicks, into the race to replace McCormack.

But in order to stop the race-baiting School Committee chairwoman, David Nelson also entered the race. Nelson, a thirty-seven-year-old attorney, was the son of Jamaican immigrants and a prominent lay leader in the Roman Catholic Church. He was determined to thwart Hicks's ambitions by cobbling together a winning coalition to deny her the nomination. Also running was state Senator Joe Moakley. Like Hicks, Moakley lived in South Boston and opposed busing but tried to maintain a moderate middle ground between his South Boston constituents and the black community's aspirations for better schools. In the cauldron of politics in Boston at the close of the 1960s, Nelson believed he could attract sufficient support to become the state's first African American in the US House of Representatives.

Hicks had first entered the political scene in the 1961 race for Boston School Committee as a school parent with a common-sense message. But after her election, as her political ambitions grew, she became the loudest voice opposed to efforts by the black community to address dramatic disparities in the quality of black neighborhood schools compared to the rest of the city. Hicks was more an opportunist than an ideologue, said *Banner* publisher Melvin B. Miller. "She was trying to decide between being the mother of school desegregation or whether she was going to go the other way. It didn't make any difference to her, but what was going to be the best result for her, and she found out that being a loud mouth got her to Congress."

During her tenure on the School Committee, as busing was eventually pushed as an antidote to addressing the deplorable state of black schools, she gained a perverse fame as the leading voice against children of different races studying together. She was aligned against the NAACP and Mel King—who had fallen short of Hicks and the other four at-large members in the 1961 race—over conditions in the Boston Public Schools. King had led advocacy efforts throughout Hicks's first term, urging School Committee members to recognize the de facto segregation created by the city's feeder system of neighborhood schools and the long history of housing segregation in Boston. Elevated to chairman of the School Committee in 1963, Hicks's clashes with black advocates made her a high-profile political lightning rod, galvanizing voters on both side of the conflict.

When faced with the link between School Committee policy and segregation, Hicks was recalcitrant. Even as the legislature passed the 1965 Racial Imbalance Act with an eye toward Boston, she would cut off advocates in hearings by insisting "there is no de facto segregation in Boston," Mel King writes, redirecting testimony to "educational matters." She deflected questions about segregation by railing against the specter of busing, raising fears about the costs and loss of parental control. Her defeat was a priority for the black community, as well as the religious and liberal backers of the civil rights movement. But their challenge was significant, as Louise had steadily maintained strong support at the ballot throughout her time on the School Committee, and even came just twelve thousand votes short of taking the mayor's office from Kevin White in 1967. In that race, she had run on the mantra, "You know where I stand," leaving no doubt about her position on the racial divide.

In Nelson, Hicks faced a deeply religious opponent who had considered entering the seminary before opting to pursue law instead. He entered an initially crowded field—with the likes of City Councilor John Saltonstall—though it was eventually winnowed down to him and two South Boston residents, Joe Moakley and Louise Day Hicks. Trained by Jesuits as an undergraduate and law student at Boston College, he was living on Munroe Street in Roxbury and practicing law downtown at the time of his run for Congress. His work on the board of Catholic Charities, and as board chair for the Boston City Hospital and the Roxbury Multi-Service Center, allowed him to rub shoulders with Boston's political elite.

At the time, "the two qualities that you needed to be successful [in Boston politics] was to be Irish and to be Catholic," said Miller. Nelson certainly wasn't Hibernian, but his deep ties to the Catholic Church and the outpouring of support from priests and nuns boosted his credibility as a candidate. Jerry Dunfey, whose sprawling political family owned the Parker House in Downtown Boston as well as other hotel properties in New England, was sitting in his Parker House office, when his friend, Boston NAACP President Ken Guscott, dropped by to bring him to Nelson's campaign announcement taking place in a hotel meeting room now named for the Reverend Martin Luther King Jr. "I come up to the room and I look in and there are nuns sitting there, there's priests sitting there, there's a monsignor, there's whites, blacks, Asians, everything," said Dunfey. "I look and I said, 'What the hell is this?' because everything at the Parker House or in Boston at the time was either all-white, all-black, all this, all that. So this really threw me off, I was completely taken by it."

Dunfey ended up getting the entire Dunfey clan behind the Nelson campaign. "All of my family, my seven brothers and my four sisters, they all got involved. My four sisters were nuns at the time, so I think they were just praying," said Dunfey. He and his brothers rode around in a motor home with a loudspeaker campaigning for Nelson, and providing financial support as well along the way.

Hubie Jones, serving at the time of the campaign as executive director of the Roxbury Multi-Service Center, also worked as Nelson's campaign manager. Jones said the candidate's support from Boston's white Catholic leadership played a significant role in boosting Nelson's electoral credibility among Boston's black leadership, which quickly rallied to his side. The campaign organized events in black neighborhoods and at Franklin Park. The Reverend Ralph Abernathy, a confidante of the late Martin Luther King Jr., came to Boston to support Nelson. Nelson attracted future fixtures of Boston's black political scene to his campaign, including Sarah-Ann Shaw, Byron Rushing, and John O'Bryant.

As Ed Brooke had four years earlier, Nelson began forming a diverse coalition of support. This backing shaped his message into a broad recognition of mutual disadvantage. Wherever Nelson campaigned, he emphasized the universal impact of policies to help all Boston's residents. "As serious as are the separate human problems—health, youth, education, housing—what is more important is the understanding that the problems are suffered with equal pain, equal injury by all people in my district," he said. His expansive message—which was also anti-Vietnam War—continued to attract a broad set of backers. Latino community leaders such as Frieda Garcia and Felix Arroyo rallied to his side.

While Nelson raced around the city to find support in every precinct, Hicks sat back, refusing multiple debates and leaving the others to battle it out. The Nelson campaign constantly had to push back on the charge that he was acting as a spoiler by splitting the anti-Hicks vote with Moakley and handing the nomination to the former school committeewoman. But that accusation papered over the fact of Nelson's growing electoral strength that portended a real shot at winning the nomination.

In the end, Hicks topped the Democratic primary ballot, beating Moakley by just about five thousand votes and Nelson by about six thousand. Nelson ended up taking Roxbury, while Hicks carried the white neighborhoods of Jamaica Plain and Dorchester even as she lost South Boston to Moakley.

While Moakley was often dismissive of Nelson's candidacy during the primary, Jones said that after the race, he wound up congratulating

Nelson for running a great campaign and winning the support of his "tremendous constituency."

Nelson's campaign changed the landscape of Boston's political scene, proving that black candidates and black communities had to be treated as major players. During the race, a *Bay State Banner* editorial had reminded readers, "Politicians downtown will be watching too. They want to see whether we back up our demands with poll power, or whether our community is just a lot of noise." Nelson's campaign rose to that challenge, registering eight thousand voters in a month and a half and securing turnout from black voters at equivalent rates to the city's white voters.

The *Globe's* coverage of Nelson evolved over the course of the campaign in a reflection of growing black political power. After publishing a July 1970 poll that showed Nelson's fledgling candidacy had zero support in the North Dorchester and Roxbury neighborhoods that were the very heart of his base, the paper later declared that "the rules of the game have changed" for Nelson's candidacy. The *Globe* would go on to publish an editorial after the primary concluding the black community "will continue to put forth candidates of great merit and show its power through the polls."

That optimism aside, Louise Day Hicks had entered Congress, setting up a similarly urgent campaign to drive her from the seat in her 1972 reelection bid. But this time around, David Nelson was out of the running. After the 1970 race, Nelson began serving as assistant attorney general under Robert Quinn, and by 1972 was in line for an appointment to a federal judgeship. For his part, Moakley's second run for the seat came as an independent. This ensured Moakley would appear on the final ballot, competing with Hicks for an electorate that had over one hundred thousand more voters. With Moakley and Nelson out of the Democratic primary, advocates who wanted to organize against Hicks needed a new candidate.

Two candidates from the black community emerged. The first was Hubie Jones, but Mel Miller pointed out that Jones lived in suburban Newton, outside of the district, prompting Miller himself to enter the race. While nothing disqualified a candidate from outside the district from running for the seat, Miller believed it was politically unwise to do so.

Moreover, Miller was concerned that the heated tone of Jones's campaign would result in a larger turnout of antiblack voters to send Hicks back to Washington.

Neither candidate came close to topping Hicks, who finished first in the Democratic primary with 21,855 votes. Nor were Jones's and Miller's combined vote totals–10,293 in all–even close to the second- or third-place finishers: Robert Crawley, who took 14,188 votes, and Boston School Committee member James Henningan Jr., who finished with 11,030. The primary finish of the competing black candidates fell far short of the broad support that Nelson, a highly respected Catholic layman, managed to draw in his 1970 run. In the final election, Hicks faced off against Moakley as an Independent, and a liberal Republican, Howard Miller, who scored an upset in his own primary. When all of the votes were counted, Moakley narrowly defeated Hicks by a mere three thousand votes and went on to serve fourteen terms in Congress.

Nelson's 1970 campaign, though unsuccessful, built on a model established by Senator Brooke to mobilize a broad coalition behind his candidacy. Not until Mel King's 1983 mayoral race would a Boston candidate of color attract such wide support. In standing up to Hicks, Nelson showed the power of a unified black electorate attracting support from other ethnic groups to make a lasting dramatic political statement.

Boston City Hall: Municipal Empowerment

The brutalist concrete of Boston City Hall cannot convey the degree of power concentrated within those walls. Boston's mayor is able to set funding levels without major City Council or School Committee meddling. The mayor retains significant local control over development, schools, hiring municipal employees, contracting, and grant making. The mayor deals with a large delegation on Beacon Hill, and has played a uniquely significant role in the state's political life. While no person of color has been able to reach that fifth floor office, the seat has remained the envy of aspiring black politicians who passed through city hall during the *Banner* years.

For black politicians in Boston, difficult access to the city's corner office has turned the focus of most political organizing elsewhere: the City Council and the School Committee. The ward-based council shifted to an at-large system of elections in 1951, raising the bar for candidates of color to join the body. It was not until 1967 that an African American, attorney Thomas I. Atkins, was elected to the council. Like Senator Brooke before him, Atkins was a transplant to Boston's black political scene. Born in Indiana before coming to Massachusetts to study at Harvard Law School, he wrote a scathing critique of the NAACP for a class paper that got the attention of Boston-branch President Ken Guscott, according to state Representative Byron Rushing. In a face-to-face meeting, Guscott, who had been interviewing for an executive secretary, hired Atkins on the spot.

Living in Roxbury, Atkins was only twenty-eight when he announced his candidacy for one seat on the nine-member at-large Boston City Council. His candidacy elicited a chorus of support from elected officials and community leaders like Mel King and Ruth Batson, director of the METCO suburban busing program. Atkins's appeal was also boosted by his work for a company formed by Celtics superstar Bill Russell. He ultimately gained seventy-one thousand votes to come in eighth and win one of the nine at-large seats. Two years later, running for reelection, he finished second.

In 1971, Atkins opted to run for mayor in a crowded field against the incumbent, Kevin White. Atkins sought to maintain his brand as a candidate for the neighborhoods, revisiting themes about "bringing city hall to you" and proposing significant neighborhood control over city services. After Atkins finished fourth that year, the incumbent White again wound up facing off against Louise Day Hicks, whose claim to fame was ignoring the city's segregated school system. Black voters rallied decisively for Mayor White in the final election. After the race, Atkins served as Boston NAACP president before moving to New York to work as general counsel for the national body.

No African Americans served on the City Council between Atkins's 1971 departure and Bruce Bolling's arrival to the council ten years later. Meanwhile, the color barrier on the Boston School Committee was cracked in 1977 by forty-six-year-old John O'Bryant. His victory capped the efforts of advocates for decades to secure a seat on the school board, with candidates stretching back to Ruth Batson's 1951 race.

O'Bryant had worked on Mel King's repeated campaigns for School Committee in the 1960s. He was a Boston Public Schools guidance counselor and teacher who also led paramedical training programs at Dimock Health Center. He had run for the School Committee in 1975 but lost in the toxic aftermath of the major desegregation ruling of the year before. In his fourteen years on the committee, O'Bryant served two terms as president, itself an historic feat. O'Bryant died in 1992, shortly after the elimination of the elected school board. But his name lives on in the local institutions that bear his name: the rigorous exam school for mathematics and science located in the heart of Lower Roxbury and the African American studies institute at Northeastern, where he taught for decades.

Jean McGuire, the first black woman to win election to the School Committee, joined John O'Bryant on the body in 1982. McGuire, director of the METCO suburban busing program, was a joint plaintiff with Mel Miller in support of a redistricting lawsuit to create a black Senate seat. McGuire also cofounded the Black Educators Alliance of Massachusetts with O'Bryant, which made waves in the polarized environment of the early 1970s by advocating for the hiring of black teachers.

From the 1970s through the early '90s, much of Boston's black politics revolved around one name: Bolling. At least one of the family's three politicians held office for a period of twenty-two years in a row.

Royal Bolling Sr. and Royal Bolling Jr. both served in the legislature on Beacon Hill, while Bruce C. Bolling served on the Boston City Council.

Bruce C. Bolling first won election to the council in 1981 as one of nine at-large members. A former director of one of Mayor White's "Little City Halls," he received White's endorsement in the race but had a considerable family base of his own. Once in office, Bolling pushed through the council passage of a 1983 linkage bill to leverage Downtown Boston development spending to fund affordable housing in Boston's neighborhoods. Mayor White vetoed the ordinance, and suggested that Bolling refile the legislation, this time creating a trust fund that would hold and spend the monies from downtown developers. The rewritten measure was filed by Bolling, passed the council, and was signed into law by White's successor, Mayor Raymond L. Flynn.

Bolling and White also clashed over the Boston Residents Jobs Policy offered by the councilor. This fight pitted black workers, organized under the United Community Construction Workers (UCCW) against the powerful developers and labor unions, as black workers fought for a slice of the development industry. After initial requests for the unions to accept black workers were rebuffed, advocates pursued an ordinance modeled on the "Philadelphia plan" to evaluate developers on their compliance with minority hiring goals. This model had proved too effective in Philadelphia, prompting court challenges to undercut its effect. That history yielded a compromise in Boston, which allowed developers to make "every good faith effort" in lieu of meeting strict requirements.

Bolling's legislation to create such a policy was vetoed by Kevin White, but Bolling kept the pressure up. White offered Bolling an executive order to the same effect, which Bolling rejected for fear a future mayor could undo the policy with the stroke of a pen. Bolling's ordinance, finally adopted in 1983, stands today.

Joyce Ferriabough, a longtime political and media consultant, advised Bolling on his policy fights and later became his wife. Like

Bolling's father, state Senator Royal L. Bolling Sr., Bruce, she said, deeply believed in reaching across the aisle and using a personable political style to get things done. Ferriabough recalls her husband's efforts to secure a maintenance contract for a black firm, a push that received resistance from fellow Councilor Albert "Dapper" O'Neil. His colleague, a colorful character given to chain-smoking, loud ties, and frequent boasts about his work as a young man as a driver for Mayor Curley, said, "he didn't know that black people did maintenance." Bolling then deadpanned, "That's what they brought us over here for. We contributed cheap labor."

After Boston's charter change, Bolling decided to run for the District Seven seat in Roxbury rather than at-large. He continued in office until he entered the 1993 race for mayor. Thomas M. Menino, who, as City Council president, had become mayor when Flynn was appointed ambassador to the Vatican by President Bill Clinton, easily cruised to victory. Until his death in 2012, Bolling continued to stand up for minority and small businesses. He ran the Massachusetts Alliance for Small Contractors, an advocacy organization he founded after his electoral career ended.

No black candidate has ever come closer to winning that coveted fifth floor office at city hall than Melvin H. King. King, who grew up in the New York Streets neighborhood of the South End before urban renewal, was a school teacher, youth counselor, and coach who had run numerous unsuccessful campaigns for Boston School Committee in the 1960s. His many dramatic protests at the Boston School Committee headquarters received widespread coverage and set him among the forefront of activists fighting for positive change for Boston's black schoolchildren. He took over the Urban League of Eastern Massachusetts in 1967, where he oversaw the movement of its headquarters from Downtown Boston to Dudley Square. He also organized the "Tent City" takeover of a Dartmouth Street parking lot in 1968, where commuters left their cars every day despite the delay in long-promised housing on the city-owned parcel. King's activism captured a key concern at the time over neighborhood "land control," particularly after bruising urban renewal battles of the 1960s. In 1972, he won election to the Massachusetts House of Representatives from the South End and used that position to fight on Beacon Hill for more progressive housing, health care, and educational policies.

Before his landmark 1983 campaign, King mounted a challenge to White in the 1979 election. In that race, he finished third, behind both White and state senator Joseph Timilty. James Jennings, a political science professor and one of the first MIT community fellows in a program organized by King, created house meetings for King during the 1979 campaign. Jennings said King's finish that year represented an achievement for "a black man, a progressive, running for office, not just tapping on the door, but the door was beginning to open. And I think that was the framework where, after the election, a lot of people realized that with a little more effort, a little more support, a little more organizing, we could win in '83."

The 1983 race took place in the backdrop of Harold Washington's victory to become the first black mayor of Chicago, raising hopes for black candidates in other cities. While aggressively running registration drives to enroll fifty-one thousand new voters, forty thousand of them black, King focused on building a "Rainbow Coalition" of supporters across the city. Forty percent of the new voters casting ballots that year were minorities.

Progressive activists from the white, Latino, and Asian communities rallied to King's campaign. When the September preliminary race rolled around, King was well-poised to make the final in a crowded field of seven candidates, including the sitting sheriff, a school board member, and three city councilors.

Banner Publisher Melvin B. Miller, however, expressed concerns that the black population in Boston formed an insufficient base to elect King as mayor, even if he made the finals. In an editorial with the headline "Stats do not predict Boston black mayor," Miller laid out a demographic analysis of black mayoral victories across the country, concluding Mel King was a long shot.

As the preliminary Election Day neared, polls showed a swell of support for King and put him within striking distance of coming in first on the ballot. In the preliminary, King pulled in 47,848 votes, just 634 shy of the first-place finisher, City Councilor Raymond L. Flynn of South Boston. King made history by becoming the first African American to win a slot in Boston's mayoral final. The *Banner* endorsed King after the preliminary, settling any question of the black support behind King's candidacy.

In the run-up to the final election, Flynn, a vocal opponent of school busing in the 1970s, presented himself as a tribune of the working class of all colors. Meanwhile, the King campaign began shifting resources to winning votes in some of the white outer wards. When the votes were counted in November, Flynn emerged victorious by a two-to-one margin.

Though ultimately unsuccessful in his bid for mayor, King's Rainbow Coalition model served as the template for the Reverend Jesse L. Jackson's 1984 presidential campaign, along with other progressive candidacies across the country. King's candidacy also helped shape Flynn's mayoral tenure, as Flynn constantly invoked racial healing during his energetic mayoralty. His first act as mayor was to deliver an $800,000 check to the widow of a black taxi driver who had been shot dead by Boston police in a show of deadly force that resulted in a federal jury award to his family.

After King's 1983 defeat, Mayor Flynn's efforts to bring development to the neighborhoods sometimes resulted in the mayor overplaying his hand. A leaked 1985 Boston Redevelopment Authority plan to rebuild Dudley Square in Roxbury resulted in accusations of plantation politics. Shortly thereafter, a provocative effort was launched, known as the Greater Roxbury Incorporation Project (GRIP), for the black neighborhoods of Boston to form a new municipality to be known as "Mandela," named after future South African president Nelson Mandela, then still imprisoned on Robben Island. The incorporation drive pushed by Andrew Jones, a documentary filmmaker and former television network producer, and Curtis Davis, a state planning expert, was long on media savvy but short on grassroots support. The Mandela campaign attracted international attention and stirred the passions of latent black nationalism. The Flynn administration mounted a scorched-earth campaign against GRIP, releasing reports showing the new municipality would face near-certain bankruptcy. In nonbinding referenda in 1986 and 1988, voters turned back the incorporation question by a three-to-one margin.

The 1983 campaign year saw the introduction of district seats to the Boston City Council and the Boston School Committee, with each body electing two black district councilors. Charles C. Yancey, the past president of the influential Black Political Task Force, won election to the District Four City Council seat while Bruce Bolling won the District Seven spot. Yancey had served as the spokesman for the charter reform efforts and helped prove the effectiveness of the new system. Once taking office, he successfully pushed for a series of projects that have benefited his Mattapan and Dorchester constituents, including the new District B3 police station and a new public library building on Blue Hill Avenue. In 1987 when B3 finally opened, "it was a very significant step for the city to make to ensure the residents of Mattapan and Dorchester of the city's concrete commitment to provide public safety services," said Yancey.

Boston's changing demographics in recent years have further empowered candidates of color. In 2009, Felix G. Arroyo (son of former Personnel Director Felix D. Arroyo) and Ayanna Pressley won two of the four at-large city council seats. Two years later, Pressley would go on to top the at-large race, the first time a candidate of color had ever achieved such a feat. In 2013, when Menino had stepped down, three strong minority candidates ran for mayor, Felix G. Arroyo, former state representative and Patrick administration veteran Charlotte Golar-Richie, and John Barros, a School Committee member who had run the Dudley Street Neighborhood Initiative. Despite favorable demographics for another minority finalist, the split vote in the black and Latino communities resulted in another all-white set of finalists. But in a show of the influence of the minority vote, state Representative Martin J. Walsh aggressively courted his preliminary rivals, winning the endorsement of all three and besting City Councilor John Connolly on the strength of winning the minority vote. After the election, he welcomed Arroyo and Barros into his cabinet.

Deval Patrick: "Together We Can"

Deval Laurdine Patrick subtitled his biography *Notes from an Improbable Life,* which aptly describes his astonishing rise in Massachusetts politics. Like Ed Brooke before him, he broke through a statewide political barrier, in Patrick's case becoming the first African American governor in Bay State history. But unlike Brooke, his 2006 election was his first run for public office—a testament to his talents, audacity, and timing. Over the course of his two terms in office, Patrick represented progressive social change and fiscal probity, maintaining balanced budgets and economic growth through the difficulties of the 2008 recession.

As a candidate, Patrick was an outsider to most of Boston's black political community. He had been raised in the heavily black neighborhoods of Chicago's South Side by his mother Emily Mae—a regular singer at church, while his father, Laurdine "Pat" Patrick, was off pursuing a career as a jazz musician. Supported by public assistance, the Patrick family turned down an apartment in the notorious Robert Taylor Homes project and moved instead to his grandparents' apartment, where Patrick, his mother, and sister took turns sleeping on the floor. A talented student, Patrick's academic abilities led to a scholarship through the A Better Chance nonprofit foundation to attend the prestigious Milton Academy just outside of Boston. "Some people will always believe that, but for Milton, I would be peddling drugs or gangbanging on the South Side of Chicago," Patrick wrote in his 2011 biography *A Reason to Believe.* "I reject that. Even back home, others had high expectations for me, and I had them for myself. Milton was a launching pad, but I always had some spring in my legs."

Armed with a Milton Academy diploma, Patrick went on to Harvard College and Harvard Law School, joining an elite private club along the way and forming networks that he would rely on in later campaigns.

After his 1982 graduation from law school, Patrick clerked for Ninth Circuit Court Judge Stephen Reinhardt in Los Angeles. While there, Patrick met Diane, his future wife, at a pumpkin carving contest. Diane, an impressive attorney who went on to make partner at Ropes & Gray, was ending an abusive marriage when she met Deval, setting the stage for his future advocacy on behalf of the victims of domestic violence. The two moved to Brooklyn, New York, in 1983, where he took his "dream job" as a staff attorney at the NAACP Legal Defense Fund, and were married the next year. In that position, he traveled widely in defense of people facing challenging cases of miscast justice. He won a new trial for an Alabama man sentenced to death, when discovery during his last-ditch appeal turned up an unseen witness statement identifying another individual as the perpetrator.

While at the Legal Defense Fund, Patrick also successfully defended three Alabama black voting rights activists targeted by then-US Attorney Jefferson B. Sessions in 1985 with charges of tampering with the absentee ballots of poor black sharecroppers. When President Ronald Reagan appointed Sessions to a federal judgeship in 1986, Patrick helped block his nomination by highlighting Sessions's use of prosecutorial discretion to chill voter assistance. Ironically, the issues that kept Sessions from joining the bench in 1986 were insufficient to stop him from becoming the nation's chief law enforcement officer—singularly responsible for the enforcement of voting rights and civil rights protections—under the Trump administration.

Patrick's law career continued as he joined the prestigious Boston law firm Hill & Barlow in 1986, as it approached its first century in existence. The firm got involved in the state's response to the savings and loan crisis of the 1980s and 1990s, with lawyers from the firm serving for seven years as special assistant attorneys general and on the task force writing new housing regulations. With Patrick's private-sector salary and Diane's income from her job as a labor attorney at Harvard, the two bought a large house in a quiet Milton neighborhood just outside of Mattapan Square. Shortly after the election of Bill Clinton, Patrick was recommended to the White House by an American Bar Association committee along with Legal Defense Fund President Elaine Jones. Patrick joined the administration as the head of the Justice Department's Civil Rights Division. It was in this role that Patrick first met and befriended Barack Obama, while Obama was still a Chicago-based organizer in the same South Side neighborhoods of Patrick's boyhood.

At the Justice Department, Patrick was put on the Equality and Fairness Task Force monitoring the practices of Texaco following the settlement of a racial discrimination case. His role there earned him the respect of the company's CEO, Peter Bijur, who offered Patrick the position of general counsel. Patrick accepted that position and stepped down from the Justice Department in 1999, but only after his relationship with Texaco was cleared by a Nixon-era federal judge. A few years later, in 2001, Patrick left for Coca-Cola, where he became executive vice president, general counsel, and secretary.

As a capable lawyer with civil rights credentials, Patrick maintained credibility within the state's liberal legal circles, even as he pursued a mostly private career. During the 2004 presidential campaign of US Senator John Kerry of Massachusetts, Patrick served on a legal "dream team" of lawyers who flew around the country tackling court challenges. After the campaign, former state Senator Dianne Wilkerson got a call from Patrick. "He had some ideas he wanted to run by me," she said. "I thought that his idea was going to be a way which we could sue and overturn the election. So needless to say, when he came to my office in the State House and told me, 'I'm thinking I'm going to run for governor,' it was a shock to me." After getting over her initial surprise, Wilkerson pressed him on whether he wanted to run or wanted to win. While candidates for public office sometimes run in races they are unlikely to win to boost their public profile, Wilkerson felt that Deval—who symbolized the opposite of current Governor Mitt Romney on nearly every front—was "everything the Democrats have not been able to deliver" and would surely win if he ran. "They get race in you, they get a black male, they get somebody who is wealthy," she said, "and you are an incredible and dynamic speaker … the Democrats are going to eat you up."

Shortly after, Patrick declared his intentions to run for the Democratic nomination for governor, "urging voters to believe," according to the 2005 *Bay State Banner* headline announcing his fledgling candidacy. And though his candidacy was panned as "improbable" and "impossible" in the press, Patrick campaigned under the slogan "Together We Can," with a message that anticipated the "Hope and Change" themes of Barack Obama's historic 2008 presidential race. Even though he was a master orator, Patrick was considered a long shot against the state's popular Attorney General Thomas Reilly from Springfield, who had a considerable head start with $2 million in his campaign's war chest, and was the center of the state's media attention. Reverend Jeffrey Brown, an active pastor at Twelfth Baptist Church in Roxbury, recalls how "everybody thought [Reilly] was a shoo-in for the nomination." Also in the race was Chris Gabrieli, a businessman, education reform advocate, and the running mate for Shannon O'Brien's failed 2002 gubernatorial bid against Mitt Romney.

At the time, blacks numbered over 425,000 in Massachusetts and made up about 7 percent of the state's population. Like Brooke before him, Patrick's electoral chances hinged on creating a broad coalition. His oratorical skills and work ethic gave him a toehold in the primary race. Meanwhile, Reilly's more plodding style and missteps in naming a flawed running mate further boosted Patrick's landmark candidacy. According to Kevin Peterson, founder of the New Democracy Coalition and a longtime voting rights activist, Patrick also got a boost from the endorsement of Reilly's old boss, former Attorney General Scott Harshbarger, whose 1998 gubernatorial campaign Patrick had chaired. During that race, Patrick mastered "inside-party politics" as he quietly visited the districts of legislators across the Commonwealth.

When primary day rolled around, Patrick beat Reilly by twenty-six points and Gabrieli by twenty-two, setting up a final election showdown with Lieutenant Governor Kerry Healey. In the run-up to the November ballot, Patrick fended off repeated attacks aimed at his legal and corporate career and even his family. "When you run for office, that's what you sign up for," Patrick wrote, while conceding the attacks took a toll on his wife.

Patrick's strong advocacy during the campaign for unionized hotel workers helped shore up support of organized labor. Major political figures in the minority community, such as former US Attorney Wayne Budd, a Republican; Suffolk County Sheriff Andrea Cabral; Cambridge Mayor Ken Reeves; and New Bedford City Councilor John Alves also helped.

But the most galvanizing black political endorsement came from the Black Ministerial Alliance. Some members of the powerful coalition of black faith leaders in Boston differed starkly with Patrick on the issue of same-sex marriage. A number of pastors criticized Patrick for siding with a recent state Supreme Judicial Court ruling, which had removed barriers to same-sex marriage in Massachusetts. But overriding their reluctance to support Patrick was their anger at the tone of Republican attacks on Patrick, which even included sending protesters dressed in prison-style orange jumpsuits to Patrick's house to accuse him of being soft on crime. That prompted the Black Ministerial Alliance to invite the candidate to a Dorchester church to "lay on hands" and pray for the success of Patrick's gubernatorial bid. The event produced powerful photos of black faith leadership reaching for Patrick and collectively blessing him together. For the Reverend Jeffrey Brown, the executive director of the Ten Point Coalition, the event was a "way of just letting people know that there's community support for the candidate."

While the Patrick campaign gained momentum, Healey had to contend with the independent candidacy of convenience store mogul Christy Mihos, who had bitterly clashed with the Romney administration while a member of the Massachusetts Turnpike Authority Board of Directors. When the November final election rolled around, Patrick beat Healey by twenty points. He won Boston with three times the votes Healey tallied, earning strong support in the white neighborhoods of South Boston and West Roxbury. Turnout in Milton and in Boston's black neighborhoods reached historic highs, and a few polling places even ran out of ballots. Patrick celebrated that night with supporters at the Hynes Convention Center, telling them, "You are every black man, woman, and child in Massachusetts and America and every other striver of every other race and kind who is reminded tonight that the American dream is for you, too."

Once in office, Patrick was slow to find his footing under the klieg lights of intense scrutiny of the rookie politician. On the policy side, however, he notched a number of victories, expanding the number of families covered under the state's health-care law, moving Massachusetts to embrace green energy, starting an impressive biosciences initiative, and pushing for criminal justice reform. He also successfully guided Massachusetts through the 2008 recession, while serving as a prominent surrogate during Barack Obama's historic White House bid.

In 2010, seeking a second term, Patrick faced Charlie Baker, a socially moderate Republican who attempted to undermine Patrick with charges of poor stewardship of the state budget. Baker, who had ably served in the administration of former Republican Governor William F. Weld, came across as strident compared to the more soft-spoken Patrick, who, faced with the latest GOP accusation, was wont to shrug his shoulders and say, "I've been called everything but a child of God." Like Healey before him, Baker had to contend with an independent candidate, this time state Treasurer Tim Cahill, who drew support from voters who would otherwise have backed Baker. Patrick took 49 percent of the election vote, besting Baker by just over six points.

By the time Patrick left office in 2015, he had made a dramatic mark on state government, appointing 40 percent of the judiciary, boosting charter school enrollment, nurturing an explosion in the biomedical industry, and overseeing the smoothest redistricting process in state history.

The remnants of Patrick's progressive campaigns for governor have had a lasting effect on Democratic politics. A new generation of black public administrators gained valuable experience under Patrick, most notably his former chief of staff, William "Mo" Cowan, whom Patrick appointed to fill the unexpired term of US Senator John F. Kerry when he left office to become secretary of state in the second Obama administration. Veterans of his gubernatorial campaigns included rising star Andrea Campbell, who defeated incumbent District Four Boston City Councilor Charles Yancey in 2015, and Patrick's budget chief Jay Gonzalez, who along with Setti Warren, the first black mayor of Newton, are running for the Democratic nomination for governor in 2018.

Since leaving office, Patrick has relocated to Bain Capital, where he promotes and oversees social-impact lending as an innovative model to attract private capital to solve social problems. He led a renewed but unsuccessful push to block Jeff Session's nomination to US attorney general, and has urged the public to "stay woke" in the divisive era of Donald Trump's presidency.

3

Three Extraordinary Protests

Sandra Larson

Many of Boston's African Americans were political activists, always ready to campaign or protest for their own rights or to protect the rights of others. Three notable examples of this proclivity are the demonstrations by Mothers for Adequate Welfare (MAW), including the 1967 sit-in that led to a police-incited riot; the protest against a proposed urban highway that would demolish neighborhoods and divide Roxbury; and the remarkable courage of local residents who took a stand against apartheid in South Africa.

The Grove Hall Welfare Sit-In and Police Riot

In early June 1967, a peaceful sit-in by a group of Boston women pushing for changes to the city-run welfare system drew a heavy-handed police response that sparked three nights of violent protest along Blue Hill Avenue where Roxbury and Dorchester meet.

Background: Mothers for Adequate Welfare

The women of Mothers for Adequate Welfare had been building a network of support and pushing for welfare system improvements for some time before the Grove Hall Welfare Office sit-in that led to unanticipated violence.

The *Banner* covered the activities of MAW extensively, starting around the time the group formed in fall 1965. Chaired by Doris Bland, the group of mostly African American women began with a simple plan to lend mutual support to one another, discuss how to improve their lot and treatment as single mothers, and grow the group to a point where it could bring pressure on city officials to provide them more respectful treatment and adequate services.

"We tried to get public housing. They don't want us. We try to get good private housing. We can't afford the rents. We can't get good jobs. We don't have the proper education," Bland said in October 1965. "This is why we have formed [MAW]. We have decided that if nobody cares about us, at least we must care for ourselves and our children."[23]

Jim Vrabel, in his book *A People's History of the New Boston*, described Boston's welfare system of that time as "undoubtedly the worst in the country." Massachusetts stood alone in the United States as the only state in which individual cities were responsible for operating the various welfare system components, including Aid to Families with Dependent Children (AFDC). While policies varied from city to city, they largely discouraged welfare recipients from working and discouraged families from staying together. Welfare offices reportedly sent workers out on middle-of-the-night raids to see if men were in the homes of welfare recipients.[24]

In spring 1966, MAW announced its intent to publish a manual of welfare rights. The group said they had requested such a manual from the city's welfare commissioner but were told the city had no funds to create it. "One of the biggest problems of mothers on welfare is that they don't know what things they are entitled to get. There are lots of health services, family services and educational and job opportunities available in the community which mothers never find out about," Bland said. "The welfare workers either don't know about these rights and services themselves, or else they don't tell the mothers about them."[25]

The *Banner's* pages that spring helped disseminate some of MAW's information, including a list of rules and regulations excerpted from the Massachusetts Public Assistance Policy Manual and a list of tenants' rights drawn up by the Boston Congress of Racial Equality.

The formation of MAW occurred in the context of broader dissatisfaction among blacks in Boston and allegations of bigotry and discriminatory treatment in many local agencies and private businesses. Complaints prompted the Massachusetts Advisory Committee to the US Commission on Civil Rights to convene open hearings on the state of Boston's black neighborhoods in March and April 1966. MAW members attended and testified about Welfare Department officials and case workers. The welfare system was just one of many areas in which blacks alleged prejudicial treatment, however, with "deplorable conditions" described in housing, education, and employment.[26]

Deep concerns were being felt in the community also about the Boston Redevelopment Authority's urban renewal plans and methods. MAW's Bland was named to a steering committee formed to oversee a larger group of local community leaders working to keep a close eye on the BRA and to keep residents informed of BRA meetings.[27]

MAW waged a number of public demonstrations to publicize its demands for improved services and treatment. In June 1966, the group held a rally on the Boston Common and marched to the State House, the mayor's office, and the Department of Welfare office. The marchers presented a set of demands for improvements in the AFDC system. As reported in the *Banner*, the demands included such basic requests as distribution of all welfare rules to AFDC mothers, provision of adequate day care so mothers could work or pursue education, an increase in the dollar amount they could earn per month while receiving welfare support, and the right to have welfare office interviews conducted privately. In addition, they wanted children to be able to save money for their future education, and AFDC mothers to have seats on the Welfare Board of Appeals.[28] They also reportedly requested extra money for Thanksgiving and Christmas dinners and asked that their children not be referred to as "illegitimate."[29]

The group's rally and its ambitions were praised by state Representative Royal Bolling of Roxbury. In a statement printed in the *Banner*, Bolling said:

> Many of the requests made by Mothers for Adequate Welfare are purely administrative matters and any forward looking welfare department could quickly put these requests, which are more than reasonable, into effect. It is axiomatic in the social work field that the people who can be helped the most are the ones that really want help and encouragement. These mothers have indicated by their march today that they have the desire and the ambition to escape from the welfare state and it is up to the administrators, both on the city and state level, to meet quickly as possible these minimum requests.[30]

Other elected officials, too, were not unsympathetic to the women's complaints. On the day of the June 1966 rally, Bland and other MAW members had managed to hold a brief face-to-face discussion with Governor John Volpe about their demands and said afterward they were "pleased" with the meeting.[31] In August, Lieutenant Governor Elliot L. Richardson announced his willingness to help seek implementation of MAW's demands. In a letter to MAW members, Richardson expressed agreement with many of the specific demands and indicated that there was a larger need for "substantial reorganization of the welfare structure."[32]

Besides waging protests, MAW members also were working on some positive community projects, such as helping to found the Educational Cooperative in November 1966, an adult education school with teachers from local colleges and the Roxbury community donating their time.[33]

But still, welfare system improvements lagged. The women persisted, gaining visibility and support.

The front page of the November 26, 1966, *Banner* featured the headline "Mothers Picket Welfare Office" above an account of some forty MAW members assembling at the city's main welfare office at 43 Hawkins Street to demand equal access to Thanksgiving turkey basket giveaways.[34] The seeming capriciousness of the Boston welfare commissioner's denial of the holiday supplement was exemplary of the sorts of slights the mothers faced in the system and the struggle to retain dignity for their families.

In December 1966, black activist and *Banner* editor Bryant Rollins, at a meeting of civil rights leaders fighting to abolish the House Committee on Un-American Activities, urged federal support of MAW. Rollins called for whites to cede more control over the black community to the black community. He said the federal government "must begin to support self-help organizations such as ... Mothers for Adequate Welfare" as opposed to sending money to assist black people into traditional welfare, educational, job training and urban renewal agencies, where he said it was wasted and misused.[35] "We must be allowed to rebuild our communities ourselves," Rollins warned. "Otherwise, frustration and discontent will increase, rebellions by Negroes will increase and the result will be something fearful to behold in our country."[36]

In early 1967, MAW leader Doris Bland spoke at a daylong institute on urban problems about the benefits of organizing, citing some changes that had been wrought in the welfare system. Also that spring, MAW was one of the groups participating in a protest against Action for Boston Community Development for cutbacks and perceived overspending on administration and downtown office space.[37]

From Peaceful Sit-In to Violence and Destruction

On Thursday, June 1, 1967, about thirty MAW members gathered inside the Boston Welfare Department's Grove Hall office at 515 Blue Hill Avenue to publicize their frustration with the department and with their treatment at the Grove Hall office in particular.

In the weeks prior, MAW had organized repeated sit-ins at the office with the aim of forcing a meeting with Boston Welfare Commissioner Daniel J. Cronin, in which they planned to present a ten-point list of their demands.

"We're here because we're sick and tired of the way the welfare department, and especially Grove Hall, treats us," said a MAW spokesperson, quoted in a *Banner* story covering one of the earlier sit-ins. "We're tired of being treated like criminals, of having to depend on suspicious and insulting social workers, and at being completely at the mercy of a department we have no control over."[38] In that sit-in, the women had planned to stay until Cronin agreed to meet with them but left around 9:30 p.m. without having achieved this end.

The group's ten demands were straightforward:

1. No recipient should be denied aid based on hearsay evidence and malicious gossip. There must be an investigation before checks are cut off.
2. Removal of police from all welfare offices.
3. Welfare workers must be available every morning to talk with recipients, not just once a week.
4. Welfare workers must respect clients and treat them as equal human beings. Workers must have the power to make decisions quickly without running to the supervisor.
5. There must be a board set up in every office, with a majority of recipients, that can act on emergency demands and policy statements without waiting for the long appeal system.
6. Welfare mothers must be appointed on all policy making boards of welfare.
7. All mothers should be able to save as much money for their children's education as they can and every dollar should be matched by the welfare department so that their children won't be on welfare, too.
8. Mothers should be able to earn $85 a month, and keep 70 percent of what they earn above the $85.

9. There should be a campaign to change the image of the welfare department. Ninety-nine percent of the recipients are honest and responsible.
10. Welfare Commissioner Daniel Cronin should be dismissed and welfare mothers should have a voice in finding his replacement.[39]

These requests were not by any means extravagant, noted long-time state Representative Byron Rushing, who in 1967 was a young community organizer in Roxbury and was well-acquainted with MAW and its aims.

"Their 'demands' were hardly even demands," said Rushing, recalling the events in a 2017 interview. "The major demand was respect. Secondary to that was to get more money."[40]

When MAW members returned to the Welfare Office on June 1, they were determined to wait Cronin out. The sit-in stretched into an overnight vigil and through the next day. Situated near a window, MAW members were able to communicate with people outside, passing notes out and receiving encouragement from a picket line of supporters that gained traction as the vigil wore on.

Former Boston City Councilor Chuck Turner, then a Roxbury activist, was inside the welfare office with MAW. He recalled a feeling of exhilaration among the group as well as compassionate behavior by the demonstrators toward the workers. "The general feeling was—for the time it lasted—a feeling of accomplishment, of having been able to assert the outrage and the concern about how things were being handled, and make our voices known," Turner said.[41]

Late in the afternoon of Friday, June 2, the welfare workers inside the building started to close the office for the weekend. The protestors had used bicycle chains to fasten the doors shut from the inside, preventing the workers from leaving. With Welfare Department staff now trapped inside, alongside MAW members, a small police detail, and a group of MAW sympathizers, additional police arrived on the scene, followed a little later by Cronin.

As reported in the *Banner*, the demonstrators wanted Cronin to respond to their demands through a loudspeaker; a local community leader suggested that, alternatively, the commissioner could climb through a window and speak to them inside. Cronin refused to speak with them if he couldn't enter through the front door.

The scene was calm until a staff member of the Welfare Office complained she was ill and needed medical attention. At that point, the police broke through the glass of the chained door to create an exit, although according to the *Banner* account a basement door had been available for egress all along.

The tension ratcheted up quickly.

The police said, "Get 'em. Beat them if you have to, but get them out of here," according to a MAW member quoted in the *Banner*, and the police then used their nightsticks to beat both women and men inside the facility. When a woman shouted out the window, "They're beating your black sisters in here," men who had gathered outside rushed into the building, only to be beaten back by police.

At this point, with demonstrators being pulled—"dragged," some reported[42]—out of the building and loaded into patrol wagons, the crowd was growing larger and more agitated. Teenagers began throwing bricks and bottles.

Some local community leaders arrived at the scene and tried to calm the police response, urging the superintendent not to expand the confrontation down Blue Hill Avenue. But the police were focused on getting the welfare workers out of the building. At the same time that Noel Day, executive director of the St. Mark Social Center, was speaking with the police superintendent, riot gear was being loaded into the building, according to the *Banner* account. This served to incite the crowd further and frustrate community leaders as they watched the confrontation escalating instead of being diffused.

By around 7:15 p.m., the building had been emptied, but the police forced the crowd down Blue Hill Avenue, and the skirmish line grew blocks long. Unruly members of the crowd aimed stones at passing cars and store windows. Some seventeen hundred police officers were now mobilized, using Franklin Park as a staging area for antiprotest operations.

Day, along with other activists and leaders, including Ellen Jackson, Reverend James Breeden, Chuck Turner, and Rushing, made contact with Mayor John Collins and the police commissioner and helped set up a communications center at the nearby office of Operation Exodus. But the police continued their heavy-handed approach, catching uninvolved passersby off guard. Jackson, a social worker, told the *Boston Globe* that some black women who were not participating in the demonstration had been clubbed by police.[43]

The community leaders also rushed to get teams out to police stations and hospitals to assist those who had been arrested or injured. Rushing and Turner would both be arrested, as well as then-Boston NAACP Vice President Thomas Atkins and dozens of others. By many accounts, police meted out physical punishment during arrests and in the stations even to those not resisting.

"I go away [to the police station], come back and it's worse. I go away to the hospital to get stitches—I come back and it's worse," recalled Rushing. "There were lots of fires, and now fire engines in addition to the police. At this point, I felt a combination of anger and disbelief."[44]

Through the night, crowds roamed the area, and by morning, windows had been smashed and a number of stores along Blue Hill Avenue had been looted or burned. Two more nights of destruction would pass before quiet returned to Grove Hall.

A Police Riot, Not a Race Riot

The disturbance received national coverage, perhaps seen as another of the so-called "race riots" that had devastated neighborhoods in other cities, including New York City, Philadelphia, and Rochester (New York) in 1964, Los Angeles in 1965, and Cleveland in 1966. A *New York Times* story began, "A mob of Negroes raged through the Grove Hall section of the Roxbury district last night, stoning policemen, looting stores and setting fires. It was the first serious riot Boston has experienced since racial tensions began developing here."[45]

Many in Boston's black community did not view the events as racially motivated, but rather as a response to aggressive police actions around a peaceful protest. The *Banner* took a strong stand, placing the blame for the escalation of violence squarely on the police. Its June 10 issue led with the blunt front-page headline, "Police Riot in Grove Hall, Scores Injured."

In an accompanying editorial, publisher Melvin Miller declared that the police had "in effect declared war on Roxbury," and that Roxbury had fought back. He decried the police behavior, noting that "the police attacked indiscriminately, beating astonished spectators, including women and children," and expressed pride that black men ran to the defense of women being attacked.[46]

"Last weekend's turmoil was a revolt against police injustice," Miller wrote. "Daniel Cronin had repeatedly spurned the frustrated mothers in their quest for a hearing. When MAW demonstrated increasing persistence, the police had ample opportunity to tamp down the anger and avoid an all-out riot, but they wouldn't listen to community leaders."

In contrast, a *Boston Globe* editorial on June 5 said, "When lawlessness breaks out, no matter how it may have been triggered, there is but one thing for the police to do, and that is to suppress it. ... [O]n the whole it appears that the police acted with commendable restraint."[47] (The editorial does go on to acknowledge that MAW's grievances were valid and that the city's blacks clearly faced discrimination and alienation.) The Boston police commissioner officially commended his department a week later for the "high quality of police service and protection ... in containing and quelling the civil disorder which erupted in Roxbury on Friday, June 2."[48]

The *Banner*'s coverage was controversial, particularly the use of the term *riot* to describe police behavior. Miller recalled being "intellectually assaulted" for his incendiary phrasing, but nearly fifty years later, still stands by it. "I'm a lawyer. I know what the definition of a riot is," he said in a 2017 interview. Citing a dictionary entry for the word, he reiterated that the police response to the MAW sit-in fits the definition. "It was appropriate for [the police] to respond to the call from the welfare office and it was lawful—but they handled it in an improper and unlawful way. So I identified them as rioters," Miller said. "And their clumsy riot injured a number of people."[49]

Could violence have been averted on June 2, 1967? Rushing, who was arrested twice that night and roughed up by police to the point of needing stitches for a head wound, believes so. "If anyone in the city had asked to talk to the black leadership about the demonstration, it could have gone differently," he said. "They would have had to be willing to negotiate, but I think they probably would have been able to do that."

Rushing noted that in retrospect, the Franklin Park staging area suggests that the police were exceptionally well-prepared, almost as if they expected a riot and showed up ready to fight. "Usually when you call the cops, one or two come, and then call for back up. But here they were, all showing up with paddy wagons and everything," he recalled. "The idea of breaking through the front door was all part of the control they wanted to show."

Not only was the police presence immense, Rushing noted, but the officers did not seem to be from Roxbury or familiar with the community. "They didn't know anybody," Rushing said, asserting that he and Chuck Turner, as local black activists, certainly should have been known to police. "Why didn't they know everybody?"

Rushing praised the *Banner*'s unflinching coverage. "The reporting by the *Banner* was remarkable. It was the only reporting done from the point of view of the community," observed Rushing. "No one else admitted that this riot was started by the police. And that was clear."

Turner, quoted in Mel King's 1981 book *Chain of Change*, said, "When the *Banner* talked about a 'police riot' it pulled the covers off the police and everybody had to look at the reality. I would say it was tremendously significant."[50]

Two weeks after the Grove Hall riot, the *Harvard Crimson* took a similar viewpoint of the police role. "It seems certain that the violence was almost exclusively precipitated by the actions of the police," concluded *Crimson* reporters examining the incidents. They went on to note that while Boston had largely been spared the violent actions in black communities that other major US cities had seen, it appeared that earlier restraint by Boston's blacks was giving way to a new willingness to act.[51]

While the *Crimson* writers raised the possibility that the blacks of Roxbury had "discovered a new tool with which to gain their goals— violence," the Grove Hall riot did not presage a new era of racial violence. Instead, the violence of June 2–4, 1967, appears to be a seminal event, resulting in lessons learned and future eruptions prevented.

Rushing draws a straight line between the devastation in Grove Hall and the successfully tempered fury in Boston less than a year later, when Martin Luther King Jr. was assassinated on April 4, 1968. "I think the immediate after-effect was how small the violence was when Martin Luther King was assassinated," Rushing said. "I think it would have been a lot worse. There was a sense in the community of, 'We're going to end up suffering the most from this if we start burning everything down.' There was more knowledge. There was also a mayoral administration that realized they had to do something."

According to Rushing, a vigorous (seemingly "endless") series of meetings that began in Roxbury in the wake of the Grove Hall riot set the stage for new, energetic community economic development efforts. After King's assassination, when an influx of federal, state, and philanthropic funding came for addressing troubles in the black community, those ten months of soul-searching and organizing had already sown seeds for positive action.

The Upshot: a Welfare System Changed, Community Wisdom Gained

After the Grove Hall violence, progress came on several fronts. Mayor Collins pledged to look into Grove Hall Welfare Office practices, and city officials—especially under the new administration of Kevin White the following year—worked to forge better relationships with black leaders and residents.

The Massachusetts legislature moved to dismantle the separate city-controlled welfare departments and move welfare administration to state control. This change came with some help from Mayor-elect White, who at that time was still Massachusetts secretary of the commonwealth. According to Vrabel in his *People's History,* "Thanks to MAW's efforts, a bill had been filed in the Massachusetts legislature that called for the state to take over responsibility for administering the welfare system. For various reasons it was stuck in committee, but Kevin White found a way to get it unstuck." White reportedly threatened to continue as Massachusetts' secretary of state while serving as mayor if the legislators didn't pass the bill, and since others wanted his position, they were persuaded.[52]

MAW kept on organizing, and the group persisted as an independent local entity even as the National Welfare Rights Organization came to town and by some accounts tried to impose its own organizing. Eventually the NWRO presence faded, and MAW continued as before.[53] Bland was named to a new board formed to work on improving the welfare system.

Vrabel ascribed a powerful impact to MAW, concluding that "this small army of women had succeeded in creating a brand new welfare system."[54]

Former state Representative Gloria Fox had crossed paths with MAW members through her organizing work with families in Roxbury and her own life as a mother living in the Whittier Street housing development. "The mothers were not treated kindly at that time," Fox noted. "They tried to negotiate, and negotiate fairly. Some might have thought they were 'pushy.' That was part of it—how they treated women was deplorable. For the first time, women, poor women, were fighting back, and they were doing it in a non-violent way."[55]

Looking back, Fox observed that the Grove Hall event, which she refuses to label as a *riot* at all, may have been a necessary step for future progress. "It resulted in some change, but it was harder for people organizing to try to work with the police. But that was what had to happen, that 'altercation,' so that it never happened again," she said.

The once-despised former Welfare Office building at 515 Blue Hill Avenue now houses Mother Caroline Academy, a tuition-free private school for girls. The Grove Hall Welfare Riot is set to be memorialized on the Roxbury Memory Trail. A work-in-progress as of 2017, the trail marker in front of the building will take the form of an obelisk bearing text recalling the riot. According to organizers, the trail markers will honor "the will to freedom and the deep desire of communities to improve the opportunities for each succeeding generation."[56] The Roxbury Memory Trail project is led by the Grove Hall Neighborhood Development Corporation with Dudley Square Main Streets, Greater Grove Hall Main Streets, The National Center of Afro-American Artists, and Earthos Institute.

Stopping the Highways

Outside Boston's Roxbury Crossing MBTA station, a large plaque displays the names of 166 ordinary citizens and community leaders who forged a unified resistance to halt a massive urban highway expansion that would have ripped through Roxbury, Jamaica Plain, the South End, and Cambridge.

The plaque is located here because the surrounding Roxbury neighborhood illustrates well the sweet and the bitter upshot of the victorious antihighway movement. If the students, workers, and families coming in and out of the busy station pause and gaze up and down Tremont Street, they see the Southwest Corridor Park and the modern buildings of Roxbury Community College, built on land cleared to make way for two highways that would have crossed here. They might also notice the weed-choked empty lot known as Parcel 3, vacant for nearly fifty years, but, like much of the cleared land, it once held homes and businesses that made up a community's beating pulse. And if passersby have absorbed the plaque's text, they are aware that if not for citizen outrage channeled into action, this area would be split apart and deeply shadowed by a five-story highway interchange carrying hundreds of thousands of vehicles each day.

Background: An Urban Highway Extension, Decades in the Planning

In the 1960s, plans for two urban highways were in the works for Boston: The "Inner Belt" would be an eight-lane ring road encircling the central city, running from Charlestown to Somerville, Cambridge, and Brookline, and through the Boston neighborhoods of Fenway, Roxbury, and the South End; the "Southwest Expressway," also eight lanes, would be a north-south extension of Interstate 95 cutting through Hyde Park, Jamaica Plain, and Roxbury, and concluding in the South End with a bypass spur that would connect to the already-built Southeast Expressway.

The idea of these Boston highways stemmed from the Massachusetts Highway Department's creation in 1948 of a Master Highway Plan for the Boston Metropolitan Area. New highways were seen as ways to boost economic activity and smooth automobile travel through and around Boston. Nevertheless, the state couldn't afford to build them on its own. In 1956, the Defense Interstate Highway Act guaranteed 90 percent federal funding reimbursements for such projects, providing sure incentive to get projects going sooner rather than later.[57] The planning history is well-chronicled in *Rites of Way: The Politics of Transportation in Boston and the US City*, along with a detailed case study of the antihighway citizen protest movement by Alan Lupo, a Boston native and longtime local newspaper reporter and columnist.

The Massachusetts Department of Public Works (DPW) began holding hearings on the plans in 1960. The earliest opposition to the Inner Belt came from Cambridge residents and from Fenway institutions such as the Museum of Fine Arts; a revised plan changed the

Fenway stretch—which would have snaked between the MFA and the Isabella Stewart Gardner Museum—to be depressed underground.[58]

But Lower Roxbury[59] stood to bear—and did bear—a particularly heavy burden, as it lay directly where the two highways were to intersect. The highway interchange would have been a huge tangle of ramps and loops as tall as a five-story building, dividing the neighborhood and looming over and isolating the Whittier Street and Mission Hill Extension housing developments as well as the planned Madison Park High School campus.[60]

While it was spared the intrusion of the highways themselves, Roxbury lost hundreds of homes, businesses, and jobs in the preparatory land-taking and demolition that proceeded for years before the plan was finally forced to a halt in 1972.

Contentious Meetings and Major Demonstrations

As awareness of the highway plans grew in the early 1960s, so did vocal opposition from various communities the plans would affect. Meetings in Cambridge and Boston drew chants, boos, and hisses against the Inner Belt; a meeting in Hyde Park drew two thousand people opposed to the Southwest Expressway; a headline for a *Boston Globe* story on a meeting at the Timilty School attended by two thousand residents of Roslindale, Hyde Park, Jamaica Plain, and Roxbury said the school was "rocked with shouts of opposition."[61]

Banner front page stories in 1965 and early 1966 raised alarm about the impending displacement of thousands of Roxbury residents. "Inner Belt to Uproot 937 Roxbury Families" dominated a front page in December 1965, and "6000 in Roxbury Sent Removal Notice" followed a few weeks later.[62]

In the South End, many blacks' homes were threatened by a third piece of the highway project, the four-lane South End Bypass under the jurisdiction of the BRA, which would tear through the short residential streets that lay between Columbus Avenue and the Southwest Corridor rail line. "Our neighbors never knew when their houses were going to be taken," recalled Ann Hershfang, a white South End resident who served on the Tubman Area Planning Council, an advisory group of blacks and whites working to stop the bypass plan.[63]

Even while voicing opposition, however, most residents and community leaders in the mid-1960s assumed the highways would be built and that all they could do in the face of government-made plans was try to alter the route or reduce the damage to neighborhoods in its wide path. But the movement gained momentum and a louder voice as opposition continued to be expressed in meetings and demonstrations over the next few years. Activism spread to more communities and eventually spurred some unexpected new alliances among them.

In 1968, the Greater Boston Committee on the Transportation Crisis (GBCTC) was formed to bring diverse opposition groups together. It included blacks, whites, and Puerto Ricans, militants and moderates, from neighborhoods and towns that had not traditionally been linked, including the South End, Roxbury, Jamaica Plain, East Boston, Charlestown, Cambridge, and suburban towns fighting highways and connector roads that threatened homes, marshland, and open space.[64] While it suffered its share of internal disagreements, the GBCTC was able to push the movement forward with greater strength through its breadth of representation.

On January 25, 1969, this diverse committee organized a major public demonstration in front of the Massachusetts State House, dubbed "People before Highways Day." Just two days after Governor Frank Sargent had assumed office after Governor John Volpe was appointed as US transportation secretary by President Nixon, more than two thousand residents from at least ten communities rallied, pressuring him to stop the plans and to review them with citizen involvement.

While Governor Sargent met with demonstrators, heard their presentations, and assured them that his administration would "never make a decision that puts people below concrete," he did not agree to stop any plans immediately, nor to stop the demolition of homes along the path. Even so, the large rally was a turning point in public and media attention to the cause.[65]

Banner Coverage: Unease and Resistance Grows in Roxbury

The *Banner* was not in existence in the earliest days of highway planning and opposition, but in 1965–66, the paper's coverage of the topic indicated that government agencies' communication with Roxbury and South End households who would be displaced by the highway was woefully inadequate.

A story about the BRA preparing to conduct a survey for the DPW of the six hundred to nine hundred families whose homes were threatened by the highways noted that "[f]ew of the agencies which deal directly with the people who are to be relocated were represented at the meeting. A majority of the persons at the meeting were non-Negro, ... and there was no person at the meeting who actually lived in the area concerned."[66] The article also indicates that "anxiety concerning Inner Belt displacements continues to rise" and that families reportedly were moving out of Lower Roxbury without waiting for the relocation assistance they were due from the DPW.

"To date, members of the Roxbury community have experienced nothing but confusion, misinformation, duplication of effort and a general lack of communications concerning the DPW's plans," an April 1966 editorial asserts.[67]

The *Banner* observed that other communities affected by the Inner Belt, even those with fewer homes at stake, seemed to be receiving more attention than Roxbury, which was facing the imminent demolition of homes, businesses, and schools as well as the prospect of major highways creating stark barriers around Lower Roxbury housing developments and the Madison Park High School campus, still in the planning stages.

In late 1967, a "meeting of concerned residents" covered by the *Banner* included pointed comments about the dramatic negative effects the highways would have on communities—not just loss of structures, but loss of space that could be used for community-serving purposes. Ralph Smith of the Lower Roxbury Community Corporation, who had issued a statement against the proposed highways, said the highways would consume space better used for Roxbury housing and economic development and would divide and isolate Lower Roxbury.

"This highway will turn out to be a new set of boundaries for the Negro community in Boston," Smith's statement said.[68]

Emerging Roxbury Leaders

In April 1968, the Boston Black United Front, an umbrella organization of black advocacy organizations, announced a twenty-one-point list of demands. One of its demands was that Inner Belt and Southwest Expressway plans be halted immediately and that any continued planning be negotiated with the black community.

Chuck Turner, then cochair of the United Front, was put in charge of organizing the Roxbury highway resistance effort. Within the United Front, Turner formed "Operation Stop," a coalition of community groups working to stop the highways in Roxbury, and Operation Stop then became active in the larger GBCTC coalition.

"It would have been monstrous," Turner recalled, describing the gargantuan interchange of the proposed eight-lane highways, whose width he said would actually have amounted to something closer to a sixteen lanes when taking into account breakdown lanes, service roads, and rail tracks in the center median of the Southwest Expressway.[69]

On July 15, 1969, Turner organized a group of blacks to hold a press conference at Columbus Avenue and Ruggles Street, on a site laid bare by the prehighway demolition. By this time, the DPW already had taken 479 structures in Roxbury, leaving 326 families displaced; 234 buildings had been destroyed.[70] "There will be no Inner Belt through our community," Turner proclaimed, holding a press release signed by black City Councilor Thomas I. Atkins and forty predominantly black groups.[71]

Turner's goal was not simply to say no to a highway. "The struggle was a conscious one to stop one thing and do another," he continues to emphasize.[72] While it was too late to save the demolished buildings and displaced families, he wanted to connect stopping the highway with securing real improvements for Roxbury's black community. "Our community does not need an Inner Belt. Instead, we need the land which the state has cleared for the Inner Belt, and we are now planning how we will use this land to meet our own needs, rather than the needs of outsiders," Turner said at the press conference.[73]

Author Lupo observed, "The DPW looked at thirty-five acres of desolation in the Madison Park district of Roxbury and saw highway interchanges. Chuck Turner looked at it and saw housing."

Former state Rep. Gloria Fox was at that time a young mother living in the Whittier Street housing development and managing the Whittier Street Service Center. The misguided highway plans—and the demolition all around her neighborhood—propelled her into an-tihighway organizing with Operation Stop.

"It was almost like we woke up one day and everything was gone," she recalled, causing not only loss of structures, but health issues from the demolition dust. "You could look down Tremont and Columbus and see the vacant land as far as the eye could see."

Creating a Unified Movement

While each neighborhood brought their own fears and goals to the highway opposition, eventually it became clear that there could be greater strength in a unified front, though that is easier said than done in Boston.

In the suburbs and in the Fenway, many of the concerns were about destruction of natural areas and urban green spaces, while human displacement and loss of economic potential were keys in others. Jamaica Plain residents were, for a time, focused more on getting the Southwest Expressway depressed below ground level than on stopping it. White opponents in East Boston, Charleston, and Cambridge may not have felt they had much in common with each other, nor with the blacks of Roxbury. "The very idea of an alliance ran counter to the insularity of Greater Boston neighborhoods," according to Lupo.[74] But somehow, in fits and starts, the movement coalesced.

"People came together and they didn't all look like us. Everyone had something to lose—transportation, community, environment," said Fox. "[Suburban activists] didn't expect city people to care about the environment, not knowing that everything plays a role as we live and die in polluted environment. Everybody has their own self-interest. But if you understand, and you're tolerant, and working on one goal, it works out. We had one purpose, one goal."[75]

Operation Stop and the larger GBCTC forged as unified a front as possible, and many credit Turner's role in it as crucial. "It was really Chuck's chairmanship that held the anti-highway movement together in the whole region," recalled Hershfang. "It was widely varying communities, from East Boston, Milton, Lexington, Cambridge, and Jamaica Plain—groups that didn't typically work together. Chuck held it together and made it strong."[76]

Pressure Builds, and a Task Force Is Swayed

Governor Sargent appointed a task force in mid-1969, with MIT Professor Alan Altshuler as chair, to study the highway plans and formulate recommendations. In November, Chuck Turner and other GBCTC members had a pivotal meeting with the task force. They used it to press their case hard.

Altshuler later said the protesters made a better case than the officials. Indeed, the task force was "radicalized" after listening to them, he said. The task force moved forward, now looking into the points GBCTC had made, reexamining their assumptions and taking a harder look at the data they'd been given.[77]

Pressure mounted on the governor to issue a moratorium on highway construction. Mayor White, after a long hesitation, came out in favor of a moratorium, joining a host of legislators and community, environmental, and religious groups. The Greater Boston Chamber of Commerce was one of the lone voices still in support of the highway construction.

The task force's report, released January 8, 1970, was harshly critical of the highway planning process. Even more damning, it laid bare that the primary reason the state had pushed so hard for the urban highways was not because they were the best investment, but solely because of the 90 percent federal funding offer.[78]

Victory—the Highway Plan Is Scrapped

Soon after the task force report release, the dominoes began to fall.

On February 11, 1970, Governor Sargent had made his decision. In a televised address, he announced a moratorium on all highway construction in Boston. He would launch a Boston Transportation Planning Review restudy that would examine not simply how the highway plans should proceed, but whether highways were the answer at all. "Four years ago ... nearly everyone was sure highways were the only answer to transportation problems for years to come," Sargent said. "We were wrong."

In 1971, Boston Mayor Kevin White halted plans for the South End Bypass.

Finally, on November 30, 1972, Sargent announced cancellation of the Inner Belt and Southwest Corridor plans.

Lasting Legacy—Community Involvement, Empowerment

In an era in which the car was king and "walkable urbanism" was not yet a buzz phrase for planners—and while Roxbury's black residents had myriad other crucial battles to wage—a dedicated, persistent, and diverse group of citizen activists rose up and stopped a highway.

Karilyn Crockett, a black Bostonian whose 2013 doctoral dissertation covers the historic struggle, cited three primary elements of that time that influenced the successful fight: an urban planning field beginning to question the trend of bypassing urban centers for suburbs; a multitude of civil rights and protest movements raising the collective consciousness; and ordinary residents demanding the right to participate in processes involving their own neighborhoods. "There was a lot at stake for people. It wasn't just about stopping a highway," she said. "It was about making decision-making and governance really reflect the will of the people."[79]

Greater Boston's successful and revolutionary upending of the prevailing highway-expansion trend spurred a major change in federal transportation funding. A 1973 provision in the Federal-Aid Highway Act allowed cities, for the first time in US history, to divert federal highway funds toward public transit and open space projects when new highway plans were successfully opposed.

This reallocation of funds and the advance thought that activists had put into planning for use of the cleared land created a silver lining on the devastation in Lower Roxbury. The Orange Line opened along the Southwest Expressway's planned route in 1987, providing new rapid transit options in Lower Roxbury and Jamaica Plain, (even as it removed transit along Washington Street in Roxbury and the South End). The Southwest Corridor Park alongside and decked over the Orange Line tracks, created a 4.7-mile swath of recreational green space that links neighborhoods from Back Bay to Forest Hills. Where the highway interchange would have loomed along Columbus Avenue, Roxbury Community College opened in a sixteen-acre modern campus in 1988, something Turner and others had recommended as a beneficial use of the land.

Another legacy of the antihighway fight, a less tangible one, is a continued high degree of citizen vigilance and involvement by Roxbury residents. The shadow of the ill-conceived highway plan and the pointless devastation of neighborhoods still looms large. Nearly fifty years later, this bitter story still surfaces quickly whenever city or state officials appear to be readying a top-down plan that will alter Roxbury's landscape.

A case in point is the city and state transportation agencies' recent tinkering with the future of Melnea Cass Boulevard, built in 1981 on one of the paths bulldozed for the Inner Belt. The availability of a pile of federal funding spurred the Boston Transportation Department and the Massachusetts Department of Transportation in 2011 to launch a redesign project for the wide, heavily trafficked boulevard.

But officials' hopes for a rapid design and construction cycle hit a snag in the first public meeting for the project, when Lower Roxbury residents and elected officials cried foul, sensing that once again, plans were being forced on a community with wounds that are still raw from the destructive highway effort. State Representatives Fox and Rushing were at that meeting and helped force it to a halt. They called for the planners to do some homework and return with a presentation that traced the history of the highway plan and acknowledged subsequent community-led planning processes, before describing any new plans.[80]

At the next meeting, the abashed city officials made some headway in repairing community relations by showing they had done their homework, and that they could speak on the troubled history of Lower Roxbury and the boulevard. "This is part of a long movement that's continuing," Fox commented after the second meeting. "We have to be community planners—but most community members don't believe they are. Then they get into a meeting like this, and they realize they're the only ones who can do it. Because they have to live with this."[81]

Years later, Melnea Cass Boulevard plans were inching along, with design proposals now significantly altered to fit community demands. At a 2015 meeting, Rushing stood up to remind attendees and presenters once again of the street's grim origins and the successful antihighway activism of the 1960s. "I don't want us ever to forget that no matter what you dislike about Melnea Cass Boulevard, if it wasn't for this community, it would have been an eight-lane highway going through here," Rushing said. "We stopped that."[82]

Local Action against Apartheid in South Africa

When Nelson Mandela was set free on February 11, 1990 after twenty-seven years in South African prisons, he made Boston one of the first stops on a US tour. As reported in the *Washington Post*, an estimated 325,000 people gathered on the Charles River Esplanade in June of that year to listen to the revered freedom fighter. Mandela expressed special thanks to Massachusetts for its leading role in action to end the repressive and racist South African apartheid system.

"Massachusetts has won a special place in our struggle," Mandela said. "I am especially grateful to you ... for leading the fight for democracy in South Africa. ... It was you who rallied around our cause when we soldiered on by ourselves. Thus, you became the conscience of American society."[83]

Prominent among the Massachusetts players who raised their voices against apartheid were black Polaroid employees whose grassroots protest movement led the firm to cut ties with South Africa, and black elected officials who spearheaded divestment of city and state government funds from banks and corporations with South Africa ties.

The Polaroid Revolutionary Workers Movement

Polaroid, headquartered in Cambridge, Massachusetts, was the first US company to cut ties with South Africa for moral reasons in the apartheid era.[84] Its action came after seven years of intense pressure that began in 1970 when two African American employees discovered the firm's ties to South Africa and risked their own livelihoods to take a stand. The workers' successful protest movement helped usher in a new awareness of the role of corporations and institutions in enabling apartheid. While the idea of sanctions and boycotts related to South Africa traces back to the 1950s, and South Africa had already been barred from the Olympics, the pressure in the 1970s on Polaroid and its ultimate cutting of South Africa ties in 1977 was something new. "Their influence was massive," said Eric J. Morgan, a professor of democracy and justice studies whose research has focused on transnational antiapartheid activism. "The Polaroid workers' movement was revolutionary in holding a U.S. corporation responsible for its relationship with South Africa, in asking U.S. power holders to confront apartheid."[85]

"You Get Involved"

In 1968, Caroline Hunter was a recent graduate of Xavier University, a historically black Catholic institution in her hometown of New Orleans. As an African American woman with a degree in chemistry she was a rarity, as she still is today. Having landed a job as a research chemist at Polaroid Corporation in Cambridge, she left New Orleans for the first time in her life. But the twenty-one-year-old was not fearful. "I didn't think it was a big deal," she recalled. "I thought you had to fall out of the nest. And it was a much better job than I would have been able to get in Louisiana—that's why I went to college."[86]

In her first two years at Polaroid, Hunter settled into her work and also sought out community service opportunities. She spoke in Cambridge public schools as part of a Polaroid youth motivation program; in Boston, she led "kitchen chemistry" classes for children at the Roxbury Multi-Service Center and taught adults in Polaroid's Inner City job training program. "That's how I was raised—you share what you have, you get involved," Hunter said. "You don't see it as activism, so much as community."

Then, on an early October day in 1970, Hunter and coworker Ken Williams, who years later would become her husband, stumbled upon evidence that Polaroid was operating in South Africa. Heading out of the Technology Square building where Williams worked as a photographer, they noticed a mock-up of a photo ID pinned to a bulletin board. It appeared to be a South African mining company badge.

"We looked at each other," she said, recalling the moment, "and Ken said, 'I didn't know Polaroid was in South Africa.' And I said, 'I know it's a bad place for black people.'"[87] Hunter knew this only because in tenth grade her class had read *Cry, the Beloved Country*, and she remembered seeing news of the Sharpeville massacre in 1960. But neither she nor Williams knew much more. This was well before antiapartheid efforts in the United States gained full steam in the 1980s. Besides, American blacks had plenty of issues to contend with closer to home.

"This was the height of the anti-Vietnam War movement, the Black Panthers—civil rights issues were prominent. This was the busing era, integration," Hunter noted. At that moment, though, the pair knew they had to press for answers.

"Before we started asking questions, we went home and looked in the encyclopedia. Then we went to the library and checked out some books and did some research," she recalled. "And we were horrified." They saw how Polaroid's ID-2 system—a camera, an instant processor, and a laminator—was supporting the intensely hated "passbook" system used by the apartheid regime to monitor and control South Africa's black majority. The pair's research and questions grew quickly into the protest and boycott effort they called the Polaroid Revolutionary Workers Movement.

They planned a rally outside the company headquarters a few days later and typed up the first of many leaflets. "Polaroid imprisons black people in 60 seconds," this one proclaimed bluntly, a twist on the firm's own instant-camera advertising. The fledgling activists went into the office on a Saturday and posted the leaflet on bulletin boards, inside restroom stalls, and even in the parking area where company executives parked.[88]

The PRWM's first rally in Tech Square included Chris Nteta, a black South African who was a local student, as a speaker. Nteta also helped PWRM develop its three initial demands:

1. that Polaroid announce a policy of complete disengagement from South Africa;
2. that the management meet the entire company and announce its position on apartheid in the U.S. and in South Africa simultaneously;
3. that the company donate all its profits from South Africa to the recognized African liberation movement in that country.[89]

Polaroid apparently was taken by surprise. Founder Edwin Land and his company had something of a reputation for progressive policies and uncommon diversity in worker hiring and advancement. Most employees were unaware of any South Africa ties, and even management wasn't sure what the issue was, according to Peter C. Wensberg, a longtime Polaroid employee and executive who included an account of PRWM's emergence his 1987 book, *Land's Polaroid: A Company and the Man Who Invented It.*

Wensberg described Hunter's single-minded focus as she called for Polaroid to denounce and leave South Africa: "She was brilliant, black, militant, and committed," he wrote. " … Her thoughts organized, her delivery swift, her demeanor alternately rational and passionate, [she] could rivet an audience."[90] Hunter and Williams quickly caught the attention of reporters local and national. Another demonstration later that same month drew one thousand participants, partly due to support for PRWM's cause by the New York-based American Committee on Africa (ACOA).[91] Polaroid had to respond.

The Polaroid Experiment

By Wensberg's account, Land and his firm attempted to address the issue without actually acquiescing to PRWM's demands. The firm decided to dispatch a multiracial group of employees to South Africa to learn more about black workers' conditions and what they wanted.

Around the same time, in December 1970, Polaroid offered a $20,000 donation to Roxbury's Black United Front. Though Polaroid insisted its choice of community funding recipient was made before the PWRM protests began, the donation stirred controversy. ("Was this 'blood money?' we wondered," recalled Hunter.) After some debate, the United Front decided to accept the donation but gave the money away to African and US black liberation groups.[92]

Polaroid's fact-finding group returned from South Africa and put forth its recommendations. Chief among them was to not disengage from South Africa but instead work to improve conditions for black workers at its distributor there, Frank and Hirsch. Dubbed the "Polaroid Experiment," the new plan also banned sales of film and equipment to the South African government and its military and police. In January 1971 Polaroid took out full-page advertisements in US major newspapers and in twenty black weekly papers to announce the plan.[93]

Polaroid's experiment in many ways foretold the influential guidelines for doing business in South Africa devised six years later by Reverend Leon Sullivan, a Philadelphia minister and the first black board member of General Motors Corporation. But in 1971, Polaroid's compromise failed to mollify the PRWM. The activists scoffed at the idea that blacks under the apartheid system would be able to openly call for foreign divestment without risking punishment and said Polaroid was opting to keep business ties for its own bene-fit.[94] In testimony before the United Nations Special Committee on the Policies of Apartheid on February 3, 1971, Hunter and Williams decried the fact-finding mission and the firm's continued ties with South Africa. "The Polaroid 'experiment' on black South Africa is an insult to the Polaroid Revolutionary Workers Movement and all those who strive for the liberation of South Africa," they testified. "Their 'experiment' offers foreign investors the pretense of the demise of apartheid through strong support of the South African racist regime." They vowed to continue pushing for an international boycott until Polaroid was forced out of South Africa or black South Africa was liberated, and urged the UN Special Committee to support PRWM's demands and to "use all its influence and power against the Polaroid Corporation."[95]

Shortly after her UN testimony, Hunter was suspended and then fired from her job.[96] Williams had already resigned. But the pair re-mained undaunted. Being unemployed, Hunter observed wryly, just gave her more time to work on strengthening the boycott effort. The PWRM continued organizing protests.[97]

In November 1977, it was revealed that the distributor Frank and Hirsch was selling Polaroid film to the South African government in spite of Polaroid's ban. At that point, the company finally severed ties with its distributor altogether. Seven years after Hunter and Williams began their movement, a key PRWM mission was accomplished. Polaroid was out of South Africa.[98]

Withdraw and Isolate or Engage and Influence?

After Polaroid cut its South Africa ties, public pressure on US corporations to pull out of South Africa grew. For Polaroid, South African sales had represented only a miniscule fraction of its business, but total US corporate withdrawal was not a trivial matter. As of 1978, more than three hundred US corporations had operations in South Africa with investments of approximately $1.6 billion, and US banks had $2.2 billion in loans there.[99]

While the PRWM and other activist groups called for nothing less than total separation, others argued that South African blacks could be best served by companies remaining there and using their presence to push for better worker conditions and an end to racist policies. A key leader in the latter school of thought was Leon Sullivan, whose "Sullivan Principles" for South Africa engagement were adopted by some 160 corporations.[100] The minister and civil rights activist's guidelines called for corporations to implement nonsegregation of races in the workplace, equal pay and fair employment practices, training programs to prepare blacks for career advancement, and improvements to the quality of life such as housing, transportation, schools, and health facilities. The Cambridge, Massachusetts, based consulting firm Arthur D. Little was engaged to monitor and rate companies on their compliance. Sullivan expanded the guidelines in 1984, directing firms also to campaign against apartheid and allow black workers full job mobility.[101] Outside the corporate realm, the Nixon and Reagan administrations favored a "constructive engagement" approach as well. And black American tennis great Arthur Ashe, who visited South Africa several times in the 1970s, espoused the view that connecting with South African blacks and learning firsthand of their struggles and hopes would be more effective in confronting apartheid than boycotting and disengaging.[102]

The engagement vs. isolation debate went on through the 1970s and '80s, but the push for withdrawal eventually won out. In 1987, with apartheid still alive ten years after his Sullivan Principles were announced and with large corporations such as Coca-Cola, IBM, and General Motors having pulled out, even Sullivan called for all corporations to withdraw from South Africa.[103]

A Legacy of Courage

Looking back, Caroline Hunter recalls no fear in launching the revolutionary movement that ended her first career and helped propel a corporate exodus from South Africa. "We were helping David battle Goliath—we were throwing rocks," she said. "We saw it as a mission, and the horror of South Africa was motivation."

Eventually, enough rocks hit their mark and the giant fell. On October 2, 1986, the US government passed legislation, despite President Ronald Reagan's veto, that imposed heavy sanctions on South Africa and forbade new business or investments there by US companies. In 1990, Nelson Mandela was freed from prison. The apartheid system unraveled. Finally, in a turn that early antiapartheid activists could scarcely have dreamed of, in 1994 Mandela himself was elected the first black president of South Africa.

Hunter went on to pursue a thirty-four-year career as a public school educator in Cambridge, teaching high school science and math, organizing school-community projects, and rising to assistant principal. She has received wide recognition for her social justice activism at Polaroid and beyond; honors have included the Massachusetts Teachers Association's Louise Gaskins Lifetime Civil Rights Award in 2011 and the National Education Association's Rosa Parks Memorial Award in 2012.[104]

Nearly fifty years after discovering the damning photo ID card at Polaroid, Hunter in 2017 was still pursuing her labor of love, working to educate today's social justice groups on how she and the PRWM used boycott, divestment, and sanctions to help dismantle South

African apartheid and how they might apply this "BDS" strategy to fight discriminatory government systems now.

She imparts to the younger activists her wisdom on the importance of focus, commitment, and building coalitions. She tells them how the PRWM waged its battle on multiple fronts, from churches to city councils, student groups and on up to the United Nations, and how they kept the fight going relentlessly.

"I haven't stopped," Hunter said. "I blame my mama for that."[105]

The Local Push for Government Divestment

Through the 1980s, a growing international protest movement forced corporations, universities, and governments to cut financial ties to South Africa, leaving South Africa increasingly isolated and under pressure to end the apartheid system. Massachusetts was a leader here, too, and its black elected officials were key to pushing divestment action in state and city government.

Massachusetts Divests Despite a Governor's Veto

Massachusetts was an early leader in divesting state pension funds from banks and corporations operating in South Africa. One of the strongest in the nation, the divestment bill was passed by the Massachusetts legislature in 1982. The bill overcame a veto by outgoing Governor Edward King in January 1983 and then was signed into law by Governor Michael Dukakis, subjecting some $90 million of state pension funds to reinvestment.[106]

The divestment effort was led in the legislature by state Representative Mel King, a black Independent from Boston, and state Senator Jack Backman, a white Democrat from Brookline. The cause was further championed by the Massachusetts Coalition for Divestment from South Africa (Mass Divest), a large coalition of antiapartheid groups that included black and Catholic church organizations, labor unions, and community groups. In addition, the involvement of TransAfrica and its leader, black MIT Professor Willard Johnson, brought the campaign to the attention of black professionals and academics.[107]

Representative King had instigated hearings on the state's South Africa connections as early as 1976, after uprisings in Soweto and other areas of South Africa that year. King and Backman first filed legislation to divest in 1979, after a report revealed that more public employee pension money was invested in South Africa than in Massachusetts. This first bill didn't pass, but King was able to get an amendment added to the state budget to bar additional pension investments in South Africa. The press for full divestment continued with the 1981 introduction of a new bill drafted by Mass Divest, hearings before the Public Service Committee, and much work by advocates to dispel fears and objections.

In late 1982, with the bill near passage, Governor King introduced a last-minute amendment that would cut the amount of money actually divested and would spare some companies, such as Ford Motor Company, that had actual plants and workers in South Africa. The bill's advocates had to decide whether to accept this watered-down version or gamble on pushing for total divestment. When Mass Divest chose to insist on the full divestment bill, King and Backman did the work of communicating this firmly to House and Senate leaders. The bill, without the amendment, was submitted to Governor King, who vetoed it. The legislature overrode the veto on January 4, 1983.[108]

The Massachusetts divestment decision served as a national model and demonstrated the efficacy of having a black and a white legislator pushing together for antiapartheid measures.[109]

The City of Boston Divests Early and Fully

In Boston, City Councilor Charles Yancey, one of two blacks on the thirteen-member council, was instrumental in crafting and pushing through a 1984 city ordinance to divest all city funds from South Africa. While Boston was not the first city to do so, its ordinance was one of the most far-reaching, spelling out total divestment with four rules:

- It prohibited retirement funds of city workers from being invested or deposited in US banks that loaned money to the government of South Africa or to South African corporations and prohibited the pension funds from being invested in stocks and bonds of companies that did business in South Africa.
- It prohibited all other public funds from being deposited with banks that made loans to South Africa or to companies doing business there.
- It required banks to sign affidavits certifying that they had no loans and offered no credit to South Africa.
- It extended the boycott to Namibia, a territory in Southwest Africa that the United Nations said was illegally occupied and administered by South Africa.[110]

The council passed the ordinance in January, and Boston Mayor Raymond Flynn signed it in June 1984. It was not an easy sell, Yancey recalled. "It was a real battle," he said. "Some of the objections had to do with the fact that many people did not see the connection between the city of Boston and the apartheid regime in South Africa."[111]

Yancey cited some of the key strategies that helped move the bill toward passage: working closely with TransAfrica and the Free South Africa Movement in Boston, holding behind-the-scenes discussions with financial institution representatives, successfully getting the ordinance placed in the Post Audit and Oversight Committee he chaired, and negotiating with white council member colleagues to bring them from indifference to support.

"My concern was that the city of Boston also had racial problems. We were suffering from racism, and one way to confront the issue here was to confront it and actively oppose it elsewhere in the world," Yancey said. "So this was a victory, to go on record opposing apartheid, opposing racism, opposing inequality." Beyond the moral victory, he noted, the city actually gained a small profit after divesting.[112]

Yancey's authorship of the ordinance garnered him national and international attention. He became active in the National League of Cities and the National Black Caucus of Local Elected Officials. In October 1985, he was invited to speak at the Conference on Municipal Investment and South Africa cosponsored by the ACOA and the United Nations Special Committee against Apartheid, held in New York City. Mayor Flynn worked to publicize the city ordinance and promote it nationally, sending letters to one hundred mayors in September 1984 urging them to enact similar laws and pressing the US Conference of Mayors to take up the issue.[113]

Yancey's antiapartheid efforts extended beyond divestment. Among other actions, on the occasion of Nobel Laureate Bishop Desmond Tutu's visit to Boston in December of that year, the councilor joined Mel King and Willard Johnson in a demonstration to demand the resignation of the South African honorary consul in Boston. "We were prepared to be arrested, to not leave unless forced out," Yancey recalled. "To our shock, after we discussed the issue and how complicit he was with the apartheid system, and we said we were not going to leave … he reached into his coat pocket, and took out a letter announcing his resignation. We were victorious."[114]

Reflecting on his decades of service on the Boston City Council, Yancey expressed satisfaction at being on the right side of history on this issue. "I made many mistakes during my 32 years on the council, but fortunately this was not one of them," he said. "The legislation played a role in the liberation of the people of South Africa, but it also allowed us to address the issue of human rights issues that take place in our own city. It allowed us to challenge the racial discrimination that continues to this day in the city of Boston." He added, "Back in 1984, not many of us were convinced Nelson Mandela would ever come out of prison alive. Boston exercised a great deal of leadership on apartheid and putting economic pressure on governments."[115]

4

A History of Law Enforcement
Yawu Miller

Introduction

A major objective of obtaining political power in the cities is to control the policies and conduct of the police force. Blacks in Boston have never had a sufficient influence on the mayor's office to achieve this. In a strong mayor form of government, one alternative is an effective civilian review board. However, blacks in Boston have as yet been unable to accomplish that. The hope now is that a larger electorate of millennials will have interests that merge with citizens of color and that together they can develop a more progressive government.

A Handful of Black Cops

Back when a he was a teenager, Billy Celester was running with the Marseilles Dukes. In the late 1950s and early '60s, membership in a street gang was not unusual for Roxbury boys. While their gang life was far more genteel than the gun violence and drug dealing that characterize contemporary gangs, those midcentury gang bangers did sometimes run afoul of the law.

And when they did, it was often one of the handful of black officers on the force who gave chase. Their names were known to all the miscreants as well as law-abiding citizens in the tight-knit black community that inhabited the South End and Roxbury neighborhoods—Joe Williams, the McLean brothers, Tom "Scotty" Scott, Herbert and Tom Craigwell, and "Long John" Smith.

Little did those officers know that Celester, the scrappy teenager they chased through the streets of the Madison Park section of Lower Roxbury, would serve on the police department with many of them and rise through the ranks to become one of the most prominent black officers on the force during the 1980s. The story of Celester's career in Boston coincides with the growth of black officers on the force and their rise from a few isolated foot patrols in predominantly black precincts to key positions in the command staff.

Early Years

The Boston Police Department was formed in 1854, but the history of policing in the city goes back to 1631, a year after the Puritan settlers arrived from England. The citizens established an all-volunteer night watch that in 1636 was taken over by the Town Meeting local government and charged with protecting the colonists from wild animals, fire, and criminals.[116]

In 1838, the city began the formation of its first police force, with six men executing constabulary duties. The Boston Watch, which by then was comprised of 120 men, continued to patrol the city separately. It wasn't until 1854 that the then-223-year-old Boston Watch was dissolved, and a new 250-member Boston Police Department was founded. By then a small but vibrant black population thrived in Boston, centered around the north slope of Beacon Hill and the West End.

In 1878 Horatio Homer, a Connecticut-born waiter and janitor, became the first black officer in the force of 746, assigned primarily to guard the entrance to the Office of the Police Commissioner in Pemberton Square. Homer, who served forty years in the department, later told a reporter he only once used force to eject an unruly visitor from the commissioner's office, grabbing the ruffian by the neck before throwing him out into the street. By the time Homer, then a sergeant, retired in 1919 at the age of seventy, the police force had grown to seventeen hundred men, but the number of black officers remained consistently low for much of the twentieth century.[117]

When Celester was a teenager, no more than twenty black officers patrolled the community. None were ranking officers, none were given prestigious assignments, and none were assigned a car.

"The black police were tough, but they were reasonably tough," Celester recalls. "If you were out of line, they would take you to task. But they weren't hostile."[118]

By the 1960s, Boston's Irish community had a lock on municipal politics and was deep into a one-hundred-year-long stretch of Irish mayors. The spoils of municipal government—jobs and contracts—had largely eluded the city's growing black community. In the Boston Police Department, the disparity in municipal hiring was particularly stark: Just thirty of the 2,805 police officers were black or Latino.

By state law, police were required to hire recruits from a list of applicants who had passed the state's Civil Service exam. But civil rights activists argued that black and Latino applicants for Boston Police and Boston Fire Department jobs were routinely passed over for jobs in favor of white applicants. "There were so few black officers, you knew it wasn't open to us," Celester said. "You could take the exam, but you knew you weren't wanted there."

The push to diversify the force began in earnest in the mid-1960s. With rising civil unrest gripping major cities across the United States, civic leaders understood the imperative to have officers on the force who knew the communities they were policing. The newly established *Bay State Banner* sought to remedy the paucity of blacks on the force by establishing at Police Station 9 on Dudley Street a training program to help blacks prepare for the civil service exam that applicants were required to pass to join the force. The *Banner* ran weekly advertisements for the program. Among those in the first class to sign up in 1965 was Billy Celester, then working as a sand blaster at the Charlestown Navy Yard.

Celester got on the force and was assigned to District 11 in Dorchester. Although the neighborhood was majority white and largely Irish, there was a sizable black community in the Columbia Point housing project. "They put me there most of the time," Celester said. "The general attitude was you were on the same job as the white officers, but you really weren't one of them. It wasn't hostile. But you weren't invited to go out for drinks or to parties with the white officers. Their attitude was, 'You guys should know your place.'"

While a number of blacks secured positions on the department through local efforts, it was clear that the blacks and Latinos who occupied the neighborhoods in the heart of the city—Roxbury, Lower Roxbury, and the South End—would not significantly increase their numbers in the department without legal action. In the *Castro v. Beecher* lawsuit, filed in 1970, the plaintiffs—six blacks and two Puerto Ricans—argued that black and Latino applicants for civil service positions in Massachusetts cities and towns were routinely discriminated against.

In 1972, US Court of Appeals Judge Frank Coffin ruled in favor of the plaintiffs with a decision that governed the hiring of police officers by the Massachusetts Bay Transportation Authority, the Metropolitan District Commission, State Police, Capitol Police, and the thirty-nine Massachusetts cities and the 143 towns that used the civil service selection criteria for their police force.

As part of this consent decree, the Boston Police Department was required to include one black or Latino candidate on the eligibility list for the police academy for every white candidate placed on the list. The consent decree did not mandate that the department hire the people of color placed on the list, but the department was required to file a report with attorneys for the NAACP Boston Branch listing the names and addresses of black and Latino candidates, the action taken with respect to their appointment and the percentage of blacks and Latinos on the force. The consent decree was to remain in effect until the percentage of black and Latino officers on the Boston police force was commensurate with the percentage of blacks and Latinos in Boston.[119]

The lawsuit was widely seen as the catalyst for a radical transformation of the Boston Police Department from a virtually all-white force whose officers were beginning to develop a reputation for brutality against the city's growing black population to a department where increasing numbers of blacks and Latinos helped shape public safety policy in the city.

In the early years, the implementation of the consent decree in Boston was anything but smooth. In 1974, then state Representative Royal L. Bolling Sr. charged that the BPD was undermining the decree by waiting to select black and Latino applicants until after other municipalities had selected applicants from the civil service list.[120] While other cities and towns hired as many as 95 percent of the black and Latino recruits applying for police positions, Boston rejected 90 percent of black and Latino applicants, Bolling noted.

Under pressure from black elected officials, change did come. By 1979, the number of blacks on the police force rose from the thirty uniformed officers walking the streets in 1967 to more than two hundred, nearly mirroring the twelve-year increase in minority employees working for the City of Boston from 3 to 17 percent.[121] Like the police and fire departments, other major city departments had increased minority hires under court-ordered consent decrees, including the Boston School Department and the Boston Housing Authority.

White police officers, police brass, and the unions representing officers and detectives frequently clashed with those seeking to uphold the department's hiring goals and those making efforts to help black officers advance through the department ranks to supervisory positions. In 1968, Herbert Craigwell became the first black deputy superintendent, in charge of community relations. In 1972, Leroy B. Chase followed suit and was appointed deputy superintendent in the department's Bureau of Administration.

By 1977, there were four black superior officers. But when then

Commissioner Joseph M. Jordan demoted Craigwell from assistant chief of Field Services to detective, taking up Craigwell's defense was the job of William Celester, then head of the Massachusetts Association of Minority Policemen (a predecessor to the current Massachusetts Association of Minority Law Enforcement Officers), who called the move an "act of total disregard and insensitivity toward the Boston black community," and joined Craigwell in a lawsuit against the department for its hiring and promotion practices.

Police Violence

The push for a more diverse police force came as the black community in Boston began to have increasingly strained relations with the department. In 1967, seventeen hundred police officers were mobilized to quell unrest after a contingent of officers began beating nonviolent demonstrators at a Grove Hall welfare office. Witnesses said demonstrators did nothing to provoke the attack and were never ordered to leave the welfare office or told they were under arrest.

In the 1980s a string of police shootings ratcheted up tensions between the department and the black community. In July 1980, patrolman Richard Bourque killed fourteen-year-old alleged car thief Levi Hart in a shooting the officer insisted was accidental. Citing discrepancies between Bourque's testimony and physical evidence from the scene of the shooting, Judge Richard L. Banks issued a report that concluded "there is ample cause to believe that the death of Levi Hart was the result of an unlawful act or acts on the part of Richard W. Bourque and that further judicial inquiry is warranted."[122] But an all-white grand jury found no probable cause to indict Bourque during an October 1980 inquest. In 1988 Hart's family was awarded $160,000 in a wrongful death lawsuit that was part of the $983,000 in settlements the department paid to victims and survivors of police violence that year.[123]

The September 1983 shooting of nineteen-year-old Elijah Pate, who officers said attempted to run them down with a stolen car, further strained relations between the department and black community members. Former *Banner* Managing Editor Brian Wright O'Connor, who lived on Haviland Street, steps from where the shooting occurred, said he was struck by the discrepancies in the police accounts of the shooting and those of eyewitnesses he encountered the night of the shooting. The police claimed Pate had attempted to use his car to run officers down. But several occupants of O'Connor's Haviland Street apartment building gave a different account. "They said [Pate] got out of the car and was running and that the police shot him from behind," O'Connor recalled. Further, O'Connor said, police asked him what he witnessed but did not interview his mostly African neighbors who, unlike O'Connor, were present when the shooting occurred.[124]

While a jury found the killing justified, many in the black community expressed deep skepticism of the ruling and the criminal justice system that rarely if ever found an officer guilty of shooting an unarmed suspect. That same year, three others were shot by Boston police. With six fatal shootings in the preceding year, there was a sharp increase from the four fatal shootings in 1981 and two in 1980.[125]

"It was a hostile atmosphere," recalled attorney Henry Owens, who represented victims of police brutality, including the family of Levi Hart. "There was a lot of mistrust between the community and the police. You had too many people being abused by law enforcement and the Internal Affairs Division was almost non-existent. Many people felt as though, if something did happen and you complained, nothing would happen."[126]

The Flynn Years

The tide began to turn as Mayor Raymond Flynn took office in 1984, following one of the most racially divisive periods in Boston's history. Flynn prevailed over former state Representative Mel King in an election that was largely split along the city's fractured racial divisions.

Two months after taking office, Flynn hand-delivered a check for the $843,498.37 settlement awarded to the widow of James Bowden, a five-foot, two-inch Boston City Hospital worker who police mistook for a six-foot-tall robber before opening fire on him as he was opening the door to his Buick. While police had maintained that Bowden had opened fire on them during the 1975 incident, attorney Lawrence O'Donnell Sr., a former police officer, presented evidence that the gun found at the scene was planted on Bowden.[127]

The administration of Mayor Kevin White had refused to pay the settlement, originally pegged at $250,000, before interest accrued. Flynn's payment and his subsequent dismissal of then-Police Commissioner Joseph Jordan were seen as signs that police-community relations were poised to turn a corner. Jordan, who was seen by many as a coconspirator in police attempts to cover up the Bowdon shooting,[128] was a frequent target for black activists who made repeated calls for his removal.[129]

In addition to the shootings, activists found fault with Jordan for another reason—suspicion of police collusion with drug dealers. The Reverend Bruce Wall, along with activist Georgette Watson, was encouraging residents of crime-infested neighborhoods to call the police and report drug dealers. "People were coming to us and giving us the names and addresses of people selling drugs," Wall recalled.[130] But it became clear that individuals in the police force were giving the names of the informants to the accused dealers, according to Wall. "The drug dealers came to the people and said 'if you go to the police again, we're going to smoke you,'" he said. "Relations with the police were bad."[131]

Allegations of police involvement in the drug trade in the black community were widespread. The Jesse Waters case stood out as a glaring example of police corruption. Waters, a dope peddler with a thirty-year record of arrests, had managed to avoid convictions and jail time until a 1983 incident during which he fired on Detective Francis Tarantino with a two-shot .22 caliber Derringer. Tarantino testified he was making a drug bust in Waters's Warren Street convenience store, opposite the Area B police station, where Waters had for years been peddling marijuana. Waters testified that Tarantino had not identified himself as a police officer and was attempting to rob the store. Waters's first shot knocked Tarantino's .38 caliber service revolver from his hand and struck the officer in the groin. Waters testified he fired a second shot after Tarantino, then on the floor, reached for his revolver. The second shot struck Tarantino in the chest, missing his heart by one centimeter.[132]

A jury refused to convict Waters of the charge of attempted murder that the district attorney attempted to pin on him but did convict the dealer of assault and battery with a dangerous weapon, illegal weapon possession and possession of marijuana with intent to distribute. Rather than serve the eight- to ten-year sentence at Cedar Junction, Massachusetts, correctional institution handed down by a judge, Waters was taken into federal custody, allegedly providing officials with the names of twenty police officers he says he regularly paid off for the privilege of peddling weed in proximity to their station house. Waters kept record of his monetary transactions with law enforcement by depositing cash directly into bank accounts bearing the names of the officers and retaining the deposit slips.[133]

In the end, however, Detective George Vest, a black officer from Mattapan, was the sole cop who went to jail in the Waters case, convicted of perjury. Tarantino's partner, who was with him during the shooting, was placed on administrative leave before retiring from the force. Tarantino, who was placed on disability for his injuries, was never charged with any offense.

The Waters case focused the media's attention on police corruption, at least momentarily, but within the black community, knowledge of police involvement in the drug trade was widespread. Wall and Watson employed a carrot-and-stick approach to their anti-crime efforts, encouraging the police to work cooperatively with the community on drug issues while at the same time threatening to expose any instances of police inaction on known drug dealers or dens. Wall circulated flyers bearing the message: "Wanted: Names of police officers selling drugs."

"When we went after the police, the community said 'these people are serious because they know who's really dealing drugs here,'" Wall commented.[134]

While black activists called on the state police and federal law enforcement officials to work with the Boston police to fight drug dealing, the police seemed unwilling to collaborate with other agencies, according to Wall. *Banner* sources at the time speculated that police officials were concerned that the intervention of outside law enforcement agencies in Boston's drug trade would uncover involvement by police officers.

Wall's demands for federal intervention continued. He and Watson began sleeping in known drug houses to draw attention to them. In 1983, he and Georgette Watson formed Drop-A-Dime, an anonymous tip line through which Boston residents could report crime and drug activity without fear of retribution from criminals tipped off by police.

Key Appointments

Flynn's new commissioner, Francis "Mickey" Roache, had headed the Community Disorders Unit, which was charged with investigating and preventing incidents of racially motivated violence in the tumultuous years of school desegregation. Roache made one of his first priorities as commissioner the diversification of the department's top brass. He appointed veteran black officers including Richard Cox, Pervis Ryan, James Claiborne, and Joseph Carter to the command staff.

"I put together goals and timetables and told the department, 'We're going to do this,'" Roache recalled in a 1997 interview. "If you're talking about implementing community policing, you can't have a department with only one minority supervisor."[135]

Black and Latino police officers made unprecedented gains during the years of the Flynn administration. Among them was Celester, who held the rank of superintendent while serving as night commander when Roache came on.

"Commissioner Roache asked me would I be willing to lose a star and become deputy superintendent in charge of Area B," Celester recalled.[136] The appointment, while technically a demotion, had its advantages. Deputy superintendents had the authority to pick who would serve as captain in the station, elevate patrol officers to the rank of detective, and transfer officers out of their district.

Roache also began forging close ties with anticrime activists in the community. "Minister Don Muhammad was one of the first people I met with," Roache told the *Banner*.[137]

Nation of Islam

Muhammad, who headed Muhammad's Mosque No. 11, had established the local Nation of Islam chapter as a major force in the Grove Hall area, at the border of Roxbury and Dorchester. Nation of Islam Minister Louis Farrakhan had resurrected the NOI in 1980, and Muhammad was his point man in Boston, propagating the group's message of black self-empowerment. In the neighborhood around the new mosque, NOI followers opened several businesses, including a small restaurant on Blue Hill Avenue.

Theirs weren't the only business enterprises flourishing in Grove Hall. The neighborhood was in the grips of an increasingly violent drug trade. New York gangs with names like the Apple Boys and the Capsule Boys were doing a brisk business in heroin and powdered cocaine that transformed nearby Elm Hill into an open marketplace for a growing number of junkies. The drug sellers were setting up elaborate networks, complete with walkie-talkie-equipped rooftop lookouts, "mules," and safe houses. At the same time, the Nation of Islam was reestablishing its presence in Grove Hall. When the New York dealers began moving their operations in from the cold, selling their drugs from inside the restaurant and other Grove Hall businesses, the Muslims drew a line in the sand.[138]

"The brother who ran the restaurant told them 'You're not going to come in here and do business,'" recalled Muhammad in a 1997 interview with the *Banner*. "The dealers said 'we're coming here tonight and we're going to clean you Muslims out of Grove Hall.'"

That night, a group of the New York gangsters showed up in Grove Hall armed with guns and knives. The unarmed Muslim men stood their ground. "We were attacked in three locations and we responded," Muhammad told the *Banner*, declining to elaborate.

Others in the area give more colorful descriptions of the melee, in which eight dealers were sent to the hospital. "They didn't kill anybody, but they kicked some serious ass," recalled Bertram Alleyne, former president of the Grove Hall Board of Trade, in a 1997 *Banner* interview. As the incidents were relayed to the *Banner*, not one Muslim was injured in the fight.[139]

Alleyne and others in Grove Hall point to the showdown as a pivotal moment in the community's war on drugs. "The Muslim brothers came into Grove Hall and commanded respect," he said. "Grove Hall would have been 10 times worse, but the criminal element was conscious of the fact that Muslims were here."

The Muslims' tenacity also showed other black clergy that the need for active participation in the war on drugs was more acute than ever. "Their effort is the one that challenged ministers to be more visible and active in the streets," Bruce Wall told the *Banner*. "Their ministers were in the hot spots long before it was fashionable. One mosque had more impact on cleaning up Grove Hall than all the churches—and there was one on every street. It was embarrassing to them."[140]

The Muslims' early show of force was just the opening salvo in a years-long effort to combat the rising tide of drugs and crime in Boston's end of a nationwide epidemic of crack dealing and associated gun violence.

Much of Boston's black community became caught in the crosshairs of the war on drugs as dealers like Darryl "God" Whiting moved large amounts of cocaine, heroin, and marijuana through their networks of convenience stores and housing projects. Whiting controlled the Orchard Park public housing development and bought businesses along Blue Hill Avenue, creating an elaborate distribution network. "They were well organized and they had a lot of money," recalled Muhammad.[141]

Muhammad and others in the Grove Hall area complained to the police about Whiting's dealing, providing information on the operation. In 1990, the Boston Drug Task Force collared Whiting and thirty of his associates, working in conjunction with Wayne Budd, an African American US attorney. The operation effectively shut down Whiting's operation.

But the vast retail network Whiting and other older dealers set up remained viable. Teens formed the street-level retail infrastructure that was the backbone of the drug trade, and, with major players like Whiting out of the way, the teens began to battle each other for territory. Crack cocaine and gangs hit the Hub with a one-two punch, beginning in the mid-1980s, and many in the city found themselves ill-prepared for the onslaught. The body count began to inch up with one after another shooting taking the lives of younger and younger victims.

In 1988, it was twelve-year-old Darlene Tiffany Moore, an innocent bystander cut down in a Humboldt Avenue shootout. Others followed—Eric Shepherd, Charles Copney, Cory Grant, Yolanda Carter, Junior Fernandez, and Louis D. Brown. Wall kept a record of slain youth on the wall of Chez Vous, the Dorchester roller rink where he ran a youth ministry. Starting with the teens killed between 1985 and 1990, Wall recorded the names of sixty-one shooting victims. "We kept updating the list because kids would come in and say you don't have my boy on there," Wall recalled. By 1995, the wall recorded 252 names.

At the same time, the Muslims were working on the street level. In 1990, a twenty-two-year-old minister named Yusuf Muhammad began working one-on-one with gang-involved youth. At the time, efforts to reach gang-involved youth were almost nonexistent. "No one wanted to be out on the streets with these young people," Yusuf told the *Banner*. "They were selling drugs. They had weapons. They were on the streets. But I looked at them like they were my brothers. Many of them were only two or three years younger than me."

Yusuf, a graduate of Xavier University in Cincinnati, and other ministers and volunteers were able to help many of the gang-involved youth obtain jobs or GEDs and move on to institutions of higher learning. Often, when gang disputes threatened to boil to the surface, Yusuf would bring the youths to Minister Don. "There was nothing like seeing Minister Don talk to the young men and seeing them get up and hug each other one night after someone was shot," he recalled.

The respect Muhammad commanded in the black community proved crucial to Commissioner Roache's efforts to improve relations there. B2 Deputy Superintendent Celester met regularly with Muhammad and other activist ministers to help diffuse gang violence. "Muhammad would sit down with me and the captain and we'd go over cases," Celester recalled. "We worked with federal prosecutors, with the probation department. We put a team together."

While some of the Muslims were working the streets, others worked in the prisons. Juvenile offenders at the former Deer Island correctional facility packed auditoriums to hear the Muslims' message of self-empowerment and redemption. In other prisons, NOI ministers such as Rodney Muhammad served as chaplains for growing Muslim congregations.

At the same time the Muslims were taking their work to the streets, Mayor Flynn's street workers program was also getting off the ground. Tracy Lithcutt, who went on to head the city's street worker program in the administration of Flynn's successor Thomas Menino, was the second man hired for the program. "We did direct outreach to the toughest kids," he told the *Banner*. "We had a feeling that if we could change their lives, it would send a message to the younger kids who saw them as role models."

Lithcutt said the street workers were able to offer the youths access to the city's resources, jobs, social services, and educational opportunities.

"A lot of the kids were selling drugs to pay rent and utility bills," he said. "They were breadwinners and were often raising their younger brothers and sisters. They never had the opportunity to go to a Patriots game or an amusement park. They were just kids. They wanted the basic opportunities that other fifteen- and sixteen-year-olds wanted."

While efforts to reach the gang-involved youth intensified, the pace of the killings continued to increase.

In May 1992, the violence hit a new low when a gang-related dispute spilled into the Morningstar Baptist Church in Mattapan. It was during the funeral service for a twenty-year-old killed during a drive-by shooting that a group of hooded youths barged into the church and chased their intended victim through the pews before stabbing the twenty-one-year-old man nine times.

The brazen act sent shock waves through the city's religious community as ministers gathered to discuss ways of stemming youth violence. Wall and a group of other activist ministers—Eugene Rivers, Gilbert Thompson, and Ray Hammond—formed the Ten Point Coalition, a group mobilized around efforts to stem black-on-black violence.

"If the last year has taught us anything, it is that the last havens in a heartless world—our schools and our churches—are no longer immune to the scourge of violence that has swept through our homes and streets," read the group's manifesto.

The coalition represented the Christian ministers' response to the crime wave—a response that incorporated street outreach, ministry, and advocacy in the courts where many young men found themselves facing serious time. The methodology was straight out of the Nation of Islam playbook through which youth ministers, many of them plucked from the ranks of the local gangs, conducted outreach to pull their former allies and adversaries out of the life. Rivers himself had learned from the NOI, accompanying their ministers on their street patrols. But now he appeared to see himself in competition with the NOI.

Despite the best efforts of law enforcement and community-based anticrime groups to gain control over the problem of youth violence, the death toll continued to creep up. The peak year for gun violence in Boston was 1990, when 152 people were killed, including sixty-two youths. It was 1993—a year during which sixteen youths under the age of seventeen were slain—when the ministers in the Nation of Islam began to grow impatient, recalled Muhammad. "They were really angry about what was going on and wanted to strike out at the drug dealers in an inappropriate manner," he told the *Banner*.[142]

Instead, Muhammad suggested they have a program urging black unity. The ministers sold a thousand $20 tickets to a special anticrime program. Despite a winter storm, seven hundred men turned out for the program, during which they were asked to sign a pledge to work toward ending youth violence. Later that year, two thousand men took the same pledge at the Strand Theatre in Dorchester when NOI head minister Louis Farrakhan addressed a packed house. *Boston Globe* columnist Derrick Jackson pointed out that in the four years prior to the Strand Theatre event, thirty children under the age of seventeen were killed by gunfire. However, in the three years from 1994 through 1996, the total dropped to seven.[143] The movement under way in Boston set the stage for the Million Man March, which saw more than nine thousand men from the Greater Boston area head to Washington, DC, in October 1995.

According to Jackson, "Of the 19 months without a youth being shot dead, 16 were after the March."[144]

Many cite the march and its message of personal accountability as a turning point in the community's response to gang violence. Sadiki Kambon, who headed the local organizing committee for the march, cited the case of one gang-involved man who at the time of the march was struggling with his responsibility for a young daughter.

"I saw him a couple of months ago with his daughter," Kambon told the *Banner*. "He said, 'I'm not in a gang any more. I'm not on the street.' The March had that kind of effect on people."

The Muslims are widely credited for piloting the cooperative approach between police and the black community, but the spirit of cooperation that was forged during the 1980s did not extend to many in the clergy. Several ministers in the Ten Point Coalition took on an adversarial relationship with the Nation of Islam. In 1994, Reverend Eugene Rivers accused NOI Minister Louis Farrakhan and members of the Grove Hall mosque with complicity in violent acts allegedly perpetrated by NOI members. Rivers and Ten Point Coalition member Ray Hammond told the *Boston Globe* they received threatening phone calls after Rivers made the allegations, but acknowledged there was no proof that NOI members made the threats.[145]

Combining a knack for grabbing headlines with a penchant for cutting deals with politicians, as well as power brokers of all stripes, Rivers came to command the media's attention and the majority of the foundation funding for anticrime collaborations in Boston. While his relationship with the local NOI members never substantially evolved beyond his early vilification of the group's leadership, Rivers enjoyed a privileged relationship with the Boston Police Department and city government during the mayoral administration of Thomas Menino, whom he supported early on in his 1993 election bid.[146]

As Rivers and his Ten Point Coalition continued to grow, NOI members continued working on their anticrime efforts without fanfare or media coverage. Rivers had effectively cornered the market on antiviolence work, controlling the lion's share of federal and state anticrime grants. At a time when the Menino administration doled out summer youth jobs to politicians like political spoils, Rivers bragged to reporters that he controlled a larger share of the city jobs than all of Boston's black elected officials combined.[147]

Seemingly sidelined by the activist Christian ministers, Nation of Islam members continued their core mission of outreach to gang members and convicts. "It's a lifetime job for us," said Minister Rodney Muhammad in 2017.[148] The Ten Point Coalition did not have much impact on the NOI ministers' work, according to Muhammad. "It was a plus for us to see that other black ministers were going into the streets and prisons. The more help we can get, even though they claimed they were doing all the work themselves—it's a plus."

Stop and Frisk

Despite vastly improved working relationships with the police department during the Flynn administration years, community residents still battled the department over what many saw as rights violations.

In 1989, neighborhood residents reacted angrily to the police department's stated policy of searching known gang members on sight. The stop-and-frisk policy, as it came to be known, came under fire from defense attorneys and community activists who argued that police used the tactic to violate the rights of criminals as well as those with no criminal ties.[149] Charges of unfair police stops and searches continue into the present. In 2014, police data obtained by the American Civil Liberties Union of Massachusetts showed that blacks were more likely than any other ethnic group to be stopped and questioned by police.

The heavy-handed tactics police employed in the black community received further scrutiny in October 1989 when a thirty-year-old store manager named Charles Stuart drove with his pregnant wife into the Mission Main public housing development in Roxbury, shot and killed her, shot himself in the stomach, and then blamed the crime on an imaginary black assailant.

The ensuing police manhunt left an indelible mark on black males living in Roxbury at the time, many of whom were subjected to public strip searches and other forms of harassment as police worked feverishly to find a black suspect who never existed. The absence of a real black perpetrator didn't prevent police from charging Willie Bennett, a black man with a lengthy rap sheet, with the murder. When Stuart's brother Matthew fingered Charles himself as the perpetrator, the department's rush to charge Bennett cast Boston police in an even more unfavorable light.

The incident and its aftermath left a discriminatory brand on the city—soul searching among journalists and white civic leaders, increased pessimism and calls for substantive reforms from black elected officials. The Flynn administration enlisted prominent attorney James D. St. Clair to conduct an analysis of the department and its management. The Report of the Boston Police Department Management Review Committee, released in 1992 and commonly referred to as the St. Clair Commission Report, found little public confidence in the department among Boston residents, noting that just 6 percent of citizen complaints against the police were sustained.

"The failure to monitor and evaluate the performance of police officers—particularly those with established patterns of alleged misconduct—is a major deficiency in the management of the Department and results in an unnecessarily dangerous situation for the citizens of the City of Boston," the report read.[150]

In addition to a recommendation that Commissioner Roache not be reappointed when his term expired in 1992, the report also recommended:

- The creation of a "Community Appeals Board, composed of both community members and police officers, charged with the task of reviewing the investigations conducted by the Internal Affairs Division and, where appropriate, returning cases for further investigation."
- That the Boston Police Department take immediate measures to begin a comprehensive shift to a community and problem-solving policing strategy.
- Better training for supervisors: "Many officers with whom we spoke were unanimous in their belief that new Sergeants are not currently provided with the necessary education and training for their new roles as supervisors."[151]

While some of the St. Clair Commission report recommendations were implemented, the call for an independent body to review cases of police abuse and misconduct—arguably the issues that led to the formation of the commission—has remained elusive. In 2007, Mayor Thomas Menino established a three-member Community Ombudsman Oversight Panel (COOP) to review civilian complaints.

The panel, which remains in existence today, has the authority to review cases only after the police department's Internal Affairs Division has completed its own investigation. The panel also reviews a random sampling of cases that have gone before IAD and is also able to review cases if complainants request they do so within two weeks of IAD completing its review.

The COOP board does not have the power to subpoena officers involved in an incident or interview witnesses but is able to review the investigations already completed by IAD and make a determination whether a case has been investigated adequately. As of 2017, current Boston Mayor Martin Walsh has maintained the COOP board, although members of the board in 2016 recommended the creation of a separate, independent board that would have the power to investigate complaints.[152]

Criminal Justice Reform

The get-tough-on-crime policies that state and federal officials made law during the dark days of the crack epidemic may have been among the factors that led to the drop in crime rates in the mid-1990s.

The Massachusetts prison population rose by 368 percent between 1980 and 2008, while the jail and house of correction population increased by 522 percent in the same period, increases primarily stemming from drug arrests.[153] Many attribute the rise in the prison population to initiatives such as the Violent Crime Control and Law Enforcement Act of 1994, a wide-ranging anticrime bill pushed by the administration of then-president Bill Clinton. The bill expanded the death penalty to cover more crimes, instituted a five-year mandatory minimum sentence for possession of five grams of crack cocaine and provided funding for hiring police and building prisons. With cities and towns plagued by drug dealing and gang-related shootings, state and local governments were adopting similar tough-on-crime laws.

But as the country's prison population continued to expand, and the higher rates of incarceration that blacks faced came even more into stark relief, black activists began pushing back on punitive policies. In the 2000 electoral season, Massachusetts voters voted down Ballot Question 8, which would have given judges the authority to commit nonviolent drug offenders to treatment programs rather than prison. The so-called Treatment on Demand question would have established a fund for drug treatment programs using money seized because of its use in drug-related crimes to fund the treatment programs. While white voters overwhelmingly rejected the question, black voters over-whelmingly supported the measure. It wasn't until 2014, when the growing opiate epidemic in predominantly white towns and sub-urbs seized the attention of white legislators and their constituents, that state policymakers began to question their get-tough-on crime attitudes.[154]

Police Force Diversity: Two Steps Back

The twenty years of the Menino administration saw many of the gains black police officers made during the Flynn years erode. For one, Menino centralized power in the department by taking the power to hire, transfer, and promote away from deputy superintendents and concentrating it more in the hands of the commissioner.[155] That modus operandi fit in with the leadership style of the newly elected mayor, who was known to take home city employees' personnel files to approve or reject any pending promotions.[156] Black and Latino men had led major city departments during the Flynn years—School Superintendent Laval Wilson (hired by the independent Boston School Committee), Directors of Personnel Roscoe Morris and Felix D. Arroyo, Boston Housing Authority Director David Cortiella, and Treasurer George Russell. During the Menino years, however, while black, Latina and Asian women held prominent positions in city government, Public Facilities Director Chuck Grigsby was the sole man of color to lead a department with a budget and a staff. That same pattern was playing out in the police department.

Deputy superintendents were reduced to figureheads in station houses, with the mostly white cadre of captains making critical decisions about the day-to-day policing of districts. Black officers who had made their way to the upper echelons of police leadership during the Flynn years, either by appointment or through civil service exams, often found their career advancement grinding to a halt. Compounding the situation, white activists and longtime City Council President James Kelly led efforts to rescind policies aimed at diversifying both the incoming recruit classes and the leadership positions in the department.

A 1980 consent decree mandating that blacks and Latinos be given preference in promotion expired in 1995, but the department had continued promoting black and Latino officers over whites with equal or higher scores on civil service exams until white officers mounted a series of challenges to the practice. In 1999, Suffolk Superior Court Judge John Xifaras upheld a 1998 Civil Service Commission decision finding that bypassing white officers violated civil service laws.[157] Then-Police Commissioner Paul Evans chose not to appeal the ruling.

Then, in November 2004, a further setback to minority hiring came when a US District Court judge ordered the department to end the practice of considering for hire one black or Latino candidate for every white candidate considered for hire, bringing to an end the thirty-one-year-old consent decree from *Castro v. Beecher*. In her ruling, Judge Patti Saris found that the department had achieved racial balance among patrolmen, 41 percent of whom were people of color in a city that was then 50.5 percent nonwhite.[158]

In the years since those rulings, classes of recruits entering the police department have become increasingly white. By 2015, two years into the administration of Mayor Martin Walsh, the share of people of color working in the department had dropped to 34 percent—23 percent black, 9 percent Latino, and 2 percent Asian.[159] By that time, Latinos represented nearly 20 percent of the city's population, blacks 25 percent, and Asians 9 percent.[160] By then the trend was clear. Successive overwhelmingly white classes of police recruits had diminished the percentages of blacks, Latinos, and Asians in the department even as the city was becoming more diverse. City officials, including Walsh, have pointed to civil service rules that give an absolute preference to veterans. Because the number of blacks and Latinos from the Greater Boston area serving in the military has dropped precipitously since the draft was abolished following the US war in Vietnam, the pool of people of color entering the force has dropped accordingly. Although police departments can supersede the veterans preference by citing a need for officers proficient in languages, such as Spanish, Cape Verdean Creole, or Haitian Creole, the Boston Police Department has done so only sparingly, despite the growing need to serve communities of people speaking such languages in the city.

Police Abuse

The apparent refusal of the city's mayor and police commissioner to implement the reforms outlined in the 1992 St. Clair Commission report seemed to signal official sanction for business as usual in the following years. Predictably, incidents of police violence against unarmed civilians and complaints of rights violations continued apace. Among the more troubling incidents was the savage beating of a plainclothes officer, Michael Cox, whose fellow officers apparently mistook him for a shooting suspect.

On the evening of January 25, 1995, Cox and his partner responded to a report that an officer had been shot in the Grove Hall section of Roxbury. Members of the department's gang unit, Cox and his partner were the first on the scene and chased the suspect down Blue Hill Avenue. When the suspect pulled onto Woodruff Avenue, a dead-end street, Cox and his partner pursued the suspect on foot. While scaling a fence, Cox was struck from behind by another officer with a blunt object, most likely a flashlight. In the ensuing beating, in which several officers were believed to have taken part, Cox was punched and kicked repeatedly, resulting in extensive internal injuries. Cox told investigators the beating stopped when the officers turned him over and one of them spotted a badge, telling the others,

"Stop. He's a cop."[161] During the subsequent investigation, none of the officers who responded to the call admitted to participating in or even seeing the beating.

Because the victim of the beating was a fellow officer, the incident offered a rare window into the use of excessive force on the department and highlighted the so-called blue wall of silence—an unwritten agreement among officers to turn a blind eye to each other's misdeeds. Coming four years after the videotaped beating of Rodney King by Los Angeles police captivated the nation and sparked riots in that city, the Cox beating seemed to spur little in the way of substantive changes in the Boston Police Department. Cox filed a civil suit against the department and was awarded $900,000 in a settlement in which neither the department nor then-Commissioner Paul Evans admitted responsibility for the actions of the officers who beat Cox. Two officers were found responsible for attacking Cox, and a third for failing to attend to Cox's need for emergency assistance. Along with another officer, all four were placed on paid administrative leave. Although none were fired from the department for their alleged actions, a fifth officer, Kenneth Conley, was fired after he testified he had run past the beating but didn't notice it. He was convicted of perjury in a criminal trial and spent thirty-four months in jail. The conviction was later overturned, and in 2007 Conley was reinstated on the force.

As alarming as the Cox beating was, a rash of police shootings, most involving unarmed blacks and Latinos as the victims, further strained tensions between the department and members of the black community. In 2001, officers shot to death three people of color. In 2002, they shot four. The fourth victim, Eveline Barros-Cepeda, was shot through her back as she and her cousin, Maria Darosa, rode in the back of her car, which was being driven by two male acquaintances. Police officer Thomas Taylor fired five shots into the car as it drove away. He later told investigators the car had struck his partner, Michael Paillant, whom he said had been standing in front of the vehicle. Darosa denied that Paillant had been struck by the car. [162] Through the two-year wave of officer-involved shootings, District Attorney Dan

Conley found no fault with the department or its officers. Barros-Cepeda's case was no different. In 2003, Conley cleared Taylor in the shooting. "The facts in this case clearly show that the officer's decision to fire his weapon was justified," Conley told reporters, adding that Taylor feared for Paillant's life.[163] In the years before social media and security cameras made images of police shootings and beatings readily available, police shootings did not spark mass protests. The seven shootings in 2001 and 2002 did lead to calls among activists and black elected officials for independent investigations into the police shootings. The department responded to criticism in 2001 with a written response noting that Boston ranked forty-ninth out of fifty major US cities for fatal shootings per one thousand violent crime arrests.[164]

It wasn't until the August 2014 police shooting of Michael Brown in Ferguson, Missouri, that the wave of mass protests against police violence sweeping the United States brought large numbers of people out into the streets in Boston.

While blacks rarely took to the streets to protest police shootings, violence, or abuse in the first decade of the twenty-first century, the disparate treatment community members experienced over the years appeared to have negatively colored their views of the department. When the department polled Boston residents on their views of policing, 71 percent of respondents citywide said they found Boston police officers "fair and respectful," but in the predominantly black Area B2 and Area B3—the Roxbury and Mattapan police districts—only 41 percent of the Roxbury respondents and 54 percent of Mattapan respondents agreed with the statement. Asked whether racial profiling was a problem, 66 percent of residents in the Roxbury precinct and 70 percent in the Mattapan precinct responded in the affirmative, versus 41 percent of respondents citywide. A police spokeswoman told the *Banner* the department had no explanation for the disparate experiences of black and white respondents.[165] "We really don't know why there's a discrepancy and we're looking further to see what is causing this discrepancy," spokeswoman Beverly Ford told the *Banner*. "We're going to find out what's happening in these neighborhoods."[166]

Anyone waiting for the department to release a comprehensive study of the underpinnings of blacks' mistrust of the department would have been sorely disappointed. But the American Civil Liberties Union of Massachusetts went on to shed light on the disparities between blacks' experience of police and those of whites. After several years of advocacy, the ACLU in 2014 secured data from the BPD showing that between 2007 and 2010, blacks represented 63 percent of all people stopped, questioned, searched, or observed in the department's database of field observations, despite making up only 24 percent of the city's population.[167] While civil rights activists and attorneys said the disproportionate number of blacks stopped by police showed police bias against blacks and a disregard for their constitutional Fourth Amendment rights against illegal search and seizure, police cited higher-than-average crime rates, arrest rates, and gang involvement of those stopped as justification for the disproportionate number of blacks stopped. But researchers found that even when controlling for prior arrests, crime rates, and gang affiliation, blacks were still more likely to be stopped, more likely to be stopped multiple times, and more likely to be searched when stopped.[168] As in other major cities where blacks were disproportionately targeted by police stops, in Boston the vast majority of the stops—97.8 percent—did not result in arrests.

A *Banner* investigation into the department's gang list, and interviews with teens who were told by police they were gang-involved, found that police can add people to their list of "gang affiliated" even on the basis of only casual contact with gang members. Further, the *Banner* found that there is no clear path for people to have their names removed from the gang list, whether they left a gang or were added erroneously to the list.[169]

Thinning Ranks

After taking office in 2013, Mayor Martin Walsh promoted to command staff positions four black men, a Latina woman, and an Asian man, bringing the total number of people of color in top positions in the department to twelve out of twenty-four. While Walsh appointed the most diverse command staff in the department's history, many black officers complain the department is losing diversity as each successive class of new recruits comes in with whites outnumbering people of color 6–1. As black officers brought onto the force under the earlier consent decrees begin to reach retirement age, black officers warn, the gains made in recent decades could be reversed.[170] While some police departments in Massachusetts have ended use of the civil service exam as an entrance requirement to circumvent the veterans' preference, and the majority-white classes resulting from that preference, the Walsh administration has shown no willingness to do so. Further, critics charge, BPD officials seldom request preferences for officers who speak languages other than English—Spanish, Chinese, Haitian Creole, Cape Verdean Creole—as a means of boosting the number of officers of color and better connecting to Boston residents who do not speak English.

Further eroding black officers' confidence in the department's commitment to diversity, Walsh administration officials have spent millions of dollars fighting high-profile discrimination cases including two that challenge the department's use of a controversial drug test that uses hair samples to find traces of controlled substances.[171] The test has been shown to yield false positives in African American hair. Although the federal government has stopped using the test, and a Superior Court justice ordered an officer reinstated after he was fired for what his lawyers say was a false positive in a hair test, the Walsh administration has continued to appeal that judgment.[172]

Electoral Gains

Black Bostonians have struggled to make gains within the Boston Police Department, only to see those gains erode in recent years. In elected law enforcement positions, however, black progress has been more linear.

In 1992, Republican Governor William Weld appointed Ralph Martin Jr. to fill the Suffolk County district attorney seat after Newman Flanagan vacated the post midterm. Martin, who had served as assistant United States attorney under Weld in the mid-1980s, changed his party affiliation from independent to Republican, becoming the first black as well as the first non-Democrat to hold the position in decades. Martin's appointment and party affiliation reflected what has long been the reality in Massachusetts: the state's smaller Republican Party with its socially liberal tradition and thin bench has presented blacks with more opportunities than the Democratic Party, which in Boston has been dominated by Irish-American politicians who have jealously guarded the spoils of office.

Although Republicans made up just 7.8 percent of Boston's registered voters in 1990,[173] Martin was able to win 58.6 percent of the vote in 1994, fending off a challenge from former Assistant District Attorney Gerald Malone, who had the backing of the unions representing Boston police patrolmen and detectives. He was elected again in 1998. Martin's electoral victory marked the first time a black candidate won a countywide election in Suffolk County. During his ten years as district attorney, Martin's office worked collaboratively with Boston police officials and community members on innovative solutions to stemming the tide of violence in Boston, Chelsea, Revere, and Winthrop—the cities and towns that make up Suffolk County.

When Weld sought a replacement for Essex County Sheriff Charles Reardon, who in 1996 pleaded guilty to corruption charges, then-legislator Frank Cousins was a natural choice. He had been elected as a Republican in 1993 to represent the First Essex District from the town of Newburyport. The Boston-born thirty-six-year-old legislator had earned the respect of party officials, who were considering him for the top GOP legislative position of minority leader, as well as that of his fellow black legislators who had appointed him chairman of the Massachusetts Legislative Black Caucus. Weld's appointment of Cousins was historic. Cousins became the first African American to become a sheriff in Massachusetts. It was also a strategic move for the party, as Cousins was able to secure reelection, fending off Democratic challengers and holding the seat down for the GOP during his twenty-one years in office.

Cousins began his two decades in office cleaning up a system that was plagued by corruption. His predecessor, Reardon, was sentenced to a year in prison for demanding gratuities from process servers—contractors who are paid to serve legal notices on behalf of the sheriff—including political donations and concert tickets.[174] Two of Reardon's deputies also pleaded guilty to similar charges. Among Cousins's first tasks were restoring public trust in the Essex County Sheriff's Office and professionalizing operation of his facilities. To that end, he instituted promotional exams and a requirement that new officers hired by the department either have an associate's degree or military service. Cousins also implemented an affirmative action policy for the office, boosting the number of people of color working in the system up from one black guard in 1996 to 18 percent of the 590-person workforce by 2002, including many Spanish-speaking corrections officers and switchboard operators to better serve a prison population that was 44 percent Latino.[175] Cousins also introduced substance abuse treatment programs, citing high levels of drug-related crimes in the county. After being re-elected three times, Cousins declined to run for a fourth three-year term.

Massachusetts saw a second African American become sheriff after Suffolk County Sheriff Richard Rouse stepped down in 2002, following a series of scandals at the South Bay House of Correction. A former Suffolk County prosecutor and assistant attorney general, Andrea Cabral, was appointed by Republican Governor Jane Swift, becoming the first woman ever to serve as sheriff. Like Cousins, Cabral came into office with a reform agenda. She helped beef up the Suffolk County jails' antirecidivism efforts, including GED programs and vocational certificates. Unlike previous sheriffs, Cabral refused to take campaign contributions from Suffolk County staff, keeping a professional relationship with the unions representing correction officers. In 2012, Cabral was tapped to serve as Massachusetts secretary of public safety by then-Governor Deval Patrick. She resigned from the sheriff's office in 2013 to accept that post.

Patrick then appointed Steve Tompkins, Cabral's former chief of external affairs, to serve the remainder of the term as sheriff. Tompkins was reelected in 2014, fending off two Democratic challengers with 61 percent of the vote. His tenure in office has been focused on care of detainees, education programs for inmates and the community at large, antiviolence initiatives, resources for addiction and mental health for inmates, and reentry programs to prepare inmates for life after incarceration.

5

The Power of Banks

Jule Pattison-Gordon

Teri Williams pauses for a moment between phone calls to sit down in the president's office at the largest black-owned bank in the country and recall how a small, struggling institution turned into the interstate force it is today.

The sixth-floor suite on Franklin Street in downtown Boston is home to OneUnited Bank, with sister branches in Florida and Los Angeles and an online system that serves customers nationwide. Its mission is dual: to be financially profitable and to build wealth in the neighborhoods it serves. Historically, members of Boston's black community were denied loans and services by major banks. For decades, community members sought to realize the vision of a bank that would serve minorities and would fuel initiatives to better their and their neighbors' lives.

"When you have a community that is in crisis and has mass incarceration, over-policing, high murder rates, even poor educational systems, it impacts people's money, real estate values and ability to make money," Williams said. "As we look at challenges in our community, economic and social justice are intertwined."[176]

Historically, small depositors have received little welcome at most banks, which focused on providing financial services to the wealthy.

When banks did court working-class customers, it often was only with the offer of a safe place to store savings, not with additional services. All too frequently, white-owned banks discriminated against minority customers—or would-be customers.

In response, visionaries set on the idea of banks that would be established by black residents and provide their communities with the financial resources necessary to build their local economies. Notable efforts to enact this vision took place in cities with substantial black populations, leading to fourteen black-owned banks coming together in 1927 to form a trade association, then-named the Negro Bankers Association.[177] The organization later changed its name to the National Bankers Association, and today lists fifty members.[178] The NBA advocates now for both minority-owned and women-owned banks.[179] Despite such efforts, challenges remain high. During 2007's prerecession months, the United States could boast forty-one banks with majority-black ownership.[180] But by 2017, the national count has dropped to twenty-three.[181]

The challenges can be steep to establishing and maintaining a bank that focuses on uplifting poorer black communities. Systemic discrimination over generations has meant that many black families have had fewer opportunities to build wealth than white families, and thus have had less to pass down to their children. As a result, even as some discriminatory policies are routed out, their impact continues to be felt through the racial wealth gap. Black banks that take on the goal of serving lower-income neighborhoods can struggle to thrive and generate profit while working with clients who may be in more precarious situations and provide them with smaller deposit amounts.

Although the path has been rocky, in 2017 Boston is home to the largest black-owned bank in the nation, OneUnited Bank. It is also the largest bank in the United States to have both black ownership and management. OneUnited's mission-influenced projects include a credit card designed to help customers repair their credit scores so they can improve job and mortgage loan prospects. Other efforts include financial literacy initiatives, collaboration with Black Lives Matter, and loans targeted at apartment owners who offer their units for below market-rate rents, thus helping combat the displacement pressures of the city's overheated housing market. The banks' financing also was instrumental to minority firms winning developer designation for a historic thirty-seven-story downtown Boston skyscraper.

In 1968, OneUnited's predecessor, Unity Bank, was launched with a similar mission: to extend loans to those often discriminated against in financial systems and to give the black community control over money—and thus determination of what initiatives and organizations get funded in their neighborhoods. When it launched, Unity Bank was heralded as the first Boston bank with a predominately black board and a mission to serve Boston's black community.

"In those days, it was difficult, say for a contractor to get a loan from a majority bank ... they were not in our community," Marvin Gilmore,[182] cofounder of Unity, recalled in a 2017 interview. "At that time, people in the community weren't getting loans from majority banks. There was a need to help small businesses, mortgages on homes. ... There was a need in Boston to have a bank to take care of needs in the community."

Bostonians also have influenced the financial policies outside of their own institutions and have enacted business approaches that model ways to be financially successful while serving smaller clients. BankBoston opened the door to extensive commercial services for urban markets; Eastern Bank has been heralded for its commitment to racial and gender diversity and community involvement, and Access Capital Strategies demonstrated how an investment fund could bring compelling returns while directing investment into low- and moderate-income communities.

Case for a Bank: Community Self-Determination

In the years before Unity Bank was established, the need for a community-controlled bank was evident. Community organizations spent much of their time grant seeking, and had to bow to conditions set by the grantors in order to survive, rather than exclusively follow their own missions, notes Mel King in his book *Chain of Change: Struggles for Black Community Development*. King is a political activist and state representative and was the first candidate of color to make it into the final mayoral election in Boston.

"Most of the private agencies in our community were founded by outside church groups and philanthropic institutions or by individuals who kept their hands on the steering wheel (and the purse strings) of services to the poor," King wrote.[183] One example: "United Community services, a social service agency, for instance, used its sway as a funder to insist that community agencies federate into the South End Settlements, the Roxbury Federation, Dorchester Settlements and others. This arrangement not only lessened each agency's autonomy but also gave United Community Services much greater influence over their agencies, their programs and how their money was spent."

Similar comment came from the late Archie Williams, a Brown University graduate and Boston University School of Law-educated attorney who founded Freedom Industries in 1968.[184] That venture was a Roxbury- and Dorchester-based[185] network of businesses designed to hire and spend within the black community in order to keep dollars circulating locally.

"Every organization I worked for was a begging organization," Williams stated.[186] "They spent a lot of time looking for, begging for funds. I had difficulty in understanding why people who had so much talent had to spend so much time away from their avowed purpose just chasing money."

Meanwhile, a bank with a civic mission and an understanding of the community could help finance significant groups and projects. This would be seen in the 1980s when OneUnited—then called Boston Bank of Commerce—provided a critical investment in the minority-led One Lincoln office tower project, including a $2.6 million loan toward the development rights for the downtown parcel on which the skyscraper was built and a $230,000 investment to kick off work.[187] The project—which resulted in the largest skyscraper built by minority developers—was made possible by the city's parcel-to-parcel linkage program, which was intended to spur economic activity in neighborhoods outside Boston's pricey inner core. Under the program, developers were offered the chance to bid on an attractive downtown parcel that was packaged jointly with a parcel in a lower-demand residential neighborhood. OneUnited's participation and financial contribution allowed a team of minority developers to amass the funding necessary to win selection and build on the downtown site as well as on the Parcel 18 site in Roxbury.[188]

Development team members Ken Guscott and Paul Chan said at the time of the thirty-seven-story tower's groundbreaking that the project demonstrated that minorities have the capacity for such notable works.[189] The team, Columbia Plaza Associates, also represented a historic collaboration of black, Latino, and Asian members. Additionally, purchase of the development rights was intended to allow the minority team to set and realize their own vision for the parcels without being beholden to outside financers, Kevin Cohee, OneUnited CEO and a Columbia Plaza Associates member, said in a 2016 interview.[190] Columbia Plaza Associates members intended to use the second parcel, located in Roxbury, as the site of a development that would generate jobs and further economic development in surrounding area.[191]

Case for a Bank: Individual Agency

In part, bank services were simply inconvenient to attain in Boston's black community: A 1967 economic survey found there was only one banking facility per every 17,500 people in Roxbury, Boston's main black neighborhood, compared to one bank for every sixty-one hundred people in the rest of the city. [192]

At other times, black residents found that banks denied them services offered to white residents. The denial of service and the power of lenders to control where and how people live exploded sharply onto the scene in the early 1970s. Federal legislators at the time launched investigation into a scheme under which a group of banks had essentially regulated exactly where in the city blacks would be allowed to get mortgage loans—down to the specific street. The practice would become known as "redlining."

In the 1960s and '70s, Roxbury was packed to overcrowding. Black newcomers were arriving from the South in search of work,[193] but finding, like many current black residents, that most banks would not offer mortgage loans—or at least, not favorable ones—for homes outside of that neighborhood.

"I had plenty of black customers interested in homes but when I went to the downtown banks for financing I got turndown after turndown. … Everyone was reluctant about taking care of the mortgage needs of black clients," said the late then-state Senator Royal Bolling, who also had been a real estate broker in Boston.[194]

Other housing pressures came from urban renewal, under which many low-income residents were displaced after their homes were razed, rebuilt, and offered for new rents above original tenants' pay grades.[195] As such, while the overall city population dropped by about 12 percent, Roxbury's population almost doubled.[196] Following the Grove Hall police-welfare riot locally and national riots over Martin Luther King Jr.'s assassination, local government began to fear that they needed to appease black residents or risk another riot burning the city, according to state Representative Byron Rushing.[197]

Out of this need emerged the Boston Banks Urban Renewal Group (B-BURG) founded in 1968, which would disperse federally guaranteed housing loans for low-income residents and specifically target them at black residents seeking to move out of the South End/Lower Roxbury area. However, unbeknownst to the public, B-BURG members agreed to offer these loans only in specific areas—the primarily Jewish parts of Mattapan and Dorchester. Residents in that area tended to be elderly homeowners who had paid off their mortgages or had mortgage loans with low interest rates and so were generating little revenue for banks.[198] Bankers took a map and drew a red line around these sections, determining to offer mortgages to black residents only within that designated area. Real estate agents and bankers worked in tandem to reap profit from black homebuyers who had few, or no, other options than to work with them.

In some cases, properties within the redlined areas were freed up by Jews who moved voluntarily to take advantage of mortgage offerings in the suburbs and encouraged by new highways providing easy access.[199] In other cases, real estate agents actively cajoled or coerced Jews into selling their homes. The agents' approaches included claims of imminent property value decline and appeals to racist fear-mongering: In more than one instance, agents told Jewish families that their children were liable to be raped by incoming black residents if they did not leave.[200] In a 1987 piece in a real estate journal, an anonymous author recalled times when violent intimidation was employed in the pursuit of acquiring homes to sell to blacks at inflated prices. "I had direct contact with people who were more blatant than I ever dreamed of being," the author wrote. "There were instances of housebreaks that were arranged only to scare people out."[201]

With properties now vacated, bankers and agents turned to black prospective homebuyers. They lured the buyers into accepting inflated home prices by providing seemingly favorable initial conditions such as automatic mortgage qualification and no down payments.[202] Because the loans were insured by the federal government, the banks would not be at risk of losing money should the borrower be unable to repay or should the homes fall into foreclosure.[203] Another incentive for black buyers to accept the banks' deals was the lack of alternative home purchase options.[204]

In many cases, a corrupt federal appraiser did little to no assessment of homes before stamping approval. As a result, the black homebuyers were loaded with homes in need of costly major repairs along with the mortgage payments for their price-jacked homes.[205] B-BURG formed in 1968; within six years, more than half of the people who bought homes under its mortgage program had lost them.[206]

According to Boston University Professor Hillel Levine and coauthor Lawrence Harmon, "Those who examined the fiscal policies of B-BURG years later [after the 1971 federal senate hearings held in Boston] would claim that the banks 'in a very subtle manner, imprisoned 80 percent of Boston's black population,' including those blacks 'funneled' into this area because it was 'the only area of Boston where incoming blacks could secure Federal Housing Administration (FHA) loans to buy houses,' save for the Jewish-dominated regions of Mattapan and Dorchester."[207] During a 1971 hearing on accusations of redlining, the Anti-Defamation League of B'nai B'rith and the Jewish Community Council of Metropolitan Boston submitted a letter stating that B-BURG had made these loan-provision decisions "with neither public knowledge nor approval."[208]

Members of Boston's black community established their first bank the same year that B-BURG was founded. While redlining had not yet emerged in public consciousness, even by that point, the power of banks' loan decisions was strongly felt.

Unity Bank

In 1966, John T. Hayden, a twenty-three-year-old graduate student at Harvard Business School, proposed the idea of a black-owned bank as a way to improve the economic situation in Roxbury, where banks serving the community were scarce. Hayden brought his proposal to Don Sneed, a resident with a background in real estate brokerage and door-to-door sales,[209] Marvin Gilmore, a World War II veteran with musical and real estate experience, and several others, urging them to turn his idea into reality.

Two years later, Sneed and Gilmore cofounded Unity Bank, a full-service, Roxbury-based institution that was run by a majority-black board of directors, in a building with a renovation designed by a black-owned architectural firm and constructed with a black-owned firm as the principal contractor. Sneed took up presidency, and Gilmore was designated one of the vice presidents.

"The opening of Unity Bank is another example of the growing strength in our community; it is an indication of a community moving to control its own destiny," stated a *Bay State Banner* article at the time.[210]

Unity's mission went beyond providing traditional banking services to the black community: In advance of the opening, Sneed said Unity would not shut the door on those who did not qualify for loans but instead offer them advice on improving their situations.

"If we have to turn a man down on a loan, we won't just say 'no,'" Sneed said. "We'll say 'no because,' and then sit down with him to help him manage his business budget a little better."[211]

To ensure residents had a stake in the bank, as well as to generate capital, the board offered stock subscriptions at $50 for five shares, what Sneed called "a poor man's price."[212] By opening day June 1968, the bank had attained more than thirty-three hundred stockholders, of whom about twenty-four hundred held fifty or fewer shares of stock, indicating that plans to engage smaller spenders had traction. Unity achieved goals for local ownership as well—more than one thousand of the stockholders were from Roxbury.[213] Larger municipal, institutional, and corporate entities including the City of Boston, Harvard, Brandeis, and Stop & Shop further bolstered the bank with deposits.[214]

For two years, Unity appeared successful. Deposits grew nearly tenfold, Unity reaped approximately $104,000 in profit during its first year,[215] and the bank's selection to receive federal post office deposits provided what Sneed said was needed capital to further its growth.[216]

However, three years in the sunny picture cracked, as untended structural problems stood poised to undermine the bank's mission. It became clear that the bank had made bad loans during the first years and now, as they came due in 1971, many went unpaid—to the tune of $1 million in loss.[217] With funds draining away, the bank verged on failure.

The exact causes were manifold. In some cases, Unity had been willing to take a chance on loans that were less likely to generate profit because staff wanted to answer a need they saw in the community, cofounder Gilmore recounted in 2017.[218]

"The problem we faced by being very open to small customers was it was very easy to borrow but not easy to pay back loans. That was a hit we took. ... The bank placed loans in areas that were not profitable," Gilmore said.[219]

Like any new bank, Unity attracted a mix of loan applicants that included poor borrowers with no true ability to repay.[220] Marilyn Anderson Chase, executive director of Roxbury Multi-Service Center Inc., said that the bank tried to serve people not being served elsewhere, but in some cases there was a valid reason they weren't being served.[221] There also were some borrowers too eager to cheat a new bank. Mel Miller, who later served as a conservator for Unity, told of a case in which a customer faked accounts receivable documents, falsely attesting that he was due to receive payments with which he could repay the requested loans, Miller said.[222]

Unity also had a paucity of workers with financial experience and as such relied on higher employee counts to balance this out, a costly approach, noted Irving Sprague, former chair of the FDIC.[223] Especially crippling was the bank's lack of experienced loan officers, as without this expertise, Unity failed to filter out some risky borrowers.[224]

"The guys at Unity did not have training in finance or money—either academic training or experience in their careers in banking," said Juan Cofield, who later would found Unity's spiritual successor bank.[225]

In some cases, the bank signed on to subordinate a loan—that is, it would sign on to jointly provide a loan with a major bank, with that larger bank lending the bulk of the money and receiving priority for repayment. If the borrower was unable to pay back the entirety of the loan, Unity would lose out. Gilmore suggested that Unity relied on the major bank's assessment of the likelihood of loan repayment, not always successfully.[226] Federal Deposit Insurance Corporation Regional Director Mark Laverick also commented years later that when it came to partially guaranteed loans, Unity made the mistake of "mak[ing] a really risky $100,000 loan to a small business and think[ing] they were all right because the loan was 90 percent guaranteed by the Small Business Administration. Well, that still cost the bank $10,000," he said.[227]

Other operational costs contributed as well: because it served primarily low- and moderate-income communities, Unity managed many small deposits, which provide less investment to the bank while generating a similar amount of work for its staff.[228]

Unity's Leaders

Many like Cofield attributed Unity's hardships in part to limited financial expertise among its leadership. Officers' backgrounds included a level of banking, political, and legal experience.

Along with Sneed and Gilmore, Unity's officers included Roy G. Guittarr as executive vice president and treasurer, Herbert L. Lyken as a vice president, C. Bernard Fulp as assistant vice president, Melanee Newkirk as assistant treasurer, and Lawrence H. Banks as clerk, according to documents provided by OneUnited Bank leadership.

Assistant Vice President Fulp formerly worked at two Boston banks and had responsibility over Unity's loan granting.[229] In October 1968, he told the *Harvard Crimson* that he believed the bank must avoid being overly cautious or let the insidious perceptions of black inferiority that were prevalent at the time make the bank afraid to take risks.

"Black institutions historically have had inferiority complexes. ... This complex can't be allowed to immobilize us," Fulp said.[230] "Every time someone comes in here I can't think, 'We mustn't take this risk because we are a new black bank.'"

Executive VP Lyken was a manager of minority vendor relations at Raytheon,[231] and clerk Lawrence Banks was an attorney and a former city councilor and state representative.[232]

Executive Vice President Guittarr was a Gloucester resident in his mid-forties by the time of Unity's opening. In October 1968, he was the only white paid employee.[233] He had attended the Bentley School of Accounting and Finance, the American Institute of Banking, and the School of Banking at Williams College[234] and brought more than twenty years of experience in banking.[235]

Newkirk served as assistant treasurer and a loan officer for Unity.[236] After Unity, she would continue involvement in finance and later become executive director of the United Black Appeal, the fund-raising branch of the Black United Front Foundation.[237] In 1974 she was appointed to the state Special Commission for Investigation and Study Relative to the Feasibility and Desirability of Establishing State Supported Development Banking Mechanisms.[238]

Along with its slate of officers, Unity opened with a twenty-two-member unpaid board of directors with members reflecting in particular political, civil servant, and entrepreneurial energy. The board included Sneed as chair, as well as Guittarr, Banks, Gilmore, and Lyken, according to documents provided by OneUnited.

When Unity Bank opened its headquarters' doors for a preview opening gala in June 1968, board of directors member Harold J. Vaughan was the one who took up the role of master of ceremonies.[239] Vaughan was an attorney with a background in real estate appraisal. He had studied at Harvard University, Stenotype Institute, Boston University, and Suffolk University School of Law.

"We are innovators," Vaughan told attendees at the preview gala,[240] "because in addition to banking services we are giving financial information and scholarships."

Vaughan also spent a time on the Randolph Finance Committee, was treasurer and director of the Resthaven Charitable Nursing Home in Roxbury, and served as district director of the City of Boston's Assessing Department. In 1972, he would be appointed special assistant attorney general of Massachusetts with a focus in the eminent domain division.[241]

Accompanying him on board was Rodney S. Brooks, who by 1972 would be serving as Suffolk County Bail commissioner, a general contractor, and a member of the Massachusetts National Guard as well as a Republican candidate for state representative.[242]

Director John G. Bynoe, a Roxbury resident and career civil servant, was known for being the first New England regional civil rights director for the federal Department of Health, Education and Welfare. He also was a World War II veteran who previously worked in the Social Security Administration and served as president of the Roxbury Community Council. Bynoe held degrees from Boston University and Portia Law School at New England School of Law.[243]

Gerald A. Jones, who served as a Unity director until his death at age forty-three in 1971, was a general supervisor for the Polaroid Corporation and the president of Job Clearing House Inc. Previous roles had him serving in the army, as store manager of a Stop & Shop, and as manager of expense administration, communications for a Bradlees department store. [244]

Director Franklin W. Holgate of Roxbury was valedictorian in his class at Boston Trade School and served as a state representative from 1965 to 1972. He was active in the Democratic Party and had co-operated a restaurant. Holgate's financial experience included selling mutual funds and providing advice on dealing with money lending institutions to a number of black entrepreneurs engaged in business startup.[245]

Attorney Baron H. Martin was a graduate of Suffolk University and the Suffolk Law School, was a justice in Roxbury District Court, and served as a legal consultant to job training centers focused on the unemployed. He was known for a variety of civic involvements, among them membership in the National Advisory Board to the Small Business Administration and Minority Entrepreneurship Program.[246]

Director George R. Skelly served on the probation staff for Boston Municipal Court, before becoming chief probation officer in 1975. He held a sociology master's degree from Boston University and undergraduate degree from St. Augustine's College in North Carolina.[247]

Rounding out the board of directors were Charles W. Downer, Eric Harriott, Wayne B. Hazard, Charles H. Lewis Jr., Robert M. Malloy, John Reynolds, John A. Seiler, Robert A. Weaver, and Donald L. Stull (not to be confused with architect Donald A. Stull, whose firm was engaged in Unity Bank's design), according to OneUnited's documents.

Too Essential to Fail

These individuals' efforts were unable to keep Unity from the brink of collapse. In an unprecedented move, the FDIC stepped in to bail out the struggling little bank. Standard procedure for the FDIC was to allow any but the largest banks to fail, then sell off its good loans and pay off depositors. But in defiance of the norms, members of the FDIC voted 2–1 to intervene. The move rested on a precedent-setting interpretation of a law allowing for rescue of a bank even at a cost should the bank be deemed "essential" to the community.

With the memories fresh of racially charged riots, especially Los Angeles' Watts, then-FDIC director Irvine Sprague feared that Unity's collapse could trigger a similar unrest, he said.

"In 1971 no one could be sure that the failure of a black bank in a rundown urban center would not touch off a new round of 1960s-style rioting," Sprague said.[248]

Sprague elected to put the bank into receivership and determined that the conservator appointed must be black lest it appear he was trying to wrest Unity from the black community.[249] The selection: Richard L. Banks, a prominent black attorney and the director of Boston Lawyers for Housing.[250] Banks was a graduate of Harvard College and Harvard Law School,[251] yet despite his legal talent, he lacked financial experience. As such, he requested the appointment of Arthur B. Dimmit, a retired white banker with forty years of banking experiences, as Unity's chief operating officer.[252] Board members, meanwhile, were retained in an advisory capacity.[253]

First Conservators

To keep Unity afloat, the FDIC loaned it nearly $2 million—another unprecedented move for the agency[254]—and helped broker a deal in which Unity borrowed about $450,000 in total from four major banks: First National, Shawmut, State Street, and New England Merchants.[255]

Following the emergency aid, Richard Banks made some progress, but Unity's debt was a steep hole to climb out of. The takeover damaged Unity's image, making it difficult to regain customer confidence, according to an anonymous federal bank regulator.[256] A level of operational mismanagement continued, with delayed bill repayments, improper bookkeeping, and loans requiring improvements.[257] While some major banks lent experienced employees to Unity for several weeklong visits, this frequent in and out added to the churn of what already was staffing turnovers.[258]

During Banks's first year, Unity tightened its loan assessment process,[259] slashed operating expenses,[260] and reduced the extent of the bank's losses.[261] By August 1972, Unity's deposits had grown by 27 percent over the previous year, and stock subscriptions once again had value. The shares that originally sold for ten dollars apiece had plummeted to a value of fourteen cents each in 1971; by August 1972, each share was worth three to four dollars.[262]

Unity would be shaped under the hands of several interim conservators. In 1973, Banks left the post to accept appointment as a justice of the Roxbury District Court. In his stead, the state commissioner of banks appointed Mel Miller, *Banner* publisher and former assistant US attorney for Massachusetts, with degrees from Harvard and Columbia Law School. Like Banks, Miller focused on reducing what he regarded as overstaffing and on refining lending assessment. Ultimately, during Miller's four years at Unity, the bank made money from operations, but the costs of bad loans made under previous management cut into capital.[263]

"The thing that hit us was outstanding loans. We didn't add much to bad loans," Miller recounted in a 2017 interview.[264]

Shaping Welfare

During Miller's time at Unity, the federal government proposed making banks responsible for food stamps dispersal. The idea was unpopular among most bankers, because it required banks to pro-vide a free extra service that made them legally liable should they mistakenly provide food stamps to an ineligible person, Miller said.[265] To avoid taking on new risk, many local banks responded that they would offer the service, but only if Unity Bank did so, something they expected the small institution to refuse because of the liability.[266]

Miller agreed to provide the new service, but on one condition. He saw an opportunity for welfare policy reform and asserted that now was the time for additional changes to be made. At the time, welfare recipients received their checks on the first and fifteenth of the month, making them easy pickings for robbers who would rifle through mail-boxes of those they knew to be on welfare. The stolen checks would then be brought to check-cashers who would look the other way in exchange for a cut.[267]

"There were two days when mailboxes are absolutely full of these checks all over the state," Miller recalled. The check-arrival dates became nicknamed "mother's day." "Ne'er do wells in the communi-ties knew who's on welfare and they would take the checks out of the mailboxes."[268]

To make it more difficult for thieves, Miller proposed a new system under which instead of mailing all checks on the same day, recipients were assigned dates spaced throughout the month. His reasoning: even if robbers were aware of which households received checks, they would not know the dates of arrival, and it would no longer be an efficient use of time to collect the few checks arriving on any given day.[269] Miller became the target of fierce backlash by those who viewed him as delaying aid to welfare mothers, but ultimately his proposal was approved by the welfare commissioner, and it rolled out, with recipients assigned check-arrival dates based on their Social Security numbers. The effectiveness of the plan in thwarting efforts to steal checks prompted other states to adopt the system change as well.

"By spreading it out over thirty days, we completely killed the [welfare theft] market," Miller recalled.[270]

Changing Banking: NOW Accounts

While Miller came to Unity under the selection of Freyda Koplow, then-Massachusetts Commissioner of Banks, she resigned two years after his appointment. Her replacement was Carol Greenwald, a Federal Reserve economist, and she and Miller clashed over several initiatives. One such instance was a 1974 dispute over how best to serve small depositors.

Greenwald had noticed what she perceived as an inequity in banking systems: Those with the means to place large sums into their deposit accounts received free checks and interest on their deposits. However, customers with small deposits were relegated to checking accounts that offered only a few free checks and no interest.[271]

Greenwald wanted to remove the disparity and allow banks in Massachusetts to provide interest to small depositors—something prevented by a 1933 federal law barring interest on any demand deposit account. Miller, however, argued that it made financial sense for bankers to pay no interest to those customers who provided them with smaller deposits. Changing this policy would have a ripple effect, he said, as banks would pass the new interest costs along as fees to customers for services and by charging for checks.[272]

"At that time, almost everybody had a bank account," Miller recalled in 2017. "Even if you had a small amount, it was a good secure place to keep your money and you could get five free checks a month—enough to pay your mortgage and other bills. You essentially got free checking and a safe place to put your money."

When in 1975 Greenwald piloted Negotiable Order of Withdrawal (NOW) accounts in a statewide program[273] it established a type of bank account that was comparable to a demand deposit account that a small depositor might open, but on which banks could provide interest. In a competitive market, one bank seizing upon this option could prompt others to do the same to contend for customers.

In later years, it would appear that this effort to help low-income earners backfired: many banks took up offering checking accounts with interest, but they absorbed the new costs by reducing or eliminating formerly free services, for instance by setting a high minimum deposit amount to avoid account fees.

Barriers to establishing a bank account continue to be an issue. In 2013, while 7.7 percent of all households nationwide were unbanked, among black households, 21.4 percent held no bank account—three times the rate for white households.[274] In 2017, OneUnited seeks to facilitate bank accounts for small depositors by offering some low- or no-fee checking and savings account options and offering financial literacy programs to dissuade people from falling prey to predatory practices.[275]

The Mattapan Dispute

During Miller's time as Unity conservator, he and Greenwald would continue to clash, and ultimately he resigned following a dispute over the acquisition of a major bank's branch in Mattapan Square. Miller opposed the acquisition, arguing that the strong presence of Shawmut Bank in the area made it unprofitable for competing banks.[276] He said he believed the bank owning the institution was willing to relinquish the branch because it had found it unprofitable, and that donating it to Unity avoided the expense and time of seeking FDIC approval to close the branch.[277]

Following Miller's departure, Unity acquired Mattapan Square and Codman Square branches from First National Bank of Boston (later known as Bank Boston), as well as State Street Bank's Dudley Street Station building, with the intention of shifting its headquarters to that site[278] The major banks offered the branches for free.[279]

Then-conservator Ted Wilkins argued for the acquisition plan, saying it allowed Unity to expand in a way that otherwise would have been impossible with its limited capital.[280] He said he believed the costs of setting up operations at the new branches would be relatively minor, and predicted the acquisitions would allow a faster increase in profit than otherwise possible.[281] Similarly, a BankBoston spokesperson said the trade-off was intended to assist Unity's growth.[282]

In 1978, however, state Representative Royal Bolling Jr., like Miller, voiced concerns that the branches were offered to Unity because the current owners struggled to make money with them.[283]

"If they [the big banks] could not turn a profit, how can Unity?" Bolling said.[284] "[This may be] a back door attempt of the big banks to walk out on the black community and save face."

BankBoston seemed to partially confirm that fear, with a spokesperson stating that the institution sought to close the branches because they had ceased to be profitable.[285]

After initially rejecting the expansion proposal, the FDIC in May 1978 approved a plan under which Unity would phase in the acquisition of the new branches. It was determined that the bank lacked the resources to assume all three at once.[286] Unity also would receive some training from First National Bank of Boston, which would also maintain a reduced presence in Codman Square. [287]

Final Conservators

By the time Miller left in 1977, he had brought the bank to the point of just breaking even and paying off debts, according to Ted Wilkins, who would be the next to assume the conservator role.[288] Wilkins said that between 1976 and 1977 the bank nearly doubled its earnings, and its deposits rose by $2 million to hit a total of $11.1 million—nearly reaching the level at the time it was founded that was a 20 percent increase over current levels.[289]

Wilkins was a forty-year-old Roxbury native and officer of Commercial Services at Shawmut Bank when he became conservator.[290] He was followed in January 1982 by Fletcher Wiley, a thirty-nine-year-old attorney for Unity and partner in the law firm Budd Reilly & Wiley.[291]

Unity received a boost in 1978 in the form of a $500,000 deposit from the state under an initiative to recognize the importance of local banks.[292] In 1979, Unity produced a profit but slipped into losses in the following two years.[293] When Wiley entered, he said the bank continued to be plagued by management issues and talent-retention issues, along with staggering debt.[294]

Unity had been under stewardship for more than a decade by this point, and its end loomed in the form of millions overdue to the FDIC and hundreds of thousands due to four major banks.[295] Bank leadership already had received one extension, sparing Unity from the original 1976 due date. Now, after entering in January 1982, Wiley had until June to repay, and he made it clear he did not see it as possible.[296] Should Unity fail on its obligation, the FDIC could liquidate it. Citing the importance of Unity to the community, state senator Bill Owens of Mattapan announced a funding drive to save the bank, but the effort fell short.[297]

From the Ashes

As Unity's chances dimmed, others saw opportunity. Nine individuals applied to the state for a charter to establish the Boston Bank of Commerce, with the vision that it would provide a range of services to individuals and commercial businesses.[298] Juan Cofield, then the vice president of Malmart Mortgage Company, proposed to become CEO. According to Cofield, he was well aware at the time that Unity was due to fail and intended to acquire its assets as a first step toward acquiring the capital needed to launch his bank.[299]

Cofield came to this idea when a friend at the Greater Roxbury Development Corporation asked him to join the organization's plan to assume Unity's assets when the bank inevitably failed. While the development corporation's plan did not come to fruition, the process connected Cofield with the banking commissioner and planted ideas around Unity, Cofield said in a 2017 interview.[300]

Unlike Unity's vision of uplifting the underserved black community, Cofield's vision for Boston Bank of Commerce was focused on the business model of generating profit by appealing to clients from as many of Boston's ethnic communities as possible, he said.[301] It would require both tailoring the marketing approach accordingly and developing relationships with business leaders in the different neighborhoods. To achieve these, he sought to recruit a diverse board, ultimately including black, Jewish, Chinese, and Irish members, he said.[302]

"I never perceived it as a black bank," Cofield said.[303] "I wanted people who were prominent in their ethnic background and ethnic communities throughout Boston. … These people certainly had contacts and relationships in their own ethnic community."

Boston Bank of Commerce was the only entity to bid to assume Unity's assets.[304] Cofield said he believed it was understood in the local finance community that the FDIC wished to continue black ownership and leadership with Unity's successor, and so favored BBC for the acquisition.[305]

Unity's debt came due, and the bank shuttered on a Friday. That very day, the Boston Bank of Commerce assumed Unity's cash, payments due from other banks, securities portfolio, physical facilities, and other assets, and opened as its own bank the following Monday.[306]

Boston Bank of Commerce

The new bank's nine-person board of directors had considerable financial experience, including the president of a venture capital corporation, a bank director, several management consultants, and the senior vice president of a mutual life insurance company.[307] The list featured Charles T. Grigsby, president of Massachusetts Venture Capital Corporation; Alton Davis, a management consultant and former chair of Data Signal Corp.; Norman Weil, a management consultant and former financial officer of Commonwealth Bank and Trust Company; Arnold M. Soloway, an economist and the president of real estate development firm Design/Housing Inc.; Herbert F. Gold, senior vice president of John Hancock Mutual Life Insurance Co.; Joseph A. Marshall, director of University Bank and Trust Co.; Eugene V. Roundtree, president of All-Stainless Inc.; and Edward

McCormack Jr., a former Massachusetts attorney general, along with Cofield.[308]

The four major banks that had provided Unity with a critical loan invested again in the form of preferred stock at Boston Bank of Commerce, and the bank established itself with more than $1.7 million in starting capital and one branch each in Roxbury, Mattapan, and on Tremont Street downtown.[309]

By many accounts, this bank had its own struggles. Leadership turnover hit quickly, as Cofield left the bank in 1983, taking with him five members. According to Cofield, he and board member Eddie McCormack, a former Massachusetts attorney general and the Irish contingent of BBC, disputed the bank's loan strategy. With consumer trust shaken by Unity's collapse, Cofield said he feared any public dispute would damage Boston Bank of Commerce's reputation. Ultimately he and several other members accepted a buyout and departed.[310]

In Cofield's place came Ron Homer, former president of the National Banker's Association and CEO of Freedom National Bank, which was the largest minority-owned bank in the nation at the time that BBC reached out to him.[311] Homer brought a shift, pushing emphasis to mortgage lending, small business loans, and nonprofit company cash management programs, along with a focus on building external relationships. He was credited with forging connections with white banks, businesses, and political groups[312] and pursuing deposits from major firms such as Raytheon.[313]

Homer said in a 2017 interview that the bank was in trouble, in part because of the conflicting visions among its initial leadership and in part because it had been opened with few funds.[314] While banks typically need about $5 million to $6 million to start, BBC had capitalized with only about $1 million, he said.

"They had lost half their capital, which wasn't hard to do given they had so little to start with," Homer said.[315] "When a bank opens up, you're going to start losing money for a while."

The bank's operations also were largely limited to collecting and holding deposits with little lending, Homer said.[316] He was able to leverage his ties in the banking community to bring in more capital, including reaching out to the then-CEO of New England Merchant Banks, who had hired him into banking out of an MBA program in 1971 and who agreed to make a loan.[317]

The bank started making loans, with a focus on mortgages and on Small Business Administration and multifamily housing developments.[318] Homer said its lending extended throughout the black community in Boston.

"We were involved in almost every facet of things that were going on within the black community," he said.[319] "There wasn't much going on that we didn't get involved in in some way."

BBC did, however, face some important decisions on the type of involvement it could have. In the early 1980s, BBC shuttered its Mattapan branch, the one that had generated controversy when Unity first acquired it from the First National Bank of Boston. The closing drew criticism for BBC for pulling back services in a largely black community. Bank leadership insisted that the branch was a costly venture and that they could not maintain it and stay afloat.[320]

In 1984, the bank lost $100,000 but became profitable the next year, producing an 18.5 percent return on equity—representing the bank's first profitable year.[321] Growth continued through 1987. During the first six months of 1987, net income rose 94 percent over the same time the previous year, total assets rose 69 percent, and deposits were up by 72 percent.[322] But the bank still struggled to raise enough capital to allow for making the larger loans that customers sought.[323]

Big Bucks and Big Changes

Teri Williams and Kevin Cohee entered the scene in August 1995 with a million-dollar investment in Boston Bank of Commerce, doubling the bank's reserves and establishing them as the largest investors in the bank's history.[324] Boston Bank of Commerce was in dire straits, according to Williams.

"Everything about the bank needed to be fixed," she said.[325]

Effects of the recession of 1991 rippled out more slowly to Boston Bank of Commerce, striking the bank in 1992 and 1993 with delinquent loans and problem credits.[326] The current management team, with Ron Homer as chair, had become lopsidedly focused on community relations and involvement, Williams said. Consequently, modernization of systems and operations were left behind.[327]

Williams had experience in bank leadership from roles in Bank of America and American Express, where she was one of the youngest vice presidents in history.[328] She earned a bachelor's in economics from Brown University and MBA from Harvard Business School. Her husband, Kevin Cohee, received an MBA and BA from the University of Wisconsin and JD degree from Harvard Law School. His entrepreneurial and business background included purchasing and growing Military Professional Services Inc., a firm that marketed credit cards to military personnel.[329]

By the time Ron Homer, a family friend, reached out to Williams and Cohee for financial help with BBC, the institution had been served a cease-and-desist order from the FDIC.[330] To turn around its profitability, Homer sought an influx of capital. Williams and Cohee hired a consultant to investigate the state of the bank and concluded it needed far more than money; it needed a new management approach.[331]

"The consultant came back and said yes [investing in Boston Bank of Commerce] could be a good investment," Williams recalled.[332] "You are going to invest $1 million, but it probably could use $3 million." Williams also was told that the bank needed intensive operational changes.

The bank's computing systems were antiquated, employees had not received raises in years, loan application evaluation procedures were not financially rigorous enough, and operations were inefficient, Williams said.[333] For now, focus needed to be on ensuring the bank stayed afloat, otherwise there would be no Boston Bank of Commerce around to serve the community, Williams said.[334]

"What we needed most was to make sure the actual bank survived," Williams said. "We needed to move it to profitability and move it to working out the problem loans and be in compliance and get the cease and desist order lifted."[335]

Homer transitioned from bank chair to president, opening the position for Cohee. Williams was appointed vice president.[336] Cohee took charge of the bank's assets and focused on establishing clear spending procedures, while Williams sought to reform daily operations, including both personnel management and systems, she said. Homer continued to do external community work.[337]

After about a year, Homer departed the bank.[338] According to Williams, Homer's focus remained different from that of the new chair and vice president.[339] In turn, Homer would go on to found Access Capital Strategies in 1997—a successful money management firm—and, in 2008, accept appointment to the MassHousing Finance Board, a quasipublic agency charged with providing funding for affordable rental housing and home purchases.[340]

Becoming OneUnited

In 1999 Boston Bank of Commerce made history by becoming the first black-owned bank to go national. BBC's small size had been constraining it from making the changes that would take it to the next level, including greater investment in personnel and updating to modern technology, Williams said.[341]

"We realized early on that Boston Bank of Commerce—[and] really a lot of black owned banks around the country—were too small to have the economies of scale that were going to be needed as banking progressed," Williams said.[342]

The solution came in 1999 when the FDIC informed Boston Bank of Commerce's leadership that Miami's People's Bank of Commerce was on the verge of failure and asked them to bid to acquire it, Williams recalls. In June 1999, People's was the twenty-fifth largest black-owned bank in the United States, but by September, it had suffered major losses, attributed to poor management and lending practices, and it was shuttered by the federal government.[343] BBC acquired most of the bank's assets as well as its deposits, soaring BBC's total assets from $37.6 million to $145 million.[344]

During their visit to Miami, Williams and Cohee were approached by a board member of Founders National Bank in Los Angeles, who sought their investment.[345] In 2001, Boston Bank of Commerce merged with that bank, following it up with a merger with LA's minority-owned Family Savings Bank in 2002.

With four entities combined, the bank had a national image and swapped out the name Boston Bank of Commerce for OneUnited to reflect this.[346] With the mergers completed, OneUnited held $500 million in total assets, vastly expanding its lending capabilities.[347] The bank's online services played an important role in its growth as well.

Faces of OneUnited

Among OneUnited's powerful resources is its personnel. In a 2015 interview with *Ebony*, Williams said her critical responsibilities include ensuring OneUnited has "the best team on the field," when it comes to directors and senior management team.[348]

As of 2017, this management team includes Sherri Brewer as security officer and chief retail officer. Brewer has a BA in economics from Occidental College and more than thirty years of banking experience including at Wells Fargo, Orange County Credit Union, Business Bank of California, and First City Federal Credit Union.[349]

The post of general counsel is held by Robert P. Cooper, who is chair of the National Bankers Association and holds a BA in economics from Yale and a JD from Harvard Law School, as well as more than twenty years of experience as a corporate attorney.[350] Cecilia Isaac brings approximately thirty years of banking experience, along with a BA and master's degree in public administration and a certificate in tax administration from the University of South Carolina, to her role as chief lending officer. Chief Financial Officer John Trotter had more than two decades of banking experience before joining OneUnited and holds a BS in business administration, with a major in accounting, from Ohio State University. Rounding out the robust team are Kimmie Jackson, lead of human resources, and James Slocum, chief information officer.

The board in 2017 included John L. Sims, a strategic planning and business operations consultant with more than thirty years of corporate management experience and a BS from Delaware State University.[351] Joining Sims is George A. Russell Jr., whose more than thirty-five years in the banking and finance industry include high-level positions at State Street Corporation and State Street Foundation and Freedom National Bank of New York, as well as the City of Boston. He graduate from Clark University and took an MBA from New York University's Stern School of Business.

Director Deloris Pettis holds an MBA in accounting from Tulane University, a BSC from State University of New York at Buffalo, and certifications in risk management assurance, internal auditing, and public accounting. She brings leadership experience in enterprise risk management and auditing and prior involvement at Bank of Boston. Serving on the board along with her is Leon Wilson, a managing director with more than thirty-five years in the banking sector and a graduate of Boston University, Virginia Graduate School of Retail Banking Management, and Harvard Business School's Program for Management Development. [352]

The board also features managing director and former Carter White House adviser Leander J. Foley and pedodontist Richard D. Carr. [353]

Mission

While at the helm of OneUnited, Williams and Cohee have the objective of using financial institutions to weave a stronger community fabric. Like many other black-owned banks, OneUnited focuses on serving low- and moderate-income communities hit by systemic inequalities, Williams said. For these kinds of banks, the goal is to assist residents in building wealth and greater community stability.[354]

"They're all sort of dealing with how to build wealth when you don't have a lot of money and with economic inequalities in the cities that they're in," Williams said. "We've constantly tried to think of ways to use the banking structure to offer services that other institutions are not offering but that would help the community."[355]

Banks traditionally are less attracted to such communities, given that it is often seen as easier to turn a profit in communities with greater concentrations of wealth. Richer customers make larger deposits, and are more likely to borrow and be able to repay loans, Williams said. They also are the kind of clientele that has demand for fee-generating services such as investment products, trust fund services, and insurance, she said.[356]

Serving a less-wealthy community means discovering creative ways to meet needs as well as to keep the bank running with profit. Lending efforts from OneUnited in 2017 include loans targeted at apartment complex owners who keep rents moderate—below 100 percent of Area Median Income, often in the range of to $500 to $1,000 per month, Williams said. For those seeking loans to rehabilitate their units, OneUnited tries to help borrowers successfully repay by basing the loan amount off the units' current rents, not off the potential rents they could generate once brought up to market. That puts lessened financial pressure on the borrower, skirting an eventuality in which the borrower has to raise rents to pay off the loan, Williams said.[357]

Credit Cards

OneUnited also has sought to leverage specialized credit cards to enhance support for community-serving institutions or help customers build the credit scores. An early experiment was the Unity Card, which offered comparable benefits to a Visa card, which debuted in 1996.[358] For every dollar charged on the card, OneUnited donated a cent to a charity. The customer selected the charity from among a menu of options that included the NAACP Legal Defense Fund, National Urban League, Thurgood Marshall Scholarship Fund, and a foundation established by the bank for donating to grassroots organizations.[359]

Cohee said at the time that the Unity Card was meant to solve a persistent problem in the black communities that OneUnited served: there were many organizations that were doing useful work in the community but that had their capacity restricted by limited funding. The card would raise the visibility of the organizations while also harnessing black consumers' dollars to fuel economic engines in their communities.[360]

"The problem is not that we don't have the organizations and people in place to work on the issues. It's that we don't have the money for these organizations to expand and improve the quality of what they're already doing," Cohee said.[361] "One of the greatest assets black people in the country possess is our economic spending power. By that I mean the $600 billion we spend buying goods and services every year. To put that in perspective, we spend more money than the entire country of Canada."

Ultimately, Unity Card would be a learning experience, Williams recalled. OneUnited had offered the card in an "unsecured" format, meaning that customers using the card borrowed money without having to put down collateral. The result: OneUnited lost money. In part, the problem was because in neighborhoods with less wealth, residents have fewer savings and are more susceptible to going into debt when hit by an unexpected life disruption such as illness, divorce, or job loss.[362] This risk was masked by some residents' good credit scores.[363]

In 2013, OneUnited revived the idea of a unique credit card after observing that many residents afflicted with bad credit resorted to using prepaid cards offered by major banks. The problem: these cards charged high fees, and using them did nothing to build credit scores.[364]

"They were becoming second class citizens in the banking world. Banks were making a lot of money off these prepaid cards but they weren't doing anything to help the community," Williams said.[365]

OneUnited issued a card—reusing the "Unity Card" name and nicknaming it "the Comeback Card"—designed to help customers bring up their credit scores. This time, the card was secured: customers could only borrow up to the amount they had deposited.[366] Bank leaders envisioned that with the card, customers would raise their scores up to the point where they could transition to or acquire a rewards credit card. By March 2017, the bank had served approximately ten thousand customers with the card, most of them low- to moderate-income families living in low- to moderate-income concentrated census tracts, Williams said.[367]

In response to nationwide instances of police killings of black civilians, OneUnited returned to credit cards to advance a social justice message, issuing its Amir Card in 2017. The card is part of a collaboration between the bank and Black Lives Matter to acknowledge the interconnectedness of economics and social justice. It depicts the image of a young black boy, and customers who sign up for the card receive notices about how to support BLM.[368]

Bank of Boston

Unity and OneUnited were not the only ones to realize the power of a financial institution with community and social justice missions. Among the others was Bank of Boston, which gained awards, publicity, and profit from developing a new business model focused on providing banking to underserved inner cities.

Gail Snowden, the daughter of social workers and founders of Roxbury's Freedom House Muriel and Otto Snowden, became the executive director of the bank's new inner-city subdivision when it was formed in 1990. Snowden held a sociology degree from Harvard and a master's of business administration from Simmons College's School of Management. Before leading the subdivision, she was the senior credit officer at Bank of Boston and had spent years winding through various financial departments ranging from retail to human resources.[369] Especially valuable: she was from the community herself and brought knowledge of community needs, and she had a solid reputation among local residents.[370]

The subdivision, named First Community Bank, was established in response to federal passage of the Community Reinvestment Act requiring banks to perform a certain level of business in the communities from which they received the bulk of their deposits. Bank of Boston took it as an imperative to go beyond basic compliance and enter a new category of business focused on often-ignored urban communities, Snowden said.[371]

"The executive leadership believed there was potentially very good business that could come if they served in the inner city adequately," Snowden recalled in a 2017 interview.[372]

At the time, minority and low-income communities were lacking services. Roxbury's Grove Hall had not had a bank for twenty-three years before First Community opened a branch there in 1992.[373] Then-Mayor Raymond Flynn celebrated the opening as a "significant move forward" for the community.[374]

Unlike other banks, Bank of Boston had not shuttered its branches in Roxbury, Dorchester, Jamaica Plain, Hyde Park, and Roslindale, although service levels had dwindled by the time of First Community's launch.[375] Bank of Boston moved seven branches in these neighborhoods from its retail branch network to the new subdivision's use.[376] First Community would be given a high level of autonomy—essentially serving as a bank-within-a-bank, Snowden said. Leadership also allowed the bank time to get on its feet and told Snowden that no individual branch had to turn a profit so long as the overall First Community division succeeded, she said.[377]

"That was an important distinction that helped us be profitable," Snowden recalled, "because at the beginning we had seven branches $700 million in deposits—which was very low—and 70 people. That was a very, very small business."[378]

Snowden sought to tailor the bank to the community. She scheduled community meetings at each branch to solicit resident feedback on what they needed and how well the bank was meeting those needs.[379] One discovery was the demand for much smaller loans—at the time, someone seeking an installment loan for purchasing furniture, a TV, or the like had to borrow a minimum of $5,000. That was too high for many who needed only a $500 minimum loan—an offering First Community soon introduced.[380]

While some bankers feared the service costs on minor loans would strip away any profit, Snowden said her aim was that with enough volume, it would balance out. A deeper fear among many bankers was that most small inner-city loans would default.[381] In part, a solution was to move away from automated business loan assessment and processing. Instead, staff members were sent into the community to visit the businesses of prospective borrowers and get a deeper understanding of their circumstances—something Snowden credited with producing better loan decisions.[382] To further bolster these efforts, First Community leadership established a business loan center at its Uphams Corner branch and hired a staff of commercial lending officers who had experience in analyzing and underwriting small business and middle-market company loans.[383]

To further serve customers, Snowden's team arranged a detailed population analysis of those living near branches in order to ensure that staff reflected the languages and other needs of the community. Along with assigning Vietnamese speakers to the Field's Corner office and multilingual staff to the Chinatown branch, the division's leadership created an internal directory listing which languages employees spoke. With the directory, a staff member could readily be called up if a customer came in needing language translation not otherwise offered.[384]

First Community advertised in local newspapers including the Chinese-English paper *SAMPAN*, the black community's *Bay State Banner*, and several Hispanic newspapers, including ads in various languages.[385] They made sure to depict loan officers and branch managers in the ads to underscore the diversity of the staff as well and that customers would be interacting with local community members. First

Community also renovated its Dudley Square headquarters to create an image designed to impress and engender trust.[386]

It took about two years for profit to show. The first year was focused on building morale, including convincing staff that they had the skills and expertise to make the long-neglected branches succeed. As part of this process, the bank staff gathered metrics and demonstrable evidence of good performance. Bank of Boston's mission, along with its data, began to attract further talent. In the second year, the bank showed a small profit, and in 1991, it was asked to expand into Rhode Island, where it started two branches. A few years later, First Community opened three branches in Connecticut.[387] First Community eventually introduced more branches in Greater Boston, and, under a new name following BankBoston's 1999 merger with Fleet Financial Group, attained branches in New York, New Jersey, and Pennsylvania.[388]

The bank division continued to grow, attracting patronage from celebrity Spike Lee,[389] winning the Community Investment Act's "outstanding" rating, becoming subject of a Harvard Business School paper, and launching its own development company to focus on smaller commercial lending in the range of $2 million to $5 million, compared to the standard $50 million minimum.[390]

"The creation of BankBoston Development Company was so unique it was recognized by the White House with the Ron Brown Award," Snowden recalled. The award recognizes companies that demonstrate deep commitment to innovative work that empowers communities and employees while furthering business interests.

Rhumbline

While some members of Boston's black community made their names in banking, others became known from different realms of finance. One notable instance was Rhumbline, a Boston-based investment advisory firm that would grow to manage funding for corporate and government clients across the nation.[391]

J. D. Nelson, who passed away in 2013, was a Roxbury native and the son of Jamaican immigrants who were active in the community.[392] His older brother would go on to become the first black federal judge in Massachusetts.[393] J. D. Nelson, meanwhile, followed high school with five years in the navy, and named his firm after the nautical term "rhumb line," meaning the most easily navigated course between two points.[394]

After returning to civilian life, Nelson studied on his own to earn a broker dealer license and delved into banking work.[395] He founded Rhumbline in 1990 after spending two years as chief budget officer of the Democratic National Committee and serving as vice president and then senior vice president of State Street.[396]

By 2001, the firm would be managing about $5 billion in assets for seventy-five clients nationwide, including government and private entities such as Goodyear Tire and Rubber, George Washington University and the City of Orlando, Florida.[397] In just three more years the client list stretched to eighty-four private and government clients in twenty-three states and Washington, DC.[398] By 2009, Rhumbline was the largest minority-owned institutional investment firm in the nation,[399] and by 2011, it was managing $23.7 billion in assets.[400]

SynCom Venture Partners

Founded in 1972 by a Boston-native, the venture capital company Syndicated Communications demonstrated the significance of who holds the purse strings in shaping society. The firm became known for providing critical equity capital investing in minority media businesses. The impact was such that Radio One cofounder Cathy Hughes labeled Syncom's owner, the late Herb Wilkins, "the gatekeeper for black entrepreneurs in the broadcast industry."[401] Clients included notable enterprises such as Radio One, Black Entertainment Televisions, BuenaVision, and Z-Spanish Radio.[402]

Herb Wilkins was born in Roxbury in 1942 and was the brother of Unity Bank's third conservator, Ted Wilkins. After attending Boston public schools, Herb Wilkins studied at Boston University, graduating with a bachelor's in 1965, and at Harvard School of Business, graduating in 1970.[403] Wilkins served as the principal in charge of management advisory services for independent public accountant firm Lucas, Tucker & Co., and as senior vice president of Boston-based venture capital fund Urban National Corp., prior to founding SynCom with partner Terry Jones.

He would expand his work to include founding SYNCOM Funds group, comprising several individual venture funds, and to be a board member of BET Holdings Inc. and Simmons-Lathan Media Group, and a director of Cowles Media Company.

In one major deal, Syncom acquired the Iridium Satellite system for $25 million, and later sold it for $436 million.[404] By the time of Wilkins's death in 2014, the companies in which Syncom invested had a market value of more than $10 billion.[405]

Wilkins was awarded the Kappa Alpha Psi Fraternity's Laurel Wreath, its highest honor, and was named to the Federal Communication Commission's Advance Committee on Minority Ownership in 1984.[406]

Access Capital Strategies

After leaving Boston Bank of Commerce, Ron Homer founded Access Capital Strategies, a money management firm that at one point would manage approximately $75 million for the state's mortgage fund and later be acquired by Royal Bank of Canada.[407]

The firm represents another way that Homer has applied a social activism lens to work in the financial industry.

Homer holds a bachelor's in psychology from the University of Notre Dame and an MBA from the University of Rochester.[408] He started out in social services work in Rochester, New York, and became critical of banks' failure to invest in low-income housing in the city.[409] When he was offered a job to place loans in low-income areas for Marine Midland Bank, he took up the opportunity.[410]

"There's a natural extension from psychology to sociology to economics," Homer told the *Boston Globe* in 1987.[411] "I realized at a bank, I could accomplish all the things I could at a social service agency but have even more impact."

Homer continued his career in finance joining the minority-owned Freedom National Bank of New York in 1979, after he tired of what he said was a climate of institutionalized racism at Midland.[412] At Freedom National, he quickly rose to CEO.[413] Homer also served as president of the National Bankers Association.[414]

When it became clear that Homer would be leaving OneUnited Bank, he sought a new way to use the financial industry to bolster urban communities.

"I came to believe over long term if you want to improve economic wellbeing of a community, you have to increase the flow of capital, rather than invest in specialized areas," Homer said in a 2017 interview.[415]

His solution would become Access Capital Strategies, an impact investing fund that by 2017 enabled banks, foundations, public funds, and other investing institutions to invest in low and moderate-income communities.[416] The firm uses clients' money to purchase securities comprised of responsibly priced loans in these communities, provided that the loans are primarily guaranteed by the United States government, its agencies, or municipalities with high credit ratings in order to reduce credit risk—the chance that a borrower defaults.[417]

By creating a specialized secondary market, the firm also provides an incentive for banks to originate more loans in these communities.[418] In some cases, Access Capital approaches originators with a proposal to buy loans that meet certain criteria, should the originators agree to issue them.[419]

Reflecting in 2017 on Access Capital, Homer said the resources had long been available to make a successful business that invested in underserved communities. He credited his decades of experience in banking with exposing him to useful tools, as well as making clear the strong potential for the kind of fund he envisioned.

"During [my years in banking], I had actively specialized in learning everything I could about government loan programs that could aid urban inner city communities," Homer said.[420] "That included FHA [Federal Housing Authority] loans, all types of affordable housing rental programs, Fannie Mae and Freddie Mac mortgage backed securities, how to get securities, etc. I learned that these assets, once they were made, performed very well—like any other asset class. And there was a high demand for them, but, ironically, the big institutions that specialized in making them still didn't devote much of their attention to low income communities or minority communities to fund these types of assets."

Among the advantages touted by Access Capital members are that traditionally-underwritten mortgages made to low- to moderate-income areas pay returns at more predictable rates than mortgages with higher balances, thus providing a more stable return for clients. [421]

The fund materialized in 1997, when Homer cofounded Access Capital Strategies with David Sand. Homer's connections in the financial community again proved useful. Through involvement in the American Bankers Association he knew a national network of bankers, and his work had brought him familiarity with Fannie Mae and Freddie Mac.[422] Homer also was friends with bankers and finance experts such as Michael Porter and Peter Lynch[423]. To launch and grow his new venture, Homer reached out to the bankers among his contacts to explain the value of his fund to their work.[424] Through such efforts, Homer and Sand raised approximately $2 million—enough to get the fund up and running.[425] The firm started with just one employee, a junior partner named Barbara Page.[426]

Bank of Boston was the fund's first investor and infused $25 million.[427] The time also was ripe for Access Capital, as the Community Reinvestment Act had been implemented in 1977 in response to redlining practices. Fannie Mae became a major investor in Access Capital, and directed some business its way. Often when bankers sought to originate loans to count toward Community Reinvestment Act requirements, Fannie Mae staff presented to them the option of selling those loans to Access Capital or investing directly in the fund, Homer said.[428]

As Access Capital grew it attracted increasing interest, including investments from state pension funds, community foundations and insurance companies.[429] In 2001, the firm hired Merrill Lynch Investment Managers as a subadviser to conduct services such as performance monitoring and management infrastructure, while the team focused on finding loans and bringing them into the fund.[430] In 2006, Access Capital switched subadvisers to the Royal Bank of Canada, after Merrill Lynch underwent a merger, and in 2008 accepted an offer to be acquired by RBC.[431] By this point, the Access Capital Strategies team comprised six people, its largest staff level.[432]

During its growth, Access Capital had expanded to manage not only its fund, but also other assets in a separately managed account.[433] Between the two strategies, Access Capital in 2017 has more than $1 billion and is among the largest mutual funds of RBC.[434] The group has done business with more than 150 banks nationwide, and currently half of Access Capital's assets come from banks with Community Reinvestment Act requirements, and the other half from traditional investors with an interest in "the idea of being able to invest in lower and moderate income communities but still have a market rate and safe return," Homer said. [435] Homer still serves as president of the fund and is involved in implementation of the funds' strategies. [436]

Eastern Bank

The model of those who recognize the social value of serving often ignored populations in a financially viable way is Eastern Bank. The oldest mutual bank in the United States, Eastern was founded to extend services to a broad customer base that included the less-affluent individuals often overlooked by banks.[437]

"We were formed [in 1818] by a group of people in Salem who looked around and saw that people were hiding money in their mattresses or burying it in the back yard to keep it safe," Nancy Hunting

Stager of Eastern Bank, executive vice president of human resources and charitable giving, said during a 2017 interview. "There were banks, but they catered to ship captains and such."

Today, Eastern actively sites branches in underserved communities, where it can benefit from lower rates of competition while also filling a social equity goal, Bob Rivers, Eastern Bank CEO, said in an interview in 2017.[438] The city of Chelsea had gone more than a decade without an Eastern branch before the bank opened one there, and Lawrence had been without an Eastern branch for twenty-three years.[439]

In the 2000s, the bank especially focused on recruiting a diverse board, as well as increasing diversity in entry-level positions as a key piece of business strategy. Including diverse voices in top decision-making levels produces more creative ideas and varied solutions, and recruiting locally allows the bank to more accurately understand its customer bases' needs and how to best serve them, Rivers said.[440] Twenty-one percent of employees were minorities, as of January 2017.[441] In 2017, the bank recruited a black president, Quincy Miller, away from his leadership position at Citizen's Bank. March 2017 elections gave Eastern a Board of Corporations on which more than 40 percent of members are women, people of color and/or members of the LGBTQ community.[442]

"Our emphasis on diversity is first a matter of mission and also a matter of business," Rivers said.[443] "Our pursuit of diversity is around producing the most robust collective mindset we can have around the table to solve increasingly complex problems in ever-changing times."

"The company has been able to adapt to changing times and the changing face of the communities it serves because of the work of people like [human resources representative Ive] Gonzalez," stated the *Bay State Banner* in 2006. Gonzalez, who at the time was responsible for the bank's diversity initiatives, told the *Banner,* "It is important to us to mirror the community we serve."[444]

Eastern's ties to and familiarity with the community are strengthened through an emphasis on volunteering, as well as a bank policy—in place since 1999—that calls for donating 10 percent of the firm's net income to charity.[445]

The strategy has paid back: Although providing small business loans is inherently risky due to the 73 percent rate of startup failure within the first three years, Eastern has managed to survive profitably as the number one Small Business Association lender in New England for seven years running, Rivers said in 2017.[446] One reason for the success is that bank staff with community connections often personally know the loan applicants and so have better ability to make wise lending decisions, Stager said.[447]

"If you know the people in the community who are running the business or doing commercial real estate development, you're in a position to make a smart decision," Stager said.[448]

In 2017, the bank also began putting a focus on a newly identified need: lending to small businesses that are several years into their lives and are now looking to scale up. In many cases, firms poised for growth find themselves in a bind: they need more equipment to increase capacity and fill larger contracts but cannot afford the equipment until they get the money from such a larger contract. That's where Eastern Bank can step in with loans, Eastern Bank President Miller said.[449]

Company efforts to recruit both diverse employees and clientele have included networking with minority organizations and professional groups, advertising in media that have readerships primarily of color, holding small business and banking seminars in the community, and providing entry-level internships and training programs to low-income high school and college students of color.[450] Additionally, the bank's reputation for diversity and community investment as well as the visibility of minorities in leadership positions helps attract more diverse workers, Rivers said.[451]

Rivers also credits the mutual bank structure with allowing Eastern to maintain a social justice focus. Under the mutual bank structure, Eastern is not publically owned or traded. Instead it is owned by a group of corporators whose members elect, and include, the board of trustees who govern the bank according to company bylaws and state law.[452] Because it does not sell stock on the public market, Eastern has no access to outside capital and instead must rely solely on its earnings. [453]

Without the pressure of stakeholders seeking to sell their stock at a profit, the bank is free to pursue growth on a gradual but steady time-line as opposed to questing for quick, sizable returns.[454] Additionally, with fewer people to please, the bank can pursue occasional outside projects they believe will help the community—such as supporting publication of certain social activism books—and other causes that could be hard to build unanimous shareholder consensus around, Stager adds.[455] In turn, she says, taking a well-thought-out targeted stance on social issues can be a profit-generator.

"When you are an advocate, you can't please everybody. From time to time, we have customers who say, because you did this, I'm going to move my account," Stager said.[456] "But we believe we have more people joining us because of the positions we take."

6

Several Major Real Estate Projects

Yawu Miller and Sandra Larson

In recent years, there has been considerable effort in Boston and other urban centers to stimulate entrepreneurship among blacks. Economic studies have indicated that insufficient involvement in business development has hindered the growth of black wealth. This chapter's focus on four outstanding real estate projects highlights extraordinary achievements by black-led developers whose successes in Boston set an example that can help other community members see possibilities and reach for opportunities.

Crosstown Center was Boston's first major black-led project, adding a Hampton Inn & Suites hotel, a large parking garage, an office building, and several retail and food establishments in Lower Roxbury. Harvard Commons created a high-quality residential neighborhood on the old State Hospital grounds at the Mattapan-Dorchester line. The One Lincoln/State Street Financial Center is one of Boston's largest commercial buildings, while United Housing owns and manages a substantial inventory of affordable rental units.

A common characteristic of these projects is that they all are private enterprise endeavors. The developers generated profits and increased black wealth. In addition, all four are of sufficiently large scale to stand out as continuing symbols of achievement.

Crosstown Center

When the Hampton Inn & Suites opened at Massachusetts Avenue and Melnea Cass Boulevard in July 2004, it was the only black-owned hotel in Greater Boston—and one of just a few dozen nationally.[457] The 175-room, ten-story hotel anchored the Crosstown Center development, which grew to include a 1,250-space parking garage, nearly two hundred thousand square feet of commercial space, and an office building. The $130 million black-led project created jobs and drew people and commerce to an underutilized location.

A Neglected Stretch

Melnea Cass Boulevard is an after-effect of the failed I-95/Inner Belt highway plans that were halted by community resistance in the 1960s and '70s. The boulevard was constructed in 1981 on a bare swath of Lower Roxbury land that had been cleared for the failed highway project. Today's wide, heavily traveled thoroughfare cuts a curving path from Tremont Street near Ruggles Station to the mouth of the Massachusetts Avenue Connector that brings traffic on and off I-93.

Development along the new boulevard came in fits and starts. The Harry Miller Company textile fabrication plant built in the mid-1990s was a sign of economic potential in the area, though the low-slung "windowless, bunker-like building" on Albany Street between Melnea Cass Boulevard and Hampden Street did little to enliven the streetscape.[458] Economic losses in the area included Digital Equipment Corporation (DEC), whose plant shut down in 1993, and StrideRite, whose manufacturing facility closed soon after.[459] The DEC and StrideRite closings robbed this light-industrial zone of more than three hundred jobs, and *Banner* coverage at the time showed local residents dismayed and angry. "Why are they pulling out of a community that needs them so much?" asked one resident; another termed the firms' departures a "tragedy," and commented, "We don't need businesses shutting down and packing up, we need businesses coming into the community."[460]

Crosstown Proposal Offers Promise of New Life

As the decade drew to a close, an exciting plan emerged. In fall 1998, black developers Thomas Welch and Kirk Sykes proposed a retail-entertainment complex to be built along Melnea Cass Boulevard between Massachusetts Avenue and Hampden Street, on land owned by the Boston Redevelopment Authority. The site included the former DEC building, which the city had purchased in 1994. Initial plans by Sykes, an architect with his own architecture and development company, and Welch, who was a housing finance expert before hanging his own shingle as a developer, included a hotel, a state-of-the-art stadium-seating movie theater, a food court, parking garage, and office building. Clearly, it stood to be the largest black-led development project in Greater Boston to date.[461]

"The Crosstown Center project was a very big deal," recalled Beverley Johnson, a Boston-based consultant who worked closely with Sykes and Welch on community and political engagement. "Black developers had done some small projects, primarily housing and affordable housing—because the city would offer different kinds of incentives to build affordable housing—but nothing on this scale. It was a really big deal for the community to have black developers be the lead owners for the hotel and the retail space as well. That played a major role in building community support—people wanted to see them succeed."[462]

The developers reported strong interest from potential retail tenants, especially in light of the expected movie theater as an anchor tenant. They gained the support of Mayor Thomas Menino and other elected officials, including state senators Dianne Wilkerson and Steven Lynch, state representatives Gloria Fox and Byron Rushing, and District 7 City Councilor Gareth Saunders, who represented the Roxbury and Lower Roxbury neighborhoods.

One reason for the project's relatively smooth progression in a city that had not been very amenable to black developers in the past may be that these developers had keen eyes for choosing the right project at the right time, on a parcel that fell outside white developers' sights.

"Not many people were looking at this piece of land as something to develop," Welch recalled, even though the location enjoyed close proximity to the Boston Medical Center and the promise of easy access to highways, the airport, and the soon-to-be-developed Boston Convention and Exhibition Center, at a lower price than downtown.[463]

Sykes said their perspective as black developers enabled them to look beyond the run-down state of the area and see its business potential. "Being a minority real estate developer can be an advantage if you can see the value in an area that other developers may not see if they only see it in one light," he told the *Banner* when the hotel opened in 2004. "Other developers didn't see the one million visitors a year to the hospital. They didn't see that when the Central Artery [Big Dig project] was completed we'd be seven minutes to the airport."[464] In a 2017 interview, Sykes elaborated on this: "It made all kinds of sense that the area had some value, given its proximity and accessibility—but people weren't looking at it that way. They were looking downtown, not looking in the black community and saying 'Hey, can we create something of value over there?' In some ways it was low-hanging fruit. You just had to have the vision to understand its connectivity to the whole infrastructure of Boston. I had a planning background and an architecture background. I knew how to look for sites that had a 'nexus' quality—nodes of activity that could be catalytic."[465]

Strong Community Support

At an early public hearing for the Crosstown proposal, covered by the *Banner* in November 1998, Representative Rushing and others urged the Boston Redevelopment Authority to fast-track the proposal in order to capitalize on the early interest of desirable cinema and retail tenants. Supporters expressed hope also that the BRA would grant the necessary zoning change from light industrial to mixed-use/commercial.[466] Black BRA Chairman Clarence "Jeep" Jones, though not typically seen at such meetings, was in attendance and "quietly watching as speaker after speaker endorsed Crosstown Center." That same month, with BRA staff reporting unanimous city and community support for the project, the BRA board voted unanimously to grant Sykes and Welch tentative designation to build the project, already titled Crosstown Center.[467] The unusual direct designation "saved a lot of time—which translates into saving a lot of money," Welch noted.[468]

Banner news coverage at the time noted a striking contrast between the overwhelmingly positive reception and consensus support for Crosstown Center and the community dissatisfaction with other local projects of the time, such as the Boston Water and Sewer Commission's large building on the former StrideRite site and a proposed Northeastern Dormitory on Columbus Avenue.[469]

The Roxbury community had become wary of developers who planned first and engaged residents later,[470] but the Crosstown development team built support by meeting with local elected officials and community groups before solidifying their plans. Beverley Johnson, who also is black, was a key player in the outreach and engagement efforts.

"Our biggest challenge was to build a broad enough level of community and political support to convince the city that the project was worth reviewing and considering for direct designation," Johnson said. "We probably spent a good part of six to eight months just building that support through one-on-one meetings ... and once we came out of that process, we established a 25-member Crosstown Community Council. After we went through that long process, support was so broad that the city decided to schedule a public hearing to further assess the level of support. The paper called it a 'love-fest'— over 75 community leaders testified in support."[471]

EEC Grant, Zoning Approval, Continued Community Buy-In

In April 1999, the Crosstown Center project received a further boost in the form of a $5 million grant from the city's Enhanced Economic Community (EEC) program. The EEC recognition stemmed from the project's job-creation potential and other facets, including the Crosstown developers' support of Transitions to Employment, a multiorganization coalition offering a job training and job readiness program serving Roxbury, the South End, and South Boston.[472] The new Transitions to Employment coalition, to which Crosstown Associates committed $1.5 million, would be instrumental in ensuring that residents of nearby neighborhoods would be eligible for jobs created by the project.[473]

Plans progressed, and a few months later, the BRA approved a zoning change from industrial use to commercial/mixed use. Testimony at the zoning hearing in favor of the Crosstown project was effusive. Community groups, politicians, and residents lined up to voice their support for the project and its developers. "The community really feels empowered by this project because the developers started out with an idea that was not set in stone until they approached the community to see what people wanted," said Sheila Grove, director of Washington Gateway Main Streets, quoted in *Banner* coverage of the hearing. Other advocates included state Senator Dianne Wilkerson, Boston NAACP President Leonard Alkins, well-known local entrepreneur Marvin Gilmore, and Pat Cusick, executive director of South End Neighborhood Action Plan. Former District 7 city councilor Tony Crayton testified, "This plan is not your average development project. There's actually a feeling that goes with this project. ... People will be able to stand inside [the Crosstown Center] and say, 'I own this building.' Even residents who don't own the building will feel like they do."[474] The BRA's vote to approve the zoning change was unanimous.

Still, the project's financing was not yet solidified.

A Setback, then Full Speed Ahead

A year later, the Crosstown Center project hit a snag when Lowes Cineplex, the expected anchor for the proposed project, backed out in June 2000. The setback came as economic prospects were declining for movie theater chains, and the Crosstown permitting process had proceeded more slowly than hoped.[475] In hindsight, developer Welch called the cinema exit a blessing in disguise. "It was a good idea at the time, but if a cinema doesn't work, it's hard to convert," he noted in a 2017 interview. "If you have an office building that doesn't work, it doesn't take much to convert it—you can spend a little money and do something else with it."

Shortly after the cinema pullout, Corcoran Jennison Co. joined with Sykes and Welch as an equity partner, and the team, now called Crosstown Associates, persevered through post-9/11 economic jitters. A major step forward came in 2002, when the project gained $42 million in low-interest, tax-exempt bonds. The project amassed a "unique financing package," as the *Boston Business Journal* termed it, that included the $42 million in bonds, a $5 million loan from the BRA and Department of Neighborhood Development, and $7 million from Boston Connects Inc., a distributor of federal Empowerment Zone (EZ) funds. All told, the city of Boston invested some $17 million in funding for the project, including cash and land costs.[476]

Construction now could move forward, and ground was broken in November 2002. The new anchor for Crosstown Center would be the hotel, a Hampton Inn and Suites.

The 175-room hotel and the associated 650-space first phase of the parking garage opened in July 2004. At an opening celebration, Sykes expressed satisfaction at a victory that was hard-won, even with the solid community support. "[W]e had to prove to the capital and financing folks that this is viable and they should invest," he said. "The community and the mayor always believed in this."[477]

The development added one hundred jobs, fulfilling one of the primary goals of the project. The EZ funds required a commitment to hire residents of the delineated EZ area, which covered parts of Roxbury, Dorchester, Jamaica Plain, South Boston, and other neighborhoods. Thanks to strong recruitment efforts in city neighborhoods, the hotel staff from the start was 93 percent people of color, and 68 percent of the full-time positions were held by EZ residents. People of color were in the majority at every level of management and staffing at the hotel.[478]

The very month the hotel opened, the Democratic National Convention came to town. In advance of the convention, Hampton

Inn and Suites was the site of a "unity gathering" held by presidential candidate John Kerry. The candidate was introduced by Senator Wilkinson, with some forty political and community leaders in attendance and a largely black audience.[479] Rooms at the Hampton Inn sold out for the convention.[480]

The new parking garage quickly drew not only hotel guests, but employees of the nearby Boston Medical Center area and of the Longwood Medical Area, which lay a couple of miles away. A Brigham and Women's Hospital bulletin promoted the garage to its LMA employees, describing it as "a brand new, well-lit parking facility with a comfortable, heated waiting area and amenities such as a coffee shop. ... [with] comprehensive security and attendant coverage 24 hours per day, 7 days per week ... easily accessible from I-93 and I-90." A local medical area shuttle service, MASCO, leased parking spaces and made frequent trips between the garage and the hospital.[481]

Sykes said the developers had anticipated robust parking demand from the surrounding Boston Medical Center and Boston University medical facilities, but had not foreseen the additional blessing of high demand from the Longwood Medical Area. Serving that need not only brought in welcome revenue, but helped garner an award from the Environmental Business Council of New England in 2003, honoring Crosstown for contaminated site cleanup and for removing some of the thousands of vehicles from I-93 that otherwise would travel each day through the black community to the LMA.[482]

Over the next several years, Crosstown Center gained retail tenants and added a 207,000-square-foot office building with ground-floor commercial space, resulting in a total of thirty thousand square feet between the office building and the hotel. Phase 2 doubled the parking garage capacity to its current 1,250 spaces.[483]

The Upshot

After the hotel's successful completion, the partners continued on to other development endeavors. Sykes felt driven to help further more public-private partnerships and make them a national model. Besides remaining a principal at Crosstown Partners, he became a principal at the New Boston Fund, a real estate and private equity fund seeking to develop similar projects with help from Empowerment Zone money in other cities, and now heads the Urban Strategy America (USA) Fund.[484] As of 2017, Thomas Welch and Associates was part of the team for the proposed Guscott Rio Grande project, contributing financial and investment analysis to a black-led effort aiming to bring 463 units of housing to Dudley Square and create the tallest tower in Roxbury to date.

Johnson, who continues to work as a liaison between developers and local communities in Boston, sees a lasting legacy in the Crosstown developers' trailblazing effort. "This project was unique in that it's very rare for the city to award a direct designation," she said. "It was also unique because we established a model that other developers could use. Our commitment to the community was that we would work with them at all phases to make sure the opportunities for jobs and Minority Business Enterprise participation continued throughout the project lifecycle. At that time, that was unusual. It became the model in Roxbury and other parts of the city."[485]

Harvard Commons

On a late-spring afternoon in 2017 in the Harvard Commons neighborhood, an elderly African American woman tended a flower garden outside her three-bedroom wood-frame house, painted a rich purple. Across the street, a young child peeked playfully out the front window of an ochre-hued house while the middle-aged homeowner pushed a lawnmower in the front yard and paused to chat with a next-door neighbor. A handful of older children came into view, bearing heavy backpacks as they strolled from the school bus stop toward home. One block over, nine additional homes were under construction, the colorful, spacious structures developed and built by Cruz Companies. A block in the other direction, along Harvard Street, the neighborhood's earliest houses resemble the single-family homes, but each contains two or three designated-affordable rental apartments.

This serene, low-density streetscape could pass for a suburb or grace a *Saturday Evening Post* cover—but the economically and racially diverse subdivision of three-, four-, and five-bedroom homes lies at the junction of Boston's densely populated Dorchester and Mattapan neighborhoods. The homes of Harvard Commons arose on land near the intersection of Morton and Harvard Streets that for nearly one hundred years held a hospital for the mentally ill and its sprawling grounds. A stone's throw away is Blue Hill Avenue, a long-struggling business corridor that has been the target of numerous revitalization efforts in recent decades.

State Representative Russell Holmes has been closely involved with the State Hospital grounds disposition over his seven-year tenure representing the Sixth Suffolk District that encompasses the site. "It is great to see high-quality higher-end units right next to affordable units," Holmes said of Harvard Commons. "There is very little high end housing stock in the Mattapan-Dorchester housing market, particularly single-families, so it adds value to the other units in the area. Now we have doctors and lawyers next to rental tenants. Middle class right next to people who need some assistance. That's a healthy mix, for this area and for the entire city. And it's rare."[486]

Former Boston State Hospital Site

The closing of the Boston State Hospital in 1979 left more than 150 acres of developable land.[487] A Citizens Advisory Committee (CAC) was formed in 1985 to study development for the site, with members appointed by then-Governor Michael Dukakis. In the years leading up to the demolition of the mental health institution's buildings, which began in 1996, a number of ideas emerged for how to best use the rare opportunity of this large land parcel spanning the Mattapan-Dorchester border. Various and sometimes competing plans advanced by city and state operatives included a domed football stadium, a state prison, a new state hospital, and a high school. Mayor Menino in 1996 proposed using the site as an industrial park with a new courthouse and back-office space for downtown firms. But local Mattapan and Dorchester community residents consistently were pushing for housing and commercial space.

"In the end, the residents won," the *Banner* reported in 2001, looking back at a bill crafted by the area's black state legislators, Senator Dianne Wilkerson and Representative Shirley Owens-Hicks that required development plans for the site to be guided by community process. Passed in 1994, the new law put the CAC in charge of approving plans.[488]

Cruz Proposes Harvard Commons

In late 1997, state officials designated Cruz Development Corporation, one of the oldest and largest minority-owned development firms in New England, as the developers of an eighteen-acre portion of the hospital site. The firm had proposed Harvard Commons, a suburban-style residential development. The 113-unit project would create a new neighborhood, with an initial phase of rental apartments and subsequent phases of single-family homes for purchase.

The Cruz proposal fit well with the CAC's criteria and was supported by CAC members and local elected officials. "The designation of the Cruz team is a step in the right direction," said state Senator Dianne Wilkerson, who represented the Second Suffolk District that includes the hospital site. "They were mentioned from the beginning by community members who specifically wanted them. People know they do good work."[489]

Jim Clark, a member of the CAC since its inception, recalled that part of the appeal of the Cruz proposal was its ultimate focus on home ownership and its unusually attractive and well-built homes. "It was a positive thing, something different, bringing new people in— homeowners who would be professors, restaurant owners," Clark said. "Back then, it was very important that we build some single-family homes, and create homeowners. And the community wanted to have homes slightly above the minimum price [for the Mattapan area]."[490]

A Family Business

The Cruz Companies—today comprising development, construction, and management segments—originated in 1948 as a carpentry company started by John B. Cruz Jr., the son of Cape Verdean immigrants. John B. Cruz III, the founder's son, is the firm's president and CEO today, presiding over some eighty employees, 90 percent of whom are people of color. Over the past forty years, Cruz Companies has built residential and commercial projects totaling over $500 million.

At the time of its Harvard Commons proposal, Cruz Development Corporation was no stranger to large projects. In Boston, the firm had played roles in developing the One Lincoln downtown skyscraper, the Reggie Lewis Track and Athletic Center at Roxbury Community College, and the new Boston Police Department headquarters. But its most significant project to date was outside Boston: the award-winning Biscayne View in Miami, a thirty-story, mixed-use development completed in 1990, with 462 apartments and ground-floor commercial space. Biscayne View won a "Pillar of the Industry" award from the National Association of Home Builders.

Looking outside Boston for opportunities was a winning strategy for a minority-owned firm, noted John B. Cruz III. Both Cruz and Thomas Welch of the Crosstown project cited the influence of Denis Blackett, one of the first black developers in Boston, on their business success. Both praised Blackett for "putting the ladder back down" for others to follow as he grew his Housing Innovations organization, creating affordable housing both in and outside Boston.[491]

"I call it the 'Yes I can' theory," said Cruz, "when you see someone like you, of your own ethnicity, make it. Coming up and trying to emulate somebody successful, whether it was in construction or development, I always had to look at a white firm. And looking at a white firm was like a Wizard of Oz Emerald City, way across this poppy field—how are you going to get there? That's how it felt. Whereas Denis was someone I could talk to. You can sort of 'draft' like race cars do, off their speed. It's very encouraging." To this day, Cruz said, he endeavors to be that role model, conveying "Yes you can" to today's younger developers of color.

"Denis gave me some advice," recalled Cruz. "He said, 'John, when you start to build your company, look to go outside of Boston, because Boston is so racist and has such a glass ceiling.' So that's why we went to Miami." In Miami, where the officials in positions to approve development were mostly Latino, the process felt different, Cruz said: "The thing that amazed me about Miami, is they didn't look at me with a sense of qualification barriers, like 'Can you do it?' because they had seen their own do it."

Proposal Reflects Personal, Business Aims

The Harvard Commons vision stemmed from Cruz's own roots in the area as well as a desire to keep building his firm's name and stature in Boston.

"It was emotionally charged for me," Cruz said. "Mattapan was a very vibrant place—fairly diverse—but Mattapan State Hospital grounds was a place that was always depressing. It was almost like driving by a prison—the gloom would come over you." As a young man, he saw Mattapan devastated by what he termed "the first sub-prime mortgage program," as real estate agents in the 1960s engaged in "blockbusting," pushing Jewish homeowners to sell in a hurry by telling them that blacks were coming in, and property values would drop. "And then they sold the homes to blacks without proper under-writing in place," Cruz continued. "You had wholesale abandonment and Mattapan went right down. That always affected me. I saw the death of a neighborhood, and it left a sad feeling. So when we got this [former State Hospital grounds] opportunity, it felt like a chance to help rebuild Mattapan. It had started coming back, but wasn't where it is today."

The project was a chance also for Cruz Companies to show its capabilities for large projects and market-rate development. "There was an opportunity to do something much bigger than we had done in Boston," Cruz said. "It was 18 acres. It had an affordable housing component, but also a market rate. We liked that because we wanted to diversify and not just be an affordable housing developer." Additionally, his own roots in a big extended family spurs Cruz to propose spacious homes, and the floor plans of the Harvard Commons houses are designed to work well for extended families. "We tend to put in a few more larger family units than the average developer will put in," he said. "That's just something in our DNA, because we've experienced the difficulty with family members trying to find housing."[492]

Harvard Commons Comes to Life

Financing was more readily available for development of affordable housing than market-rate units, so the strategy for Harvard Commons was to build the affordable rental component first. Creating attractive buildings that resembled single-family homes would bring color and life to the site early on, making it easier for potential homebuyers to imagine their new home in a neighborhood that didn't exist yet.

After several years of delays, including a wait for environmental cleanup and a $2 million state-issued infrastructure grant, Cruz Companies broke ground on Harvard Commons in 2004. The $10.5 million phase I was complete in August 2005, creating forty-five new rental apartments in two- or three-unit houses, widely spaced apart with landscaped yards. Two new streets—Senator Bolling Circle and Snowden Way—wound through the complex, which still was mostly empty land. The goal of making the designated-affordable apartments look like permanent homes was achieved. "We have had about 250 people thinking these are for-sale homes and asking to buy them," noted Dan Cruz at the time. "That is a lot considering there are no signs saying they are for sale."[493]

Then came the construction of for-purchase homes, which were added gradually between 2007 and 2017. A few homes were built on spec so buyers had something to look at, but in order to avoid having a costly inventory of unsold homes, with construction loan interest, real estate taxes, and insurance costs accruing, the ownership homes were largely constructed as each was purchased. Another $1.93 million MassWorks grant helped fill in additional infrastructure.

The last phase of Harvard Commons was nearly complete as of mid-2017, with only five lots unsold. The project had already had a ripple effect on black community wealth. The firm averaged 71 percent utilization of minority-owned business enterprises during a decade of construction, and 76 percent of worker hours went to minority hires.[494] Home prices at Harvard Commons have risen to the point where some of the early buyers could sell in 2017 at $50,000 to $150,000 more than they paid. The Harvard Commons homeowners are a diverse group, with the majority of them black and others Caucasian, Asian, East Indian, and Latino. They represent many stages and walks of life, including retirees, young couples, police officers, businesspeople, PhDs and lawyers.[495]

Looking back at the project, which survived the Great Recession, John B. Cruz III recalled defying the odds of making any sales at all during the downturn and of asking $400,000 or more for homes in that part of Boston. "People thought we were out of our minds, in a market with [nearby] triple-deckers going for $150,000 to 250,000," he said. But the first home sold for $419,000. Some other early sales topped $500,000. As of mid-2017, the average sale price for new homes in the final phase of construction was more than $600,000, for three- to five-bedroom houses with attached garages, landscaped front yards, and plenty of other "bells and whistles" such as whirlpool tubs.[496] Dan Cruz, the firm's senior vice president and a cousin to John Cruz III, added, "I think about those first three houses, when there was still 13 acres of vacant land and piles of dirt around. The people who bought were rightfully concerned about their futures. … It took 12 or 15 homes before people saw it as a neighborhood."[497]

The State Hospital site still has fourteen undeveloped acres, and the CAC in 2017 continued to oversee plans that were likely to bring additional housing.[498] Representative Holmes said developer interest has been heightened by the projects already in place, which include a MassBiologics campus and a sixty-seven-acre Massachusetts Audubon Society nature center as well as the residential development. Summing up the impact of Harvard Commons, Holmes said, "We deserve properties like these in the community. We can't just have affordable. We have to have people with upward mobility stay in the neighborhood. This development is critical for the entire area. It really will be an anchor for generations to come."[499]

One Lincoln

Not many black real estate developers can claim credit for a skyscraper. But a group of black, Chinese, and Latino developers in Boston succeeded with a million-square-foot office tower that leaves an indelible mark on the city's skyline, etched in gray granite and glass. The road to success wasn't easy. Individually, the black, Asian, and Latino developers had hit numerous roadblocks in their efforts to break into the upper ranks of the city's lucrative real estate development field. Together, they surmounted those obstacles and achieved a remarkable feat. Paving the way for their success was a broader push for inclusion in Boston.

In 1983 Mayor Raymond Flynn was elected by a two-to-one margin with 128,578 votes to former state Representative Melvin King's 69,015. But the lopsided victory was far from a mandate: votes split cleanly along race lines. King, the first African American to make it to the mayoral primary, had galvanized a coalition of black, Latino, Asian, and progressive white voters that Flynn knew he would need to win over to shore up his support in the racially divided city. While blacks were effectively locked out of the city's political power structure, their formidable showing at the polls indicated a great desire in the community to break the barriers that traditionally kept them out.

Paul Chan and Ken Guscott, principals of Kingston Bedford Joint Venture,
with partner John B. Hynes III (center) stand before the thirty-six-story,
one-million-square-foot office tower at One Lincoln Street, the largest real estate
project in the country that was developed by African American and Asian investors.

In the city's real estate development field as well, blacks were pushing against long-established barriers to inclusion. While blacks' political successes in Boston have taken a long, linear track, black developers were able to break into the city's skyline in a dramatic fashion, thanks in part to the growing clout of the black electorate. Paving their way for the advancement of minority developers were two important players in city government: District Seven City Councilor Bruce Bolling and Boston Redevelopment Authority Director Stephen Coyle. Bolling was elected to the City Council in 1981 as one of the so-called "Kevin Seven" a cadre of up-and-coming Bostonians endorsed by then-mayor Kevin White. White's blessing, however, didn't extend to what would become one of Bolling's signature legislative victories: parcel-to-parcel linkage. That legislation did not move forward until Flynn became mayor.

In 1982, when Bolling authored the law, city officials knew they were sitting on a gold mine. For decades, the City of Boston owned parking garages and vacant parcels of land in the downtown area on which developers were now looking to build. The linkage law required that developers building commercial projects downtown pay five dollars for every square foot over one hundred thousand square feet into a fund for the development of affordable housing. While Mayor Kevin White was resistant to implementing linkage, Flynn, who had run a populist campaign and supported affordable housing, was supportive. In hiring the progressive Coyle to lead the BRA, Flynn sought an ally who could bridge the gap between the prosperity flourishing in the downtown area and the unrealized opportunity of the vast expanses of vacant land in Roxbury. Coyle, who earned his bachelor's degree from Brandeis University, a master's from the Kennedy School of Government at Harvard University, and a juris doctor degree from Stanford Law School, was no city hall insider. As director of the BRA, Coyle took linkage a step further. He pushed the BRA Board to make a formal determination that blacks, Latinos, and Asians in Boston had been excluded from the city's construction boom and proposed a parcel-to-parcel linkage program that would require developers of select downtown parcels to invest in the development of parcels in the city's predominantly black community, with minority investors controlling at least 30 percent interest in the venture.[500]

Coyle and other officials in the Flynn administration saw the city-owned land as a means to leverage greater development in the city's underdeveloped neighborhoods, to build more affordable housing and to provide opportunities for black, Latino, and Asian real estate investors and construction firms that had long been unable to penetrate the city's insular real estate development circles. Under Bolling's linkage law, the city would require those bidding on the city-owned parcels downtown to invest a portion of the proceeds from their projects into developments in the predominantly low-income communities in Roxbury, the South End, and Chinatown. BRA officials said the program would "create opportunities for minority developers and individuals to be equity participants in both downtown and neighborhood development."[501]

The Kingston Bedford parcel was the last major downtown parcel the city sold through its linkage program. Early on, the late Joseph Warren, who was an administrator with Northeastern University, and the then-Boston Bank of Commerce officer Ron Homer met with Flynn, urging him to make the parcel available to minority developers.[502] Flynn was initially skeptical that the minority developers would have the wherewithal to develop an office tower on a downtown parcel. No minority-led development team had ever taken on a project of that size in Boston or undoubtedly anywhere else in the country.

Under the parcel-to-parcel linkage program, the Kingston Bedford parcel was paired with Parcel 18, a vacant plot of land at the intersection of Melnea Cass Boulevard, Columbus Avenue, and Ruggles Street. Boston Redevelopment Authority officials saw in Parcel 18 the potential to revitalize an economically depressed section of the city. Many of the businesses and homes in the area had been cleared during the late 1960s to make way for the planned extension of Interstate 95 through the Boston neighborhoods of Hyde Park, Roslindale, Jamaica Plain, Roxbury, and the South End, and the planned inner belt highway, which was to cut through Roxbury, the Fenway, Cambridge, and Somerville. The plan was scrapped in the face of fierce opposition from neighborhood residents, but not before the state had taken and cleared land along what is now Melnea Cass Boulevard and along Columbus Avenue between Jackson Square and Ruggles Street, leaving a vacant wasteland.

City officials surmised Parcel 18 had the potential to hold seven hundred thousand square feet of office space, create four thousand new jobs and absorb a portion of the city's projected job growth, primarily through the construction of so-called back office space, offices where businesses' administrative functions are undertaken.[503] At the same time, the city expected that development on the Kingston Bedford parcel would generate up to $7 million ($15.4 million in 2017 dollars). Half of that funding was to go to the creation of affordable housing in Roxbury and Chinatown.[504]

Ruggles Center

Ken Guscott and Paul Chan were the leaders of a new group, Columbia Plaza Associates, which was launched in 1986. The principals of the group represented Chinatown and Roxbury, the communities that were tied together through the city's parcel-to-parcel linkage program. Guscott grew up in Roxbury, not far from Parcel 18. Chan represented the Chinatown community in which the Kingston/Bedford parcel was sited. Initially the Chinese and black investors formed separate groups. But both sides saw the advantage of strength in numbers. "Minorities need to get together and work together," Guscott told the *Banner* in a 2000 interview. "Remember, the Chinese were as mistreated in America as the black people were. The Chinese and Latinos were all hungry immigrants like my people were."[505] In all thirty-seven black, Latino, and Chinese investors put up funds for the project—twelve investors from or associated with Roxbury and twenty-five associated with Chinatown. Prominent minority investors included Boston Bank of Commerce Chairman and CEO Kevin Cohee, Guscott, John B. Cruz III, attorney Fletcher "Flash" Wiley, Consuela Thornell, Stanley Chen, Edward Dugger, Peter Bynoe, and Wayne Budd. The partners prevailed in a 1987 competitive bidding process and pooled their funding to come up with a $2.5 million initial investment. Additional early financing came from the black-owned Boston Bank of Commerce, now OneUnited Bank, which put up $230,000 for planning work and an additional $2.6 million toward the development rights for One Lincoln Street.

The developers sought to build out Parcel 18 first, with plans for a four-building complex including office space, a hotel, and a parking garage. With backing of then-Governor Michael Dukakis, the development team was set to move forward with the Massachusetts Water Resources Authority as the anchor tenant for the development. That deal fell through, however, as South Shore lawmakers successfully angled for the MWRA to be relocated to the Quincy Shipyard. The legislative wrangling set the developers back but did not derail the project. In 1991 then-governor William Weld agreed to move the state's Registry of Motor Vehicles to the Roxbury site. Construction on the project, named Ruggles Center, began in 1992 and was completed in 1994. The initial victory was short-lived, however. Almost immediately, Registry employees, many of whom were resistant to the relocation to Roxbury, complained of poor air quality. The agency pulled up roots and moved into offices in downtown Boston after only five months. With the anchor tenant gone and investors on the hook for remediation work to the building's interior and HVAC system, the development team struggled to maintain payments on the loan used to construct the building. Bank of America foreclosed on the building in November 1996. Northeastern University, then expanding rapidly in Lower Roxbury, purchased the building in a $17 million deal approved by the Boston Redevelopment Authority in June 1997. Columbia Plaza Associates remained partners with Northeastern on other planned projects on the site, including a parking garage.

In 1999, Northeastern University officials signed a contract with Columbia Plaza Associates for the joint development of a parking garage that was to be built on Parcel 18–2 and Parcel 18–3A, land over which the minority group had development rights. Under the contract, Columbia Plaza Associates was entitled to 30 percent of the net profits.[506] In a 2013 lawsuit, the minority developers charged that Northeastern reneged on its promises, failing to provide accounting for net receipts generated by the $16 million Renaissance Parking Garage and failing to pay to the minority developers 50 percent of those receipts as stipulated in the contract. Instead, Northeastern paid itself $100 per year pursuant to an agreement for sixty years to operate the garage. Columbia Plaza Associates also sought fair rental value for a three-tower dormitory complex Northeastern built on Parcel 18–3A without the necessary consents from minority investors.

In 2017, a judge ruled that Northeastern had no contractual obligation to pay Columbia Plaza Associates because the 1999 agreement stipulated that the university would create a joint venture with the development team. Because no joint venture was ever agreed upon and because the developers waited more than four years to file an unfair business practice lawsuit, the judge ruled, Northeastern owed Columbia Plaza Associates nothing. The developers filed an appeal to the court ruling.[507]

Breaking Ground Downtown

The 1994 foreclosure of Ruggles Center, the planned site of the Registry of Motor Vehicles, did little to deter the minority developers' forward momentum. That setback was a road bump in the fifteen years of deal-making the team undertook before construction on One Lincoln Street got under way. During that time, the team weathered an economic downturn and a change of mayoral administrations, raised funds, invested their own funds, and formed partnerships with major developers.

The economic recession of 1990 and its slow recovery nearly brought the project to a halt. During that time, the Columbia Plaza team borrowed $6.5 million from their venture partner, Met Structures, a subsidiary of the MetLife insurance firm. In 1997, when Met Structures sought to sell its stake to a New Hampshire-based company, the Columbia Plaza team bought out their former partner to regain 100 percent equity of the project. The team then brought in developer Don Chiofaro, who had previously developed the 1.7-million-square-foot International Place office tower complex. Chiofaro's mandate: to find tenants and financing for the venture. But by 1999, Chiofaro's designation expired with no substantive progress on either front. Columbia Plaza Associates turned its attention to John B. Hynes, principal of the New Jersey-based firm Gale & Wentworth. The son of a Boston newscaster and grandson of former Mayor John B. Hynes, the developer had secured the rights to purchase a parcel of land adjacent to the One Lincoln Street garage for $20 million.

Hynes formed partnerships with Morgan Stanley Real Estate Fund and the State Teachers Retirement System of Ohio and convinced them to put up the funding to purchase the adjacent parcel and the $15 million to buy the garage. He secured the permits necessary to break ground. Columbia Plaza still needed a tenant. Fortunately Marshall Carter, the chairman and chief executive officer of the State Street Corporation, was in need of new office space. It helped that Roxbury-raised George A. Russell was executive vice president for community affairs at State Street. Russell had begun at State Street in 1974, working as a credit analyst, served as treasurer of the City of Boston and its chief comptroller, and president and chief executive officer of Freedom National Bank of New York. With Carter and Russell's commitment to community investment, One Lincoln Street was an easy yes. State Street signed a letter of intent for six hundred thousand square feet, ensuring financing would go forward for the project.

Shovels were in the ground by spring of 2000. At that time, One Lincoln was larger than any other office construction project built in Boston over the preceding ten years.[508] At thirty-six stories and more than one million square feet of office space, the $360 million building gave black-, Latino-, and Asian-owned firms the opportunity to take on work on a major project. "What you learn by going through the process is sometimes better than the money," developer John Cruz III told the *Banner*.[509]

As part of the process, the team underwent one experience familiar to most real estate developers: a lawsuit. Chiofaro took his case to Suffolk Superior Court in 2002, alleging that Columbia Plaza Associates stopped cooperating with him as it gravitated toward Gale and Wentworth. He sought a share of the profits the Columbia Plaza partners earned from the project. In 2004, a fourteen-member jury decided that Chiofaro had not fulfilled the duties required of him, and therefore there was no breach of contract with Columbia Plaza Associates.

The lawsuit was a minor bump for the team, whose members were benefitting from the experience of working on a major construction project. Among those gaining next-level expertise on the building was longtime contractor David Lopes, one of six foremen at One Lincoln. His participation and his relationships with minority subcontractors helped the developers maintain a workforce that was 32 percent people of color—a rare feat during that era of tight control over construction jobs by majority white building trade unions. Among those securing contracts was Webster Engineering, a black-owned firm that handled the excavation for the project, which included a below-grade nine-hundred-car garage. "When you have equity in a project, you sit at the table when decisions are made," Ruggles Bedford Associates partner Ken Guscott told the *Banner*. "It makes a difference."[510]

When the massive One Lincoln project was completed in 2003, the minority developers had earned their victory through perseverance and ingenuity. By then, the anchor tenant, State Street Bank, changed the building's name to State Street Financial Center. Columbia Plaza Associates, eager to reap the rewards of their seventeen-year-long venture, were ready to sell. Codevelopers Gale & Wentworth and the other investors were on board with the plan, and set a floor of $650 million, State Street's initial offer. With the city's economy in full recovery and office space running at a premium, they had little trouble finding interested buyers. On February 3, the building, renamed State Street Financial Center, sold to Pennsylvania-based American Financial Realty for $705 million, doubling the $350 million the developers and investors had plowed into the project. The $671-per-square-foot price was at that time the highest ever paid for commercial real estate in Boston. By comparison, the John Hancock Tower had sold for just over $300 a square foot a year earlier.[511] The Columbia Plaza investors received 15 percent of the proceeds of the sale, growing their $5.5 million investment to $44 million. The building generated $16 million in linkage fees for projects in Chinatown and Roxbury.[512]

United Housing Management

United Housing Management's headquarters is located in a two-story brick building in Grove Hall, located within walking distance of many of the more than twenty-one hundred units the firm owns and manages. One of the largest black-owned businesses in Boston, UHM employs more than sixty people and collects annually more than $23 million in rents.

In Boston—a city where more than 20 percent of all housing units are subsidized by state or federal government—property management is a big business dominated by large firms, many of which manage units across the country. That a local black-owned start-up firm has been able to carve out a formidable share of the market is remarkable.

The story of United Housing Management begins in the early 1980s, when a large swath of the city's housing subsidized by the US Department of Housing and Urban Development (HUD) was in crisis. The housing units, sited in Roxbury and Dorchester and owned by Granite Properties, were in violation of city housing codes and sorely in need of repairs. With the support of local officials, HUD foreclosed on the 107 multifamily brick buildings. At the time, the more than two thousand units constituted the largest block of HUD-foreclosed buildings in the country.[513]

In the 1960s and '70s, HUD had invested heavily in affordable housing projects in Boston, providing federally insured mortgages for the construction of large developments including Warren Gardens, Marksdale, St. Joseph's, Academy I and II, and Roxse Homes. While private and nonprofit developers were able to build developments on land cleared through its urban renewal program with those funds, many failed to pay the HUD-backed mortgages on the developments and to maintain the developments, forcing the agency to foreclose on and reacquire the projects.

In the case of the Granite properties, the HUD intervention was aimed at stabilizing a tract of deteriorating absentee-owned housing that began a rapid decline in the late 1960s as many of Boston's white residents fled for the suburbs taking with them the capital necessary for community investment. The intervention worked in the short term and provided lucrative tax breaks for real estate investors, but by the early 1980s, the code violations were building up. In pushing out Granite Properties, HUD officials hoped to dispose of the build-ings, most of which were constructed in the first decade of the 1900s. Under the administration of President Ronald Reagan, who advocated shrinking the nation's housing agency, HUD may easily have sold the housing to one of the city's or state's large real estate firms. However, a coalition of local officials including Mayor Raymond Flynn, Governor Michael Dukakis, and community activists called on the agency to sell the units off gradually, allowing for profit and nonprofit entities to purchase the buildings and preserve affordability.[514]

Long Bay Management, then led by brothers Cecil, George, and Kenneth Guscott, bought twenty-five of the buildings, for a total of 217 units. The units they purchased, most of which were in the Elm Hill area, make up the core of United Housing Management's current portfolio.[515] After the 1987 purchase of the Granite Properties, Long Bay continued to build its stock of affordable housing, naming each new development after a town in Jamaica, the Guscott brothers' par-ent's country of origin. The acquisitions grew Long Bay's portfolio—Morrant Bay Apartments, a 129-unit, scattered site development in Dorchester; Boston Bay, eighty-eight units in buildings in the Grove Hall area; Hope Bay, forty-five units in three Dorchester buildings.[516]

Back in 1987, when Long Bay Management acquired the Granite Properties buildings for $1.7 million, most of the senior management of United Housing Management was senior staff working at the firm. Guscott, who throughout his career placed an emphasis on hiring and doing business with people of color, first approached his senior management team about acquiring a portion of Long Bay's portfolio in the late 1990s. Guscott then was seeking to sell off Nazing Court, a 150-unit complex on Seaver Street, opposite Franklin Park. He and Long Bay Partner Cecil Guscott, his elder brother, approached the managers.

"They said, 'You guys run the company now,'" recalls Bynoe, UHM's senior portfolio manager. "'You should put together a plan.'"

In their initial effort, as the team spent months putting together a plan, they were outbid by a competing management firm that paid more than twice the managers' original offer.

"It was a painful, but necessary lesson," Bynoe says. "We made critical errors in closing the deal. The lessons we learned led us to where we are today."

In 2002, the management team came back under the leadership of John Strodder and developer Otis Gates and put together a deal to purchase 750 units from Long Bay's portfolio. That deal got UHM off the ground. As the Guscotts divested themselves of their affordable properties and property management business, the UHM principals offered the twenty-four staff members at Long Bay jobs with their new firm. All accepted.

In the tradition of the Guscotts, UHM prioritizes hiring people of color and contracting with businesses owned and run by people of color. Contracts for snow removal, janitorial services, exterminators, landscapers, legal services, insurance, security, and accounting services are with minority-owned firms. In 2010, for instance, 74 percent of the firm's contracts went to minority-owned businesses and 28 percent went to woman-owned businesses. By comparison, WinnResidential—the state's largest property management firm— that year reported hiring only 43 percent MBEs and 20.5 percent WBEs.[517] UHM essentially has an affirmative-action plan to provide opportunities for local and minority-owned businesses.

In many ways, the firm's success with contractors of color is baked into its DNA. "A lot of the contractors we work with originally worked for Ken [Guscott]," Bynoe said. "He got them started and helped them get financing, working with Unity Bank to help them obtain lines of credit."

"One of the nicest compliments we receive is when we send a contractor to do work on our building," Bynoe says. "They say 'We know how to find your properties. You have the nicest buildings on the block.'"

7

Strategies for Employment Diversity

Anthony W. Neal and James Jennings, PhD

Introduction

The 1964 Civil Rights Act banning employment discrimination everywhere in the United States inspired black-led initiatives to expand employment opportunities for black Bostonians. Prominent activists such as Tom Brown of the Jobs Clearing House; Charles "Chuck" Turner, along with Mel King and others, who were key organizers of the Boston Jobs Coalition; and several others worked tirelessly to find gainful employment for black Bostonians. Despite opposition from employers, unions, and others who sought to maintain the status quo, these black leaders utilized innovative and effective strategies to place blacks in what were then considered good-paying jobs. The battles for racial and economic justice are not yet over in Boston and elsewhere in Massachusetts. Several studies document challenges faced by black people in seeking access to economic resources.[518] Earlier struggles reflected key themes that are still relevant today for the pursuit of local economic equity and justice.

The following case studies highlight the efforts of several black men and their organizations that were seeking greater employment opportunities. Their work was covered mostly in the *Bay*

State Banner. However, black women like Melnea Cass, Sarah-Ann Shaw, Sister Virginia, and Doris Bunte, who also served as the first African American woman elected to the Massachusetts House of Representatives in 1972, all played an enormous role in the over-all account of the black community economic struggles.[519] Although Latinos and Asian Americans were much smaller in numbers compared to blacks during the period covered in this chapter, they also faced community-wide economic challenges. Russell Lopez's book, *Boston's South End: The Clash of Ideas in a Historic Neighborhood* (2015) highlights economic challenges facing Latinos, for example. Mario Luis Small's *Villa Victoria: The Transformation of Social Capital in a Boston Barrio* (2004) is a historical case study of the founding of the Inquilinos Boricuas en Accion (IBA), the first Puerto Rican-led community development corporation in the nation. A dissertation by Michael Liu, "Chinatown's Neighborhood Mobilization and Urban Development in Boston" (University of Massachusetts Boston, 1999), describes longtime struggles for economic justice in Boston's Chinatown.

Boston's Black Population and Employment Levels

Between 1950 and 1960 Boston's black population grew by 57 percent. While the total population in Boston in 1960 was 697,197, the black population was 63,165 or 9.1 percent of the total.[520] The median income in Boston during that period was $3,243. For blacks it was $2,369.[521] By 1968 Boston's black population had increased to approximately 88,000.[522] The overall unemployment rate in the city that year was 3.1 percent, but for residents of the South End, Roxbury, and North Dorchester, where most of the black population at the time resided, it was more than double that at 6.8 percent. Eighty percent of the people in Roxbury were considered underemployed—their full talents were not being exploited. Median income in the South End, Roxbury, and North Dorchester was $4,224, compared to $6,300 nationally. [523]

By the 1970s the unemployment rate for blacks was still about twice that of whites. Nationally the unemployment rate for blacks in 1973 was 9.4 percent, compared to 4.9 percent for whites.[524] That year, Boston's population was 16.3 percent black and 4.6 percent other people of color.[525] The high black unemployment rate was not due solely to racial discrimination on the part of private employers but also to the actions and nonactions of public agencies, such as the Boston Housing Authority and the Department of Public Works. In 1973, only 8.5 percent of the city's workers were black people. Other people of color comprised only 1.7 percent of all city workers.[526] Adding urgency to the struggle for equal employment opportunities was that Boston's black community rapidly grew to 104,596 by 1970.[527]

Patterns of Discrimination

In the 1960s, blacks occupied a disproportionately large segment of low-level positions, such as domestics and janitors, and they were severely underrepresented in the economy's mid- and upper-level positions. Sociologist Stephan Thernstrom reported the following occupational breakdown for black males in 1970: professional (11%); manager, proprietor or official (5%); clerical worker (11%); sales worker (3%); craftsman (17%); operative (25%); service worker (19%); and laborer (8%).[528] A hidden problem here was underemployment—blacks working below their skill level or potential skill level. The major barrier to equal employment opportunity in Boston's job market was racial discrimination—or antiblack animus—as evinced by an employer's refusal to disclose information about job vacancies to qualified black applicants, and its refusal to hire them. For example, the Urban League of Greater Boston had launched an effort in 1965 to convince Boston City Hospital (BCH) to provide periodic lists of job vacancies, but the hospital refused. The NAACP also met repeatedly with BCH officials in an attempt to obtain lists of job openings and job descriptions, to no avail. Moreover, though the hospital's repeated explanation in 1968 for not employing blacks in clerical positions was that it couldn't find qualified applicants, over a twelve-month period the Urban League's executive director, Mel King, helped to identify and send thirty qualified black applicants to the BCH, seeking clerical positions. And despite a continuing critical shortage of clerical help and dozens of job vacancies at the hospital, not one of those applicants was offered a job.[529]

Another barrier to black employment was an employer's use of preemployment aptitude tests. These tests did not measure the person's ability to perform the essential functions of the job but worked a hardship on otherwise-qualified black applicants. Thus, under the guise of metrics supposedly to measure qualifications, the employer and union practice of nepotism, or the reserving of entry-level job vacancies for relatives and friends, combined with union-bargained seniority systems, denied black people access to better paying mid-level jobs.

Pressure on employers to hire more blacks increased after the passage of Title VII of the Civil Rights Act of 1964, which banned discrimination against individuals in hiring, firing, and terms and conditions of employment based on race, color, religion, sex, and national origin, and also called for the creation of governmental agencies to enforce the law. Under Title VII, Congress established the Equal Employment Opportunity Commission (EEOC) to monitor civil rights compliance in the workplace. A year later, President Lyndon B. Johnson issued Executive Order 11246, creating the Office of Federal Contract Compliance (OFCC). The OFCC was given permanent status within the Department of Labor and charged with the responsibility of ensuring that firms being awarded federal contracts hired minority workers. By the fall of 1966, Title VII cases began appearing in the federal courts.

Jobs Clearing House

Thomas J. Brown and the Jobs Clearing House is an uplifting story of how a personally successful, highly educated black used his professional status to benefit others. Brown and his nonprofit corporation found midlevel administrative jobs for thousands of people of color in Boston. Brown was born in Fall River, Massachusetts, in 1925, where he attended B.M.C. Durfee High School. A popular student, he sang in the chorus and glee club and was a member of the track team. His 1942 graduating class voted him "best personality."[530] Brown subsequently served three years in the army during World War II before returning to Fall River. He enrolled at Brown University, graduating with a bachelor's degree in English in 1950. Afterward, he worked at Raytheon as a project coordinator in the early 1950s.[531]

By 1963 Brown utilized his winning personality to become an account executive for the Marvin and Leonard Advertising Agency in Boston. He was the only black man with such a job in the city at that time. On Labor Day 1963, while employed at the advertising agency, he founded and became executive director of the Jobs Clearing House Inc. (JCH), a nonprofit corporation at 600 Washington Street in downtown Boston, whose purpose was to locate and provide middle management and midlevel administrative jobs for black Bostonians. "Our job at the Clearing House," Brown explained, "is to narrow the gap in employment by encouraging employers to hire Negroes who need training in order to become productive."[532] Neither the job applicant nor the hiring company paid a fee for this service. Grants from Harvard University, the Ford Foundation, and Boston's business community paid the rent. In addition to carrying a full-time responsibility as an account executive, Brown worked at the JCH at least two hours during the evenings, and he worked as well on weekends, taking no compensation.[533]

In the 1960s black employment at the midlevel was low, regardless of schooling level. "Getting a job as an elevator operator or a low-level clerical job was all that a black person could hope for then," remarked Melvin B. Miller, publisher of the *Bay State Banner*. "Tom Brown pushed for middle management jobs for black people, moving them up and changing their lives," he said.[534]

Due in part to pressure applied by black activist groups such as the NAACP, Greater Boston businessmen as a group actively tried to recruit black employees in 1964.[535] But their efforts were in large part successful due to Brown as well, whose employment agency had registered two thousand black job applicants and placed seven hundred of them in jobs at 295 companies by Christmas 1964.[536]

Brown felt it his moral duty to focus his free time and effort on finding black people meaningful work. When asked by a local reporter in 1964 why he went to the trouble of providing the service, Brown replied, "Give me one reason why I shouldn't try to help other Negroes. Give me one reason." Clearly, he wasn't in it to make money. He told the reporter, "I'm in this because somebody's got to do it."[537] Brown knew that the "situation" of high black unemployment in Boston was not going to be solved in his lifetime, but he, with the help of his wife, Inez, made every effort to place black people in good jobs.

In 1965 Brown left the advertising industry to become special assistant to Edwin H. Land, founder of Polaroid Corp. There he used his office and his very affable personality to open doors to equal employment opportunity. "From Ed Land's office, he would call top executives of big companies and they would take his calls," said Miller, adding, "He would tell company CEOs, 'I was down at your office the other day and didn't see one black face. What's going on?'" Brown made it difficult for them to refuse to hire blacks.

When corporate executives claimed that they could not find qualified black job applicants, Brown and Miller worked together harmoniously to deliver them. Miller ran ads in the *Banner* posting JCH job vacancies at no cost, and candidates went to the JCH. This was one of the ways that the *Banner* became a major employment source for blacks. Another way was through its regular column, "The Job Scene," which provided information on job openings. Brown told a reporter in 1965 that the problem of jobs in Boston was basically a misunderstanding between blacks and white employers that required better communication. "The white man believes the Negro labor pool is largely unskilled," he said, "and the Negro, in turn, either doesn't know or doesn't dare believe that the 'off limits' sign has been yanked down in most places."[538] For his job-finding efforts, Brown was honored by the Association of Business and Professional Women of Boston, who presented him with the Human Relations Award at its annual Sojourner Truth Award Luncheon on June 13, 1965.[539] Alan Monroe, the first black branch officer of the First National Bank of Boston—indeed the first black to achieve such a position at any bank in Boston—owed his success to Brown. In December 1966, Monroe told the *Banner*, "Tom referred me to the First and has done much over the last three years to help me get where I am today."[540] In addition to fulfilling the obligations of his day job at Polaroid and running the Jobs Clearing House, Brown presented free lectures on how to obtain employment. For example, on the evening of February 14, 1966, he gave one at the Egleston Square branch of the Boston Public Library entitled, "Jobs for Negroes: Where They Are and How to Get Them."[541] Five days later, he gave another one on "Negroes in the Job Market" at the Calvary Baptist Church in Lowell.[542]

In 1968 Brown estimated that 80 percent of the people in Roxbury were underemployed—not working up to their skill level or potential skill level.[543] In the first half of that year, the JCH filled 110 clerical positions with black workers.[544] According to agency records, the nonprofit corporation eventually connected more than ten thousand Boston area residents to jobs during its thirty-year history.[545] Few individuals amassed a record like Brown's. But he sacrificed a lot. He became an uncompromising champion of the employment rights of his people even though he knew it would ultimately diminish his status within the white power structure. Top business executives were not always pleased with someone so committed to equal employment rights. Brown died of cancer June 24, 2013, at Milton Hospital.

New England Telephone's Hiring Efforts and Freedom House

Prior to 1968 the New England Telephone and Telegraph Company (NET&T) had a horrible record when it came to employing African Americans. In 1943 it employed fewer than twelve blacks out of a workforce of about twenty thousand. By 1950, that number had more than doubled, but the workforce, too, had increased to twenty-seven thousand.[546] NET&T employed fewer than 150 people of color in 1964, out of a workforce of thirty-five thousand.[547]

Allen G. Barry took over as president of the telephone company in October 1963. He did not want to carry the stigma that attaches to engaging in employment discrimination. He was aware that discrimination complaints had been filed with the FCC against other telephone companies, such as Southern Bell. In 1964, Barry authorized E. Eric Butler, then-director of recruiting for NET&T, to adopt the Massachusetts Plan for Equal Employment Opportunity—a plan devised to make every effort to employ blacks and other people of color.[548] That year, Butler also served as employment opportunity chairman for Freedom House, a nonprofit community-based organization in the Grove Hall section of Boston. Freedom House was founded in 1949 by social workers and activists Muriel and Otto Snowden as a catalyst for promoting equality and access to quality education for lower-income communities of color throughout Boston. In his capacity as employment opportunity chairman for Freedom House, Butler scheduled a job fair on December 15, 1964, for blacks seeking employment. The job interviews were conducted by New England Telephone and seven other Boston employers: Boston Gas Company, First National Bank of Boston, First National Stores, H. P. Hood & Sons, Liberty Mutual Insurance Company, Shawmut National Bank, and the Gillette Safety Razor Company. The job fair offered a wide range of jobs, from assistant advertising managers to night porters. Some of these jobs required high school diplomas and others required college degrees.[549]

Due in large part to the efforts of Butler and NET&T Vice President Bruce Harriman, whose responsibilities included public relations, the telephone company made progress on its commitment to hire more blacks. In 1965 it dropped two of its three pre-employment tests because it concluded that they measured acquired knowledge, rather than the fundamental ability to learn. It went a step further by contacting applicants who had been rejected in the past for failing the knowledge tests and offering them jobs. NET&T also used the *Banner* as a major means of communicating information on job opportunities.

At the Washington Park Shopping Mall in the heart of Roxbury, NET&T also set up a mobile employment office, which was unusually successful. The first visit netted sixty-one female job applicants over three days, sixteen of whom were hired on the spot.[550] In an effort to allay the suspicions of black men and recruit them for jobs, the telephone company staffed its mobile office with black male employees. Thus, recruiting in the Roxbury community and enlisting black employees to help with that recruitment were effective strategies in increasing the employment of people of color at NET&T. Those efforts and others, such as the creation of a summer work program for black male high school and college students and a Teenage Employment Training Skills (TEST) program, netted modest gains in minority employment. By 1968, NET&T employed about 580 people of color, who comprised about 1.5 percent of its thirty-eight-thousand-member workforce. A telephone company official that year remarked that all those hired under the new arrangement had "proven capable of handling jobs assigned."[551]

On April 26, 1968, the employees of NET&T went on strike rejecting the company's final offer of a 7.5 percent wage increase.[552] The bargaining committee of the largest union, the 13,500-member International Brotherhood of Telephone Workers, had been negotiating since March 15, 1968, for a substantial across-the-board wage increase for its crafts people, noncrafts employees, and clerical workers. All of the reporting on the strike focused on wages, but one unspoken battle of management was to make up for missed opportunity by allowing qualified blacks to enter NET&T at midlevel. Indeed, the real barrier to midlevel black employment had been the seniority system, and historically, white union employees had engaged in the practice of nepotism—filling entry-level job vacancies with their relatives and friends. After 128 days, the longest strike in Bell Telephone history ended on August 31, 1968.[553]

The Boston Urban Coalition

There were other significant black-led efforts to address the problem of black unemployment. After organizing in closed door meetings in December 1967, the Boston Urban Coalition, a group of more than two hundred business, union, and community leaders, went public in March 1968, intending to attack poverty and reduce black unemployment in the city by using the powerful muscle of the private sector to create jobs. Among the members of that coalition were black leaders Thomas J. Brown of the Jobs Clearing House; Kenneth I. Guscott, president of the Boston branch of the National Association for the Advancement of Colored People (NAACP); Reverend James P. Breeden of the Massachusetts Council of Churches; Melvin H. King, executive director of the Urban League of Greater Boston; and Bertram Alleyne of the South End Manpower Corp. (SEMCO).[554] However, only four months after the coalition went public, in July 1968, all five black leaders resigned over its failures, noting in their letter of resignation to Robert Slater, chairman of the policy-making steering committee, "It is our judgment that the Urban Coalition in Boston has proven itself unwilling or unable to take the steps necessary to add significantly to the energies available to meet the urban crisis." They suggested that the coalition work directly with community organizations and elected black officials in order to give black people a say.[555]

Boston Water and Sewer Commission

Dennis R. Tourse was appointed general counsel for the Boston Water & Sewer Commission (BWSC) after *Banner* publisher Melvin Miller was named a BWSC commissioner. Both were committed to expanding job opportunities there for people of color. Tourse was born on April 3, 1940, in Ridgewood, New Jersey. His mother cleaned houses for a living. He graduated from Ridgewood High School in 1958 and attended Bates College in Maine, where he played the position of halfback on the football team. He graduated with a BA in 1962 and then worked for an insurance company. Eligible for the draft, Tourse attempted to sign up for the Army Reserve, but he was rejected. So he attended the US Naval Officer Candidate School at Newport, Rhode Island, in 1963, graduating in 1965. He became a signal officer, one of three hundred black officers out of eighty-seven thousand, and the second black officer on the aircraft carrier Essex—the most decorated ship in the navy at that time. He was also a communications officer who actually had top-secret clearance. Tourse became a reserve and a special service officer who was stationed at the Naval Air Station in New York.

After leaving the Navy Reserve, Tourse went to work for IBM in 1967 as a sales representative. His sales territory was midtown Manhattan. The person who got him hired was John Lewis, a tremendous sales representative and mentor. Tourse recalled that IBM management chewed him out for wearing a button-down blue oxford shirt. "One had to wear a white shirt, a dark suit and a striped tie at IBM," he said, adding, "I probably was not cut out to be a businessman in corporate America."[556]

Tourse left IBM and enrolled at Harvard Law School, graduating in 1970. That year, he became the first black man hired at the law firm of Sullivan & Worcester. He worked there for about six months and then found employment at the Massachusetts Law Reform Institute. After staying there a year, he decided that he really wanted to practice law. He ran into a partner at Sullivan & Worcester, who told him that the firm was disappointed that he left and wanted him to return. So he went back and stayed for five years.

In 1973, two years after Unity Bank & Trust Company was placed in receivership, then-State Banking Commissioner Freyda Koplow appointed Melvin Miller conservator of the bank.[557] Unity Bank had been organized in 1968 by a group of Greater Boston black businessmen. In 1971, it was about to collapse, and the banking commission was not going to allow that to happen. While Miller was holding down that appointment, he made Tourse's firm, Sullivan & Worcester, counsel to the bank, for which Tourse, who had corporate law and real estate experience, did proxy work. Under Miller's stewardship the bank's operations became profitable for the first time. He resigned as conservator of the bank effective February 4, 1977, to devote his full time to other professional activities.[558]

When the City of Boston was running a deficit, Boston's Water & Sewer Department was spun off into a separate entity in 1977 to balance the City of Boston's books at the request of Mayor Kevin White. That year the Massachusetts Legislature, pursuant to a home rule petition entitled the Boston Water and Sewer Reorganization Act of 1977, established the Boston Water and Sewer Commission (BWSC) on July 18, 1977. In accordance with the enabling act, ownership of the wastewater collection and storm water drainage system and the water distribution system was transferred from the City of Boston's Department of Public Works (DPW) to the BWSC in August 1977. The BWSC was created to solve the city's water and sewer program's growing deficit, which was $26 million in 1977.[559] Virtually all of the BWSC's 325 employees came from the DPW. The BWSC, which was responsible for the delivery of water and sewer services to over ninety thousand Boston customers, became a subdivision of the Commonwealth of Massachusetts. The Enabling Act also provided for the establishment of a three-member Board of Commissioners. Mayor White appointed Melvin Miller as one of the three unpaid commissioners of the BWSC, the other two being John Howe, CEO of the Provident Institution for Savings bank, and Michael Rotenberg, a successful real estate investor.

Miller, who was then vice chairman of the BWSC as well, stated, "When I was appointed I could hardly find any black workers in the office or in the field. There weren't many blacks and they weren't treated with respect."[560] Joseph F. Casazza, who had been appointed DPW commissioner by Mayor White in 1968, was not known as a leader in hiring a diverse workforce. In 1976, the Lawyers' Committee for Civil Rights under Law of the Boston Bar Association filed a class action lawsuit against the DPW on behalf of three black men, claiming that they were illegally denied employment at the DPW. The suit charged the department with racial discrimination in hiring and promotion and accused Commissioner Casazza of appointing provisional and temporary white employees "on the basis of patronage, friendship or influence to the detriment of minority persons," who traditionally had "fallen outside the sphere of influence and patronage." The lawsuit also claimed that these temporary white employees then gained a disproportionate advantage in obtaining permanent civil service jobs. The city and the state Civil Service Commission were accused of failing to publicize job openings and upcoming examinations in the black neighborhood, failing to recruit blacks, and failing to correct the belief that the DPW discriminates against minorities.[561] According to the City of Boston's January 1977 figures, 17 percent of Boston's population was black and about 6 percent was Spanish-speaking people and other people of color; however, the DPW, with a payroll of 1,064 workers, was more than 96 percent white.[562]

Tourse and Miller set out to expand job opportunities for people of color at the BWSC. They helped to create and implement an affirmative action program. On January 23, 1978, the commissioners appointed African American Charles Scales, a Midwesterner with an extensive engineering background, as executive director of the BWSC. He worked there for only a few months.[563] Rajaram Siddharth became the commission's director of administration, and Eleanor Matthews became deputy director of personnel. In June 1978, the commissioners presented the Boston City Council with a proposal to spend $1.2 million to hire 131 employees and to eliminate all legal restrictions on the amount of money that could be spent on those employees. The council approved both requests.[564] Over the next few years, according to Miller, the BWSC began hiring blacks in substantial numbers.

The commissioners were authorized to sell revenue bonds. Goldman, Sachs & Co. prepared the underwriting for the first bond issue. Garland E. Wood, an African American who had established himself at Goldman as the numbers guy in public finance, was assigned the task. He came to the investment bank from Columbia University, where he earned an undergraduate degree in economics and an MBA. Goldman had somewhere between forty and fifty partners. Miller had repeatedly asked David Clapp, the partner overseeing Wood at the time, "When is Garland going to become a partner? You guys have to have a black partner." Wood became a partner in 1986—Goldman Sachs' first and only African American partner. In 1992, *Black Enterprise* named him one of the "25 hottest blacks on Wall Street."[565] He had retired by 1996, having left the firm at age fifty-nine.[566]

In 1980 Miller became chairman of the commission and managed its operating budget of $193.2 million. The following year, he joined Tourse and Harrison A. Fitch in cofounding Fitch, Miller & Tourse, a primarily corporate law firm. The BWSC agreed to bring a significant amount of business to the firm. Tourse became outside counsel for the agency and, later, a special examiner.

The BWSC had been headquartered in South Boston. The commissioners purchased land in Lower Roxbury in March 1998 and moved their headquarters to 980 Harrison Avenue. The handling of the BWSC's deal to move its headquarters to the old Stride Rite building in Lower Roxbury was not welcome by residents and prompted many to charge that blacks continued to be left out of the loop in public planning schemes in their own neighborhoods. Tourse urged the BWSC to set up a hearing process for complaints. Roxbury residents wanted jobs. They believed that if a large employer such as the BWSC came to their community, it had to hire people in that community.

For six months, an abutters group of activists met with BWSC representatives and asked that they make significant concessions to the neighborhood. They had hoped to get specific commitments from the BWSC to give Roxbury residents priority when filling job openings at the agency; however, the BWSC made no specific hiring commitments at that time. It did agree to fund a "part-time job development specialist position" at the Enhanced Enterprise Community to find candidates for open BWSC positions within the city's Enhanced

Enterprise Community. It also agreed to provide commercial driver's license training to two residents of the Roxbury community in each calendar year and to do outreach by sponsoring a job fair once a year.[567] Tourse believed that, in addition to increasing the number of employees of color at the BWSC, putting its headquarters in Roxbury was one of their major accomplishments.[568]

Charles "Chuck" Turner and the Boston Jobs Coalition

For more than three decades Charles "Chuck" Turner has been unrelenting in his efforts to get Roxbury residents their fair share of the city's construction jobs. His work at the Third World Jobs Clearing House and the Boston Jobs Coalition opened thousands of jobs to people of color in Boston. Originally from Ohio, Turner came to Massachusetts in 1958 to attend Harvard University and graduated four years later with a bachelor's degree in government.[569] He began to participate actively in black community affairs. In 1968 he cofounded a coalition of black community self-help organizations called the Black United Front of Boston (BUF), of which he and John Young became cochairmen. Among other things, the BUF advocated community control of local institutions such as schools and increased black employment in state and local government.[570]

Boston residents had traditionally taken a backseat to suburban workers on city construction jobs. Before 1970, local, state, and federal efforts to increase minority hiring in the construction trades were a dismal failure. After a series of negotiations among several parties, including representatives of the Building Trades Council, the Associated General Contractors of Massachusetts and other industry groups, and the Black Community Construction Coalition (BCCC), an association of several black community groups established in February 1970, they signed the "Boston Plan" on June 18, 1970. Under the plan, the construction industry was to set up a training program for workers of color in various construction trades and to add at least two thousand of those workers over the next five years.[571] The plan was to be administered by a board of directors equally representing black workers, the industry, and the unions. The NAACP and the Urban League denounced the plan at the outset, charging that the administrative setup left control of entry into construction industry jobs in the hands of the building trades unions and the employers, who had a vested interest in maintaining the status quo. Those black organizations also believed that a lack of strict enforcement provisions made Boston Plan ineffective.[572] The plan failed a year later.[573]

The signing of the Boston Plan, however, did not dissuade activists like Turner and members of the BCCC from picketing construction sites where contractors employed few blacks. On August 20, 1970, they picketed a Boston City Hospital construction site, charging that only ten of the one hundred workers on the project were black, and demanding that the contractor, Perini Company of Framingham, increase that number to fifty.[574] They were arrested and charged with disorderly conduct, loitering, and blocking a public way.

In 1976 the Commonwealth's minority hiring policy had a "30-10-5" formula. This meant that if a contractor's job was in a predominately black or Spanish-speaking area (South End, Roxbury, North Dorchester), the work crew had to be at least 30 percent minority. If it was outside the "impacted areas," at least 10 percent of the workforce had to be minority, and if it was outside the city, the crew had to be 5 percent minority. Speaking for the Third World Construction Task Force in July 1976, Turner proffered that the state's percentage in the "impacted areas" should have been increased from 30 to 50 percent for workers of color, as this would ease tensions between white and minority workers, since each would have a "fair share of the city jobs."[575] He did not see it solely as a racial issue but one that involved "the rights and fairness of Boston workers."[576] After months of negotiation and debate, the task force accepted the state's terms.

In August 1976 the Construction Industries of Massachusetts Inc. (CIM), an organization representing about two hundred contractors, subcontractors, and other companies involved with highway or transportation construction contracts with the state's Department of

Public Works and the Massachusetts Bay Transportation Authority, filed a suit charging that the state's Department of Transportation and Construction was discriminating against white contractors by setting aside 30 percent—or $5 million—of the work on the South Cove Tunnel to minority contractors. The 30 percent formula was based on an affirmative action order issued by Governor Michael S. Dukakis that contractors doing business with the state employ more workers of color. The lawsuit, in Turner's view, was a "continuing effort" by the construction industry to prevent public officials from increasing minority participation on construction jobs through policy decisions.[577] The $500 million Southwest Corridor project, which involved relocating the Orange Line and improving railroad and other transportation facilities, was expected to create eighteen thousand jobs.

Turner was appointed executive director of the Third World Jobs Clearing House (TWJCH) in 1976. This South End-based organization combined the forces of the black, Latino, and Chinese communities to recruit and train people of color for work in the construction industry and to obtain construction jobs for them. It had a no-dues structure and asked nothing of the workers it placed except that they do a day's work for a day's pay.[578] Though not a union, the TWJCH served as a hiring hall for people of color. In 1976, Mayor Kevin White included the TWJCH in Boston's Comprehensive Employment and Training Act (CETA) program with a $195,000 grant. The clearing house had exceeded its goal of placing 360 minority construction workers in jobs during its first year of existence.

Many workers of color believed that the Third World Construction Worker's Association (TWCWA), a private group formed in January 1976 by black, Chinese, and Latino workers, enabled the TWJCH to surpass its target figure of 360 placements.[579] In March 1976 Turner and workers from the TWCWA began demonstrating at construction job sites to protest inadequate minority hiring on construction projects in communities of color. Twenty-six people were arrested at the Madison Park High School construction site; they were later tried and found not guilty of trespassing. After only two weeks of demonstrations, the workers received fifteen job orders, compared to the fifty-five job orders the TWJCH had produced during its first five months of operations.

Not only were the TWCWA's series of job actions, which had succeeded in shutting down some construction job sites in the spring of 1976, effective, they prompted about two thousand mostly white suburban union construction workers to demonstrate at Boston City Hall on May 7, 1976, protesting what they called "harassment" by minority groups demanding employment. William Cleary, president of the Association of Building Trades Unions, said that the TWCWA wanted nonunion workers hired for construction jobs and that the union officials wouldn't stand for it because there wasn't enough work for their own members, including blacks.[580] Under pressure from the construction unions, the Boston City Council opposed funding the TWJCH, and by a vote of 9–0, it amended the city's proposal for 1977 CETA funds to exclude it. The council claimed that Turner and several TWJCH employees supported the activities of the TWCWA, who, in addition to picketing construction sites, was the main proponent of a 50 percent hiring quota for people of color on all city-funded construction jobs in Boston's communities of color.[581]

On November 2, 1976, faced with opposition from the Boston City Council, Mayor White approved an order effectively dropping the TWJCH from Boston's budget for the training and placement of workers of color. Calling White's decision "disappointing," Turner said that the mayor chose to make it not on what was "just and right but only on what satisfied political expediency."[582] The TWJCH's funding was terminated though no legal basis had been established by the city for ending it. A legal battle and great controversy ensued over the issue. The US Department of Labor warned that the action of the Boston City Council and the mayor could result in the total loss of the CETA monies, which funded eighteen other city agencies.

When US Labor Department officials, in a letter dated November 29, 1976, told Mayor White that he had until December 29 to rescind his order to cut TWJCH funding, or the city's request for $7.5 million in federal funds under CETA would be jeopardized, he made arrangements to resubmit to the Boston City Council a proposal to restore funding to the TWJCH for the months of January and February 1977, on the following conditions: (1) that there be no job actions on the part of members of the TWJCH, (2) that a liaison committee be formed to resolve differences between the Building Trades Council and the TWJCH, and (3) that the program be monitored and evaluated by the Mayor's Office of Affirmative Action.[583]

According to Turner, the real issue was that the construction trade unions' policies and referral systems unjustly deprived Boston construction workers, white people as well as people of color, of a fair share of the jobs on construction projects in the city, and that the white construction workers of Boston had no leadership.[584] "[I]t is apparent to blacks, Spanish-speaking and Chinese," he said, "that the problem of white people in Boston is not us. The problem is how are they going to get a fair share of the economics of this city—the same problem we have."[585] Reflecting on that period, Turner recalled, "I realized we were both fighting for the same thing—jobs. All we had to do was unite the two groups under the employment umbrella of residency to break the power of the suburbs. If the economic system is such that those on the bottom view each other as enemies, then chaos will result."[586] Turner's assessment of the construction jobs situation in Boston led to only one possible solution. He said that it necessitated "an alliance between the communities of color and white communities in Boston"—one that would hopefully reduce racial tensions. After months of work, forty-two organizations from eight neighborhoods, including the Third World Jobs Clearing House,[587] joined together to form the Boston Jobs Coalition.[588]

On September 6, 1979, Turner announced that the Boston Jobs Coalition had reached an agreement with Boston Mayor Kevin White's administration on a hiring policy that would give preference to Boston residents on publicly funded or subsidized construction projects.[589] Set forth in the mayor's executive order, the new policy required that at least 50 percent of the workers be Boston residents, that 25 percent be minorities, and that 10 percent be women.[590] It also made federal and state funds available for on-the-job training for unskilled, inexperienced workers.[591] Turner noted, "With residency coupled to affirmative action for workers of color and women, the policy was viewed as a fair way to cut the pie."[592] In October 1979, White extended the hiring policy to all construction dependent on long-term tax agreements under Chapter 121A of state law.[593] Before the executive order went into effect, up to 80 percent of those employed on city construction jobs lived outside of Boston. That percentage dropped significantly during the first year of the policy, when close to 40 percent of the jobs went to city residents.[594] Turner noted that the policy was aimed at providing eighty thousand construction jobs and $1.6 billion in wages for Boston residents during the 1980s.

Opposition to Hiring Boston Residents

The construction industry and organized labor opposed any insistence that nonunion blacks be employed in city construction projects. Moreover, they made it quite clear that they objected just as much to sharing construction jobs with white Bostonians as sharing them with workers of color. In a lawsuit filed by the Massachusetts Council of Construction Employers and organized labor[595] against Mayor White and others to challenge the new policy, the Supreme Judicial Court of Massachusetts, on August 28, 1981, declared the mayor's 50-25-10 executive order unconstitutional, in violation of the Commerce Clause.[596] Immediately after that ruling, the percentage of city construction jobs going to Boston residents dropped to 34 percent, then to a low of 28 percent by the end of 1982.[597]

The state court ruling, however, was appealed to the United States Supreme Court, and on February 28, 1983, Judge William Rehnquist, writing for the majority, held that when local government enters the market as a participant, it is not subject to the restraints of the Commerce Clause. Thus, the city was not prevented from giving effect to the mayor's 50-25-10 executive order.[598] Once that order was reinstated by the US Supreme Court, the Boston City Council, by a vote of 8–0 on September 28, 1983, passed a new ordinance consistent with Mayor White's executive order.[599] By the time the council had passed the jobs ordinance, the Boston Jobs Coalition had collapsed under the weight of internal racial tensions.[600]

Changes in tax laws eliminated the requirement for downtown developers to use the 121-A tax benefit. As a consequence, advocates for the new jobs policy saw that private industry was no longer covered. Remnants of the Boston Jobs Coalition placed political pressure on Mayor Raymond Flynn, who had replaced Mayor White in 1983.[601] In response to that pressure, on July 12, 1985, Mayor Flynn signed an executive order extending the Boston Jobs Policy, which had covered publicly assisted projects, to include major private construction, including ten downtown construction projects. Flynn predicted that, in three years, the policy would create 6,500 construction jobs for Boston residents, 3,250 jobs for people of color, and 1,300 for women.[602] Turner attended Flynn's signing ceremony. He remarked, "Past experience has shown that an active cooperative effort on the part of the city, community and construction industry is essential if policies are to be effectively implemented."[603]

Turner noted that figures for the first half of fiscal 1988 showed that "on private construction projects, totaling $1.3 billion, Boston residents got 29 percent of the hours worked; workers of color, 25 percent, and women, 3 percent. On public projects during the same period, totaling $371 million, residents got 39 percent, workers of color, 25 percent, and women, 3 percent."[604] Although these figures did not live up to the 50-25-10 requirement of the Boston Jobs Policy, it was a significant improvement over 1980, when the executive order was first implemented.

On December 14, 1990, Turner, who was at that time chairman of the Roxbury Neighborhood Council, joined Reverend Graylan Ellis-Hagler and several black elected officials and community leaders[605] in picketing the site of Roxbury's new $4.5 million post office building, vowing to continue until neighborhood residents made up 50 percent of those employed on the construction project. Turner told a reporter, "Our standard is that for every hour worked by a worker from outside our community, there will be an hour worked by a worker from our community on every trade." He added, "We understand people will try to make it look as if we are in the wrong. ... But if we don't stand up for our rights to a fair share of the work in our community, who will? ... If we don't take action to see that those in our community who have the skills can work on construction jobs in our community, how can we persuade our children to develop skills?"[606] As a result of the picketing, Suffolk Construction Company, the federal project's general contractor, agreed to hire one-third of its workers from Roxbury.[607]

Out of the protests at the Roxbury post office site was born the Greater Roxbury Workers' Association (GRWA), a volunteer group of union and nonunion construction workers. Its goal, according to Turner, its cofounder and chairman, was to evolve beyond the basic demand for jobs and become a clearinghouse to help workers save money, buy housing, and assist newcomers in job training.[608] On May 9, 1991, the GRWA began picketing a site on Washington Street in Jamaica Plain, where the Methuen Construction Company was replacing old sewers under a city contract. A dozen demonstrators were arrested.[609] A month later, on June 6, members of the GRWA staged a sit-in, occupying Mayor Raymond Flynn's office for five hours. At a news conference that day on City Hall Plaza, Turner said, "To have a major construction project of $3 million going forward without community residents on the job is a travesty of economic justice. We want neighborhood work to go to neighborhood workers." After lengthy negotiations with the GRWA, city officials contacted the Methuen Construction Company and requested that all new hires on the sewer project come from minority neighborhoods of Boston, and that half of those new hires be members of the GRWA.[610] For more than thirty years, Chuck Turner has been a relentless champion of black employment on construction projects in Boston, particularly in predominately black and Latino neighborhoods in the city.

Kenneth I. Guscott and the NAACP

Before becoming one of Boston's most prominent African American real estate executives, the late Kenneth I. Guscott served as president of the Boston branch of the NAACP for six years. Sworn into office on January 1, 1963, in addition to trying to eliminate segregation in public housing and public schools, he concentrated much of the civil rights organization's efforts on placing unemployed blacks in jobs. Guscott worked with several employers, including his own, General Dynamics Corporation in Quincy, where he was employed as a nuclear engineer.[611] During the week of August 15–20, 1966, the NAACP and General Dynamics cosponsored a special Job Opportunity Week to recruit black employees. At that time, the company employed about two hundred blacks.[612] A total of 309 people applied for jobs at the Quincy division of General Dynamics during Job Opportunity Week, and of that total, 255 qualified as potential employees or trainees. Guscott stated at that time, "This program demonstrates that there is a reservoir of manpower available in minority groups—a reservoir of ready, willing and able people who are looking for opportunities to work or improve themselves."[613] He also negotiated with several other companies to begin black recruitment drives.[614]

Almost a year before the General Dynamics-sponsored Job Opportunity Week, in October 1965, the NAACP's New England Regional Conference of Branches, of which the Boston branch of the NAACP was a member, instituted a selective buying boycott to pressure three major Massachusetts bakeries to employ blacks. Only the Wonder Bread Company had employed a black salesman. The Nissen Baking Company, the Sunbeam Company, and the Ward Baking Company had all refused to employ black salesmen, even though they all enjoyed a considerable market in the black community. The executive board of the conference called upon all members of the black community to buy only from such baking companies that recruited blacks as salesmen. The Boston members of the committees for the New England Regional Conference of Branches included

Guscott, Thomas J. Brown, Kivie Kaplan, Harold Vaughn, and Ruth Batson.[615]

As head of the Boston branch of the NAACP, Guscott not only pressured private employers to hire blacks but also local government agencies. Testifying before a state Senate committee on August 17, 1966, he charged that hiring procedures in local agencies resulted in discrimination, as those agencies employed far fewer blacks than their 9.6 percent ratio in Boston. Guscott cited as an example a federal investigation of the Boston Housing Authority (BHA), which revealed that 461 whites were employed by the BHA, compared to only nineteen blacks. He recommended that Boston Mayor John F. Collins take several steps to ensure equal employment of people of color, including: sending a directive to all city department heads to request a survey of people of color in their employment and their positions; directing department heads, within two weeks after the survey, to state how they intend to improve the employment situation for people of color; and setting up an agency to police a program for increased minority employment. Guscott said that the mayor should also consider the use of people of color when filling nonsalaried city agencies and boards.[616] Focusing on jobs, Guscott observed to the more than one thousand guests at the Seventh Annual Awards Banquet of the NAACP on December 3, 1966, "The Civil Rights Movement has changed. No longer is it a movement with demonstrations and marching with signs. Today the opportunity is for us to get jobs so that men can be men, bringing home paychecks, instead of unemployment checks."[617]

In October 1967, Guscott created the nationally acclaimed Positive Program for Boston (PPB), a tax-exempt arm of the NAACP Special Contribution Fund, and named his longtime friend and close aide Robert Montjoy as its director. Funded by financial contributions from foundations, individuals, and Boston's business community, the PPB was active in the field of job opportunities, among other areas,[618] and it placed one thousand people in jobs in its first year. "One of the valuable aspects of this program," Guscott told a reporter in November 1968, "is that it has the flexibility to go where the needs are.

We're not rigid like most other programs."[619] The PPB had been such a success that agencies in other cities were modeling their programs after it.[620]

On June 3, 1970, Guscott became the first black president of Action for Boston Community Development (ABCD), the city's community action poverty agency. As president, he coordinated board decisions on the allocation of ABCD's $18 million annual federal funding and programs ranging from Head Start to the Neighborhood Youth Corps.[621] In 1970, ABCD operated thirteen Neighborhood Employment Centers, plus four orientation and training centers, including the OIC.[622]

In 1972, Guscott and his brothers, Cecil and George, founded Long Bay Management Company, a property management, development, and construction company. By the year 2000, the company owned and managed three thousand units, primarily in Roxbury, and had provided jobs for hundreds of community residents. "We want to house people and build businesses to employ these people," Guscott told the *Banner* in 1993.[623] Dudley Square Main Streets Director Joyce Stanley remarked, "His projects always engaged at least 80 percent minority workers and services. He didn't just talk about hiring minorities. He made it happen."[624] Guscott died on March 6, 2017. He was ninety-one.

Opportunities Industrialization Center (OIC)

In addition to the efforts of black churches, there were other efforts involving campaigns to expand economic opportunity in the black community.[625] Opened in the summer of 1966 at the old Robert Gould Shaw House, 11 Windsor Street, Roxbury, the Opportunities Industrialization Center Inc. (OIC), headed by its founding executive director Reverend Virgil Wood, was a nonprofit, self-help job training program for the unemployed in the South End, Roxbury, and North Dorchester. Bertram M. Lee of Chicago became the new executive director in 1967.[626] Among the OIC's special features were basic education, black history classes to instill pride, and job skills training. It also had neighborhood recruiters who went into poolrooms and barrooms to give job information to the hard-core unemployed.[627] Initially, the OIC had to struggle to raise funds for its modest job training program, but its success in helping seriously disadvantaged community residents attracted support, first from the federal government through Action for Boston Community Development (ABCD), and then from the business community, the general public, and the state.[628] In March 1968, the OIC moved to the Hibernian Hall Building at 184 Dudley Street. That year, on $500,000 in federal funding, it employed a staff of nearly eighty and had almost four hundred enrollees in its job training program. And with classes in secretarial science, IBM keypunch, electronics, telephone switchboard, and graphic arts, the OIC was able to place more than two hundred people of color in jobs. On June 1, 1968, Gary Robinson took over as executive director of the OIC, succeeding Lee, who became vice president and general manager of EG&G Roxbury Inc., a new business, recently formed by EG&G, to provide job opportunities and training for Roxbury area residents.[629] By 1970, the OIC was training about one thousand people a year.[630]

To help qualified blacks obtain employment in Boston, the Urban League of Greater Boston, headed by Executive Director J. Westbrook McPherson, launched the Skills Bank Project on June 1, 1964. The purpose of the project was to help locate and list qualified young men and women in a broad array of skills, crafts, and professions, and to direct them to companies with openings.[631] McPherson is noteworthy for his accomplishments in the area of increased black employment and for the renewal of the Urban League's On-the-Job Training Project from the US Department of Labor. He resigned as executive director on February 27, 1967.[632]

8

Boston's Media History

Robin Washington

In the spring of 1987, an earnest young man appeared at the Boston Association of Black Journalists' monthly meeting at the Harriet Tubman House in the South End. He sat quietly in one of the steel and plastic stacking chairs and could have been mistaken for a member, perhaps a new face in town, as the regulars arrived and mingled. Then, having made arrangement with the group's president, he was introduced and gave a presentation.

Though some in the group were aware of his work, most were surprised to learn he had spent the last few months studying them, or more intently, their employers, and was now ready to unveil his findings.

"To better understand how the local media portray Boston's black community, I monitored news reports from a sample of newspapers and radio and television stations for one month during the summer of 1986," Kirk Johnson informed them in his introduction to "Media Images of Boston's Black Community," a study by the William Monroe Trotter Institute, a black think tank at the University of Massachusetts Boston.

"In the major media, 85 percent (39 of 46) of the news items reinforced negative stereotypes about blacks," he reported, offering as examples stories headlined "Man convicted in funeral home thefts,"

"Residents protest neighborhood trash dumping," and "Man slays wife with baseball bat." Lest there be any doubt, Johnson translated the hidden messages in the stories as, "Blacks are thieves," "Blacks are dirty," "Blacks live violent lives and die violent deaths."

Only 22 percent of the stories contradicted prevailing assumptions about blacks, indicative, Johnson suggested, of stories driven by mostly white news personnel who were "more likely to report stories that align with their preconceptions of blacks than they are to report stories that challenge those preconceptions."

Johnson, then thirty-two, was himself a journalist in a broad definition of the term, though not trained as such. An environmental science graduate of Duke University with a master's in technology and human affairs from Washington University in Saint Louis, he had most recently been in Washington, DC, as an analyst for the Environmental Protection Agency and staffer of the Center for Science in the Public Interest. Three years before the BABJ meeting, he arrived in Brookline to join the staff of the naturopathic *East-West Journal*. Later, he would work as a researcher on the second installment of the PBS documentary series *Eyes on the Prize*, one of Boston's and the country's most significant black journalistic projects.

Though his credentials did support social analysis skills, "I was not a trained academic," he recalls thirty years later, and he happened on the UMass project almost by accident. "I answered an ad"—probably in the *Bay State Banner*—"for a researcher at the Trotter Institute. They had gotten a grant and needed someone to conduct this research, which would get the official stamp of the university on it."

Johnson's analysis was by no means the first of how the city's news outlets portrayed the communities of color they ostensibly covered. Indeed, nearly two decades earlier, the Boston Community Media Committee had united media power brokers with community activists to soul-search and painfully assess their coverage, pledging to integrate their virtually all-white news staffs. The committee's work, examined in detail later in this chapter, would make real headway toward changing the color of Boston's news, though their work would be imperceptible to Johnson, who was unaware of how much progress had been made in the twenty intervening years.

Johnson's study wasn't the most damning account of race in the media, either. The *Boston Globe* in 1983 had included an evaluation of failings by the media, including the *Globe* itself, in an examination of race relations in Boston by a black and white reporting team. Their report included passages such as:

> "When the senior editors of The Boston Globe meet at 10:30 every morning to plan the next day's paper— deciding which stories to cover and which are likely to run on page one—nine persons attend. None is black.
>
> "Practically and politically, the underrepresentation of blacks in Boston institutions has meant disenfranchisement to blacks who make up of a fifth of the city's population. Black interests and feelings are largely ignored when institutions make the decisions that shape the city."

The coverage would win a Pulitzer Prize, including for Ken Cooper, a black member of the reporting team.

And though packed with facts and figures, Johnson's study was not the most complete. It had a glaring omission in neglecting to include Channel 7 (then WNEV) among the TV stations monitored, which Johnson explained was deliberate because the station then was partially owned by black investors. From 1982 to 1986, the investors, with an ownership share of 14 percent, comprised what was then the largest minority-group stake in an American television station. But that partial ownership did not automatically dictate editorial control of news or total staff sensitivity to issues of communities of color, and BABJ members expressed surprise at WNEV's omission in the analysis. Johnson was in turn surprised by their reaction. "Should I have included them?" he asked. Most definitely, responded the journalists, including those working at the then-CBS affiliate.

The young researcher also acknowledged a technical glitch that may have affected his findings: the inadvertent erasure of several hours of recorded newscasts. Nevertheless, his study received notice, enough to earn both attacks on its veracity from some news outlets and hand-wringing pledges to do better by others. And if history is an indication, it had a lasting impact in further examinations of race in media, with numerous subsequent academic papers citing it to the present day.

What was most remarkable about Johnson's effort was simply that he did it; a fluke, he says, that he attributes to a director at the Trotter Institute having secured a grant allowing it to be published. "It didn't say anything that any black journalist didn't already know," recalls Johnson, who went off to complete a PhD at the University of Illinois and became a professor of sociology and African American studies at the University of Mississippi. The difference was that it presented its message with the imprimatur of a university.

Other African American academics would come to town—the BABJ would occasionally be visited by some—and after making initial jaunts between Dudley and Harvard squares, would quickly identify social wrongs and endemic disenfranchisement in a city otherwise brimming with intellectual and political capital. Their suggestions to conduct similar studies in hopes of spotlighting those disparities would invariably be dashed with cold water by native Boston blacks or seasoned transplants with answers of "We did that" or, indeed, "Don't bother."

Why? Was Boston's African American community resigned to second class citizenship or settling for crumbs? Or were the fresh-eyed, enthusiastic newcomers who expected to find in Boston a black community as powerful as those in Chicago or Detroit misunderstanding something?

A cogent explanation is offered by Byron Rushing, a black Massachusetts state representative from the South End first elected in 1982 and retaining his seat for thirty-five years as of this writing. With a face both cherubic and serious, and a shock of hair reminiscent of Frederick Douglass, in whose footsteps he travels daily from the South End to the State House, Rushing is also a historian who served thirteen years as president of Boston's Museum of African American History. His assessment of black Bostonia—including what is "wrong" with black Bostonia—is a prerequisite for anyone delving into the city's social dilemmas and inequities, especially with an eye toward combating them.

"There are no black Boston Brahmins," he says, invoking the term for the city's self-effacing long-ancestored power elite. "There are no descendants of Crispus Attucks walking around," even if the enslaved, and later presumably freed, African was the first to die in the revolution that created the United States of America.

Rushing's point is that Boston, unlike other northern cities, did not have a large industrial base to attract refugees in the Great Migration fleeing the Jim Crow South. And indeed the numbers back Rushing up. In the forty years between 1900 and 1940, the size of Boston's black population rose by only 104 percent. While this may seem like a large increase at first glance, during just the ten years between 1910 and 1920, Philadelphia's black population rose by 500 percent.

In the population shifts of African Americans following the two world wars, those who did make it to Boston found few occupations in the nonindustrial, banking, and commerce hub open to them beyond menial work. A Rushing classic is his characterization of Marcus Garvey, who, arriving in Boston from Jamaica on a United Fruit Company boat (the corporation was headquartered in the city), proclaims, "This is not where I want to be!" before lighting out for New York to start an Afrocentric revolution.

Boston's black population would finally begin to grow after the Second World War, but, Rushing notes, "1970 was the first year that most black Bostonians were born in Boston." The growth continued until 2000, he says, but then stagnates as Asian, Latino, and other communities of color increase. "In the 2000–2010 Census, we're (black people) the exact same percent," he says.

A Proud and Pronounced Legacy:
Blacks in Colonial Media and Beyond

Still, the few blacks who did permanently call Boston home did so with an outsized contribution. Like Attucks, they rocked both the Cradle of Liberty and the nascent republic as a whole. To the day, history records the beginnings of an African American literary and newspapering tradition with the publishing of fourteen-year-old Phillis Wheatley's first poem, "On Messrs. Hussey and Coffin," in the *Mercury* of Newport, Rhode Island, on December 21, 1767. A full volume of poetry followed, published both in the colony and in England in 1770. While considered gifted and "remarkable for her race" (some historical interpretations suggest she was trained as such by her slaveholders as a living demonstration that black people could be taught European customs and culture), she was not necessarily an anomaly nor even the first American of African descent recorded as mastering the English literary form. Across the state in Deerfield, another black woman, Lucy Terry, penned in 1746 the poem "The Bars Fight," chronicling a deadly skirmish with Native Americans in that frontier village.

The black literary tradition continued beyond Massachusetts' abolition of slavery in 1783, with writers fueled by their stake in the continuing fight for freedom nationwide. As white abolitionist William Lloyd Garrison began publishing his fiercely antislavery newspaper, the *Liberator*, in Boston in 1831, his protégé (and Rushing's doppelganger) Douglass was frequenting Faneuil Hall and other Boston meeting places as an orator and writer. Sixteen years later, Douglass followed Garrison into publishing, founding the *North Star* in Rochester, New York. Beyond the single issue of slavery, records show the emergence of a Boston black press with the Civil War-era publication of an edition of New York's the *Pine and Palm*, described as "devoted to the interests of freedom, and of the colored races in America."

African Americans also worked in the nineteenth century

mainstream press, including at the two newspapers that survive to this day. In 1885, J. Gordon Street moved to the *Boston Herald* after ending an earlier stint at the *Boston Traveler* (both forebears of today's *Herald*) when its editors objected to Street, the *Traveler's* only black reporter, publicly identifying himself with the paper. The far more accepting *Herald* kept Street's employ even while he simultaneously wrote for a dizzying array of national newspapers and published his own black-oriented title, the *Boston Courant*. Its contemporaries were the *Boston Advocate*, the *Boston Leader* and the *Boston Co-Operator*, giving the city four black titles out of 154 published nationwide by 1890, some running into the early twentieth century.

In 1888, the *Boston Globe* hired Robert Teamoh, a Boston Latin grad and journeyman newspaperman who quickly earned "an enviable reputation as a news-gatherer and writer." He also became a director of the Globe Athletic Club, complementing another sports role he held as secretary of baseball's Negro National League. In the days before simultaneous political and journalistic avocations presented themselves as a conflict, Teamoh kept his *Globe* reporting job after his election to the Massachusetts House of Representatives in 1894.

A Bostonian was also founder and publisher of the *Woman's Era*, the first national newspaper published by and for African American women. Josephine St. Pierre Ruffin was also a charter member of the NAACP and founder of the American Woman Suffrage Association and the local League of Women for Community Service, a black woman's group that still exists today in a South End brownstone. WBZ-TV reporter Sarah-Ann Shaw was one of its presidents in the modern era.

In the twentieth century, Dorothy West would follow Wheatley as a prodigy, also publishing her first work at age fourteen, in the *Boston Post*. She became an important figure in the Harlem Renaissance and returned to the Bay State and established a long-running column in the *Martha's Vineyard Gazette*, along with regular appearances on WMEX radio, counting her as one of Boston's first black broadcast personalities.

Most significantly, though, was William Monroe Trotter, for whom the UMass institute would be named. An 1895 Phi Beta Kappa graduate of Harvard University, Trotter in 1901 started the *Boston Guardian* as an outlet for his fierce criticism of Booker T. Washington's accommodationist policies of race relations. He also took on Washington's political opposite, Garvey, who after his quick departure from Boston to New York founded his Back-to-Africa movement. With W .E. B. DuBois, Trotter convened both the Niagara Movement and its progeny, the NAACP. The *Guardian* was the uncompromising voice of each.

Trotter died in 1934, his newspaper outliving him and his fiery rhetoric by more than two decades. If it fought its founder's quixotic battles, it also chronicled the more mundane yet colorful everyday lives of black Bostonia. One example was the platform the *Guardian* offered talents such as sportswriter Mabry "Doc" Kountze of Medford, later the paper's editor, who was instrumental in securing a Boston Red Sox tryout of Jackie Robinson in 1945. The tryout was little more than a sham, and two years later, the Brooklyn Dodgers signed the Negro League star to change baseball and America forever. Had the Red Sox been serious, the team would have been the first in Major League baseball's modern era to integrate; instead, it was the last.

Kountze was also the first black journalist granted a press pass to Fenway Park. Years later, when asked what he found newsworthy there for a black newspaper audience, he enthusiastically replied, "We wrote about the 'Cubans'!"—a reference to darker-complected players who invoked, or invented, ancestry from the Caribbean island.

The *Guardian's* last recorded issue was 1957. Coinciding with it was the *Boston Chronicle*, whose publishers, Alfred Houghton and William Edward Harrison, hailed from the islands, representative of Boston's growing Caribbean population, and took a more conservative, or at least don't-rock-the-boat, position politically. The *Chronicle* continued to publish until 1960. That left only Boston's mainstream press to document the blossoming of the civil rights movement, some indeed admirably. One of note was WGBH, then the educational channel before the advent of National Public Radio and the Public Broadcasting System, which broadcast the 1963 March on Washington live from the nation's capital. The station also aired live a sit-in against de facto segregation at Boston School Committee headquarters two weeks later, early rumbles of what would become the desegregation crisis of the 1970s.

From the Guardian to the Banner

A qualifier is due to Rushing's assertion that there were no black Boston Brahmins walking around: there may have been one. With roots in the city dating to 1880, Melvin Miller was born with as much privilege as could be expected in black Bostonia. He grew up in Roxbury's H-Block neighborhood, a parcel around Munroe Park named for Harold, Harrishof, and Holworthy streets and Humboldt Avenue and populated by the Boston contingent of W. E. B. DuBois's talented tenth. With Boston Latin School, Harvard College, and Columbia Law School diplomas in hand, he initially planned "to become a well-heeled lawyer," seizing on opportunities then opening up for well-credentialed blacks at the time the nation was reversing one hundred years of postslavery Jim Crow with the Civil Rights Act of 1964 and Voting Rights Act a year later.

But those achievements were not happening without great sacrifices and setbacks. The signing of the Civil Rights Act came amid the disappearance and murders of three Congress of Racial Equality workers in Mississippi and racial unrest across the country. Abandoning his white-shoed ambitions, Miller instead took a job as an assistant US attorney and, perceiving a void in the black community, decided to start a newspaper.

Not amused was Miller's father, a stern man who like many of his generation found accomplishment in the US Postal Service, one of the few avenues of government employment or nonmenial jobs anywhere open to African Americans. Born in 1896, John J. Miller rose to become a supervisor in the Boston Post Office, appointed to that position by US Speaker of the House John W. McCormack. After a few issues were published, the elder Miller questioned his son about the risky venture, which required him to hawk papers.

"He asked, 'You making any money doing that?'" recalls Miller, then thirty-one, suggesting his father knew the answer before he responded.

"I said, 'No, Dad.'

"He said, 'You like doing that?'

"'Not especially.'

"'Then why don't you find something you don't like that makes money?'"

The elder Miller was not the only one the young publisher needed to impress. After William Monroe Trotter's death, Trotter's sister Maude, a Wellesley grad, took over the *Guardian*. At her passing two decades later, her husband, Harvard class of 1896 graduate Charles Steward, followed suit, using his earnings as a dentist to finance the by-then occasional issues.

Miller called on the ninety-five-year-old Steward, to get his grace for the new venture. Dr. Steward responded by speculating why he had lived so long. "He said, 'I guess I've just been waiting for you,'" Miller recalls. Steward greeted him, and then proceeded to grill him to see if Miller knew what he was in for.

A Slow Start

With the reluctant support of his father and the aid of a business partner, Otis Gates, another Boston Latin grad from Roxbury who went to Harvard College and obtained an MBA from the Business School, Miller was ready to begin publication. But business realities came quickly. After a short time the *Banner* ceased publishing. But what seemed like a final edition was only a hiatus. The struggling entrepreneurs regrouped, in part by the young lawyer leaving his government job and taking no salary while getting the paper on its feet—one of numerous times Miller would endure such a sacrifice for his journalistic venture. Soon the *Banner* resumed publication.

WGBH and "Say Brother"

If there was ever a justification for a black view—or regardless of color, a more truthful view of how the white media was parachuting into the black community to depict incidents affecting blacks—it was in recounting a violent confrontation between police and welfare rights demonstrators in Grove Hall on June 9, 1967. Mainstream media called the encounter that left scores injured and broken glass in the storefronts of "Agency Row," a swath of social service organizations, a "riot." The *Banner* headline agreed—but with a significant and distinctively different qualifier, declaring: "Police Riot in Grove Hall."

Racial tensions remained high in Boston, much fueled by the struggle to end segregation against an intransigent Boston School Committee. The issue plagued many northern cities with distinctly separate black and white neighborhoods as the civil rights movement shifted following the 1954 Supreme Court decision in *Brown v. Board of Education* outlawing legalized separation solely by race. In Boston, Chicago and other cities, rights activists charged the school systems had deliberately built schools in decidedly black and white areas in order to preserve and perpetuate neighborhood segregation.

Yet even with its share of protests and active chapters of national civil rights movement organizations such as the Congress of Racial Equality, unrest in Boston paled compared to the rest of the country. A month after the Grove Hall incident, a riot raged in Detroit for four days, taking forty-three lives and leaving fourteen hundred buildings burned. Two years earlier, in August 1965, thirty-four people perished in Los Angeles' Watts riots, triggered by police assault of a black motorist.

After the Detroit riot, President Johnson appointed a commission to look at the causes and possible prevention of urban disorder.

It was released the last day of February, a Leap Day that may have allowed extra time but still not enough to prepare for even greater violence scarcely more than a month away with the assassination of the Reverend Dr. Martin Luther King Jr., when riots raged in at least a hundred cities across the country.

Except in Boston, where, for once, media may have quelled racial strife, not blithely contributed to it. Assisting was the Hardest Working Man in Show Business.

By happenstance, James Brown had been scheduled to perform in Boston on April 5. At first Mayor Kevin White decided to cancel or postpone the concert but was persuaded not to by Tom Atkins, a black city councilor elected the year before. The two of them also convinced WGBH-TV to broadcast it live from the Boston Garden.

If the notion was that an angry black person who was about to bash an appliance storefront window might notice the TVs on display were all showing James Brown playing live and have a change of heart, well, however stereotypical, it basically worked. Boston was spared the destruction. WGBH, already an early leader in the budding public television universe, more than earned its stripes as a public trust.

As for the concert at the Garden, Brown deftly handled a few over-enthusiastic fans, and during introductions took the microphone from Atkins to welcome White as "a swinging cat." The show was a classic.

WGBH has never been shy about embracing its community responsibility that night or the idea that there ever should have been any question that it would. While television was invented in the 1920s and radio three decades before that, the station unabashedly traces its roots even before the telegraph. An 1836 bequest by John Lowell Jr. endowed the Lowell Institute, WGBH's forebear, for the purpose of presenting free "public lectures for the benefit of the citizens of Boston." In WGBH's eyes, James Brown was simply following the likes of Louis Agassiz and Charles Dickens in continuing the Lowell legacy of attracting the top-name talent of the day.

The success of Brown's peacemaking performance notwithstanding, it was clear to anyone in the post-April 4, 1968, world that social ills would not be solved by a one-night stand, regardless of the level of talent. A decade later, longtime WGBH general manager and chairman David Ives recalled:

> The realization was born that all previous programming, of which WGBH had done a lot on black problems and black issues, amounted to whites doing programs about blacks. It was felt perhaps it was time blacks had the opportunity to say what they thought and what they had the right to express about their problems.

The vehicle for that expression would be a weekly television series, *Say Brother*. The show would be an opportunity, wrote Sarah-Ann Shaw, an early contributing reporter, "to expose the true facts about black history through music, song, discussions, art, drama, fashion, and educational scholarship." It also represented "another door being cracked open slightly by white America" that held particular significance because "it opened the door to TV land, a place where blacks had been sorely underrepresented for years."

Say Brother made its debut on July 15, 1968. The station did not short-shrift the show and provided it with a healthy budget, at the same time endowing it with a talented staff. An early producer was Ray Richardson, described by Shaw as "a brilliant young man" who "never wavered in his commitment to portraying all facets and accomplishments of black life."

Richardson expounded on that on *Say Brother's* first anniversary, stating:

> We attempted to create an outlet for many of the viewpoints that exist in our community and to deal with political, educational, and cultural activities relevant to black people. We have had successes, occasional failures, and many memorable incidents.

Unfortunately, the show would experience a too memorable incident leading to a contentious and ultimately tragic fallout. Richardson, who had been becoming increasingly critical of decisions by station management, sometimes publically so, defied a warning not to broadcast an obscenity in a July 23, 1970, ninety-minute special on the African American community of New Bedford, Massachusetts, and conditions leading to unrest in that city earlier in the month. "Due to the graphic language of those interviewed for the program, and due to the fact the program was aired in its entirety against the wishes of WGBH management, *Say Brother* Producer Ray Richardson was fired after the broadcast," reads a description of the program posted by WGBH in its online historical collection. Station management also announced plans to cancel the show or, as *Jet Magazine* reported, to "drop the all-Black program ... and replace it with another all-Black show," sparking protests. The show was resumed, a new producer was hired, and a community committee established to assure the "interests of the black community were represented" and to create "an open dialogue between staff and management, so conflicts could be addressed and additional firings forestalled."

If that was a less-than-satisfying resolution for Richardson, an even graver conclusion followed. Vacationing in Mexico not long afterward, he was swimming in Acapulco when he was caught in an undertow or rip current or other circumstances, leading to his death at twenty-four. In a period of untimely deaths of political and social change leaders, his loss was mourned by community members as something that would not have happened had he not been fired and subsequently been traveling in Mexico.

Yet *Say Brother*'s influence would grow during these years, with the hiring of experienced producers such as Topper Carew to join already skilled staff members like Stan Lathan. With Marita Rivero, later a top WGBH executive as general manager, they would take the program national in 1975 as arguably the nation's premiere African American nonfiction television venue. The next year, long before "people of color" was used widespread to refer to nonwhites, the show adopted a multicultural format to present programming about Native American, Latina/o, and Asian concerns. In 1981 it would return as a black show.

Say Brother would receive many accolades—countless Emmys and other awards—and a degree of quality most measurable in the achievements of its alumni. Carew and Lathan would go on to distinguished Hollywood careers as the creators of numerous prime-time sitcoms, specials, and other shows.

Others include Shaw, Henry Hampton of Blackside Inc., the creator of the groundbreaking PBS series *Eyes on the Prize*, Barbara Barrow-Murray, Juanita Anderson, Calvin Lindsay, Lovell Dyett, Elliott Francis, June Cross, Darren Duarte, and Beth Deare.

Deare, the producer from 1978 to '88, once articulated the show's focus after reviewing audience data showing its viewership was in fact majority white. Though at first glance that might imply the content should be changed to better reflect the interest of white viewers, she vehemently disagreed, saying, "Absolutely not. If those watching this are white people, then they're watching it because it is a black show."

That changed ten years and three producers later, when the station announced a name change from the 1960s soul-surviving *Say Brother* to *Basic Black*. Referring to viewership data similar to what Deare had reviewed, producer Carol Johnson told the *Globe* that a majority of viewers were white and that she wanted to make the program seem:

> Less dated, more contemporary, a sign of the times. I wanted it to be classy and elegant, reflective of a certain standard. To me, that's what basic black is.

Like the *Banner*'s account of the Grove Hall police riot, *Say Brother* would often report on individuals, issues, and incidents through a black lens presenting a completely different, if not contradictory, perspective than the mainstream white media—even in the decision of which facts to incorporate in the telling.

One example is *Whatever Happened to Donald Johnson?* The

documentary told the story of a model-student teen once lauded by Mayor Ray Flynn spied driving a Greyhound bus by police. Assuming he had stolen it, they gave chase, with Johnson turning into Roxbury and its hilly, narrow streets. He was finally stopped by a gauntlet when police opened fire, riddling the bus head-on with bullets and killing him.

What the *Say Brother* crew found and other media did not, however, was that the bus was not stolen but loaned to Johnson by a Greyhound staffer, well aware of his passion, and knowledge, of buses, plus his skill at driving them. The youth had in fact driven buses around the facility, if not with official permission, certainly with the knowledge of those responsible for them.

"It was an unknown driver who, according to his mom, was mentoring his desire to become a bus driver and had let Donald take the wheel a few times," recalls Elliott Francis, *Say Brother's* host who was also producer of the documentary.

"The spot news footage of the shooting was also exclusive to WGBH. The tip for the story came from a producer at *The 10 O'Clock News* who approached me with the footage. She said although they did day of coverage, there were no plans to follow the story and she thought it deserved more."

The result was that a story initially presumed to have concerned a black male doing something wrong and illegal turned out to have another side, and the wrong committed by someone else. Donald Johnson had been, and still was until his death, a model teen.

One of thousands of programs in nearly fifty years, the show symbolized the power of a black story, told by black journalists in search of the truth.

The Best Intentions—and Actual Progress: The Boston Community Media Committee

Even before the King assassination, the relationship of major media to the black community was severely questioned. One critic was Hall of

Fame Boston Celtics player-coach Bill Russell. In June 1966—at the conclusion of their still-unbroken eighth consecutive NBA championship season—Russell convened a meeting at Slade's, his restaurant in Lower Roxbury, with forty news executives. His warning was that violence affecting other cities could take root in Boston unless they did something.

The *something* was the Boston Community Media Committee, a joint group of the city's media power brokers and minority community organizers, including school integration activist Ruth Batson, NAACP President Ken Guscott, and Shaw, then director of the Northern Students Movement in Grove Hall's Agency Row. The group identified as its objectives both increasing black employment in the media and improving coverage, specifically citing "the phraseology used by reporters in regards to events in the black community." *Boston Globe* editor Tom Winship was selected as chairman.

After an initial dormancy, the BCMC's activities jump-started with the release of the Kerner Commission Report (officially, the National Advisory Commission on Civil Disorders) on February 29, 1968. Appointed by President Johnson, the commission was charged with investigating the causes of riots in several cities the year before. Famously concluding: "Our nation is moving toward two societies, one black, one white—separate and unequal," the report gave a specific charge to media to:

- Expand coverage of the Negro community and of race problems through permanent assignment of reporters familiar with urban and racial affairs, and through establishment of more and better links with the Negro community.
- Integrate Negroes and Negro activities into all aspects of coverage and content, including newspaper articles and television programming. The news media must publish newspapers and produce programs that recognize the existence and activities of Negroes as a group within the community and as a part of the larger community.

- Recruit more Negroes into journalism and broadcasting and promote those who are qualified to positions of significant responsibility. Recruitment should begin in high schools and continue …

Certainly nothing had changed thirty-five days later when the Reverend Dr. Martin Luther King Jr. was assassinated in Memphis. More cities burned, even if Boston was spared.

For whatever reason—the fear of violence, the economic benefits of tapping of a potential black media market, and quite possibly the simple altruism of wishing to do the right thing, Boston's white power structure sensed the urgency. The BCMC stepped up efforts, assembling an unprecedented gathering of more than 120 media power brokers and bona-fide community leaders for a two-day retreat in Dublin, New Hampshire. Also attending was a representative from the US Justice Department's Community Relations Service, an agency formed to encourage implementation of the Kerner Commission's recommendations.

If the commission's report, the 1967 riots, Russell's warnings, the King assassination, and the more widespread riots in its wake weren't enough, the participants were jolted by yet another impetus in the weeks leading up the gathering on June 28–30. On June 5, Senator Robert Kennedy, the head of Massachusetts' most famous family after the tragic deaths of his brothers, was himself shot to death while campaigning for the Democratic nomination for president.

Despite that dark shadow, the Dublin conference saw enthusiasm and unity. Yet not long after, the ardor began to wane as the organizers sought to reconcile the gathering's expenses.

Financial commitments also affected the committee's long-term operation as media members were assessed dues to cover expenses, including the salaries of an executive director and secretary. Still, there were hard numbers showing positive results. Directly after the Dublin conference but more likely attributable to efforts following Bill Russell's come-to-Jesus meeting at Slade's, media outlets reported significant new hires. "Channel 4 now has 15 black people (10 in full time, five temporary) as opposed to four in 1967," read a tally from August 1968. "Channel 5 employs three blacks. Channel 7 has 10 full-time, one coming next week, and two summer trainees. ... Radio reported that eight stations now have 21 black employees compared to a total of five a year ago. ... The press reported that there are now 110 black employees on four papers, working as columnists, reporters, typesetters, photographers, artists, copy editors, and trainees."

Boston media weren't alone: During the King assassination riots, newspapers and broadcast entities across the country were suddenly hiring African American reporters and cameramen as white journalists were physically attacked by rioters. Blacks who previously had been denied these positions as "unqualified," despite many attending journalism schools or working years for the black press, found themselves members of a quickly minted "class of 1968" for whom previously insurmountable qualifications were suddenly waived.

Maurice Lewis, who got his start in broadcasting on Armed Forces Radio before moving to Boston and eventually holding weekend anchor spots at Channels 7 and 4, recalls the ascendancy of WBZ reporter Charlie Austin:

"Charlie was transferred from the mail room. They (taught) him the ins and outs of reporting from the street," Lewis recounts. A solid journalist, Austin would report for the station for decades.

Shaw too was tapped by WBZ. With her civil rights movement experience directing the Northern Students Movement, she had been asked by WGBH to host *Talking Black*, a three-part public affairs program before the launch of *Say Brother*, which she also joined. WBZ general manager Win Baker approached her immediately as the BCMC was gathering steam.

"He asked me that summer, and I came to 'BZ that fall," she recalls of Baker's invitation in 1969.

For its part, the BCMC fostered an innovative way to train those who truly lacked television production experience in order to increase minority hiring. The group contracted with Blackside, a black-owned production company founded by Henry Hampton, which would later produce the groundbreaking PBS series *Eyes on the Prize* that created the civil rights movement as a discipline of American history. With station support, the committee funded NIGHTTRAIN, a training program in television production utilizing station facilities in off-hours, during which the stations would broadcast participants' work. A steady pipeline of NIGHTTRAIN graduates began to supply the production ranks at Boston TV stations, for which black cameramen and film (later video) editors were no longer an anomaly.

If there was discontent by media outlets, whether over dues-paying or otherwise, there may have been more so with minority community members unhappy at the rate of progress in reaching the committee's objective. By 1973, a Boston Minority Caucus of "dissatisfied black media members" had spun off from the committee, drafting its own "nine-point program to end 'racism and indifference' in the Boston media":

1. Employ 25 percent minority personnel at all levels.
2. Grant 25 minority educational grants in communications.
3. Name minority members to boards of directors.
4. Provide a minimum one-hour prime time to minority-oriented programs on all radio and TV stations.
5. Provide at least one page of coverage per issue "by, for and about minority peoples" in all newspapers, including one column in Spanish.
6. Set up a formal recruitment program for minorities.
7. Provide at least five minutes of news in Spanish each day on radio and TV.
8. Make BCMC a central agency for all recruitment and job openings, given preference to "local minority group people."
9. Provide regular sensitivity training conducted by minority group organization for all media personnel involved in gathering, reporting and dissemination of news.

How much hope the caucus had in achieving those goals is anyone's guess, but one was accomplished with surprisingly little fanfare. The *Boston Globe* named Carlos Quintero a columnist and ran his Spanish-language work weekly in the '70s.

The bolting of the disaffected Minority Caucus foreshadowed a general unraveling of the BCMC. Financial woes, continued disagreements over dues, and operational difficulties persisted, including basic questions of the goals of the committee. A Saturday Open House in May 1970 asked: "Are you young, black or Spanish speaking? Of high school or college age? ... Interested in finding out how a newspaper, radio or television station works?" The solicitation offered "Your chance to actually see inside a television and radio station, a newspaper plant and to talk with the people who work there!" It did not promise any jobs, however, emphasizing, in all caps: "THIS IS A COME AND SEE PROGRAM ONLY! THERE WILL BE NO INTERVIEWING OR JOB PLACEMENT AT THIS TIME!" Records show one hundred media participants and only thirty-three "young guests" attended. "The low attendance appears to be a reflection that Radio, Television or newspapers, possibly, aren't capable of delivering a message that can attract black-Puerto Rican kids," the *Globe's* Dexter Eure wrote to his fellow committee members in his "report on last Saturday's first 'Careers in Media' Day."

"We might examine ourselves even further," he continued, "by acknowledging had we had a full response, many of us were poorly equipped to 'communicate' with poor young blacks."

Despite such setbacks, if through nothing else other than its existence, the BCMC did keep minority hiring top of mind in Boston media for a decade and a half. Records kept by Muriel Snowden show its demise in 1983 amid continuing squabbles of its media members paying for, and to some extent controlling, its executive director. If nothing else, hires like Shaw and Austin and the many trainees from NIGHTTRAIN mark its lasting legacy. Its existence also marked Boston as one of the few cities that in some way heeded the recommendations of the Kerner Commission Report, as well as the warnings of Bill Russell. BCMC's model could be replicated today, if media executives today want to discuss it.

Slade's is still there, and meeting space is available.

Doing It Ourselves: The Blackside Story

In 1987, few American history departments at the nation's universities offered a concentration in the civil rights movement. Not quite twenty years had passed since the assassination of the Reverend Dr. Martin Luther King Jr., and only the year before did Americans officially celebrate the first national holiday marking the slain leader's birth. The thousands of nonviolent black foot soldiers and their allies who walked with King, literally or figuratively, put their lives on the line in twenty-five years of campaigns for equality and justice. They had endless stories to tell, but few thought of them as history lessons.

That changed with the January 1987 premiere of the six-part PBS series *Eyes on the Prize*. The documentary told the story as narrative history, from the lynching of Emmett Till through the passage of the 1965 Voting Rights Act. Captured on film were the participants themselves—both those who fought to end segregation and those seeking to uphold it—whose fresh and uncontaminated memories were gold as primary source history.

The person bringing that history to the fore was one who lived it, Henry Hampton. Marching not quite with King but John Lewis, on March 7, 1965, he was far in the back of the crowd of six hundred attempting to cross the Edmund Pettus Bridge in Selma, Alabama. It was there that police unleashed a torrent of nightsticks against them to dub the day Bloody Sunday.

"We were standing there on the bridge," Hampton told WGBH's Chris Lydon in 1994. "There were cameras buzzing overhead … the president and federal government in all its power was there. We had terrific villains. … a formidable opposition who were literally killing people."

If Hampton left that attack with a limp, he was actually unharmed; it was a preexisting condition that was the vestige of a childhood bout with polio. But what he witnessed did leave a mark, one that he vowed then to document to the world.

"I looked around and said to myself, not being a native Southerner … 'This could make a terrific movie.'"

That cinematography would have to wait. Hampton was then not yet a filmmaker, but nor was he a disinterested bystander. One of the few black staff members of the Unitarian Universalist Church, he was part of a delegation to Selma that included the Reverend James Reeb, also of Boston. Two days later after the attack on the bridge, Reeb was walking to attend a meeting with King when he was approached by a group of white men and attacked. He died two days later, on March 11—instantly becoming the subject of worldwide news reports and a martyr to the movement forever, no doubt further sealing Hampton's belief in the power of the civil rights story and the necessity of telling it.

Hampton was born in Saint Louis in 1940 to a black surgeon and his stay-at-home wife. He received a bachelor's in English at Washington University and in 1963 joined the staff of the Unitarian church in Boston in a public relations role that took him to Selma and around the world.

In 1968, he went on his own to start Blackside Inc. in the South End, as a production house for documentary and industrial films. It also became a training ground for black production personnel through the NIGHTTRAIN project. Coordinated by the Boston Community Media Committee, it arranged for Boston television stations to provide off-hour airtime and facility use for trainees. Between NIGHTTRAIN and Blackside's ongoing work, the company was estimated to have trained some two hundred minority producers, technicians, and researchers.

A decade into running his own company, Hampton picked up the promise he made to himself to document the movement. He struck an initial deal with Capital Cities Communications, then a chain of ABC-affiliated commercial TV stations. It fell through, and his idea was also shot down by Steve Fayer, a writer with whom he had collaborated. "I told him, 'Nobody cares about colored people and nobody cares about civil rights,'" Fayer told the public media newspaper *Current* in 1998. Not giving up, Hampton asked Fayer to indulge him by writing some treatments together, and the project was launched.

But not paid for. "We were halfway through production, and there was not enough money to carry on," Jon Else, one of the series' producers, told *Current*. "The roof leaked. There were 30 people on staff, and tempers were hot. There was not enough cash to meet next week's payroll."

Hampton mortgaged his house, not only to meet the payroll but send a message of his commitment to the staff. He also exhibited smart business sense in forging an agreement with WGBH to serve as the presenting station, but not the producers, for national broadcast on PBS. The producing credit would remain with Blackside, which also retained the copyright.

The series won instant acclaim. Innumerable honors included a Peabody, a duPont-Columbia Gold Baton, several Emmys, and an Oscar nomination. *TV Guide* called it the best documentary of the year and *Time* the best of the decade. Suddenly, civil rights history *was* history, and master's and PhD programs across the country began getting thesis proposals for research on previously untold aspects of the movement.

Hampton wasn't done with the story, however, and set to work on a second series, *Eyes on the Prize II*, chronicling the period from 1965 until the King assassination. Yet despite the awards and accolades, he found it harder to raise money for *Eyes* 2 than *Eyes* 1. Eventually prevailing, he again garnered support from WGBH.

Blackside was anything but a one- or two-hit wonder. Among more than fifty major films and media projects were *The Great Depression*, *War on Poverty*, *Malcolm X: Make It Plain*, and *I'll Make Me a World*. After years of scraping by for money to fund his productions, he produced the latter—a retrospective about blacks in the arts—with an $800,000 grant from the National Endowment for the Humanities.

Individually, Hampton was awarded fourteen honorary degrees, a Loeb Fellowship from Harvard University, and the Charles Frankel Prize from President George Bush for outstanding contribution to the humanities.

It was a contribution that ended too soon. First suffering from lung cancer, Hampton contracted the bone marrow disease myelodysplasia in 1998. At fifty-eight, he died after surgery to repair a hematoma in his brain, according the *New York Times*.

His sisters continued to run Blackside, and after a copyright expiration issue that prohibited *Eyes on the Prize* from being broadcast and used in schools, WGBH collaborated to again make the series available. In the now cottage industry that civil rights movement stories have become, there are newer, more updated documentaries of the struggle, as well as thousands of books, plays, and other works inspired by Hampton and his producing protégés.

But none had the groundbreaking power of that first telling, conceived by a visionary who saw the movement's horror and triumph firsthand, and always kept his eyes on the prize.

An Urban Voice: Kendell Nash, WILD, and Sunny Joe White

"This is Information Ten-Nine-Oh!"

For a twenty-year run, those words prefaced the news reports of WILD-AM. The AM station operated only when the sun shined, and the newscast that followed was fairly barebones, mostly rewrites of the daily papers as similar stations did. Some years, the news director for the black-oriented station may have been white. But the flavor was undeniably black and focused toward the community outside its Dudley Square studio.

"When I arrived [in Boston] in 1973, the only commercial radio station in Boston playing 'soul' music was a small AM station, WILD, that was on the air sunrise to sunset," Jacquie Gales Webb, a lifelong radio professional, told the Emerson College alumni magazine.

At night, she said, "those who loved Black music turned to the college stations for soul, jazz, and R&B"—including Emerson's WERS-FM. That's where Webb worked as a student and where WILD program director Sunny Joe White heard her jazz program and recruited her.

WILD had just been acquired that year by Sheridan Broadcasting, which switched its format from rock and roll to urban contemporary. At its 1946 start it had been classical, and in 1966 became the first Boston station to target a black audience with what Billboard called then the "Black Top 40."

In 1980, Kendell Nash of Nash Communications Corp. purchased WILD from Sheridan for $1 million, becoming Boston's first black-owned radio station. That same year, White left WILD for KISS-108. Nash soon applied for a twenty-four-hour broadcasting permit, only to be blocked by an opposing applicant. The matter headed to the courts.

Even with the limited signal, WILD cemented its following and groomed new personalities. "I began serving an internship at WILD-AM in Boston under a [program director] named Steve Crumbley, who wanted a Caribbean announcer and didn't know that Bermuda was not really the Caribbean," Elroy Smith, better known to WILD listeners as simply Elroy, said in a 2006 interview.

The internship paid off, both for Elroy, who eventually succeeded White as program director, and for the station. It was particularly evident one day in 1983, when Elroy dropped the needle on a single performed by a group of preteens from the Orchard Park Housing Project practically outside his window. The song was "Candy Girl," and New Edition catapulted into fame. It also was a career moment for the Roxbury boy group's manager, Maurice Starr.

Meanwhile, White was at WXKS-FM, rechristened KISS-108 and reinventing its elevator music programming into a Billboard top-rated station in Boston. He also became a part owner of the station. Its audience had been white and became multicultural with his revamped format.

History almost repeated itself when Starr, cast off from New Edition, re-created his formula with a group of white teens dubbed New Kids on the Block. This time, White would be among those to first play the group.

In 1984, White won industry accolades with Billboard's award as radio's "Top Major American Market" programmer of the year. The next year, White made an attempt at TV, becoming the first host for the short-lived *Boston Beat* program on Channel 66, a Saturday night feature broadcast from 10 p.m. to 2 a.m. and recorded on-location at Boston's clubs.

Later, Nash sought to give his old program director a run for his money with an attempt to buy a major suburban FM station that he would convert to an urban sound, with Elroy heading it up, the *Herald* reported in 1992. But that August, Nash, fifty-four, died of leukemia. His FM plan and dream of broadcasting WILD twenty-four hours remained unrealized.

Bernadine Nash took over for her husband and eventually succeeded in getting the station a full-time signal. In 2001, she sold WILD to the black chain Radio One for approximately $5 million.

White too would pass before his time, from a heart attack, at forty-two. Long active in the fight against AIDS, he was remembered and honored years after his death by the AIDS Action Committee, which marked its twenty-fifth anniversary recognizing twenty-five people, White among them, in 2010.

A Station of Our Own—Almost

The Minority-Minority Ownership of Channel 7

You may not know from watching its sitcoms or newscasts, but Boston's Channel 7 was once owned by a consortium of investors that included the largest minority group member participation in the country.

That's the careful, and accurate, way of putting it. For a while during the 1980s and '90s, the shorthand in the black community may have described the station as black-owned.

In fact, people of color never controlled a majority of the station, and only comprised 14 percent during the group's direct involvement in the ownership and operation of the station from 1982 to 1986. No television channel in Boston has ever been more than 51 percent black-owned. But it's understandable and forgivable if the impression grew to outsized dimensions. In 1978, a few years before the group's involvement at Channel 7, only one station out of 965 nationwide was controlled by African Americans. As of 2015, that had grown to twelve out of 2,119—and that was following a dramatic jump from only two black-held licenses the year before.

The story of how Boston's Channel 7 came to have the then-greatest minority ownership stake begins in Los Angeles. In 1965, less than a month after the Watts riots, RKO General Inc. filed with the FCC to renew its license for KHJ-TV Channel 9. A smaller, local LA broadcast company filed an application of its own for the airwaves, saying it would better serve the community and uphold the public trust.

So began a twenty-three-year legal battle that eventually expanded to antitrust actions and US Justice Department involvement, culminating in the denial of RKO's license renewal in LA.

That sparked a similar contest in 1969 over RKO's license in Boston to operate Channel 7, then with the call letters WNAC-TV. Two competing companies each filed petitions for the license. One was Community Broadcasting of Boston Inc., headed by David Mugar, whose family owned the Star Market supermarket chain. The other was the Dudley Station Corp., headed by black entrepreneur Bertram Lee.

After nine years, the FCC had not yet decided on the license, and the matter was mired in court. RKO's parent company, meanwhile, entered a consent decree with the Securities and Exchange Commission regarding business practices.

Sensing that RKO's license for WNAC was vulnerable, Mugar

and Lee merged their companies to form New England Television Corporation (NETV.) The new company forged a settlement with RKO in which it would sell its WNAC license to NETV if the FCC found for RKO.

After the settlement was reached, RKO reevaluated the value of its physical assets at WNAC, determining they were worth more without the license than with it. The company then petitioned to the FCC that its license indeed should not be renewed and completed the sale to NETV.

New England Television Corporation did not take over immediately. Another black entrepreneur, Thomas W. Jones, challenged NETV's petition, but was eventually rejected on technical grounds. On June 6, 1980, the FCC ruled that NETV was the sole remaining applicant, and the de facto winner. Two years later, its broadcast began.

The new ownership company was 14 percent minority and included seven black owners—Lee, Ruth Batson, *Banner* publisher Mel Miller, Henry Hampton, Thomas Brown, Elaine Moragne, and Judge Baron Martin—and twenty-three whites. Among them were Win Baker, the former general manager of WBZ Channel 4; former Watergate attorney Terry Lenzner; Theodore Jones of the classical radio station WCRB; former MIT president Jerome B. Wiesner; Mort Zuckerman of the *Atlantic Monthly*; John Chase; computer genius Edward Fredkin; Dr. George Tuttle; and Dr. Henry M. Morgan, dean of Boston University School of Management.

Expectations and Accomplishments

Along with its minority participation, the new group held the distinction of being Boston based, distinguishing it from WBZ Channel 4, owned then by the national Westinghouse Broadcasting chain, and WHDH (later WCVB) Channel 5, a Metromedia property. The latter also was the result of a rare license revocation by the FCC, which had stripped the frequency from the Boston Herald-Traveler company in 1972, in part because of an evolving push to ban newspaper ownership of television stations in the same market. An earlier local group had first acquired the station from the Herald-Traveler, then sold it to Metromedia, which in 1985 sold it to the Hearst Corporation.

The cache Channel 7 earned by being Boston's sole locally owned VHF station brought with it high expectations, if not excitement. Batson described her ambitions invoking the failures of media, and television in particular, cited in studies such as the Kerner Commission Report fourteen years earlier.

"Broadcasting has not been open to all people," she told the *Globe*. "Right now, if people turn on their television, they're inclined to think there's only one kind of person living in Boston, and that's not true."

Saying she hoped the station would begin to rectify that in its programming, she addressed the equal concern identified by the Kerner Commission and Boston Community Media Committee of minority hiring, calling jobs her first priority.

"My one hope is that we maintain our goals from 13 years ago to increase the number of minority people on both sides of the camera."

That hope was realized: in two years, the station reported doubling the number of minority staffers, to 20 percent, though the figure was disputed in a *Globe* report critical of the new owners' accomplishments, citing the station's EEOC filings showing minority employment at 18.5 percent. Regardless, it was still now the highest of the city's major stations, edging out WBZ-TV's at 18.1 percent and WCVB-TV at 17.4. The jump at Channel 7 would be one reason why Kirk Jackson would waive WNEV from his racial analysis of Boston media three years later.

The station received kudos for stronger public service announcements, particularly those about AIDS during the early stages of the epidemic, when discussions of the disease were shunned if not taboo on television. Likewise, its "Priority One anti-crime campaign" received praise and awards.

In another effort to beef up its local presence, the station scored a coup in snagging two big-name personalities to head its news team:

Robin Young, who had gained a large following as host of WBZ's *Evening Magazine* before joining NBC News, and Tom Ellis, Channel 5's popular top anchor.

Most ambitious was *Look,* a two-hour afternoon magazine show conceived by GM Baker to replicate *Look* magazine on television.

But *Look* did poorly in the ratings and proved expensive to produce for a station whose new ownership was already burdened by having to pay $15 million for the license fight alone. Baker cut it to an hour before replacing it with *New England Afternoon* and game shows. Ratings for its programming as a whole failed to catch on, with Channels 4 and 5 soaring ahead. The poaching of Ellis from Channel 5 inadvertently led to that station creating the very popular husband-and-wife news team of Chet Curtis and Natalie Jacobson, while the folksy and endearing black female, white male team of Liz Walker and Jack Williams hit the right buttons for Channel 4 to soar.

A ratings report in February 1984 showed Channel 7, though still third, gaining on its two rivals, but only after abandoning some local content in favor of popular if mindless nationally syndicated game shows such as *Wheel of Fortune.*

Though for entirely different reasons and unrelated except in a shared cast of characters, Channel 7's money woes mirrored those that one of its coowners was simultaneously experiencing. Blackside's Henry Hampton was in the throes of production of *Eyes on the Prize* and short of funding, unable to meet payroll. After a failed deal to sell the series to the Capital Cities chain of television stations, he turned to the commercial station in which he had an interest, if not influence.

"For $3 million, the station could have broadcast the most prestigious program in Boston history and silenced many of its critics about the lack of quality and minority programming," the *Globe's* Ed Sigel wrote after the series' PBS premiere in early 1987. "It would have made some, if not all, of the money back by syndicating the series."

That was only speculation; there is no way of knowing if one of the hallmarks of public television would have been the same on commercial TV, or if WNEV's owners would have been successful selling it to other stations, especially if, as would have likely been the case, it did not do well in the ratings at the third-place station. (Ratings of PBS programming are almost universally lower than even the most dismal major-market commercial stations.) Regardless, history simply didn't work that way.

In the end, for many reasons—debt from the long license fight, expenses higher than anticipated, and well-heeled competitors fueled by national chain ownership—the reign of local ownership with a significant minority share did not long endure. In 1986, just as Jackson was completing the research from which he had exempted WNEV because of its partial minority ownership, Mugar bought out most of his partners. (Miller was one who stayed on.) For the others, an upshot was a huge buy-low, sell-high profitability; though perhaps oversimplified, one analysis suggested Bertram Lee's original $10,000 investment returned $14 million.

(Another decision likely driven by the wish to foster a more local imprint was acquiring the now-defunct WHDH call letters that had previously been used by Channel 5 before its license was stripped from the Herald-Traveler company. The familiarity may have worked, but it may also have sewn more confusion, accentuated a decade later when Channels 4 and 7 swapped their NBC and CBS network affiliations respectively. A viewer watching WHDH over the decades and its channel switches would have seen ABC programming in the 1970s, the CBS lineup in the late 1980s and '90s, then NBC's in the 2000s. After New England Cable News appeared on the scene and was acquired by NBC Universal, the affiliation migrated again in the 2010s, and WHDH at this writing is independent.)

Eventually, Channel 7 would become a rating powerhouse, but not with the local team. In 1993, Mugar sold the station to Sunbeam Television Corp. of Miami for $215 million. The buyer was known for the flashy "crime-oriented and tabloid-style" newscasts, the *Wall Street Journal* reported, of WSVN, its flagship Miami property that it would replicate in Boston.

The Boston Association of Black Journalists

When the National Association of Black Journalists was formed in Washington, DC, in 1975, "You could have held the meeting in a phone booth," Al Fitzpatrick, the longtime editor of Ohio's Akron *Beacon Journal,* was fond of saying.

He was referring to the minute number of black journalists at mainstream, or white-owned, news outlets nationwide. But if you took him literally, it would have to be a pretty large booth: In Washington to cover a national meeting for their respective organizations, the black journalists who agreed to start the organization would later be counted as its forty-four founding members.

Or perhaps with an asterisk, it should have been forty-five.

"I was at an earlier meeting, in Philadelphia," recalls Sarah-Ann Shaw of Boston's WBZ-TV, who was among those calling for the new group. She had attended an earlier meeting where the idea was ruminated on before an attendance sheet was passed around and a name chosen at the Washington gathering.

The name choice would not have been difficult; there had been various associations of black journalists around the country over the years, not the least of which was the National Negro Newspapers Publishers Association, comprised of the black press. But two groups comprised largely of black journalists in the white press were already going full-steam: The Philadelphia Association of Black Journalists, founded in 1973, and the Boston Association of Black Journalists, begun two years earlier, in 1971.

"We wanted to know who else was out there, where they were and what they were doing," Shaw says of organizing the group. The organization coincided with the bolting of more radical members of the Boston Community Media Committee as its quasiindependent Minority Caucus, and Shaw and others remember attending meetings of both, if not in the same space and time.

"We had meetings at the Freedom House (the Roxbury settlement house founded by husband-and-wife Otto and Muriel Snowden, the latter the longtime secretary of the BCMC)," recalls Maurice Lewis, an Armed Forces Radio veteran who ventured to Boston in 1968. He eventually rose to weekend anchor (often called a ghetto position for the number of blacks in the stations' big chairs who were absent during the week, until WBZ's Liz Walker was tapped for the top spot) at Channels 7 and 4.

"There were lively meetings where we talked about how to create paths for high level employment that basically didn't exist," Lewis continues. Most of those paths were word-of-mouth. Members who knew of openings at their newsrooms would unhesitatingly pass them on to others in the group, and after the national counterpart was started, the job fair at its annual convention became its biggest attraction and likely the largest such event in the industry, attracting as many as two hundred exhibitors or more and thousands of applicants.

BABJ's everyday activities were more modest but no less effective, with the organization taking strong stands on coverage of the black community and employment issues, with the group's officers often going against their own bosses. In early 1990, a firestorm followed the revelation that a white suburbanite, Charles Stuart, had shot and killed his pregnant wife, then shot himself superficially to cover up the crime, which he blamed on a fictitious black man. The BABJ hosted a forum, moderated by Harvard Law School Professor Charles Ogletree, holding accountable media executives who had been duped by Stuart's ruse, which resulted in a three-month spree by police of stopping and frisking innocent black males. The program was broadcast nationally on CSPAN.

More parochially, the organization led a multiracial coalition challenging Channel 7 in 2001 when it announced a wholesale canceling of all but one of its targeted-audience public affairs programs, including *Asian Focus, Jewish Perspective, Revista,* and *Higher Ground.* The only one to be spared was the black-oriented *Urban Update,* which would be made more multicultural to incorporate the canceled shows and moved to a taped morning show from a live spot leading into Saturday's early evening news, where it frequently won its rating slot.

The BABJ-led group prevailed, and the shows were saved, though *Urban Update* was moved, and its longtime producer, Vicky Jones, a former BABJ president and NABJ national board member, was let go.

Many other BABJ members held prominent positions in the national organization, including as president (Greg Lee), vice president print (Gayle Pollard), vice president broadcast (Callie Crossley and Alexis Yancey), secretary/treasurer (Lee), and parliamentarian (Robin Washington.) Also, Shaw's WBZ colleague Allison Davis did attend both founding meetings to be counted among the forty-four.

Yet the national group's signature event, its annual convention, eluded Boston for years.

"We never had it in Boston," Shaw said in 2014, "because Boston had a bad reputation insofar as the treatment of black people is concerned."

The occasion for Shaw's observation was the first year the convention was held in Boston, thirty-eight years after its founding. It changed through the efforts of Lee, who, following his term as NABJ president, enlisted the city's convention and visitors bureau to join him in making a pitch during a national board meeting in Boston.

"They were telling us," the new NABJ President Bob Butler, a San Francisco radio news reporter originally from Chelsea, related then, "that Boston had changed and they wanted us to help them tell the rest of the country and the world that Boston was not the Boston you remember from the busing crisis."

Those memories were counterpointed, if not nearly erased, by the second day of the August 2014 convention, when Red Sox and *Boston Globe* owner John Henry invited the journalists to the upper deck State Street Pavilion at Fenway Park. Many of the local black journalists—let alone their national peers—had never been to the elite club, if to Fenway Park at all.

"I would venture to guess that the event," WCVB-TV's Karen Holmes Ward said soon afterward, "probably was the largest concentration of people of color that was ever in the State Street Pavilion."

To be precise, not everyone attending the national convention, which attracted some two thousand attendees, made it to the ballpark event, which had to be first come, first served. Seating capacity of the club was capped at five hundred.

But it certainly was larger than a phone booth.

A Lasting Legacy

Members of the Boston Association of Black Journalists may have been proud to at long last host the national meeting, but they certainly didn't spend all those years waiting for someone else to bestow recognition on them. Throughout the Boston chapter's history, its members worked tirelessly to network, nurture, and give notice to the world of the hundreds of black journalists who indelibly shaped the profession locally and beyond.

Any attempted listing of them would be incomplete; what follows is one measure of accomplishment: those black journalists who have covered black Bostonia for two decades or more. But that gives short shrift to those of briefer tenures who nonetheless left a significant impact, and any omission is humbly acknowledged.

A BABJ program book from a 1993 event offers one example of the organization's effort to document these accomplishments. "Anchored in Achievement" honored three black female television anchors—Liz Walker of WBZ, Pam Cross of WCVB, and Rehema Ellis of WHDH. Walker would have been instantly recognizable throughout Massachusetts as half of the prime-time, ratings-leading, male-female/salt-and-pepper duo with Jack Williams. A Boston import from Little Rock, Arkansas, (where she knew Bill and Hillary Clinton), Walker was so much a household name that an unwed pregnancy echoing that of Candice Bergen's fictitious sitcom anchor "Murphy Brown" gave her a moment of national fame. It only subsided when Walker left WBZ's top spot after twenty-one years to enter Harvard Divinity School, eventually becoming pastor of Roxbury Presbyterian Church.

The crest of Ellis's fame was still in the future at the time of the gala, coming a year later when she left Boston to become a national correspondent for NBC News. Though she was raised in the city and made her mark there, she also worked in Pittsburgh. Her Boston career may have had impact but did not have the longevity of others.

Cross, conversely, would occupy a Boston anchor chair the longest of the trio, albeit in a weekend position that black journalists often called the ghetto spot at stations far beyond Channel 5. She would total thirty-five years as an anchor (with weekday reporting duties) before retiring in 2016.

Yet none of them was the first. One of the most prominent was Janet Langhart, who in 1973 joined Channel 5's *Good Morning!* (later *Good Day!*) after starting out in Chicago four years earlier at WBBM-TV. She left Boston for New York's WOR and *Entertainment Tonight*, BET, and other national work. Her marriage to former Maine Senator and US Secretary of Defense William Cohen rekindled her public life, including as a celebrated author of a play about an imaginary meeting between Anne Frank and Emmett Till.

A native of Springfield who was a young reporter at the *Banner* before joining the *Herald* for its coverage of the school desegregation crisis, Gwen Ifill would also go on to national fame—as a broadcaster. After stints at the *Washington Post* and *New York Times*, Ifill joined PBS's *Washington Week in Review* and later held the coanchor spot on the *PBS NewsHour*. Her untimely death from cancer came at age sixty-one in 2016.

Another national anchor called Boston home, though in the reverse order when Carole Simpson of ABC News chose the city and teaching at Emerson College following her departure from the network. She also indirectly made an impact on WBZ's local airwaves when her daughter, Dr. Mallika Marshall, became the station's medical reporter.

Back on the Hub-to-the-world route, Tanya Hart cut her teeth at Channels 7 and 4, the latter as longtime host of the *Say Brother* counterpart *Coming Together*. Hart left in 1990, first with her own BET celebrity show and later for red-carpet reporting on the E! Network and

American Urban Radio Networks. Another WBZ colleague, Soledad O'Brien, worked studiously as an associate producer and writer before going in front of the camera at San Francisco's KRON and NBC's *Weekend Today,* leaving to anchor CNN's morning program. In 2013 she formed her own production company.

In radio, Audie Cornish of WBUR went on to anchor National Public Radio's *All Things Considered.*

NABJ cofounder Maureen Bunyan worked at WGBH in the 1970s before embarking on a thirty-year-plus career as a prime-time anchor in Washington, DC.

And those were just the women. As noted, early *Say Brother* pioneers Stan Lathan and Topper Carew graduated to prolific Hollywood careers, with Carew creating the sitcom *Martin,* the feature film *D.C. Cab,* and many other productions, and Lathan directing and producing the *Def Comedy Jam* and Dave Chappelle specials, along with the series *Moesha, The Steve Harvey Show, Real Husbands of Hollywood,* and many others. He is also the father of actress Sanaa Lathan.

Ron Allen of WCVB went national as a correspondent for NBC News, and WBZ's Hampton Pearson began a two-decade-plus career at CNBC in 1995.

The *Boston Globe's* premiere long-form writer, Wil Haygood, joined the *Washington Post* and received widespread acclaim for his articles and for his book, *The Butler: A Witness to History,* the basis for a major motion picture.

Greg Moore, the *Globe* metro editor who rose to managing editor, became one of very few blacks to hold the top editor spot at a US daily (there are typically fewer than a dozen at any one time out of about one thousand papers) when he took the reins of the *Denver Post,* leading it to multiple Pulitzer Prizes. He also chaired the Pulitzer board.

After seventeen years in Boston, Robin Washington similarly took the top spot in the newsroom of the *Duluth News Tribune,* garnering more national awards for that paper than all before combined in its history. He returned to Boston media after leaving the Minnesota paper, previously having worked for the *Banner,* the *Herald,* and "every station except Channel 7"—a joke he shared with Carmen Fields, whose credits included the *Globe*, co-anchor of WGBH's *The 10 O'Clock News* and every station except Channel 5.

Lovell Dyett bested them both by completely hitting for the Boston network affiliate cycle, notably as a longtime anchor at Channel 7 and host of its unapologetic *Black News*. His mellifluous voice was even better known as a thirty-year-plus talk show host on WBZ-AM.

Maurice Lewis was an Armed Forces Radio veteran who also became a Channel 7 anchor and presence on multiple Boston frequencies before eventually anchoring TV news in Chattanooga.

Likely the first black anchor in Boston if not nationally was Terry Carter, a Brooklyn, New York, native and Northeastern University grad who already had television acting credits on his resume by the time he joined WBZ in 1965. He held Channel 4's big chair until 1968, afterward concentrating fully on Hollywood with veritable roles such as Sgt. Joe Broadhurst on *McCloud* and Colonel Tigh on *Battlestar Galactica*.

Black broadcast talent who made Boston the mainstay of careers of twenty years or more include Cross and her Channel 5 colleagues Karen Holmes Ward, Jim Boyd, and Rhondella Richardson; Delores Handy of Channel 7 and WBUR; Lester Strong, Garry Armstrong, and Byron Barnett of Channel 7; and WBZ's Charlie Austin and Walt Sanders, who Sarah-Ann Shaw notes preceded her at the station in the class of '68.

Standard-bearers in Boston sports broadcasting include AM local stars Coach Willie Maye of WILD and Jimmy Myers of WBZ, WEEI, and WTKK. Reaching a decidedly different listenership, Callie Crossley is host of WGBH-FM's *Under the Radar*, capping a longtime affiliation with the TV side of the public broadcasting powerhouse as well as a national producer for ABC News based in Boston. She was also the Academy Award-nominated producer of two documentaries in the first *Eyes on the Prize* series. Tessil Collins first hit WBZ's airwaves as a college student in the 1970s, still producing radio at WGBH forty years later.

Behind the scenes are numerous producers, techs, and camera people, three of whom were honored by the BABJ the year before the gala toasting the women anchors: Richard Chase of WBZ, Bob Wilson of WCVB, and Thurman Toon of then-WNEV. Others on the front lines of news stories were WGBH's Dasal Banks, widely recognized as gifted and later plying his trade as a successful freelancer in Hollywood; and Alex Washington. Wesley Williams began as a film processor, then film editor at Channel 7 before being trained as a cameraman. Ralph Griswold was a cameraman at WBZ before moving for twenty-plus years at WFXT.

Channel 7's Victoria Jones was a longtime producer of news and public affairs, including *Urban Update*. Barbara Barrow-Murray, Beth Deare, Calvin Lindsay, and Marita Rivero accounted for decades of leadership at *Say Brother,* with Rivero later becoming WGBH's general manager of radio and television. Bob Glover helped create and run children's programming and other shows at Channels 2 and 7. June Cross was a producer for WGBH who worked at CBS News and later executive-produced acclaimed national documentaries.

In print, George Forsythe was a fixture at the *Boston Herald* and its then-sister papers in the 1960s and '70s (with one writing project culminating in the muckraking documentary *Titicut Follies.*) Much later at the *Herald,* Leonard Green would have the distinction of being a columnist with two separate tours of duty before doing the same for the *New York Post. Banner* alum Gus Martins became a longtime pro soccer writer on the *Herald's* sports staff. The *Herald* in 2015 named Zuri Berry a deputy managing editor, likely the highest ranking African American in the paper's history.

As an active participant in the American Society of News Editors' call for newsroom racial parity by the year 2000 (later revised to 2025 when that goal fell pitifully short), as well as leadership in the Boston Community Media Committee, the *Globe* posted far more impressive numbers. Derrick Jackson's opinion page column, a Pulitzer finalist and winner of numerous NABJ awards, has run for more than three decades. Adrian Walker has matched that tenure in the metro section, picking up a black columnist slot, if all but unofficial, previously penned by Bob Jordan and Dexter Eure, a *Globe* circulation employee recruited for the newsroom as part of the class of '68. Larry Whiteside was a baseball writer and the first African American beat writer to receive the prestigious J. G. Taylor Spink Award from the Baseball Writers' Association of America. A black voice was the ultimate arbiter of Boston society dos and don'ts with John Robinson holding down that beat for many years.

Ken Cooper, a coauthor of the *Globe's* Pulitzer Prize winning series on race in 1984, left for the *Washington Post* but returned to Boston, writing for the *Banner* and producing for WGBH radio. Renee Graham is a longtime opinion writer. Glenda Beuel was the letters editor for many years. Michael Frisby similarly went to the *Washington Post* after a notable career at the *Globe*.

Behind the scenes, Paula Bouknight is an assistant managing editor and the newsroom recruiter. Bonnie Foust is a veteran sports copy editor. Copy editor Michelle Johnson became one of the creators of boston.com, ushering the *Globe* into the then-new World Wide Web. She later turned to academia as a journalism professor at Boston University.

Then there is the *Banner*. At a regional NABJ conference in Springfield in the early 1990s, publisher Melvin Miller, accepting an honor from the group, asked everyone in the room who had ever worked for or contributed to the *Banner* to stand—and at least two-thirds of the sixty or so present rose. Many of that alumni are mentioned above, including Ifill, Ellis, Cross, Washington, Banks, and Martins. Others no less notable include Steve Curwood, an early *Banner* managing editor who later created and hosts the long-running Public Radio International show *Living on Earth*; Brent Staples, who took the unusual path from the *Globe* to the *Banner*; Yawu Miller; and photographer Don West.

With Miller attesting that "the *Banner* has always been an equal opportunity employer," its roster has included white and other non-black journalists dedicated to documenting an accurate portrait of

African Americans. Those include arts writer Kay Bourne, who was the *Banner's* longest-standing employee and whose archive of Boston's black arts scene is nothing short of a historic treasure trove; Brian O'Connor, one of the *Banner's* longest-serving and prolific managing editors; and Miller's wife, Sandra Casagrand, who has guided the newspaper, if not saved it in economically trying times, as copublisher and creator of niche products.

As stated earlier, it is futile to attempt listing them all. But it's also impossible to imagine news coverage in Boston without these trailblazers, or the contributions of any one generation without the influences who came before.

Indeed, the venerable Old South Church, which prides itself on creating nothing short of the United States of America out of "a dispute between the deacons of Old South and the King," has sought in recent years both to atone for its acquiescence to slaveholding among its seventeenth- and eighteenth-century congregants and to pay homage to its black forebears. Phillis Wheatley was a devout attendee whose worship had to be granted permission by her owner. Yet she persevered and mastered the skills of a nascent communications industry, putting "pen and parchment—to great effect," the Reverend Nancy S. Taylor said in honoring the poet at the church's Phillis Wheatley Sunday in 2016. Also being lauded that day and connected to that history was Sarah-Ann Shaw, who used "the medium of her day—television—to equally great effect," Taylor said.

Echoing over three hundred years, that great effect endures.

9

Boston's Early Years
Anthony W. Neal

Efforts to Thrive in Revolutionary Times

Africans first arrived in Boston on December 12, 1638, when the slave ship *Desire* landed on its shores from Providence Island in the Bahamas.[633] They were purchased as slaves by people in Boston. In colonial Massachusetts the black population rose from 295 in 1650 to 2,150 by 1720. In the 1780s enslaved blacks in Massachusetts brought so-called "freedom suits' against their owners to gain their liberty. African Americans such as Prince Boston, Juno Larcom-Thistle, Elizabeth "Mum Bett" Freeman, and Quock Walker successfully sued their masters for their freedom. In their lawsuits, Freeman, and later Walker, claimed that their enslavement was incompatible with the Massachusetts Constitution, which had been ratified in 1780. Article I of that Constitution declared that "all men are born free and equal." The 1783 finding in the Quock Walker case was considered to have implicitly abolished slavery in Massachusetts.[634] In fact, by the 1790 US Census, no slaves were found residing in the state.

Even before American independence, enslaved blacks seemed to believe that the ouster of the British would improve their state. Crispus

Attucks, in a confrontation he had led against British troops, became the first martyr of the American Revolution on March 5, 1770. As historians James and Lois Horton noted, "When the Revolution began, African Americans from Boston and elsewhere in the commonwealth immediately joined in the struggle for independence."[635] At the Battle of Bunker Hill on March 17, 1775, black Minuteman Peter Salem from Framingham was the first to kill a British officer, Major Pitcairn.[636] On April 19, 1775, Prince Estabrook, an enslaved black man and a Minuteman private who lived in Lexington, Massachusetts, was the first black patriot wounded on Lexington Green during the Battle of Lexington and Concord, the first official battle of the American Revolution.[637] Colonel George Middleton led the Bucks of America, an all-black military unit, during the American Revolution. Indeed, about twelve hundred African American troops from Massachusetts served in the American Revolutionary War.

The Right to Vote

In 1781, the black man's right to vote was established in Massachusetts by the proceedings of Paul Cuffee and his brother John. The country's first prominent black entrepreneur, Paul Cuffee made his fortune as a successful whaler, shipbuilder, and ship owner. When he and his brother were asked by the Town of Dartmouth to pay a personal tax, they objected, arguing that since they were not allowed to vote, they should not be required to pay taxes. They petitioned the selectmen of the town to determine whether "all free negroes and mulattos shall have the same privileges in this said Town … as the white people have." After much discussion, the town authorities conceded that taxpaying and the privilege of voting should go together.[638]

The Antislavery Movement

Some of the earliest free black communities were established in Boston. Before the Civil War, the city was one of the hotbeds of antislavery activism. Many black citizens of Boston figured prominently in the crusade to end slavery in the United States. In fact, many of the Hub's abolitionists were African Americans. The most prominent were David Walker; William Cooper Nell; Lewis Hayden and his wife, Harriet; Charles Lenox Redmond and his wife, Sarah; Edwin Garrison Walker; Robert Morris; and John S. Rock.

In 1829, David Walker, one of Boston's most outspoken critics of American slavery, wrote the seminal book *Appeal to the Coloured Citizens of the World*. In his incendiary publication, he exhorted enslaved black men to rise up and fight "in the glorious and heavenly cause of freedom."[639] Walker's book had a major influence on abolitionists during the three decades immediately following its release. One year after the book's release, William Lloyd Garrison formed the New England Anti-Slavery Society in Massachusetts. In 1842, federal marshals captured fugitive slave George Latimer in Boston. Local abolitionists raised funds to purchase his freedom. In 1849, fugitive slaves William and Ellen Craft, disguised as an enslaved manservant and a white male, respectively, escaped slavery in Georgia and settled down in Boston.

With Benjamin Weeden and others, William Cooper Nell established the New England Freedom Association in 1843. In 1850, it merged with the Boston Vigilance Committee, whose purpose was to assist fugitive slaves after the passage of the Fugitive Slave Act of 1850. Targeted by the act, countless escaped slaves who passed through Boston found refuge at Lewis Hayden's residence, 66 Southac Street.

While working as a waiter at the Cornhill Coffee House on February 15, 1851, Shadrach Minkins, an escaped slave from Norfolk, Virginia, was captured by a US deputy marshal under the Fugitive Slave Act, and held at the US Courthouse. Members of the Boston Vigilance Committee led by Lewis Hayden stormed the courthouse, rescued Minkins, and helped him escape to Canada. In May of 1854 in Boston, US deputy marshals took into custody Anthony Burns, an alleged fugitive from the "service and labor" of Charles F. Suttle, a merchant of Alexandria, Virginia. After a large local crowd made an unsuccessful attempt to rescue him from the courthouse, he was returned to slavery after a trial.

Outstanding Achievements in Public Office
Remarkable State Representatives

Black participation in Boston's electoral politics between 1866 and 1946 resulted in the election of fifteen African American representatives to the Massachusetts State House. The first black men elected were Edwin Garrison Walker, the son of abolitionist David Walker, and Civil War veteran Charles Lewis Mitchell. On November 6, 1866, Charlestown residents of Ward 3 elected Walker to the Massachusetts General Court as a Republican.[640] That same day, Boston residents of Ward 6 cast 837 votes for Mitchell, picking him for state representative as well.[641]

Walker passed the bar examination in May 1861, becoming the fourth African American to gain admission to the Suffolk Bar. As a state representative, he gained a considerable reputation as an able debater and eloquent orator, invariably commanding the respect and attention of his colleagues.[642] He not only championed women's suffrage, but he was also part of a small minority who had voted against ratification of the Fourteenth Amendment to the US Constitution, believing that it fell far short of guaranteeing African Americans full citizenship rights. To Walker, full citizenship meant being politically vested, so he preferred an amendment that affirmatively prohibited the disfranchisement of any citizen based on color.[643] He eventually became an independent and, throughout his life, was a fearless and outspoken advocate on behalf of African Americans.

As a Republican, George Lewis Ruffin was elected to his first of two terms in the Massachusetts Legislature by residents of Boston's Ward 6 on November 2, 1869, making him the fourth African American elected to that body.[644] He would also become the first African American graduate of Harvard Law School, in 1869, the first elected to the Boston Common Council on December 14, 1875, and—years later on November 19, 1883, when he was confirmed as a judge on Charlestown Municipal Court—first African American north of the Mason-Dixon Line to hold a judicial office higher than magistrate.[645]

On November 7, 1882, Boston's Ward 9 elected Republican Julius Caesar Chapelle to the State House. He served from 1883 through 1886.[646] In 1885, he introduced a bill to amend the state's public accommodations law, adding skating rinks to the list of places where racial discrimination was prohibited.[647] Residents of Ward 9 elected Republican William Oscar Armstrong state representative on November 2, 1886. He served for two years.[648] Armstrong introduced and carried through a bill in 1887 appropriating $10,000 to erect a monument to Crispus Attucks on the Boston Common. Before that, on December 9, 1884, he was elected to the Boston Common Council, where he served two successive one-year terms.[649] Elected on November 7, 1893, Republican Robert Thomas Teamoh, a reporter for the *Boston Globe*, served two years as state representative.[650] During that time, he introduced and passed legislation further amending and strengthening the state's public accommodations law.[651]

Representing the Fifth Middlesex District as a Republican, William Henry Lewis, another Harvard-educated lawyer, served in the State House and as a member of its judiciary committee in 1902.[652] In his reelection bid on November 4 that year, however, he was defeated by Democrat Frederick S. Dietrick by a narrow margin of 134 votes.[653] That loss not only signified a personal defeat for Lewis; it marked the beginning of a four-decades-long absence of black representation in the State House, as no African American would serve again until 1947. He was Republican Laurence Harold Banks of Roxbury, who won in the Ninth Suffolk District on November 5, 1946, defeating Democratic Representative Dennis P. Glynn, 4,656 votes to 3,944 votes.[654]

The First Aldermen

Harvard-trained attorney Clement Garnett Morgan, a scholar, inspirational speaker, and civil rights leader, became the first African

American elected to the Cambridge Board of Aldermen on December 15, 1896. In fact, he is believed to be the first black alderman elected in any city north of the Mason-Dixon Line and east of the Mississippi.[655] Morgan was also the first African American elected to the Cambridge Common Council. He was elected on December 11, 1894, and served two consecutive one-year terms.[656]

Captain William James Williams, another Harvard-educated lawyer, crossed the color line on December 1, 1900, becoming the first African American elected to the Chelsea Board of Aldermen.[657] He served successive terms as alderman and alderman-at-large from 1901 until the Great Chelsea Fire of 1908. He provided crucial leadership during that chaotic period, opening the doors of his home and taking in many of the city's black residents. Williams served consecutive terms as alderman and alderman-at-large in Chelsea again from 1912 to 1919.[658]

The First Black School Committee Members

Prior to 1977, two African Americans served on the Boston School Committee.[659] The first was Harvard Medical School honors graduate Dr. James Thomas Still, who was elected as a Republican to a three-year term on December 15, 1874.[660] The second was Harvard Medical School graduate and obstetrician Dr. Samuel Edward Courtney. He was elected as a Republican to a one-year term on December 15, 1896, and reelected to a three-year term the following year.[661]

Other Public Sector Positions of Honor

In addition to elected office, African Americans in Boston actively sought appointed positions in local, state, and national government. Acting on Booker T. Washington's recommendation, President Theodore Roosevelt directed Henry P. Moulton, US attorney of Boston, to appoint outstanding criminal lawyer William Henry Lewis third assistant US attorney in January 1903, making him the first African American to hold that position.[662] In October 1910, President William Howard Taft announced Lewis's nomination as the first African American assistant attorney general of the United States—the highest office in the executive branch of government offered to any black man at that time.[663] Despite strong opposition from southern senators, his nomination was confirmed on June 14, 1911.[664] The *Boston Globe* called Lewis "one of the most important lawyers in the United States."[665]

Appointed by Mayor James Michael Curley on December 24, 1917, North Carolina-born Lucius Sumner Hicks—an honors graduate of Boston Latin School who attended Harvard and acquired a bachelor of laws degree from Boston University School of Law in 1908—became the first African American to serve as assistant corporation counsel for the Law Department of the City of Boston.[666]

A popular athlete in both high school and college, Matthew Washington Bullock, a Dartmouth College graduate and Harvard-trained attorney, served as a college football coach, a college professor and administrator at what is now Morehouse College, special assistant attorney general for Massachusetts, and the first black chairman of the Massachusetts Board of Parole and Advisory Board of Pardons. In 1924, Attorney General Jay R. Benton tapped Bullock as special assistant attorney general for Massachusetts, where he was responsible for assisting the Metropolitan District Commission in performing any legal work that arose out of the construction of the Northern Artery—a highway running from Boston to Somerville's Wellington Bridge.[667] In 1927, Governor Alvan T. Fuller appointed him to the Massachusetts Board of Parole and Advisory Board of Pardons.[668] Succeeding governors reappointed him to the Board of Parole on which he served until 1936, when he was named division director of the Department of Correction—a six-year appointment.[669] Bullock returned to the parole board in 1943. The following year, Governor Leverett Saltonstall appointed him parole board chairman for a five-year term at an annual salary of $9,000, making him the first black man to serve as chairman and, likely, the highest paid one in public service in Massachusetts at that time.[670] As a parole board member, Bullock promoted reasonable prison reform, advocating a policy of separating adult convicts from juveniles, and urging a policy of preparing prisoners for release as the major objective of all correctional institutions.[671]

The eldest son of noted attorney James Harris Wolff, James Graham Wolff, a graduate of Boston Latin School and Harvard College, became a prominent lawyer in the Hub, working in the Suffolk County District Attorney's Office for sixteen years, serving as assistant corporation counsel for the Law Department of the City of Boston from 1930 to 1934, and serving as assistant attorney general for the Commonwealth of Massachusetts from 1949 to 1953.[672]

In 1931, Governor Joseph B. Ely appointed African American John T. Lane, a graduate of Suffolk University Law School,[673] clerk of the Boston Juvenile Court, where he served for twenty-nine years.[674] A recognized authority on penology, Lane authored several bills relating to juvenile delinquency, some of which were enacted.[675] In 1959, Governor Foster Furcolo appointed him to the Massachusetts Board of Parole, and Governor Endicott Peabody reappointed him in 1964.[676] Lane also served as president of the Boston chapter of the NAACP.

Outstanding Civil Rights Leaders

William Monroe Trotter was the leading civil rights advocate in Boston at the dawn of the twentieth century. He was born April 7, 1872, in Chillicothe, Ohio. His parents, James Monroe Trotter and Virginia Isaacs Trotter, moved to Boston when he was just seven weeks old. In 1890, he graduated from Hyde Park High School with honors and was unanimously chosen valedictorian of his class.[677] The first African American Phi Beta Kappa graduate of Harvard University, Trotter received his bachelor's degree magna cum laude in 1895 and his master of arts degree in 1896.[678] Three years later, on June 27, 1899, he married Geraldine Louise Pindell, and they moved into a two-story wood frame home at 97 Sawyer Avenue in Dorchester. On November

9, 1901, Trotter and George Washington Forbes, an Amherst College graduate, first published the *Boston Guardian*, a weekly paper that advocated social equality and full citizenship rights for black people. The major civil rights publication of its time, the *Guardian* acted as a watchdog, reporting acts of lynching and discrimination against African Americans throughout the country. Trotter demanded fair play and that unrestricted opportunity in America be afforded to black and white men alike. With Archibald Grimké, he founded the Boston Literary and Historical Association in 1901 "to promote the intellectual life of the community."[679] He established the Boston Equal Rights League as well and was a founding member of the Niagara Movement and one of the early organizers of the Boston branch of the NAACP. A staunch opponent of segregation and discrimination, for years he championed the civil rights of all African Americans. Trotter claimed that he was not a personal enemy of black leader Booker T. Washington, but a "political enemy." He said that Washington was doing great work in Alabama, but that he ought to stay there and not interfere with politics in the North and endeavor to lead black people politically. He believed that Washington had been trying to control all the political appointments for blacks through President Taft, and if Washington had gotten out of politics most black northerners would have backed him in his work.[680]

Trotter was a persistent critic of President Woodrow Wilson as well. Leading a delegation of the National Independence Equal Rights League on November 12, 1914, he met Wilson at the White House. Though the meeting was scheduled for fifteen minutes, it lasted nearly an hour. Trotter told the president that he found fault with his administration's policy of segregating white and black civil service employees in government departments.

Trotter published the *Guardian* until his death on April 7, 1934. His sister, Maude Trotter Steward—a Wellesley College graduate who cofounded and became president of St. Mark Musical and Literary Union, and who had served as associate editor of the *Guardian*—took over the paper, along with her husband, Dr. Charles "Doc" Steward, a dentist. She published it until 1955.[681] The paper ceased publication with the death of Dr. Steward in 1967.

Outstanding Achievements in Businesses

Early Successful Businesspeople

Born in 1819, Joseph Scarlett was said to be more affluent than any other black citizen of Boston, and he made it sweeping chimneys in the 1840s and 1850s. Having inherited the chimney-sweeping business from his father, John E. Scarlett, who owned a shop at 40 Brattle Street in the West End,[682] Joseph Scarlett had a monopoly in that line of work for many years. He invested thousands of dollars of his earnings in real estate.[683] Scarlett, who understood his value as chimney sweep, once said, "If a man doesn't know what he's worth, he will never get it."[684] He owned considerable property in Boston, Cambridge, Chelsea, and Charlestown, valued collectively at $40,800. Scarlett died on October 14, 1898. In his will, he left bequests to the North Russell AME Zion Church and the Home for Aged Colored Women.

Born a slave in 1811 in Smithfield, Virginia, abolitionist and philanthropist Nathaniel Springfield was one of the most affluent black men in Boston. He escaped from slavery and fled north, first to New Bedford, then on to Boston in 1846. Initially a blacksmith, he learned the straw business from a man named Peter Smith and eventually purchased the business from him. Though not an educated man, Springfield peddled straw by the bundle and, by thrift, invested his savings in real estate and accumulated property valued at between $70,000 and $80,000.[685] He died in 1896. In his will, he left bequests to the Home for Aged Colored Women, the Charles Street AME Church, St. Paul's Baptist Church, and the Twelfth Baptist Church, where he served as a deacon.[686]

As a young woman, Christiana Carteaux Banister, known professionally as "Madame Carteaux," moved from Rhode Island to Boston, where she embarked on a career as a wigmaker and hairdresser. By the 1850s, she owned a successful chain of beauty shops in Boston and Providence. She and her husband, Edward Mitchell Banister, a hairdresser and award-winning landscape artist, were active in the abolitionist movement and supported the formation of the famed Fifty-Fourth Massachusetts Regiment during the Civil War.

Joshua Bowen Smith of Cambridge entered the catering business around 1850 and became an excellent caterer—one of the most noted in the country. He continued catering until his death in 1882. In the 1860s, he became owner of an elegant building on Bulfinch Street. He also served as a state representative in 1873 and 1874.

Makers of Wigs and Hair Products

Born in 1853 in Petersburg, Virginia, Gilbert C. Harris, the Hub's most successful wigmaker, moved to Boston in 1876 and found employment at a hair products store. After learning as much as he could over the next fourteen years about the hair products business, with a capital outlay of $38, he launched Gilbert & Company at 732 Washington Street. Each year, Harris's hair products company stocked goods valued from $6,000 to $8,000.[687] He offered theatrical and street wigs for sale and to let, ready-made and to order, and cleaned and dressed them as well.[688] Before long, his company would provide wigs to theatrical groups all over the United States. One of the best wigmakers of his time, Harris owned the largest wig and toupee manufacturing business in New England by 1910.

Madam Mary L. Johnson, a wigmaker, "scientific scalp specialist and hair culturist," and her husband, Dr. W. Alexander Johnson, founded the Johnson Manufacturing Company in 1899.[689] They sold their hair goods and toiletries out of Johnson's Hair Store at 798 Tremont Street. Distributed all over the United States since 1900, the "famous Johnson Hair Food" was touted as "the most scientific pomade yet discovered for growing, beautifying and softening the hair."[690] In addition to their hair products outfit, they operated the Johnson School of Beauty Culture, where they offered a variety of services, including manicuring, shampooing, scalp massage, facial massage, hairdressing, and scalp treatment. The school's graduating class of 1915 consisted of seventeen young black women, each engaged in her profession and doing well.[691]

Madam L. C. Parrish, a hair culturist, started a wig-making and hair-weaving trade for black women in Boston.[692] She manufactured scalp and hair products and operated a beauty school for more than seventeen years at 95 Camden Street.[693]

Noteworthy Tailors and Dressmakers

At the close of the nineteenth century, the most successful African American tailor in Boston was John Henry Lewis. Born in 1847 in Heathsville, North Carolina, to slave parents Anna and John H. Lewis, he made his way to Boston and, in the 1870s, became one of the city's most noted clothiers. Known for his "bell trousers," Lewis owned a clothing store on Washington Street for more than thirty years. He had become wealthy by 1896 primarily because affluent customers, black and white, had patronized his establishment. Revealing how he succeeded in business, Lewis said, "If you produce what someone wants, he never questions who the maker is. He will buy. I have found during my 20 years of business that to succeed in business you must have the ability to turn out good work. You must have industry, pluck and common sense."[694]

Mrs. Phoebe Ann Glover, a dress designer and dressmaker, was one of Boston's more affluent black women. Born Phoebe Ann Whitehurst, likely around 1841 in Norfolk, Virginia, she was the daughter of Martha and Edward Whitehurst.[695] With her younger sister, Hester, and brother, Manuel, she moved to Boston to live with her uncle, Coffin Pitts, a clothing dealer who owned a shop at 36 Brattle Street. Around 1873, Glover opened a dressmaking shop at 31 Winter Street. According to her daughter, Georgiene, the volume of her dressmaking business allowed her to employ as many as thirty-five women during the busy season.[696] In 1907, Glover moved her shop to

418 Newbury Street in Boston's Back Bay, where it remained until her death in 1916.[697]

News Dealers

In the late nineteenth century, James R. Hamm formed what would become one of the oldest news dealer companies in Boston. He first traveled to the Hub in 1879 but soon left for New York City and gained experience in the news dealer field. Hamm returned to Boston in 1884. Three years later, with $800 to start his newsstand company, he bought out a run-down business for its inventory and established James R. Hamm & Company—an outlet that sold newspapers, books, periodicals, stationery, and small wares. Over a six-year period, Hamm's annual sales increased, requiring him in 1893 to move his business from 71 Cornhill to 46 Howard Street in the West End. There it remained for more than twenty-five years.[698] A Boston correspondent for the *New York Age* reported that Hamm's "display of magazines, newspapers, popular novels and other goods" was "as good as any shop of the sort in that section of the city." Everything in his store was systematically arranged, and with a roster of devoted customers, he did in excess of $10,000 a year in business. By 1907, Hamm enjoyed the distinction of having the oldest business of its kind in the West End.[699]

Morticians

At the dawn of the twentieth century, Basil F. Hutchins, a National Negro Business League member, operated a funeral home equaled by few others—a large elegant building, located at 797–99 Tremont Street and equipped with a chapel, showroom, morgue, and every modern convenience. Hutchins advised, "In case of death anywhere, call upon us to arrange your affairs."[700] He was one of the leading black property owners of his day.

Undertaker Benjamin F. Jones arranged funerals at 639 Shawmut

Avenue for as low as $65. He urged potential customers not to "make arrangements until you see our $65-funerals." Jones opined, "We furnish funerals as low, if not lower, than any other undertaker in Boston."[701]

Hoteliers

In the late nineteenth century Joseph Lee became one of the most-talked-about hotel proprietors and restaurateurs in New England. In 1880, he started managing boarding houses and ran them well.[702] Two years later, he leased the Woodland Park Hotel, a summer inn standing in the middle of a sand bank on the corner of Washington Street and Woodland Avenue in Auburndale—one of the villages of Newton.[703] A man of business acumen and ambition, Lee saved his money, purchased the hotel in 1883, built additions to it, and enlarged and beautified the grounds. His investment in the Woodland Park Hotel must have become profitable by 1886 as that year the *Boston Daily Advertiser* listed him as one of "Newton's rich men"—among the town's large taxpayers.[704] He paid an annual tax of over $1,000 on property valued at $75,000.[705] Open to visitors throughout the year, the elegant guest house provided unrivaled facilities for hosting class suppers, dinner parties, and other social functions. During this time, Lee owned the Abbotsford as well, a top-quality hotel at 186 Commonwealth Avenue in Boston.[706] Indeed, the *Advertiser* reported that the proprietor "proved himself one of the most successful and pleasing hotel men in New England."[707] In 1898, Joseph Lee opened the Squantum Inn, a summer resort at Squantum Park, located at the end of the Quincy & Boston Electric Railroad in Squantum—a coastal neighborhood in the northernmost section of Quincy, Massachusetts.[708] Boston Mayor Thomas Hart, Governor John Bates, and Massachusetts State House representatives were among the inn's regular diners. Also an inventor, Lee acquired US patent no. 524,042 for a dough-kneading machine in 1894 and secured US patent no. 540,553 for a bread crumbing machine in 1895.

In 1915, Reddick James Royster, a native North Carolinian, was the proprietor of the Hotel Melbourne—an elegantly furnished establishment at 805 Tremont Street.[709] He was a barber, real estate broker, and notary public as well.[710]

Bankers

Attorney David Eugene Crawford is best known for establishing what was at that time the only black-owned bank in the Northeast. In 1910, with $100,000 of capital, he founded the Eureka Co-Operative Bank at 930 Tremont Street in Lower Roxbury and served as its secretary, treasurer, and largest stockholder.[711] By November 1911, African Americans had deposited $50,000 in the bank—a considerable sum back then.[712]

Finding that some of Boston's banks had discriminated against African Americans, attorney and philanthropist Edgar Pinkerton Benjamin and others successfully petitioned for a bank charter. And in November 1921, at 806 Tremont Street, Benjamin established the South End Cooperative Bank, of which he became founding president. Under his unfaltering leadership, nearly seventy-five bank customers received assistance in buying their own homes by 1927, and approximately three hundred African Americans were put on the road to independence through thrift and regular savings. According to a local newspaper report, the South End Cooperative Bank had grown "from a beginning of thirty depositors" to "more than three hundred, with a total balance of approximately $150,000 accumulated through regular monthly deposits averaging $5 for each member of the bank."[713]

Born in Grenada, British West Indies, Nathaniel Theodore Julien, a clerk and stenographer, immigrated to the United States with his wife, Mary, in 1922, and, with members of St. Cyprian's Episcopal Church, he founded the Boston Progressive Credit Union (BPCU) in 1929.[714] With more than three thousand largely West Indian members and $500,000 in its treasury, the BPCU opened a new bank building at 1079 Tremont Street in April 1953.[715] The successfully run

$2.1 million credit union was acquired by the Home Savings Bank of Boston on January 1, 1981.[716]

Real Estate Investors and Brokers

At the turn of the twentieth century, Jesse Goode Associates, also known as the Jesse Goode Real Estate Trust—a group of about twenty black men, most of them waiters—pooled their savings and invested in real estate. They took title to property located at 27 and 31 Windsor Street in Lower Roxbury and 110 and 112 West Concord Street in the South End.[717]

At 714 Shawmut Avenue, J. Edward Stephens managed the Boston Real Estate Exchange, a company "organized with a view to securing desirable homes for Afro-Americans in and about greater Boston."[718] D. M. Riddick, a real estate and insurance broker, conducted business at 7 Water Street, Boston. The Eureka Realty Company, at 888 Main Street, Cambridge, also bought, sold, and rented real estate.

Outstanding Achievements in the Professions

Noteworthy Lawyers

On May 5, 1845, Macon Bolling Allen became the first African American licensed attorney in Massachusetts. He moved to Charleston, South Carolina, in 1868. In 1847, Robert Morris, an abolitionist and civil rights activist, became the second black licensed lawyer in the state. In 1849, Morris and Charles Sumner challenged the legitimacy of segregated schools in *Sarah C. Roberts v. City of Boston*.[719] They lost the case but a state law integrating schools was signed into law by Governor Henry J. Gardner on April 28, 1855.[720]

Attorney James Harris Wolff served his country honorably during the Civil War and demanded nothing less than full citizenship rights for African Americans.[721] He attended Harvard Law School for two years and gained admission to the Suffolk Bar on June 26, 1875.[722] In

1886, Wolff, Edward Everett Brown, and Edwin G. Walker established the firm of Walker, Wolff & Brown at 46 School Street—the first black law firm in Massachusetts.[723] Wolff, according to Brown, was "a practical, well-read, common sense lawyer, thoroughly conversant with the abstruse problems of commercial law." He also possessed a profound knowledge of constitutional law and, with skill and ability, argued important cases before the Supreme Judicial Court of Massachusetts.[724] In 1891, Wolff served as chairman of the South End Equal Rights Association, which typically met at Equal Rights Hall, 161 West Springfield Street.[725] He also served as vice president and president of the Wendell Phillips Club and was a member of the Crispus Attucks Club. On February 14, 1905, members of the Massachusetts Grand Army of the Republic, a veteran's group whose membership consisted of honorably discharged Civil War veterans of the Union Army, Navy, Marine Corps, and Revenue Cutter Service, elected Wolff department commander. Held at Faneuil Hall during the organization's thirty-ninth annual meeting, the election was the first instance of an African American comrade being chosen to fill the Massachusetts GAR's top post.[726] In 1910, Wolff delivered the Fourth of July Oration at Faneuil Hall. In his address, entitled "The Building of the Republic," he traced the development of American democracy and showed reverence for the country's black soldiers.[727] The *Boston Herald* called him "one of the most prominent Negro lawyers" in Massachusetts.[728]

For more than fifty years, Butler Roland Wilson devoted his time, talent and energy to combating racial discrimination on behalf of African Americans in Massachusetts. He acquired a bachelor of laws degree from Boston University School of Law in 1884.[729] In 1887, Wilson helped establish Boston's Colored National League, of which he became corresponding secretary.[730] That same year, the newly formed West End League of the Massachusetts Woman Suffrage Association elected him its vice president.[731] In 1893, Wilson and then-Harvard-law-student William Henry Lewis were instrumental in lobbying the Massachusetts Legislature to amend the state's public accommodations law, extending its reach in prohibiting racial discrimination to include barbershops and other public places. Wilson was a member of the American Red Cross, and he served on several boards. On January 9, 1900, he was elected auditor and one of the directors of the Home for Aged Colored Women.[732] The lawyer was also secretary of the Harriet Tubman House.[733] In addition to becoming, with Lewis, the first African American members of the American Bar Association on August 27, 1912, Wilson was a member of the Massachusetts Bar Association.[734] He was a charter member and the third president of the Boston Literary and Historical Association,[735] a first grand counselor of the Knights of Pythias, a thirty-third degree Mason, supreme counselor of the Scottish Rite Lodges of America, and an Odd Fellow as well.[736] Wilson possessed rare oratorical gifts, and his reputation as a powerful advocate was well earned.[737] An exceptional attorney, he demonstrated a relentless commitment to performing racial uplift work and often donated his services on behalf of the poor. As an early organizer of the Boston branch of the NAACP, Wilson became the association's first secretary in 1912. In fact, he and his wife, Mary, directed much of its early activity. He and attorney Clement Morgan, working on behalf of the NAACP in 1913, persuaded the board of directors of Boston's YMCA to eliminate its discriminatory swimming pool policy.[738] On November 12, 1914, Wilson marshaled and led a group of black Bostonians to successfully challenge the public schools' use of the book *Forty Best Songs*—a volume of songs containing the words "darkey" and "nigger," compiled by James M. McLaughlin, director of music for the Boston Public Schools.[739] Wilson often spoke publicly on issues of race. For example, on February 15, 1922, at the Franklin Street Congregational Church in Somerville, Massachusetts, he delivered an address titled "The General Race Problem in the Country."[740] In the early 1920s, Wilson became the official president of the Boston branch of the NAACP and served in that capacity until 1936. He was a member of its national board of directors as well.[741] On May 19, 1938, George W. Coleman, president of the Ford Hall Forum, presented Wilson with its gold medal, annually awarded to the Massachusetts citizen who has "rendered prominent service to human welfare."[742] Butler Roland Wilson passed away in Boston at the age of seventy-nine on October 31, 1939, leaving behind three of his six children: his two sons, Butler Jr. and Francis, and his daughter, Lola.[743]

Attorney Edward Everett Brown held leadership positions in several black organizations. He was elected vice president of the Colored National League on January 13, 1891,[744] and reelected to that office on January 17, 1893.[745] Additionally, Brown served as president of both the Wendell Phillips Club and the Crispus Attucks Club in 1899.[746] In 1907, he was appointed assistant health commissioner of Boston, where he headed up the tenement house division, a new department of the Board of Health. He managed a workforce of housing inspectors and prosecuted cases of Boston landlords who failed to maintain sanitary housing conditions.[747] Brown also served as Boston's deputy tax collector in 1912.[748] About him, the *Boston Post* reported, "Mr. Brown's career has been a fortunate one in Boston, and at all times he has been foremost in the educational work here attempted for the benefit of his race."[749]

Attorney and author Archibald Henry Grimké, an 1874 graduate of Harvard Law School—in fact, the second African American graduate—was a civil rights leader and a major intellectual who lived much of his life in Boston. In 1889, he wrote for the weekly paper the *Boston Beacon*. Later, he was a contributing writer on the staffs of the *New England Magazine*, the *Boston Herald* and the *Boston Traveler*.[750] He devoted much of his spare time to literary pursuits. His several works include: *William Lloyd Garrison, the Abolitionist* (1891); *The Life of Charles Sumner, the Scholar in Politics* (1892); *Why Disfranchisement is Bad* (1904).[751] In 1901, Grimké and William Monroe Trotter founded the Boston Literary and Historical Association "to promote the intellectual life of the community." Grimké served as the organization's first president.[752] He also served as US consul to Santo Domingo from 1894 to 1898 and as president of the American Negro Academy from 1903 to 1919. He became vice president of the NAACP in 1916.[753] That organization awarded him the Spingarn Medal in 1919 for his distinguished service as an author, scholar, and president of its Washington, DC, branch.[754]

The son of former slaves, William Louis Reed was elected state representative by residents of Ward Nine on November 5, 1895, and held positions in the Executive Department of the State House during the term of fourteen governors. After leaving the State House, Reed accepted a position as deputy collector of Internal Revenue in June 1898.[755] On December 21, 1899, he was installed as Most Worshipful Grand Master of the Prince Hall Grand Lodge, an office he held until 1902.[756] In 1900, Mayor Thomas N. Hart appointed him deputy tax collector of Boston,[757] and in 1902, Governor Winthrop Crane, a Republican, picked him for executive messenger—a political appointment at the State House. Channing Cox, the outgoing governor of Massachusetts, appointed Reed executive secretary of the Governor's Council on January 7, 1925.[758] When he turned seventy years old, many people expected him to retire from the position. But on April 8, 1936, after obtaining an attorney general opinion that the executive secretary is a public officer and not subject to retirement under state law, the Executive Council unanimously reappointed him to the post. In presenting Reed's name for reappointment, Governor James M. Curley said, "Because of his exemplary conduct and outstanding ability, he has merited and enjoyed not only the goodwill but affection of every governor, regardless of politics."[759] Reed died on February 5, 1943, at the age of 76.[760]

Julian David Rainey, a 1917 graduate of Suffolk Law School, became the second African American lawyer to join the legal staff of the Boston Elevated Railroad Corporation as assistant counsel in 1920.[761] In the fall of 1924, he accepted a one-year appointment as a professor at the Suffolk Law School. Initially a Republican, Rainey left the party to become a Democrat and was named national director of the black division of Alfred E. Smith's 1928 presidential campaign committee.[762] In 1930, Mayor James M. Curley appointed him assistant corporation counsel for the Law Department of the City of Boston, making him the highest-paid black man in public service in all of New England. Employed in that position for four years at an annual salary of $5,000, Rainey defended the city against claims for property damage and personal injury.[763] He also worked as a special attorney in the office of the US attorney general and served as a special adviser to President Franklin D. Roosevelt.[764] On March 6, 1936, Joseph D. McGrath, acting on behalf of the president, chose Rainey as an alternate delegate-at-large to the Democratic National Convention in Philadelphia.[765] About five months later, on July 29, James A. Farley, chairman of the Democratic National Committee, appointed him director of its black division in the East.[766]

Rainey was a staunch proponent of antidiscrimination legislation. In the *Boston Globe* of March 22, 1941, appeared a letter he wrote to the editor, urging Massachusetts Senate Republicans to back a bill prohibiting racial discrimination by hospitals that conduct training schools for nurses. He noted, "Intelligent white people and colored people have signified their desire that this bill shall pass. The Democratic leadership of the Senate has expressed its determination to support this bill. It is now up to the Republicans to show where they stand in the fight against discrimination and intolerance in Massachusetts."[767] On March 13, 1945, Rainey appeared on behalf of the local branch of the NAACP at a Massachusetts legislative hearing and testified in support of a measure prohibiting racial discrimination in employment.[768]

A star athlete at Harvard University, William Clarence Matthews acquired a bachelor's degree from the school in 1904, took graduate courses there the following year, and went on to attend Boston University School of Law, from which he received a bachelor of laws degree in 1907.[769] He gained admission to the Massachusetts Bar on August 21, 1908.[770] Matthews embarked on a successful career in public service. He was appointed athletic instructor for the Boston Public Schools in 1908,[771] special assistant US district attorney in Boston in 1912,[772] chairman of the black division of the Republican National Committee in 1924, and special assistant to the attorney general of the United States in 1925.[773]

John Winfield Schenck, a native of Charlotte, North Carolina, was appointed assistant US attorney in Boston by President Warren

Harding in 1922.[774] In that position, he handled most of the immigration cases in Massachusetts until 1933, having been reappointed by President Coolidge. Schenck was also appointed public administrator for Suffolk County by Republican Governor Charles F. Hurley in 1937, a position he held until his retirement.[775] The *Boston Globe* called him "the dean of Negro lawyers in Boston."[776]

Pioneering Physicians

On May 19, 1849, Dr. John Van Surly DeGrasse acquired his medical degree with honors from the Medical School of Maine at Bowdoin College, becoming the third black graduate of an American medical school.[777] By July 1853, he had established a medical practice at 40 Poplar Street in Boston.[778] He advertised it in the *Liberator*, an antislavery newspaper copublished by William Lloyd Garrison. Having earned a good reputation by his skill and persistent effort, in August 1854, DeGrasse became the first African American in the state to gain admission to the Massachusetts Medical Society. The *Boston Investigator* reported that it was probably the first instance of such an honor being conferred on a black man in the United States.[779] Commenting favorably upon his induction, another local newspaper reported that many of the city's most respected physicians consulted DeGrasse whenever medical advice was needed, and that the Boston medical profession had "done itself honor" in "discarding the law of caste, and generally acknowledging real merit, without regard to the hue of the skin."[780] Governor John A. Andrew commissioned DeGrasse as an assistant surgeon in the Union Army. He was mustered in on May 18, 1863, and mustered out on November 1, 1864. In recognition of his brief service with the Thirty-Fifth in Beaufort, South Carolina, and Jacksonville, Florida, the governor awarded him a gold-hilted sword from the Commonwealth of Massachusetts.[781]

A preeminent mid-nineteenth-century abolitionist, teacher, dentist, doctor, and finally lawyer, Dr. John S. Rock was one of Boston's most eloquent and uncompromising champions of the rights of African

Americans. Rock graduated from the American Medical College in Philadelphia and married Catherine Bowers in 1852. The couple moved to Boston the following year. After Rock set up his medical practice at 86 Cambridge Street, the Boston Vigilance Committee, an integrated abolitionist organization, commissioned him to provide health care to ill fugitive slaves.[782] On the advice of his doctors, Rock gave up his medical practice in 1860 because of deteriorating health. Undaunted, he pursued a legal career. Through perseverance and diligent study, he gained admission to the Suffolk Bar on September 14, 1861, on a motion of Thornton K. Lothrop, making him the fifth African American attorney to practice in the courts of Boston.[783] On February 1, 1865—the day after the House of Representatives passed the Thirteenth Amendment to the Constitution of the United States to abolish slavery—Rock became the first black man to be admitted to practice before the United States Supreme Court.

Dr. Rebecca Crumpler was the first African American woman in the United States to acquire a medical degree. In 1852, she moved from Pennsylvania to Charlestown, Massachusetts, to pursue her passion: working as a nurse. On April 19 that same year, she married Wyatt Lee, a laborer from Prince George County, Virginia.[784] The doctors under whom Rebecca Lee served recommended her to the faculty of the New England Female Medical College (NEFMC) in Boston's South End. Lee enrolled at the NEFMC in 1859 when few blacks were admitted to medical schools.[785] On March 2, 1864, Charles Demond, president of the NEFMC, conferred the degree of "Doctress of Medicine" upon her and two other women.[786]

In 1864, a widowed Rebecca Lee married Arthur Crumpler and practiced medicine briefly in Boston before moving to Richmond, Virginia, where she treated ill freed people through the Freedmen's Bureau. Created by Congress on March 3, 1865, the Freedmen's Bureau provided free health care, education, and technical assistance to emancipated slaves, thereby easing their transition to freedom. Upon returning to Boston in 1869, Dr. Crumpler performed her "work with renewed vigor, practicing outside, and receiving children in the house for treatment; regardless, in the measure, of remuneration."[787] In 1883, she published *A Book of Medical Discourses in Two Parts*, a valuable volume of medical advice written primarily to educate women on the various ways of preventing deadly diseases. It was dedicated to "mothers, nurses, and all who may desire to mitigate the afflictions of the human race."[788] Described in her early sixties as "tall and straight, with light brown skin and gray hair," Crumpler was a "very pleasant and intellectual woman, and an indefatigable church worker."[789] The *Boston Sunday Globe* of July 22, 1894, reported that she was "the one woman who, as a physician, made an enviable place for herself in the ranks of the medical fraternity."[790]

Dr. James Thomas Still, a foremost African American physician, practiced medicine in Boston during the late nineteenth century. He studied chemistry, saved his money and, in 1867, enrolled at Harvard Medical School.[791] Still graduated with honors in 1871, having presented his thesis on hay asthma and hay fever, and he set up a medical practice at 21 Grove Street in Boston.[792] The doctor contributed many articles to medical journals and other publications and wrote one noteworthy book.[793] Published in 1889, his work, *Don't Tell White Folks, or Light Out of Darkness*, was intended to shine light on issues of race.[794] In his book, he advised that black people should be educated "in the best colleges of our country," as he believed that would "spurn true education and elevation." As noted previously, in 1874 he was the first African American elected to the Boston School Committee. From 1877 until 1890, Still served on the board of directors of the Home for Aged Colored Women. He was Boston's most widely known and respected African American physician, and a most skillful one. More for the love of his profession than for what it paid, he attended to sick black Bostonians up until the time of his death in 1895.

Remarkable Physicians

Dr. Augustus Riley served on the faculty of Harvard Medical School for over three decades. He was born November 17, 1878, in Riley,

Alabama.[795] The fourth child of Sarah "Sallie" McCreary, a former slave of mixed race, and Confederate Captain Thomas Mercer Riley Jr., he attended Fisk University one year but took a bachelor's degree from Oberlin College in 1903. After graduating from Harvard Medical School in 1907, he trained for a year at Boston's Long Island Hospital and studied surgery for a year at Massachusetts General Hospital. Riley initially set up his medical practice at 868 Beacon Street.[796]

Beginning his teaching career at Harvard Medical School in 1911, Riley served on its faculty for thirty-five years. He was on the faculty of Tufts and Boston University schools of medicine as well. It was possible for Riley to teach at a time when these medical schools discriminated on the basis of color because when he applied to Harvard, he kept his African ancestry a secret. He identified himself as Caucasian and passed for white.

In 1940, Riley was named head of the Middlesex Medical School in Waltham, Massachusetts, a position he held for two years. He was appointed to the surgical staff of Boston City Hospital and assigned to reorganize the genito-urinary division of its outpatient department. During his career at Boston City, he was in charge of the genito-urinary division and was later made visiting surgeon in urology and chief of urological service. Dr. Riley was a consultant to Boston City Hospital and Mount Auburn Hospital when he retired in 1965.[797] He died on May 17, 1966, leaving behind a daughter, Mrs. Claire Neikirk.

Dr. William Augustus Hinton is noteworthy for developing a test for syphilis and publishing a book on its treatment. Born the son of Maria and Augustus Hinton on December 15, 1883, in Chicago, Illinois, he obtained a bachelor's degree from Harvard College in 1905. Hinton earned the Wigglesworth Scholarship two years in a row and graduated cum laude from Harvard Medical School in 1912.[798] Three years later, he became the director of the Wassermann Laboratory—the Massachusetts state laboratory for communicable diseases, located at Harvard Medical School. There he developed the famous Hinton test for syphilis.[799] In 1936, the Macmillan Company published his textbook, *Syphilis and Its Treatment*. Dr. Hinton died of diabetes on August 8, 1959, in Canton, Massachusetts.

Born in 1879 in Forsyth, Georgia, the son of Taylor and Bathsheba Worthy, Dr. William Worthy earned his medical degree from the Boston College of Physicians and Surgeons in 1908. A year later, he established a medical practice at 676 Shawmut Avenue and subsequently moved it to 239 Northampton Street.[800] Worthy was a member of the Massachusetts Medical Society, the South End Medical Club, and the National Medical Association.[801] In 1916, he served as trustee and treasurer of the Charles Street AME Church.[802] In 1929, Worthy and Dr. Walter O. Taylor, cochairing a committee that included *Boston Guardian* editor William Monroe Trotter, persuaded Boston City Hospital to admit black high school graduates Frances Harris and Letitia Campfield into its nurses' training program.[803] Dr. Worthy died in Boston on May 20, 1954, at the Peter Bent Brigham Hospital, survived by his wife, Mabel; his son, William Worthy Jr.; and his three daughters, Myrtle, Ruth, and Helen.

Elected as a Republican from Ward Eleven to the Boston Common Council on December 13, 1904, Dr. Isaac Lincoln Roberts served three consecutive one-year terms as councilman.[804] After completing his studies at Leonard Medical School, he did postgraduate work at Harvard Medical School in 1911. He set up a practice at 35 Grove Street and served on staff at Massachusetts General Hospital. In 1916, Roberts was installed as Most Worshipful Grand Master of the Prince Hall Grand Lodge, a position he held until 1926—longer than anyone else except John T. Hilton and Prince Hall himself.[805]

After obtaining a bachelor's degree from Livingston College in 1897, a doctor of medicine degree from Leonard Medical School in 1901, and performing postgraduate work in London, Dr. Cornelius N. Garland, an Alabama native, moved to Boston around 1902.[806] Dr. Garland purchased a small building at 12 East Springfield Street in the South End and, on February 25, 1908, formally opened to the public the Plymouth Hospital and Nurse's Training School—a fifteen-bed infirmary managed on a semicooperative plan participated in by local black churches and organizations.[807] He was assisted by Dr. Columbus W. Harrison, who worked as an assistant surgeon at the hospital for ten years,[808] Dr. Benjamin E. Robinson, who conducted a practice at 404 Columbus Avenue, and Dr. Theodore E. A. McCurdy. The local press provided the following description of the medical facility:

> In addition to several wards, there is a nurse's ward, an out-patients' ward, an operating room, and office and a dining room. The wards are named after the church organizations which contributed toward their furnishings, and will continue to maintain them. The wards are to be known as Taborian, Love and Charity, Columbus Avenue AME Zion Church, Emma Spiller, Mt. Hebron, and Charles Street AME Church.[809]

Plymouth Hospital provided essential health care to Boston's African American community and gave black physicians an opportunity to perform clinical work when other hospitals in the city refused to grant them privileges.[810] The hospital also offered nurses of color a training program at a time when they were denied admission to other nursing schools in Boston.[811] Plymouth Hospital closed in 1929, when Boston City Hospital began admitting blacks to its medical and nursing programs.

In 1909, Dr. Garland was elected secretary of the surgical section of the National Medical Association.[812] He was also vice president of the New England Medical, Dental and Pharmaceutical Society.[813] He devoted twenty years of his life to conducting the affairs of Plymouth Hospital while carrying on a successful medical practice.[814] He died in 1952.

Dr. Andrew Berkley Lattimore, who practiced medicine at 28 Warwick Street, is remarkable for serving on the Boston Common Council in 1887 and in the Massachusetts legislature from 1889 to 1890.[815]

Dr. Solomon Carter Fuller, the nation's first black psychiatrist, made significant contributions to Alzheimer's disease research and the development of American psychiatry. He graduated from Livingston College in May 1893, receiving his bachelor's degree with honors. The following year, in March, he headed for Brooklyn, New York, where he attended Long Island College Hospital, working his way through the medical school as a waiter in a boarding house. Later that year, in the fall, Fuller transferred to Boston University School of Medicine. While there, he worked for $4 a week as an elevator operator in a high-rise apartment building on Commonwealth Avenue. He acquired his medical degree in the spring of 1897.[816] After Fuller graduated from medical school, his neurology professor, Dr. Edward P. Colby, impressed with his aptitude, arranged for him to meet with Dr. George Adams, superintendent of the Westborough Insane Hospital,[817] a state facility located thirty-five miles west of Boston, established on June 3, 1884, "for the care and treatment of the insane, upon the principles of medicine known as homeopathic."[818] Dr. Adams immediately hired Fuller as an intern in the hospital's pathology laboratory. He spent most of his time there performing unpleasant work—autopsies—the purpose of which was to collect and analyze tissue sections from deceased mentally ill patients. The Westborough Insane Hospital promoted him to pathologist in 1899. That same year, Boston University School of Medicine appointed Fuller instructor of pathology, making him the first African American to hold such a post at a medical school other than Howard or Meharry.[819] He was best known for two important accomplishments: his contributions to the medical literature in the field of psychiatry and his groundbreaking research on Alzheimer's disease—a degenerative neurological disorder in which memory, judgment, and the ability to reason progressively deteriorate. The doctor published papers in several medical journals, presenting his first, "The Report of Four Cases of Pernicious Anemia in Insane Subjects with a Consideration of the Nervous Sequelae of the Disease," on April 10, 1901, at the sixty-first annual meeting of the Massachusetts

Homeopathic Medical Society.[820] In 1901, the pathologist published his paper in the *New England Medical Gazette*.[821] From November 1904 to August 1905, he performed further research in Germany at the psychiatric clinic of the University of Munich, studying under Professors Alois Alzheimer and Emil Kraepelin, the latter described by some as the father of modern scientific psychiatry.[822] In an effort to improve his skills in analyzing brain tissue and its relation to mental illness, Fuller took courses in pathology and worked in an Alzheimer's lab as a neuropathologist, performing anatomical and histological preparations, followed by microscopic examination of the resulting brain samples.[823]

Fuller served on the staff of Westborough State Hospital forty-five years—twenty-two years as pathologist and twenty-three as consultant—and, for many of those years, edited the *Westborough State Hospital Papers*, a journal reporting the medical research of the hospital's staff.[824] He was a visiting neurologist at Massachusetts Memorial Hospital for eleven years and a consultant neurologist to Massachusetts General Hospital for ten. He was also a consultant to Marlborough Hospital and, for thirty years, remained a consultant to the State Hospital of Allentown, Pennsylvania.[825] In Tuskegee, Alabama, the psychiatrist offered assistance in the development of the Veteran's Administration Hospital, whose aim was to provide medical care to African American veterans in the South. Though Fuller himself did not work at the facility, he helped train its black psychiatry staff.

In 1943, Livingstone College conferred the honorary degree of doctor of science upon Fuller at his fiftieth class reunion and proclaimed him one of the school's outstanding alumni. On January 16, 1953, at the age of eighty, Fuller died of diabetes mellitus and gastrointestinal cancer at Framingham Union Hospital. In recognition of his contributions, in 1974 Boston University, through an act of the Massachusetts Legislature, opened the Dr. Solomon Carter Fuller Mental Health Center—a ten-story building located at 85 East Newton Street in the South End.

Noteworthy Dentists

Originally from Oswego, New York, Dr. George Franklin Grant traveled to Boston to attend Harvard Dental School, where he graduated with distinction in 1870, becoming only the second African American to acquire the degree of doctor of dental medicine.[826] In 1882, he was elected president of the Harvard Dental Alumni Association.[827] Grant was a founding member and later president of the Harvard Odontological Society. An inventor as well, he invented and patented the oblate palate—a prosthetic device that allowed patients to speak more normally. Additionally, on December 12, 1899, he acquired US patent no. 638,920 for his invention of a golf tee.[828] An authority in the field of dentistry, Grant was the first African American employed as a faculty member of Harvard Dental School. From 1871 to 1874, he was an assistant in the Mechanical Department, and from 1875 to 1884, he was a demonstrator in mechanical dentistry. He became an instructor in the treatment of cleft palate and cognate diseases in 1884.[829] Grant set up a dental practice at 86 Pinckney Street in Boston.[830] Charles W. Eliot, president of Harvard University, was one of his private patients. A generous man, Dr. Grant treated patients who were unable to pay for needed dental care, and when they thanked him, as they often did, he would earnestly advise, "Now, don't say anything about it! Do your work as well as you can, and be kind; that will be the best reward you can give me."[831]

Dr. Alfred Pierpont Russell Jr., an active participant in community affairs, practiced dentistry in Boston for nearly sixty years. He was educated at St. Paul Normal and Industrial School in Lawrenceville, Virginia. He acquired a bachelor's degree in 1905 from Howard University and then moved to Boston to attend Harvard Dental School, from which he graduated at the top of his class with a doctorate of dental medicine in 1908.[832] Russell set up a dental practice at 5 Park Square, where he specialized in cleft palate treatment.[833] In 1923, he became the first African American to serve on the visiting staff of Forsyth Dental Infirmary for Children in Boston.[834]

Blazing a trail for black women with a career that spanned decades,

Dr. Jessie Katherine (Gideon) Garnett was the first black woman to graduate from Tufts University School of Dental Medicine and the first to practice dentistry in Boston. She graduated from Girls' High School in 1916 and then attended Tufts College and Tufts University School of Dental Medicine.[835] On June 21, 1920, Tufts University School of Dental Medicine conferred upon her the degree of doctor of dental medicine, making her the first black woman graduate of the dental school. She opened her first dental office at 795 Tremont Street—at the intersection with Camden Street in Lower Roxbury.[836] By 1929, she had relocated with her family to 80 Munroe Street, Roxbury, and built an office behind her residence.[837] Before disabling arthritis in her hands forced her to retire in 1969, Dr. Garnett had practiced dentistry for nearly fifty years. In 1926, she became a charter member of the Psi Omega Chapter of Alpha Kappa Alpha Sorority. She was also a member of the board of Freedom House, a nonprofit community-based organization in the Grove Hall section of Boston, and a member of the NAACP and the Urban League. She served on the boards of the Boston YMCA and St. Mark's Congregational Church in Roxbury as well.

Notable Pharmacists

Robert H. Carter was the first African American certified pharmacist in Massachusetts, the Board of Registration in Pharmacy having certified him on January 5, 1886. He attended New Bedford High School and, as a teenager, worked as a drugstore delivery boy for New Bedford pharmacist William P. S. Caldwell. Impressed with his honesty, Caldwell offered him a two-year apprenticeship in pharmacy. Carter diligently studied a textbook on the compounding of medicines and mastered his trade by the age of twenty-one.[838] From 1876 to 1907, he owned drugstores in New Bedford and Boston.[839] In 1876, Carter established his first drugstore at 135 Purchase Street in New Bedford, and around 1901 he opened an apothecary, Robert H. Carter & Co., at 1443 Tremont Street in Roxbury.[840]

In 1892, Dr. Thomas William Patrick Sr., a man of foresight, energy, and ambition, established the successful Patrick School of Pharmacy at 19 Essex Street in Boston, where he trained about five thousand pharmacy students—most of them white. He operated his school until about 1937.[841] An 1894 graduate of the Boston College of Physicians and Surgeons, Dr. Patrick owned an apothecary at 13 Blossom Street.[842] A member of the National Negro Business League, he presented a paper in August 1903, before its fourth annual conference in Nashville, titled "The Negro in Pharmacy and as Druggist."[843] In 1906, he published, *Patrick's Course in Pharmacy*, and later wrote the book *Essentials of Prescription Compounding*.[844]

In 1913, Dr. William A. Smith, a North Carolina native, established Bay State Pharmacy at 840 Tremont Street. He subsequently incorporated his business, becoming its president and treasurer. Dr. Smith remained at the helm of his company until 1927, when he died.[845] Boston's only black-owned drugstore in 1913, Bay State Pharmacy thrived on Tremont Street for more than thirty years.[846]

The First Black Licensed Nurse

Born in Roxbury on April 16, 1845, to Charles and Mary Jane (Stewart) Mahoney, Mary Eliza Mahoney entered the nursing program of the New England Hospital for Women and Children in Boston on March 23, 1878. She was awarded a diploma on August 1, 1879, becoming the first African American licensed nurse in the United States.[847] After practicing nursing for more than forty years, Mahoney died in Boston on January 4, 1926. In recognition of her outstanding example to nurses of all races, the National Association of Colored Graduate Nurses (NACGN) established the Mary Mahoney Award in 1936. When the NACGN merged with the American Nurses Association in 1951, the award was continued. Mahoney was inducted into the Nursing Hall of Fame in 1976 and the National Women's Hall of Fame in 1993.

The First Black Schoolteachers

Elizabeth N. Smith, the daughter of John J. Smith, was the first African American schoolteacher appointed to a racially integrated school in Boston. She graduated from the Wells School in 1864 as a "City Medal Scholar" and, during the spring and summer term of 1868, enrolled in a teacher training program at the State Normal School at Salem, Massachusetts.[848] From 1869 to 1874, Smith provided instruction at a primary school on Joy Street in the Phillips School District. Years later, from 1894 to 1899, she taught at the Sharp School, a primary school on the corner of Anderson and Pinckney streets. She was active in charitable causes as secretary of the Colored Women's Refuge Aid Society and as treasurer of the benevolent fund of the Female Benevolent Firm—at that time the second oldest club composed exclusively of black women. She also served as vice president of Ruth Circle, a black women's club in Boston that did much to help in the charitable work of the city.[849]

Florida Y. Ruffin, the daughter of Josephine and George L. Ruffin, was the second African American schoolteacher hired by the city.[850] Ruffin graduated from Girls' High School in 1879 and from the Normal School in 1880. The Boston School Board first appointed her special assistant teacher for the Phillips School District on October 12, 1880. It named her instructor on probation on October 25, 1881, and confirmed her as an instructor on January 23, 1883.[851] She taught at the Grant School, a primary school on Phillips Street, from 1881 until 1888, when she married Ulysses Archibald Ridley Jr., a well-known tailor.[852]

Maria Louise Baldwin, a gifted speaker, civic leader, and one of the nation's preeminent educators, was the first black public school teacher and school principal in Cambridge. She attended the Sargent Primary and Allston Grammar schools in Cambridge, subsequently enrolled at Cambridge High School, and passed through its full English course. Baldwin was awarded a diploma in July 1874, becoming one of only two young black women in a graduating class of sixty-seven students.[853] The following year, she successfully completed the Cambridge Teachers' Training School's program of study. On November 16, 1882, the Cambridge School Board held its regular monthly meeting, at which time it selected Baldwin to teach at the Agassiz School,[854] a primary grade school at the corner of Sacramento and Oxford streets.[855] Thanks to her exceptional ability, Baldwin soon ranked high among the teachers in Cambridge.[856] In the autumn of 1889, the board appointed her principal of the Agassiz School, and years later, master, making her one of just two women in the Cambridge Public Schools and the only African American in New England to hold such a post. Baldwin supervised an all-white staff of twelve teachers who were responsible for about five hundred students—almost all of them white.[857] For more than forty years, she served faithfully at the Agassiz School.

Baldwin was the first president of the League of Women for Community Service Inc. (LWCS) as well. Organized under her leadership in 1918 as the Soldiers' Comfort Unit, and headquartered at 428 Massachusetts Avenue in Boston, the LWCS was incorporated in 1920 to undertake charitable, civic, educational, and social work for the benefit of the community.[858] The civic welfare organization purchased the old Farwell estate at 558 Massachusetts Avenue—a station on the Underground Railroad before the Civil War—and formally opened it to the public on March 24, 1920. It established a soup kitchen as the first activity in its new home to avert malnutrition in neighboring school children.[859] Baldwin remained president of the organization until 1922, when she died.

Epilogue

The challenge confronting every African American is to achieve and prosper despite the continuing impediment of racial discrimination. Unfortunately, the general prognosis is for failure. Many of the media reports of black poverty, crime, and social disorder indicate that failure is to be expected. This is a depressing prospect for young blacks preparing to find their role in the world. And it is also discouraging to those who might like to work for social change but are unwilling to spend their efforts on a "lost cause."

There is some relief from the despair with stories of individuals who have overcome the hazards of life as an African American and developed business or professional competence. However, *Boston's Banner Years* is more than accounts of successful black individuals. It is the story of a black neighborhood in Boston, a major city, that has functioned over the years as an effective incubator for talented residents. Numerous creative and productive residents of color have emerged.

It is impractical to attempt to mention all of the achievements by Boston blacks, but since Boston is recognized as the Athens of America, it is appropriate to note several outstanding achievements in academia. The top post in a college is the president. Boston-bred Clifton Wharton Jr. is the first black to be president of a major college. He assumed that post at Michigan State University on January 20, 1970.

In 2017 there are four black college presidents in office in the

Greater Boston area: Dr. Paula Johnson at Wellesley, M. Lee Pelton at Emerson, Deborah C. Jackson at Cambridge College, and Dr. Valerie Roberson at Roxbury Community College. Keith Motley just stepped down as chancellor (equivalent to president) of UMass Boston. Jackie Jenkins Scott left Wheelock last year and Ronald Crutcher moved on from Wheaton College in 2014 after ten years in office. Ted Landsmark also left as president of Boston Architectural College in 2014 after seventeen years of service.

A few outstanding academicians also to be noted are Dr. Adelaide Cromwell, who is now emerita. She helped establish the African Studies Center at Boston University in 1959 before such programs were at all popular at major universities. Another is the late S. Allen Counter, who was a professor at Harvard Medical School and director of the Harvard Foundation for Intercultural and Race Relations; he was also an internationally recognized explorer. And there is Henry Louis Gates Jr., who is a Harvard professor, a literary critic, a prize-winning filmmaker, a public intellectual, and director of Harvard's Hutchins Center for African and African American Research.

Since Massachusetts has the oldest constitution and a historic commitment to the rule of law, some prominent black jurists should be noted. Harry J. Elam became the first black chief justice of the Boston Municipal Court in 1978; Frederick L. Brown became the first black judge on the Massachusetts Court of Appeals in 1976, and Roderick L. Ireland became the first black chief justice of the Massachusetts Supreme Judicial Court in 2010.

Despite the success stories, racial discrimination persists in Boston, and the racial imbalance case that led to busing in public schools has caused Boston to have the reputation as a racially hostile city. There is a growing awareness that in order to become a truly metropolitan city, Boston has to be recognized as essentially devoid of racial bias. In order to attain that state, residents must develop an informed awareness of ethnic groups other than their own. One purpose of *Boston's Banner Years* is to enable readers to have a greater understanding of Boston's African American history and culture.

Education

Many reporters who came to cover Boston's education conflict in the 1960s assumed that the city's public schools had always been segregated as they had been throughout the South. It is remarkable to note their surprise when they learn that Ruth Batson, Mel King, Ellen Jackson, and Melvin Miller all went to racially mixed public schools. None of those old-school Boston students believed that their academic success was enhanced by the presence of white students in the classroom.

Photo credit: Photo by Boston Public Schools
Miss Forsyth's musical ensemble, 1944, sixth grade. Henry L. Higginson School, Roxbury. Miss Forsyth, second row, sixth from left; Melvin Miller, first row, sixth from left; Dan Holgate, third row, third from left, the only member of the ensemble who succeeded in music as an arranger and music director for Broadway musicals.

In the eighteenth century there was a substantial contingent of black families that would just as well have all-black schools rather than endure the insults of biased whites. For a period of time back then, blacks were permitted to attend only designated all-black schools. As many now know, racial integration won the day when the state legislature passed a statute outlawing racial discrimination in the selection of students for a public school. That was in 1855.

For many years when segregation returned, well before Judge Arthur Garrity issued his opinion in *Morgan v. Hennigan* in 1974, the Boston School Committee had been indifferent about their violations of state law. Since no one was aggressively enforcing compliance, it is more than likely that there was little awareness of the breach, especially since the financial penalty amounted to peppercorn in today's dollars.

While those black families in Boston that were interested in local history knew about the Benjamin Roberts case that challenged racial discrimination in Boston schools, many believed that blacks had won the case. The lesson learned was that you win by fighting injustice. Indeed, had Roberts not pressed forward, the legislature would not have acted to change the law. Over time, the concept of taking a stand had become considered to be the same as winning. In numerous public policy issues, there is still a historical requirement to stand up and protest against injustice or the lack of education.

Political Power

For political success, it is necessary to have a substantial base of voter support and the funds to finance a campaign. Both assets were once deficient in Boston's black community. As recently as 1940, only 3.1 percent of Boston residents were African American and their economic status was limited.

In the seventy-five years or so since then the black population has grown to 25.33 percent, a significant bloc. However, the great ethnic diversity of the black community still makes it difficult to develop a reliable consensus. Haitians, Cape Verdeans, and Latinos have different histories from the descendants of those who were held in slavery. Those differences are disappearing over time, but unity is still elusive.

The most exciting political developments have been by those

candidates who are able to transcend ethnic barriers because of the strength of their character, talent, and personality. It is not reasonable to expect another Senator Edward W. Brooke or a Governor Deval Patrick anytime soon. Nonetheless, there is a historic reluctance in the black community to be barred from entering the political fray because of race.

Major Protests

The continuing campaign for equality and civil rights has created the image of African Americans as a people involved in constant protest. Indeed, Boston has been in the front lines of the battles. We have chosen three of those protests for *Boston's Banner Years*, all of which have unique attributes.

Grove Hall Riot

The so-called race riot in Grove Hall of 1967 was not a race riot at all but was a community's reaction to an unjustified police assault. The police overreacted to a demonstration by Mothers for Adequate Welfare, an interracial organization of women on welfare. Undoubtedly the police anticipated community violence because of the race riots in other cities, so they struck first.

One of the worst aspects of the situation is that the major media took the side of the police and seemed to justify their reaction because of property damage. Little attention was given to the injuries to citizens as a result of abusive police conduct.

At any rate, Boston is now mistakenly added to the list of cities that suffered race riots in the 1960s.

Apartheid Opposition

Rarely can ordinary citizens cause a major change in US foreign policy. When black workers at the Polaroid Corporation discovered that their photo technology had become a significant device to enforce racial apartheid in South Africa, they put their jobs on the line and rebelled. Ultimately, Polaroid Corp. withdrew from South Africa,, and the US government required US companies still operating there to abide by the procedures of the Sullivan Principles to allay the impact of racial discrimination.

Local residents opposing injustice had thus helped to end the undemocratic policies in another country.

I-95 Protest

This protest demonstrated the capacity of Roxbury residents to work with people from other neighborhoods on a major protest movement. Participants were multiracial. After an extended period of cooperation, the destructive plan was abandoned by state government, a blessing to all.

Law Enforcement

In the early days of the *Banner* there were only a few black officers on the police force. It has been a great challenge over the years to increase the number of local residents in the police department and to assure that those who are qualified for promotion get the opportunity.

Nation of Islam

Beyond the operation of local and federal law enforcement has been the Nation of Islam. The local mosque under the leadership of Minister Farrakhan's ambassador Don (Straughter) Mohammad prevented the establishment of major new drug gangs in Grove Hall and the Dudley Square area. The account of these interventions reported in *Boston's Banner Years* indicates the great capacity of the Nation of Islam to end major criminal ventures that have plagued some black communities.

The capability results from the extraordinary respect for Minister Farrakhan, who was raised in Roxbury, among African Americans across the nation. He called for a Million Man March in Washington, DC, to be held on October 16, 1995, and it happened. There had never been a convocation of that size in the nation's capital, and predictions were that the turnout would be embarrassingly low. After all, only 250,000 came to Washington for Martin Luther King's "I Have a Dream" speech in 1963. That crowd included people of all races and both men and women.

But black men from all over the nation came to Washington at Farrakhan's request. The National Park Service reported the size of the crowd as only four hundred thousand, much larger than the MLK event but still quite short of one million. However, sensing that this number was inaccurate, a TV news bureau engaged Farouk El Baz, a Boston University professor and director of the Center for Remote Sensing, to determine the size of the crowd using satellite analysis. Professor El Baz reported a base crowd size of 837,244, with a 20 percent variance that would provide for attendance in excess of one million. He was able to perform his analysis only later in the day after many attendees had already left, so the crowd size that he analyzed was even less than it was earlier.

Members of the Nation of Islam have shown great discipline and courage in confronting major crime elements. Rather than obtain the social benefit of such resources, the media have relentlessly pilloried Minister Farrakhan. They have never publicized that in the decades with Farrakhan as the organization's leader, there has never been an act of violence against others, even against those who declare themselves to be hostile. This has been a lost opportunity for the development of institutions to provide peaceful prosperity for urban blacks.

Economic Development

Studies indicate that the development of wealth among Boston's African Americans is deficient. Too many people have been left behind in America's fast-changing economy. Several chapters in the book point out some efforts to help blacks to succeed economically.

Building a Bank

It is natural for ethnic minorities to want to establish a bank they can trust. The chapter on the Colonial era lists some early efforts, but the "Building a Bank" chapter shows how Unity Bank became the Boston Bank of Commerce, and finally OneUnited Bank, the largest black-owned and managed bank in America. It is extraordinary for Boston, with a relatively small black population, to be the home office of such a financial institution.

Real Estate Projects

Office buildings are big and can demonstrate substantial business acumen to construct. The real estate project that produced the home office of State Street Corporation is an example of a successful effort by a competent and determined group of black businessmen to build a skyscraper. A description of that project indicates what it takes to be successful in real estate. Other projects by blacks in Boston indicate the variety of the real estate industry.

Employment Efforts

Of course the basic economic activity is to have a job. Blacks were not waiting around for good fortune to come their way. The problem has always been that racial discrimination often forecloses employment of qualified black applicants at the better jobs. We have provided information on some of Boston's outstanding projects to provide job opportunities.

Boston's Media History

There has always been an effort to report news from a black perspective as well as from the point of view of those in society's major positions. So much of the news and information comes from national sources that Boston's influence is limited. This chapter records efforts of African Americans in Boston to be included. As a result of the efforts of the black community, Boston was the only city to comply with the recommendations of the 1968 Kerner Commission Report to involve the black population in the process of covering local news.

But the greatest accolades for work in the media go to the nationally acclaimed *Eyes on the Prize,* a graphic cinematic account of major elements of the civil rights movement that was produced by the late Henry Hampton's Blackside Inc. in 1987. International journalists reported on various aspects of the civil rights movement, but Hampton produced an authentic black perspective account from his offices and studio in Boston.

Colonial Era

The title of this book indicates that it covers the years 1965–2015. However, readers undoubtedly would want to know who are these African Americans in Boston, and where did they come from. This chapter shows that the population of black forefathers, and mothers for that matter, was small, and the people were feisty and ambitious. Fortunately, Massachusetts is not primarily an agricultural state, so there was no need for blacks in the fields. The alternative to being a house servant was to develop a craft or engage in commerce. Whichever route the people chose, they developed a sense of racial equality that has survived over the years.

A Promising Future

There is still very far to go to eliminate racial discrimination from American society and to repair the damage it has already caused. Consequently there is a risk in writing about successes. Some conservatives could insist that the record of achievement of some blacks indicates that the problem is not as severe as protestors insist. Also, those who are still suffering from the affliction of racial discrimination might believe it is inappropriate to focus on the successes even while so much adversity persists.

Indeed, there are numerous stories of sustained commitment by blacks whose efforts still led to failure. It has always been a marvel that so many blacks have had success stymied by bigotry. Yet they have kept hope alive. Therefore, it is of great value for people to be reminded of blacks who are successful, as an inspiration for them and their children. Sometimes people are unaware that many of the doors formerly closed are now open for those with the talent and qualifications.

The Writers

Sandra Larson is a regular journalist at the *Bay State Banner*, primarily covering Boston's African American community. For eight years, Sandra has developed considerable knowledge about urban conflicts and economic development issues. She holds an MS in urban and regional policy from Northeastern University and a BS in Conservation Biology from the University of Wisconsin-Madison.

Yawu Miller, as a graduate of Milton Academy and Dartmouth College, where he majored in English, has always had an awareness of precise language being a major learning tool. As a deputy director of the Public Policy Institute he instructed participants in how to write to influence support on public issues. He is now senior editor at the *Bay State Banner*.

Anthony W. Neal has for some time been aware of the influence of black history on current attitudes. That induced him to major in American history at Brown University, after preparing at Concord Academy. After earning a JD from the University of Texas School of Law, he became a staff attorney at Greater Boston Legal Services where he could help low-income clients. Neal continues writing while practicing law.

Neal's experience with legal issues surrounding unemployment qualified him to collaborate with **James Jennings**, who had been professor of urban and environmental policy and planning at Tufts University from 2001 until he became emeritus. Jennings received a BA from Hunter College and a PhD in political science from Columbia University.

Brian O'Connor graduated cum laude as a Kissinger Scholar from Harvard College. After a stint as an English teacher at St. Albans School in Washington, DC, he left for the Grenoble University in France to develop his French. Upon his return, O'Connor immersed himself in journalism, serving as managing editor at the *Bay State Banner* and later in political strategy. He became communications director for former US Representative Joseph P. Kennedy II and has continued in that status as vice president of public affairs in Citizens Energy Corp. **Peter C. Roby**, who collaborated with O'Connor, is a political activist focused on New England's Cape Verdean community. He graduated summa cum laude from Northeastern University, where he majored in English and philosophy. He also earned a master's degree in English.

Jule Pattison-Gordon is a 2013 Phi Beta Kappa graduate of Carnegie Mellon University and completed Columbia University's Summer Publishing Course. She has a profound interest in writing, publishing, and editing. Pattison-Gordon is a former journalist for the *Bay State Banner.*

Robin Washington has had an extensive media career, including as the chief editor of a daily, Minnesota's *Duluth News Tribune.* He has also produced the 1995 PBS documentary *You Don't Have to Ride Jim Crow.* In his early career, Washington was managing editor of the *Bay State Banner,* a position that makes him especially qualified to write the chapter on the media.

Endnotes

1   *The Cultural Matric: Understanding Black Youth*, by Orlando Patterson, 557.
2   Ibid., 544.
3   *Yale Bulletin and Calendar News Stories* 26, no. 1, Aug. 25-Sept. 1, 1997.
4   Prince Hall, "Extract from a Charge Delivered to the African Lodge, June 24th, 1797, at Menotomy," Evans Early American Imprint Collection / Text Creation Partnership, University of Michigan library system, 10 and 12. http://quod.lib.umich.edu/e/evans/N24354. 0001.001/1:2?rgn=div1;view=fulltext. See also "Prince Hall, 1735–1807," *Africans in America*, WGBH Boston, http://www.pbs.org/wgbh/aia/part2/2p37.html.
5   Stephen Kendrick and Paul Kendrick, *Sarah's Long Walk: The Free Blacks of Boston and How Their Struggle for Equality Changed America*. (Boston: Beacon Press, 2004), 71–72.
6   Stanley K.Schultz, *The Culture Factory: Boston Public Schools, 1789-1860*. (Oxford: Oxford University Press, 1973), 167.
7   Kendrick and Kendrick, *Sarah's Long Walk*, 84.
8   Kendrick and Kendrick, *Sarah's Long Walk*, (no page cited).
9   Kendrick and Kendrick, *Sarah's Long Walk*, 73–74.
10 "An Act concerning Public Schools," 1845 Mass Acts 214, http://archives. lib.state.ma.us/actsResolves/1845/1845acts0212.pdf.
11 "Reports of the Annual Visiting Committee of the Public Schools of the City of Boston," (Boston, 1845), quoted in Robert H. Bremmer, ed., *Children and Youth in America: A Documentary* (Cambridge, MA: Harvard University Press, 1970), I, 526, quoted in James E. Teele, *Evaluating School Busing: Case Study of Boston's Operation Exodus* (New York: Praeger, 1973), 3.
12 Schultz, *The Culture Factory*, 187.

13 Schultz, *The Culture Factory*, 194.

14 Schultz, *The Culture Factory*, 197–98.

15 *Roberts* v. *City of Boston*, 59 Mass. (5 Cush.) 209 (1850).

16 *Roberts* v. *City of Boston*.

17 *Dred Scott* v. *Sandford* 60 U.S. 393. The Library of Congress maintains a platform on this at https://www.loc.gov/rr/program/bib/ourdocs/ DredScott.html.

18 Horace Mann founded and edited *The Common School Journal* in 1838, which provided the template that modern public education continues to follow. The Internet Archive maintains a freely downloadable copy at https://archive.org/details/commonschooljou00manngoog. For more on Boston's current dilemma with respect to its legacy, see David Rhode, Kristina Cooke, and Himanshu-Ojha, "The Decline of the 'Great Equalizer,'" *Atlantic*, Dec. 19, 2012. https://www.theatlantic.com/ business/archive/2012/12/the-decline-of-the-great-equalizer/266455/. See also quotes from the Horace Mann League of the USA, http://www. hmleague.org/quotes-by-horace-mann/.

19 See Matthew Delmont and Jeanne Theoharis, "Introduction: Rethinking the Boston 'Busing Crisis,'" *Journal of Urban History* 43, no. 2 (March, 2017), 194. DOI: 10.1177/0096144216688276. See also Delmont and Theoharis, endnote 15, "Ruth Batson, 'Statement to the Boston School Committee,'" in *The Eyes on the Prize Civil Rights Reader*, ed. Clayborne Carson, David Garrow, Gerald Gill, Vincent Harding, Darlene Clark Hine (New York: Penguin, 1991), 598.

20 *Morgan* v. *Hennigan*, 379 F. Supp. 410 (D. Mass 1974) 482, aff'd 509 F. 2d 580 (1st Cir. 1974), cert denied, 421 U.S. 963 (1975).

21 Ibid., 476.

22 Ibid., 484.

23 "Welfare Mothers Form Protest Group," *Bay State Banner*, Oct. 9, 1965. https://search.proquest.com/docview/371335088.

24 Jim Vrabel, *A People's History of the New Boston* (Amherst: University of Massachusetts Press), 81.

25 "MAWS Group Plans Welfare Info Book," *Bay State Banner*, Feb. 5, 1966. https://search.proquest.com/docview/371334676.

26 "U.S. Committee Hears Discrimination Charges," *Bay State Banner*, Mar. 19, 1966. https://search.proquest.com/docview/371335614; the "deplorable conditions" quote is from Jason Sokol, *All Eyes Are upon Us: Race and Politics from Boston to Brooklyn* (Basic Books, 2014), 134.

27   "Results of Meeting," *Bay State Banner*, May 28, 1966. https://search. proquest.com/docview/371334465.

28   "Mothers March," *Bay State Banner*, July 2, 1966. https://search.proquest. com/docview/371332428.

29   Sokol, All Eyes Are upon Us, 134.

30   "Rep. Bolling Praises Welfare Mothers March," *Bay State Banner*, July 9, 1966. https://search.proquest.com/docview/371332986.

31   "Volpe Confers with Welfare Mothers," *Bay State Banner*, July 16, 1966. https://search.proquest.com/docview/371331569.

32   "Lt. Governor Supports Demands of MAWS," *Bay State Banner*, Aug. 20, 1966. https://search.proquest.com/docview/371333263.

33   "Education Coop Offers Opportunity for Adults," *Bay State Banner*, Nov. 5, 1966. https://search.proquest.com/docview/371331256.

34   "Mothers Picket Welfare Office: Protest Calls for Equal Distribution of Thanksgiving Allowances," *Bay State Banner*, Nov. 26, 1966. https:// search.proquest.com/docview/371331993.

35   Ibid.

36   "Kinoy Urges HUAC Abolishment," *Bay State Banner*, Dec. 17, 1966. https://search.proquest.com/docview/371331555.

37   "Delegation Protest At City Hall: Community Agencies Charge ABCD with 'Senseless Spending of Poverty Funds,'" *Bay State Banner*, Mar. 18, 1967.

38   "Welfare," *Bay State Banner*, June 3, 1967. https://search.proquest.com/ docview/371356782.

39   "List Demands: MAW in U.S. Protest," *Bay State Banner*, June 10, 1967. https://search.proquest.com/docview/371347950.

40   Byron Rushing, interview by author, Mar. 8, 2017, Boston.

41   Chuck Turner, interview by author, Mar. 15, 2017, Boston.

42   F. J. Taylor, "Police, Mothers Tell Different Stories on Riot's Start," *Boston Globe*, June 4, 1967.

43   William Fripp, "From Quiet Vigil to Melee," *Boston Globe*, June 3, 1967.

44   Rushing interview.

45   John H. Fenton, "A Welfare Protest Spurs Boston Riot; Scores Are Injured." *New York Times*, June 3, 1967.

46   "Roxbury Fights Police Attack," *Bay State Banner*, June 10, 1967. https:// search.proquest.com/docview/371341762.

47   "Disaster Strikes in Boston ... and the City Seeks an Answer," *Boston Globe*, June 5, 1967.

48 "McNamara Cites Police Riot Control," Boston Globe, June 13, 1967.

49 Melvin B. Miller, interview by author, Mar. 20, 2017.

50 Mel King, *Chain of Change* (Boston: South End Press, 1981), 58.

51 Jonathan Fuerbringer and Marvin E. Milbaur, "Roxbury, Quiet in the Past, Finally Breaks into Riot; Why Did Violence Occur?" *Harvard Crimson*, June 15, 1967. http://www.thecrimson.com/article/1967/6/15/roxbury-quiet-in-past-finally-breaks/.

52 Vrabel, *A People's History*, 90.

53 Vrabel, *A People's History*, 91.

54 Vrabel, *A People's History*, 91.

55 Gloria Fox, interview by author, Apr. 3, 2017, Boston.

56 "Roxbury Memory Trail," 2016, http://roxburymemorytrail.org.

57 Alan Lupo, Frank Colcord, and Edmund P. Fowler, *Rites of Way: The Politics of Transportation in Boston and the US City*. (Boston: Little, Brown, 1971), 13–14.

58 Ibid., 14.

59 Lower Roxbury is the area of Roxbury that abuts the South End, west of Massachusetts Avenue. Its other boundaries are variously described as Tremont Street/Columbus Avenue on the north, Harrison Avenue on the south, and what is now Melnea Cass Boulevard on the west (see United Neighbors of Lower Roxbury, http://unlr.org/pages/about_lower_roxbury.html) or extending to Martin Luther King Boulevard on the south and Washington Street (to Seaver Street) on the east (see Ronald Bailey's *Lower Roxbury: A Community of Treasures* (Boston: Lower Roxbury Community Corporation and Afro Scholar Press, 1993).

60 Vrabel, *A People's History*, 142.

61 Anthony Yudis, "Roxbury School Rocks with Shouts of Opposition to S.W. Expressway," *Boston Globe*, Oct. 23, 1962.

62 Ronald Bailey, *Lower Roxbury: A Community of Treasures* (Boston: Lower Roxbury Community Corp. and Afro Scholar Press, 1993), 28.

63 Ann Hershfang, telephone interview by author, Apr. 13, 2017.

64 Lupo, *Rites of Way*, 42–43, 50–61; GBCTC formation also covered briefly in Vrabel, 145–45.

65 Lupo, *Rites of Way*, 47–49.

66 "Wider Community Participation Sought: BRA to Survey Families in Inner Belt Path." *Bay State Banner*, Feb. 5, 1966. https://search.proquest.com/docview/371334619.

67 "A New Problem with the DPW's Inner Belt," *Bay State Banner*, Apr. 16, 1966.

68 "Threatened Communities Oppose Highways," *Bay State Banner*, Sept. 14, 1967. https://search.proquest.com/docview/371347738.

69 Turner interview.

70 Lupo, *Rights of Way*, 57.

71 Lupo, *Rights of Way*, 58.

72 Turner interview.

73 "United Front Protests Inner Belt," *Bay State Banner*, July 17, 1969. https://search.proquest.com/docview/371333490.

74 Lupo, *Rites of Way*.

75 Fox interview.

76 Hershfang interview.

77 Lupo, *Rites of Way*, 89–90.

78 Lupo, *Rights of Way*, 97.

79 Sandra Larson, "Roxbury Forum Revisits 1960s Anti-Highway Fight," *Bay State Banner*, Mar. 20, 2014. https://search.proquest.com/docview/1516364073.

80 Sandra Larson, "Melnea Cass design meeting sparks anger," *Bay State Banner*, Oct. 20, 2011. Retrieved from https://search.proquest.com/docview/905950189.

81 Larson, "Strides made at Second Meeting on Melnea Cass Blvd. Design," *Boston Banner*, Dec. 22, 2011. https://search.proquest.com/docview/916002883.

82 Larson, "City Floats Latest Cass Blvd. Plan at Community Meeting," *Boston Banner*, Apr. 23, 2015. https://search.proquest.com/docview/1676880064.

83 Kenneth J. Cooper and Christopher B. Daly, "In Boston, Mandela Hails State's Leadership In Anti-Apartheid Drive," *Washington Post*, June 24, 1990. https://www.washingtonpost.com/archive/politics/1990/06/24/in-boston-mandela-hails-states-leadership-in-anti-apartheid-drive/ae9cd4cc-54f6-441d-8ccb-0f4992ac5e4a.

84 Eric J. Morgan, "The World Is Watching: Polaroid and South Africa," *Enterprise & Society* 7, no. 3 (September 2006), 520–49, 522. http://www.jstor.org/stable/23700835.

85 Eric J. Morgan, interview by author May 15, 2017.

86 Caroline Hunter, interview by author Mar. 23, 2017, Cambridge, MA.

87 Hunter interview.

88 Hunter interview.

89 PWRM, "Statement by the Polaroid Revolutionary Workers Movement to the United Nations Special Committee on the Policies of Apartheid, February 3, 1971," African Activist Archive, Michigan State University.

90 Peter C. Wensberg, *Land's Polaroid: A Company and the Man Who Invented It* (Boston: Houghton Mifflin, 1987), 161–2.

91 Morgan, 2006, 531.

92 Hunter interview; also Carl W. Sims, "Polaroid Gift Will Go to S. Africa, Cairo, Ill.," *Bay State Banner*, Dec. 24, 1970. https://search.proquest.com/docview/371273266.

93 African Activist Archive, introductory paragraph for the PWRM collection. http://africanactivist.msu.edu/organization.php?name=Polaroid+Revolutionary+Workers+Movement; For an example of Polaroid's published announcement, see "An Experiment in South Africa," *Bay State Banner*, Jan. 14, 1971. https://search.proquest.com/docview/371273228.

94 Hunter interview.

95 PWRM, "Statement by the Polaroid."

96 Leonard Edgerly, "Polaroid Officials Suspend Blacks Leading Boycott," *Harvard Crimson*, Feb. 12, 1971. http://www.thecrimson.com/article/1971/2/12/polaroid-officials-suspend-blacks-leading-boycott/; also Hunter interview.

97 Hunter interview.

98 Wensberg, *Land's Polaroid*, 167.

99 Derek Reveron, "Small Group of Activists Puts Pressure On Big Firms to Get Out of South Africa," *Wall Street Journal*, Feb. 23, 1978.

100 "Sullivan Principles' Author Hopes for Change," Business Day, *New York Times*, Oct. 22, 1986.

101 Paul Lewis, "Leon Sullivan, 78, Dies; Fought Apartheid." *New York Times*, Apr. 26, 2001.

102 Eric J. Morgan, "Black and White at Center Court: Arthur Ashe and the Confrontation of Apartheid in South Africa," *Diplomatic History* 36, no. 5 (2012): 815–41.

103 Cecilie Ditlev-Simonsen, "Sullivan Urges Total S. Africa Exit," *Chicago Tribune*, June 4, 1987. http://articles.chicagotribune.com/1987-06-04/business/8702110089_1_south-africa-rev-sullivan-disinvest.

104 Cambridge Public Schools, "Former Math Teacher And Assistant Principal, Caroline Hunter Awarded For Her Contributions To Civil Rights," 2012. http://crls.cpsd.us/cms/One.aspx?portalId=3045383&pageId=3599232Brannen. Also see "Anti-Apartheid Stance Garners Ultimate Reward," *Vineyard Gazette*, May 17, 2012. https://vineyardgazette.com/news/2012/05/17/anti-apartheid-stance-garners-ultimate-award and

National Education Association, "2012 Rosa Parks Memorial Award." http://www.nea.org/home/51340.htm.

105 Hunter interview.

106 Mass Divest, "Make it in Massachusetts, Not in South Africa: How We Won Divestment Legislation," 1983, 1. American Committee on Africa pamphlet accessed from the African Activist Archive, Michigan State University. http://africanactivist.msu.edu/document_metadata.php?objectid=32-130-CB4.

107 Ibid.

108 Mass Divest, 1983, 4.

109 David Goodman, "The 1980s: The Anti-Apartheid Convergence" in *No Easy Victories: African Liberation and American Activists Over a Half Century, 1950–2000*, edited by William Minter, Gail Hovey, Charles Cobb Jr. (Africa World Press, 2007), 155.

110 Cheryl C. Sullivan, "Boston mayor urges US cities to divest South African investments," *Christian Science Monitor*, Sept. 20, 1984. http://www.cs-monitor.com/1984/0920/092042.html.

111 Charles Yancey, telephone interview by author, Apr. 13, 2017.

112 Yancey interview.

113 Sullivan, "Boston mayor urges," 1984.

114 Yancey interview.

115 Ibid.

116 History-BPDNews.com.

117 Ibid.

118 2016 interview with William Celester.

119 U.S. District Court for the District of Massachusetts - 365 F. Supp. 655 (D. Mass. 1973) Apr. 15, 1973, Pedro CASTRO et al. v. Nancy BEECHER et al.

120 "Bolling criticizes police department's minority hiring," *Bay State Banner* (1965–1979); Boston, Mass. [Boston, Mass] Feb. 28, 1974: 6.

121 Jane Shaw, "Mayor fields tough questions at Boston candidates' forum," *Bay State Banner (1965-1979)*; Boston, Mass. Nov 1,1979: 3.

122 Eileen McNamara, and William Doherty, *Globe* staff, "US jury declines to indict Bourque," *Boston Globe*, Oct.17, 1980.

123 Sean Murphy, "Police lawsuits cost city millions," *Boston Globe, Nov. 28, 1991*.

124 March 2017 interview with Brian O'Connor.

125 Richard Higgins, "Witnesses challenge police on shooting," *Boston Globe*, Sept. 8, 1983.

126 1996 Banner interview.

127 Robert A. Jordan, "A Triumph For The Truth," *Boston Globe*, Apr. 12, 1986.

128 Ibid.

129 1997 interview with Min. Don Muhammad.

130 1997 interview with Bruce Wall.

131 Ibid.

132 "The dealer and his dope: weighing Jesse Watters's vested interest," the *Boston Phoenix*, Sept. 9, 1986.

133 March 2017 interview with Banner Publisher Melvin Miller.

134 Yawu Miller, "Muslims Play Key Role," *Bay State Banner*, 1997.

135 Ibid.

136 March 2017 interview with William Celester.

137 Miller, "Muslims Play Key Role."

138 Ibid.

139 Ibid.

140 Ibid.

141 Yawu Miller, "Grassroots efforts contributed to drop in Boston's crime rate," *Bay State Banner*, Mar. 6, 1997.

142 Ibid.

143 Derrick Z. Jackson, "Another reason crime has fallen: black leadership," *Boston Globe*, Feb. 28, 1997.

144 Ibid.

145 David Armstrong, "Five black ministers say Farrakhan a'hypocrite'" *Boston Globe* (pre-1997 Fulltext) - Boston, Mass., Mar. 11, 1994.

146 Yawu Miller, "Dorchester rev. raises ire in black community,", *Bay State Banner*, 16 Oct. 1997: 1.

147 Ibid.

148 March 2017 Muhammad interview.

149 Police gang-search policy continues to ignite debate, *Bay State Banner*, K. Charles Peterson, Oct. 12, 1988.

150 Report of the Boston Police Department Management Review Committee, 1992.

151 Report of the Boston Police Department Management Review Committee submitted to: Mayor Raymond L. Flynn (St. Clair Commission Report) Jan. 14, 1992.

152 Police oversight panel recommends creating separate office for complaints against officers, *Boston Globe* - Boston, Mass., Ransom, Jan., May 10, 2016.

153 "The Failure of the War on Drugs: Charting a New Course for the Commonwealth," Massachusetts Bar Asssociation Drug Policy Task Force, David W. White Jr., 2008.

154 Y. Miller, "White lines: changing attitudes toward addiction," *Bay State Banner*, Aug. 11, 2014.

155 March 2017 interview with Billy Celester.

156 1994 interview with former City of Boston Human Resources Director Roscoe Morris.

157 Curtis, S. (1999, Dec. 23). Court nixes police promotion policy. *Bay State Banner*. Retrieved from https://search.proquest.com/docview/367426287?accountid=31796.

158 J. Schwab, Court rules against police hiring policy. *Bay State Banner, Dec. 2, 2004.*

159 City of Boston 2015 Workforce Report.

160 Data Access and Dissemination Systems (DADS). "American FactFinder – Results". census.gov.

161 D. G. Yosifon, "Police, cox settle for $900k," *Bay State Banner*, Feb. 18, 1999.

162 Schwab, Jeremy, *Bay State Banner*, Sept. 12, 2002, 1.

163 Y. Miller, "DA's investigation clears cop in shooting," *Bay State Banner*, Sept. 4, 2003.

164 Sukhtian, L. (2001, July 26). "Activists call for commission to investigate police shootings," *Bay State Banner*.

165 Y. Miller, "Police survey: Profiling a problem for Roxbury, Mattapan residents," *Bay State Banner*, May 20, 2004.

166 Ibid.

167 Y. Miller, "ACLU study finds blacks disproportionately targeted by police stop-and-frisks," *Bay State Banner*, Oct. 8, 2014.

168 Ibid.

169 J. Pattison-Gordon, "'Gang' label can have serious consequences for Hub teens," *Bay State Banner*, Sept. 24, 2015.

170 March 2017 interview with MAMLEO President Larry Ellison.

171 Y. Miller, "Civil rights activists calling for police dept. reforms," *Bay State Banner*, July 16, 2015.

172 Y. Miller, "Black cops suing department over 'false positives' in hair tests," *Bay State Banner*, Aug. 19, 2015.

173 F. Butterfield, "Black Republican Is Appointed District Attorney for Boston Area," *New York Times*, July 3, 1992.

174 P. Nealon, "Former sheriff gets one-year sentence," *Boston Globe*, Dec. 4, 1996.

175 Y. Miller, "Sheriff shuns campaign trail, focuses on family." *Bay State Banner*, Jan. 3, 2002.

176 Teri Williams, interview by author, Mar. 3, 2017.

177 "History," National Bankers Association. Accessed Apr. 20, 2017. http://www.nationalbankers.org/history.htm.

178 "History," National Bankers Association.

179 "History," National Bankers Association.

180 Jeanne Lee "Why America needs black owned banks," *USA Today*, Feb. 16, 2017. Accessed Apr. 20, 2017.

181 Lee. "Why America needs black owned banks."

182 Marvin Gilmore, telephone interview by author, Jan. 11, 2017.

183 Mel King, *Chain of change: struggles for black community development* (Boston: Hugs Press, 2016).

184 "The CEO of Freedom," *Brown Alumni Magazine*, April 2003. Accessed Apr. 14, 2017. http://www.brownalumnimagazine.com/content/view/1013/40/; "Archie Williams: Man in the News," *Bay State Banner*, Oct. 23, 1965. Accessed April 2017.

185 "The CEO of Freedom"; "Archie Williams."

186 "King, *Chain of change.*

187 Williams interview.

188 Howard Manly, "One Shining Example," *Bay State Banner*, Sept. 9, 2010. Accessed December 2016. https://search.proquest.com/docview/751931053?accountid=31796.

189 Wenty Bowen, "Minority investors breaking ground on Lincoln St. project," *Bay State Banner*, Apr. 6, 2000. Accessed 2016.

190 Jule Pattison-Gordon, "Northeastern University case revolves around public land," *Bay State Banner*, Oct. 26, 2016. Accessed December 2016.

191 Pattison-Gordon, "Northeastern University case."

192 "Unity Bank Chartered," *Bay State Banner*, June 29, 1967. Accessed December 2016.

193 Hillel Levine and Lawrence Harmon, *The Death of an American Jewish Community* (Plunkett Lake Press, 2012).

194 Levine and Harmon, *Death of an American Jewish Community.*

195 Levine and Harmon, *Death of an American Jewish Community.*

196 Levine and Harmon, *Death of an American Jewish Community.*

197 Jule Pattison-Gordon, "How urban renewal shaped Boston; Look at the past as city plans for future,"*Bay State Banner*, Mar. 3, 2016. Accessed December 2016.

198 Levine and Harmon, *Death of an American Jewish Community*.

199 Levine and Harmon, *Death of an American Jewish Community*.

200 Levine and Harmon, *Death of an American Jewish Community*.

201 Levine and Harmon, *Death of an American Jewish Community*.

202 Levine and Harmon, *Death of an American Jewish Community*.

203 Levine and Harmon, *Death of an American Jewish Community*.

204 Levine and Harmon, *Death of an American Jewish Community*.

205 Levine and Harmon, *Death of an American Jewish Community*.

206 Levine and Harmon, *Death of an American Jewish Community*.

207 Levine and Harmon, *Death of an American Jewish Community*.

208 Levine and Harmon, *Death of an American Jewish Community*.

209 "Unity Bank Plans in Final Stages," *Bay State Banner*, Apr. 22, 1967. Accessed December 2016; "Unity Bank Meets," *Bay State Banner*, Nov. 2, 1967. Accessed December 2016.

210 "Front is Largest Depositor in Unity Bank," *Bay State Banner*. Accessed December 2016.

211 "Unity Bank Meets," *Bay State Banner*, Nov. 2, 1967. Accessed December 2016.

212 "Unity Bank Plans in Final Stages," *Bay State Banner*, Apr. 22, 1967. Accessed December 2016; Unity Bank Chartered," *Bay State Banner*, June 29, 1967. Accessed December 2016.

213 "Unity Bank Opens for Business," *Bay State Banner*, June 27, 1968. Accessed December 2016.

214 Donald Lowery, "Unity—Good Idea Gone Bad," *Boston Globe*, Aug. 10, 1982. Accessed December 2016.

215 Lowery, "Unity—Good Idea Gone Bad."

216 "Unity Bank chosen as postal depository," *Bay State Banner*, July 9, 1970. Accessed December 2016.

217 Lowery, "Unity—Good Idea Gone Bad."

218 Gilmore interview.

219 Gilmore interview.

220 Lowery, "Unity—Good Idea Gone Bad."

221 Lowery, "Unity—Good Idea Gone Bad."

222 Miller interview.

223 I. H. Sprague, "Unity Bank: The Essentiality Doctrine is Established," in *Bailout: An Insider's Account of Bank Failures and Rescues* (Washington DC: Beard Books, 2000), 37.

224 Sprague, "Unity Bank," 37.

225 Juan Cofield, interview by author, Mar. 10, 2017.

226 Gilmore interview.

227 Sprague, "Unity Bank," 37.

228 Lowery, "Unity—Good Idea."

229 Mona Sarfaty, "Soul Business—Roxbury's Unity Bank," *Harvard Crimson*, Oct. 28, 1968. Accessed April 2017.

230 Sarfaty, "Soul Business."

231 "Unity Bank on Road to Stability, Says Report," *Bay State Banner*, Aug. 31, 1972. Accessed April 2017.

232 "Atkins and Banks Run for Council," *Bay State Banner*, Aug. 24, 1967. Accessed April 2017.

233 Sarfaty, "Soul Business."

234 "Unity Bank Moves to Open Here," *Bay State Banner*, May 6, 1967. Accessed April 2017.

235 "Organizers Speak at Business School—Unity Bank—Issued License to Sell Stock Subscriptions 100,000 Shares," *Bay State Banner*, Aug. 31, 1967. Accessed April 2017.

236 "Who's news," *Bay State Banner*, Jan. 31, 1974. Accessed April 2017.

237 "Who's news."

238 "Who's news."

239 "Unity Bank Opens for Business," *Bay State Banner*, June 27, 1968. Accessed April 2017.

240 "Unity Bank Opens for Business."

241 "Harold Vaughan named special assistant Attorney General," *Bay State Banner*, May 11, 1972. Accessed April 2017.

242 "Brooks sees candidacy as 'change,'" *Bay State Banner*, Oct. 12, 1972.

243 "Bynoe New Regional HEW Director," *Bay State Banner*, Aug. 3, 1967; "John Byone, longtime Rox activist, dead at 82," *Bay State Banner*, Aug. 20, 2009.

244 "Jones, Polaroid supervisor dead at 43," *Bay State Banner*, Aug. 10, 1972. Accessed April 2017.

245 Bob Pinderhughes, "Franklin Holgate, local activist, dies," *Bay State Banner*, May 30, 1974. Accessed April 2017.

246 "Baron Martin to Emerson Board," *Bay State Banner*, Dec. 4, 1969. Accessed April 2017.

247 "Death notices," *Bay State Banner*, July 27, 1978. Accessed April 2017.

248 Sprague, "The Essentiality Doctrine," 38, 47–48; Radin, Charles A. "Regulator's Eye-View of Greed; FDIC Chief: Most Failures Happen Because Some Go; 'Too Far Too Fast,'" *Boston Globe*, Dec. 1, 1998. Accessed December 2016.

249 Sprague, "The Essentiality Doctrine," 45–46

250 "Unity Bank sets $2 million," *Bay State Banner*, Aug. 5, 1971. Accessed April 2017.

251 Luix Virgil Overbea, *Bay State Banner*, June 12, 1997. Accessed April 2017.

252 Sprague, "The Essentiality Doctrine," 45–46.

253 Sprague, "The Essentiality Doctrine," 50.

254 "Unity Bank sets $2 million." *Bay State Banner*, Aug. 5, 1971. Accessed December 2016.

255 Mercedes Palmer, "Wilkins to be Unity Bank conservator," *Bay State Banner*, Feb. 3, 1977. Accessed December 2016; Donald Lowery, "State shuts down Unity; a new bank takes over," *Boston Globe*, July 31, 1982. Accessed December 2016.

256 Lowery, "Unity—Good Idea."

257 Sprague, "The Essentiality Doctrine," 50.

258 Lowery, "Unity—Good Idea"; Sprague, *Bailout: An Insider's Account*, 50.

259 "Unity Bank on road."

260 "Unity Bank on road."

261 Lowery, "Unity—Good Idea."

262 "Unity Bank on road."

263 Lowery, "Unity—Good Idea."

264 Mel Miller, interview by author, Jan. 13, 2017.

265 Miller interview.

266 Miller interview.

267 Miller interview.

268 Miller interview.

269 Miller interview.

270 Miller interview.

271 Miller interview.

272 Miller interview.

273 Charles Belle, "Business in the Black: NOW Hurts Blacks," *Sun Reporter* (San Francisco), Dec. 27, 1975. Accessed December 2016.

274 "'Payday' loans risky business," *Bay State Banner*, Mar. 6, 2013. Accessed December 2016.

275 Williams interview.

276 Miller interview.

277 Miller interview.

278 "Unity Bank to move headquarters in July," *Bay State Banner*, June 29, 1928. Accessed April 2017.

279 Dan Swanson, "Bank closings spark debate with several points of view," *Bay State Banner*, Apr. 6, 1978. Accessed April 2017.

280 Jonathan Fuerbringer, "Bolling questions motives of banks," *Boston Globe*, Jan. 11, 1978. Accessed April 2017.

281 Swanson, "Bank closings spark debate."

282 Fuerbringer, "Bolling questions motives."

283 Fuerbringer, "Bolling questions motives."

284 Fuerbringer, "Bolling questions motives."

285 Swanson, "Bank closings spark debate."

286 Dan Swanson, "Plan worked out for Unity expansion." *Bay State Banner*, May 11, 1978. Accessed May 2017.

287 Swanson, "Plan worked out."

288 Palmer, "Wilkins to be Unity."

289 "Unity Bank to move headquarters in July." *Bay State Banner*, June 29, 1978. Accessed December 2016.

290 Palmer, "Wilkins to be Unity."

291 Donald Lowery, "Wiley Named Conservator of Unity Bank," *Boston Globe*, Jan. 1, 1982. Accessed December 2016; Donald Lowery, "Help for a Troubled Bank," *Boston Globe*, Jan. 10, 1982. Accessed December 2016.

292 Kay Bourne, "$500,000 in state funds deposited in Unity Bank," *Bay State Banner*, May 18, 1978. Accessed December 2016.

293 Lowery, "Unity—Good Idea."

294 Lowery, "State shuts down Unity"; Donald Lowery, "Unity Conservator Closes Books; Wiley Confident Boston Bank of Commerce Will Succeed," *Boston Globe*, Aug. 5, 1982. Accessed December 2016.

295 Lowery, "State shuts down Unity."

296 Patricia Gatto, "Drive Started to Save Unity," *Boston Globe*, June 3, 1982. Accessed December 2016.

297 Gatto, "Drive Started to Save."

298 Donald Lowery, "Area businessmen plan minority-owned bank," *Boston Globe*, May 12, 1982. Accessed December 2016.

299 Cofield interview.

300 Cofield interview.

301 Cofield interview.

302 Cofield interview.

303 Cofield interview.

304 Lowery, "State shuts down Unity."

305 Cofield interview.

306 "Lowery, "State shuts down Unity."

307 Lowery, "Area businessmen plan."

308 Lowery, "Area businessmen plan."

309 Lowery, "State shuts down Unity."

310 Cofield interview.

311 Douglas M. Bailey, "Banking Turnaround as a Healthy Minority-Owned Bank Emerges, Skeptics Become Believers." *Boston Globe*, Aug. 4, 1987. Accessed December 2016.

312 Bailey, "Banking Turnaround."

313 Bailey, "Banking Turnaround."

314 Ron Homer, telephone interview by author, Apr. 26, 2017.

315 Homer interview.

316 Homer interview.

317 Homer interview.

318 Homer interview.

319 Homer interview.

320 Gregg Patterson, "B.E. Bank of the Year: Banking on Boston." *Black Enterprise*, June 1986, 150. Accessed December 2016.

321 Patterson, "B.E. Bank of the Year," 150.

322 Bailey, "Banking Turnaround."

323 Bailey, "Banking Turnaround."

324 Robin Washington, "Bank seeks to tap black dollar power to assist social services," *Bay State Banner*, Oct. 12, 1995. Accessed December 2016.

325 Williams interview.

326 Williams interview.

327 Williams interview.

328 William, Garth, Sr. "One United Bank Appoints Teri Williams as President," *Chicago Citizen*, July 26, 2006. Accessed December 2016.

329 "Board of Directors," OneUnited Bank. Accessed Apr. 27, 2017. https://www.oneunited.com/about-us/company-profile/board-of-directors/#kevincohee.

330 Williams interview.

331 Williams interview.

332 Williams interview.

333 Williams interview.

334 Williams interview.

335 Williams interview.

336 Washington, "Bank seeks to tap."

337 Williams interview.

338 Beth Healy, "OneUnited CEO absent as fight rages over church," *Boston Globe*, Mar. 22, 2012. Accessed December 2016.

339 Williams interview.

340 "In the news," *Bay State Banner*, Nov. 11, 2009. Accessed December 2016.

341 Williams interview.

342 Williams interview.

343 Sarah Curtis, "Boston Bank of Comm. acquires Florida bank." *Bay State Banner*, Sept. 16, 1999. Accessed December 2016.

344 Curtis, "Boston Bank of Comm."

345 Williams interview.

346 "Protecting community interests," *Bay State Banner*, Apr. 5, 2012. Accessed December 2016.

347 "One United Bank becomes Nation's Largest Black-owned Bank," *Messenger Magazine*, October 2003. Accessed December 2016.

348 Gil Robertson, "Cool Jobs: Meet OneUnited Bank Prez Terrie [sic] Williams," *Ebony*, July 24, 2015.

349 "Meet the Management Team," OneUnited Bank. Accessed Apr. 27, 2017. https://www.oneunited.com/about-us/company-profile/management/.

350 "Meet the Management Team."

351 "Board of Directors." OneUnited Bank. Accessed April 27, 2017. https://www.oneunited.com/about-us/company-profile/board-of-directors/#kevincohee.

352 "Board of Directors."

353 "Board of Directors."

354 Williams interview.

355 Williams interview.

356 Williams interview.

357 Williams interview.

358 "Boston Bank of Commerce Launches Unity Visa with Support from African American leaders," *New York Voice*, Oct. 1, 1996. Accessed December 2016.

359 "Boston Bank of Commerce."

360 Washington, "Bank seeks to tap."

361 Washington, "Bank seeks to tap."

362 Williams interview.

363 Williams interview.

364 Williams interview.

365 Williams interview.

366 Williams interview.

367 Williams interview.

368 Williams interview.

369 Gail Snowden, telephone interview by author. Jan. 18, 2017.

370 Snowden interview.

371 Snowden interview.

372 Snowden interview.

373 "Bank of Boston Opens Grove Hall Branch," *Bay State Banner*, June 18, 1992. Accessed December 2016.

374 "Bank of Boston."

375 Snowden interview.

376 Snowden interview.

377 Snowden interview.

378 Snowden interview.

379 Snowden interview.

380 Snowden interview.

381 Snowden interview.

382 Snowden interview.

383 Gail Snowden, "Re: Request for an interview with Gail Snowden." Email message to author, Mar. 30, 2017.

384 Snowden interview.

385 Snowden interview.

386 Snowden interview.

387 Snowden interview.

388 Snowden, "Re: Request for an interview."

389 Donna Wilson, "Bank expands lending in commercial market," *Bay State Banner*, Oct. 7, 1993. Accessed December 2016.

390 Snowden interview.

391 "Hilton Picks Rhumbline to Manage Retirement Funds," *Los Angeles Sentinel*, Feb. 14, 2001. Accessed December 2016.

392 Wenty Bowen "Firm charts course for pension funds," *Bay State Banner*, May 6, 2004. Accessed December 2016.

393 Bowen, "Firm charts course."

394 Bowen, "Firm charts course."

395 Bowen, "Firm charts course."

396 Bowen, "Firm charts course."

397 "Hilton Picks Rhumbline."

398 Bowen, "Firm charts course."

399 "Rhumbline Advisors," *Black Enterprise*, May 9, 2009. Accessed May 2017.

400 Alan Hughes, "75 Most Powerful Blacks on Wall Street," *Black Enterprise*, Nov. 7, 2011. Accessed May 2017.

401 "Herb Wilkins, investor in BET and Radio One, dies at 71," *Bay State Banner*, Jan. 9, 2014. Accessed December 2016.

402 "Herb Wilkins, investor in BET."

403 "Herb Wilkins, investor in BET."

404 Hughes, "75 Most Powerful Blacks."

405 "Herb Wilkins, investor in BET."

406 "Herb Wilkins, investor in BET."

407 Howard Manly, "State treasurer invests $1.2b with minority-owned businesses," *Bay State Banner*, Dec. 22, 2005. Accessed December 2016.

408 Ron Homer, "In the news," *Bay State Banner*, Nov. 26, 2009.

409 Bailey, "Banking Turnaround."

410 Bailey, "Banking Turnaround."

411 Bailey, "Banking Turnaround."

412 Bailey, "Banking Turnaround."

413 Bailey, "Banking Turnaround."

414 Bailey, "Banking Turnaround."

415 Homer interview.

416 Homer interview.

417 Homer interview; RBC Global Asset Management, *Access Capital Social Impact* brochure, 2016.

418 Ron Homer, "Re: Interview about Access Capital, Bank of Boston" email message to author, May 4, 2017.

419 Homer, "Re: Interview about Access Capital."

420 Homer interview.

421 RBC Global Asset Management, Access Capital Bridging the Divide Between Wall Street and Main Street brochure, 2016.

422 Homer interview.

423 Homer interview.

424 Homer interview.

425 Homer interview.

426 Homer interview.

427 Homer interview.

428 Homer interview.

429 Homer interview.

430 Homer interview.

431 Homer interview.

432 Homer interview.

433 Homer interview.

434 Homer interview.

435 Homer interview.

436 Homer interview.

437 Nancy Huntington Stager, "Re: Book interview," email message to author. Mar. 31, 2017.

438 Bob Rivers, interview by author, Feb. 16, 2017.

439 Stager, "Re: Book interview."

440 Rivers interview.

441 "Embracing Diversity," Eastern Bank. Accessed January 2017. https:// www.easternbank.com/site/about_us/Pages/diversity.aspx.

442 Eastern Bank, "Eastern Bank Corporation elects new Board members at 199th Annual meeting," news release, Mar. 29, 2017. Accessed Mar. 29, 2017.

443 Rivers interview.

444 Vidya Rao, "Bank's diversity initiatives are paramount to success," *Bay State Banner*, Sept. 12, 2006. Accessed December 2016.

445 Nancy Huntington Stager, interview by author, Feb. 16, 2017.

446 Rivers interview.

447 Stager interview.

448 Stager interview.

449 Quincy Miller, interview by author, Feb. 16, 2017.

450 Rao, "Bank's diversity initiatives."

451 Rivers interview.

452 "Corporate Governance," Eastern Bank. Accessed April 27, 2017. https:// www.easternbank.com/corporate-governance/.

453 Rivers interview.

454 Rivers interview.

455 Stager interview.

456 Stager interview.

457 Jeremy Schwab, "Community fetes opening of new black-owned hotel," *Bay State Banner*, July 7, 2004. Also see this discussion of Crosstown and black hotel ownership as of 2003: Carlo Wolff, "African-Americans blaze hotel trails in Houston and Boston," National Association of Black Hotel Owners, Operators & Developers. http://www.nabhood.net/home/index. php?option=com_content&view=article&id=178&Itemid=192.

458 Yawu Miller, "Developers seek to build theatre on Melnea Cass Blvd.," *Bay State Banner*, Sept. 10, 1998. https://search.proquest.com/docview/367388964.

459 Boston Redevelopment Authority, "The Boston Economy 2004: Turning the Corner," September 2004. https://www.bostonplans.org/getattachment/a0287798-1f07-4d58-8437-305758f4be82.

460 Richard Thorpe, "Stride Rite, Digital to Close Down," *Bay State Banner*, Dec. 24, 1992. https://search.proquest.com/docview/367304598.

461 Miller, "Developers seek to build."

462 Beverley Johnson, telephone interview with author, July 29, 2017.

463 Thomas Welch, interview with author, June 12, 2017, Hampton Inn & Suites, Boston.

464 Jeremy Schwab, "Black-owned hotel creates over 100 jobs," *Bay State Banner*, July 29, 2004.

465 Kirk Sykes, interview with author, June 28, 2017, Jamaica Plain, Boston.

466 Yosifon, Dec. 12, 1998.

467 Yosifon, "BRA designates developers for Crosstown cinema site," *Bay State Banner*, Nov. 19, 1998.

468 Welch, June 12, 2017.

469 Ibid.

470 David G. Yosifon, "Community rallies behind Crosstown cinema plan," *Bay State Banner*, Dec. 12, 1998.

471 Johnson, July 29, 2017.

472 Yawu Miller, "Crosstown team gets $5 million in EEC funds," *Bay State Banner*, April 22, 1999.

473 Miller, April 22, 1999.

474 Sarah Curtis, "Crosstown project clears zoning hurdle," *Bay State Banner*, July 29, 1999.

475 Yawu Miller, "Cinema pulls out of Crosstown deal," *Bay State Banner*, June 29, 2000.

476 Mark Micheli, "After 5 years on drawing board, Crosstown work begins," *Boston Business Journal*, Nov. 20, 2002. https://www.bizjournals.com/boston/stories/2002/11/18/daily26.html.

477 Jeremy Schwab, "Crosstown project clears funding hurdle," *Bay State Banner*, Oct. 17, 2002.

478 Schwab, "Black-owned hotel."

479 Patrick Healy, "Kerry Hones Campaign Themes," *Boston Globe*, July 13, 2004. http://archive.boston.com/news/nation/articles/2004/07/13/kerry_hones_campaign_themes/.

480 Northeastern School of Architecture, "Case Studies: Transitions of Trust," Oct. 16, 2011.

481 *BWH Bulletin*, "Crosstown Center Garage Provides Parking for BWH Staff," Feb. 6, 2004. http://www.brighamandwomens.org/about_bwh/publicaffairs/news/publications/DisplayBulletin.aspx?articleid=1942.

482 Sykes, June 28, 2017; Environmental Business Council of New England website, http://ebcne.org/wp-content/uploads/2014/05/The-James-D.P.-Farrell-Award-for-Brownfields-Project-of-the-Year.pdf.

483 Thomas Welch, email communication, Aug. 1-2, 2017.

484 Schwab, July 29, 2004.

485 Beverley Johnson, July 19, 2017.

486 Russell E. Holmes, telephone interview with author, July 10. 2017.

487 Boston Redevelopment Authority, "Boston State Hospital, Current Proposals," Classic Reprint Series, Feb. 1, 1973.

488 Yawu Miller, "Boston State Develop Plans Move Forward," *Bay State Banner*, Nov. 22, 2001. https://search.proquest.com/docview/367441591.

489 Yawu Miller, "Cruz Designated to Build on Boston State." *Bay State Banner*, Sept. 11, 1997. https://search.proquest.com/docview/367334157.

490 Jim Clark, telephone interview with Sandra Larson, July 25, 2017.

491 John B. Cruz III, July 12, 2017; Tom Welch, July 12, 2017.

492 Cruz, July 12, 2017.

493 Jeremy Schwab, "New Housing Opens on Boston State Site," *Bay State Banner*, Oct. 11, 2005. https://search.proquest.com/docview/367297118.

494 MBE/worker utilization figures via email from Dan Cruz, July 18, 2017.

495 Edgar Carrera, Cruz Companies senior project manager, interviews with author at Harvard Commons July 16, 2017 and by telephone 8Aug. 4, 2017; also see Jenifer McKim, "Dorchester developer has a new vision for city homes," *Boston Globe*, Dec. 4, 2011. http://www.bostonglobe.com/2011/12/04/harvardcommons/mMa3vokFQ89BTVsI9Mne3N/story.html.

496 John B. Cruz III, July 12, 2017, and Edgar Carrere, interview with author, Harvard Commons, July 16, 2017.

497 Dan Cruz, interview with author, July 12, 2017, Boston.

498 Jim Clark, July 25, 2017.

499 Russell E. Holmes, July 10, 2017.

500 Lawrence W. Kennedy, *Planning the City upon a Hill: Boston since 1630*, University of Massachusetts Press, Apr. 27, 1994, 229.

501 Ibid., 230.

502 Yawu Miller, "Minority developers savor success with one Lincoln," *Bay State Banner,* Aug. 14, 2003.

503 Parcel To Parcel Linkage Program Interim Report: Kingston Bedford/ Parcel 18, Boston Redevelopment Authority, May, 1986.

504 Howard Manly, "One shining example," *Bay State Banner,* Sept. 9, 2010.

505 Wenty Bowen, *Bay State Banner;* Apr.6, 2000, 3.

506 Howard Manly, "Minority developers file suit against Northeastern Univ.," *Bay State Banner,* Aug. 14, 2013.

507 Jule Pattison-Gordon, "Court rules against minority firms in land use, profit sharing dispute," *Bay State Banner,* Jan. 18, 2017.

508 Richard Kindleberger, *Boston Globe,* Apr. 8, 2000, C.1.

509 Yawu Miller, "Minority developers savor success with One Linclon," *Bay State Banner,* Boston, Aug.14, 2003, 2.

510 Ibid.

511 Thomas C. Palmer Jr., "One Lincoln fetches a towering $705m," *Boston Globe,* Feb. 3, 2004.

512 Manly, "One shining example."

513 Peter Canellos, "Grove Hall restored 'granites' to give tenants lease on new life," *Boston Globe,* Jan. 13, 1989.

514 Desiree French, "Low-income project is made brand new," *Boston Globe,* Feb. 13, 1988.

515 Ibid.

516 Interview with United Housing Management principals, August 2016.

517 Manly, Howard, *Boston Banner,* Jan. 13, 2011.

518 See Bruce Mohl and Coleman M. Herman, "No Seat at the Table" *Commonwealth Magazine* (Nov. 15, 2013), for a social and economic profile of Blacks in Massachusetts today; see J. Jennings, et al, *Blacks in Massachusetts: Comparative Demographic, Social and Economic Experiences with Whites, Latinos, and Asians,* William M. Trotter Institute, University of Massachusetts Boston (December 2015); and for an overview of Boston's political history, see Melvin King's *Chain of Change* (South End Press, 1981).

519 See James Vrabel, *A People's History of the New Boston* (University of Massachusetts Press, 2014) for some discussion about the activism of Black women; also, King, ibid.; but the *Bay State Banner* has covered the work and impacts of these and other Black women extensively.

520 US Bureau of the Census, *Statistical Abstract of the United States: 1968* (Washington, DC, 1968), 21; Omar M. McRoberts, *Streets of Glory: Church and Community in a Black Urban Neighborhood* (Chicago:

University of Chicago Press, 2005), 18; "New England Luring Educated Negroes," *Berkshire Eagle*, Tuesday, Oct. 24, 1961, 14.

521 Robert C. Hayden, "A Historical Overview of Poverty among Blacks in Boston, 1950–1990," *Trotter Review* 17, no. 1, Article 8 (2007), 139.

522 Alexander Auerbach and Thomas Oliphant, "Boston Business Going to Work on Negro Unemployment," *Boston Globe*, May 19, 1968, 82.

523 Auerbach and Oliphant, "Boston Business Going to Work," 82.

524 <https://data.bls.gov/pdq/SurveyOutputServlet> accessed July 19, 2017.

525 Robert A. Jordan, "Will HUD Withhold Boston Funds to [E]nsure Hiring of Minorities," *Boston Globe*, May 11, 1977, 17.

526 Jordan, "Will HUD Withhold Boston Funds to [E]nsure Hiring of Minorities," 17.

527 These figures were reported in Stephan Thernstrom, *The Other Bostonians* (Cambridge: Harvard University Press, 1973), 179, Table 8.1.

528 Thernstrom, *The Other Bostonians* (Cambridge: Harvard University Press, 1973), 179, Table 8.10.

529 Carl M. Cobb, "Employment: an Illness at Boston City Hospital: 30 Qualified Blacks Not Hired," *Boston Globe*, June 25, 1968, 1.

530 *The Record Book: B.M.C. Durfee High School Yearbook 1942*, 24, 92, 114.

531 J. Lawrence, "Thomas J. Brown: Created Job Placement Agency for African-Americans," *Boston Globe*, July 16, 2013, B-12.

532 "Tom Brown Discusses Employment on WNAC," *Bay State Banner*, Sept. 10, 1966, 1.

533 Sue Davis, "Jobs Clearing House: A One-Man Show," *Bay State Banner*, Oct. 16, 1965, 7.

534 Interview with Melvin Miller on July 13, 2017.

535 "For Negroes, Business: Growing Cooperation," *Boston Globe*, Sunday, Jan. 3, 1965, B-18.

536 "For Negroes, Business: Growing," B-18.

537 John B. Value, "Tom Brown's Big Question: 'Why Shouldn't I Help Other Negroes," *Boston Globe*, Dec. 25, 1964, 44.

538 Davis, "Jobs Clearing House: A One-Man Show," 7.

539 "Business Women to Honor Negro," *Boston Globe*, Sunday, June 13, 1965, A-33.

540 Martin Gopen, "The Job Scene: A First at the First," *Bay State Banner*, Dec. 3, 1966, 6.

541 "Lectures," *Boston Globe*, Feb. 14, 1966, 30.

542 "NAACP Workshop Hosted by Lowell," *Bay State Banner*, Feb. 12, 1966, 2.

543 Alexander Auerbach and Thomas Oliphant, "Boston Business Going to Work on Negro Unemployment," *Boston Globe*, Sunday, May 19, 1968, 82.

544 "Employment: an Illness at Boston City Hospital: Thirty Qualified Blacks Not Hired," *Boston Globe*, Tuesday, June 25, 1968, 1.

545 Lawrence, "Thomas J. Brown; Created Job Placement Agency for African-Americans," B-12.

546 Hayden, "A Historical Overview of Poverty among Blacks in Boston, 1950–1990,"138; "WLB Approves Wage Increases in Four Decisions," *Boston Globe*, Mar. 18, 1943, 5; "Phone Co. Offers $2-$5 Raises to 27,000 Workers," *Boston Globe*, Oct. 11, 1950, 8.

547 John B. Value, "Much-Traveled Executive Keeps N.E. Phone Ringing: Profile In N.E. Business," *Boston Globe*, Feb. 13, 1964, 45; Alexander Auerbach, "New England Telephone Recruits the Ghetto," *Boston Globe*, Mar. 31, 1968, B1.

548 Ian Menzies, "A Quiet Plan to Aid Negroes," *Boston Globe*, Tuesday, July 14, 1964, 21.

549 "Negro Job Interviews Scheduled by Eight Firms," *Boston Globe*, Thursday, Dec. 3, 1964, 6.

550 Susan Davis, "N. E. Telephone Company Pioneers in Recruiting Negroes," *Bay State Banner*, Jan. 7, 1967, 13; Alexander Auerbach, "New England Telephone Recruits the Ghetto," B1.

551 Auerbach, "New England Telephone Recruits the Ghetto," B1.

552 Ken O. Botwright, "14,000 Idle in N.E.T.," *Boston Globe*, Apr. 27, 1968, 2.

553 Frank Donovan, "Phone Workers End Their 128-Day Strike," *Boston Globe*, Sept. 1, 1968, 1.

554 Lupo, "Boston Urban Coalition Tackles Jobs, Housing," 24.

555 Robert A. Jordan, "Five Blacks Quit Urban Coalition," *Boston Globe*, July 18, 1968, 1.

556 Interview of Dennis Tourse on June 13, 2017.

557 Laurence Collins, "Unity Bank Has Rapid Rise," *Boston Globe*, Aug. 19, 1973, A106.

558 "Miller Quits Unity Bank," *Boston Globe*, Jan. 26, 1977, 21.

559 Peter Cowan, "Average Water Bill in Boston to Jump from $89 to $132," *Boston Globe*, June 22, 1978, 3.

560 Miller interview.

561 William F. Doherty, "Suit Filed to Withhold $14 Million from Boston: Second Action Against DPW Charges Discriminatory Hiring Practices, Seeks to Block Funds," *Boston Globe*, Nov. 30, 1976, 3.

562 Robert A. Jordan, "Will HUD Withhold Boston Funds to Insure Hiring of Minorities?" *Boston Globe*, May 11, 1977, 17.

563 "Scales Ousted as Water-Sewer Director in Hub, *Boston Globe*, June 22, 1978, 3.

564 Cowan, "Average Water Bill in Boston to Jump from $89 to $132," 3.

565 Caroline V. Clark and Frank McCoy, "25 Hottest Blacks on Wall Street," *Black Enterprise* (October 1992), 47.

566 "Where Are They Now?" *Black Enterprise* (October 1996), 94.

567 David G. Yosifon, "Abutters Say BWSC Concessions Inadequate," *Bay State Banner*, Nov. 5, 1998, 1.

568 Tourse interview.

569 Diane E. Lewis, "Extortion or Inclusion," *Boston Globe*, Aug. 18, 1992, 37.

570 "United Front's 21 Demands to Business, Government," *Boston Globe*, Apr. 9, 1968, 16.

571 Thomas Oliphant, "Plan Signed for Bringing 2,000 More Blacks into Building Trades," *Boston Globe*, June 19, 1970, 3.

572 Thomas Oliphant, "2 Black Groups Denounce Minority Plan," *Boston Globe*, June 28, 1970, 45.

573 "Jobs for Blacks in Building," *Boston Globe*, Nov. 12, 1971, 18.

574 Thomas Oliphant, "Boston Plan for Minority Hiring Seen in Danger after BCH Protest," *Boston Globe*, Aug. 21, 1970, 1.

575 Robert A. Jordan, "Solution Possible in Minority Hiring," *Boston Globe*, July 29, 1976, 13.

576 Robert A. Jordan, "Proposals—and Problems—of the Southwest Corridor," *Boston Globe*, July 15, 1976, 23.

577 Robert A. Jordan, "Decision Due in White Contractors' Suit of 30% Minority Formula," *Boston Globe*, Sept. 2, 1976, 24.

578 Chuck Turner, "No Dues Structure at Clearing House," *Boston Globe*, Dec. 29, 1976, 30.

579 Dan Swanson, "Minority Construction Gains Have Cost Years of Struggle," *Bay State Banner*, Jan. 26, 1978, 9A.

580 Gary McMillan and Robert J. Anglin, "2,000 Workers Demonstrate at City Hall Plaza," *Boston Globe*, May 8, 1976, 1.

581 "White Reportedly Will Still Withhold 3d World Funds," *Boston Globe*, Dec. 14, 1976, 7.

582 David Rogers, "White Yields to Council Pressure, Drops 'Third World' CETA Funds," *Boston Globe*, Nov. 3, 1976, 24.

583 Walter Haynes, "U.S. Tells White: Restore Third World Job Center or Lose $7.5 M," *Boston Globe*, Dec. 8, 1976, 3; Cislyn Munroe, "3rd World Job Agency Funded Once Again," *Bay State Banner*, Jan. 13, 1977, 1.

584 Turner, "No Dues Structure at Clearing House," 30.

585 Chuck Turner, "Q & A: Minority Construction Workers Want Larger Share of Job Pie," *Boston Globe*, Dec. 5, 1976, 2.

586 Nick King, "Boston: Jobs Policy Goes to Court," *Boston Globe*, Nov. 28, 1982, A1, A4.

587 Turner resigned from his position as executive director of the TWJCH in March 1979 to become full-time director of the Fannie Lou Hamer Memorial Housing Foundation, the housing development arm of the Clearinghouse. Other groups that comprised the Boston Jobs Coalition included the South Boston Clergy Association, the Jamaica Plain Neighborhood Development Corp., the Tenant Policy Council of Boston, the United South End Settlement House, the South End Project Area Committee, the Dennison House, the Dorchester House, and the Oficina Hispana.

588 Chuck Turner, "Sharing the Pie: The Boston Jobs Coalition," *Labor Research Review* 1: no. 12, Article 4, (1988), 82–83.

589 Carr, "White OK's Job Pact Favoring Residents," 11.

590 The relevant portion of the mayor's order is as follows: (1) On any construction project funded in whole or in part by City funds, or funds which, in accordance with a federal grant or otherwise, the City expends or administers, and to which the City is a signatory to the construction contract, the worker hours on a craft-by-craft basis shall be performed, in accordance with the contract documents established herewith, as follows: a. at least 50% by bona fide Boston residents; b. at least 25% by minorities; c. at least 10% by women ... For purposes of this paragraph worker hours shall include work performed by persons filling apprenticeship and on-the-job training positions ... (2) Each department of the City of Boston contracting with any private corporation or person for such construction projects, shall include in all such contracts the provisions of the City of Boston Supplemental Minority Participation and Residents Preference Section to insure compliance with this Executive Order ... (3) The Equal Employment Opportunity Contract Compliance Office of the City of Boston through the awarding Authority shall be responsible for monitoring and enforcing the provisions of this Executive Order and the contract provisions established in accordance therewith.

591 Robert B. Carr, "White OK's Job Pact Favoring Residents," *Boston Globe*, Sept. 7, 1979, 11.

592 Turner, "Sharing the Pie: The Boston Jobs Coalition," 84.

593 "White Reaffirms Policy on Jobs," *Boston Globe*, Mar. 21, 1980, 17.

594 Nick King, "Boston: Jobs Policy Goes to Court," *Boston Globe*, Nov. 28, 1982, A1, A4.

595 The other plaintiffs were the Massachusetts State Building and Construction Trades Council, AFL-CIO; the Building and Construction Trades Council of the Metropolitan District, AFL-CIO; individual contractors incorporated in Massachusetts; contractors incorporated in Rhode Island; and members of sixteen trade unions.

596 *Massachusetts Council of Construction Employers v. Mayor of Boston*, 384 Mass. 466, 425 N.E.2d 346 (1981).

597 King, "Boston: Jobs Policy Goes to Court," A4.

598 *White v. Mass. Council of Constr. Employers*, 460 U.S. 204 (1983).

599 Ed Quill, "Jobs for Hub Law Passed," *Boston Globe*, Sept. 29, 1983, 1.

600 Turner, "Sharing the Pie: The Boston Jobs Coalition," 85.

601 Turner, "Sharing the Pie," 85.

602 Michael K. Frisby, "City Seeks to Enforce Hiring Rule," *Boston Globe*, Nov. 1, 1985, 24.

603 Kirk Scharfenberg, "Resident Jobs Plan Passes a Milestone: Mayor Expands Program Beyond Public Projects," *Boston Globe*, July 21, 1985, A17.

604 Turner, "Sharing the Pie: The Boston Jobs Coalition," 86.

605 They included Boston School Committee member Juanita B. Wade, City Councilor Bruce C. Bolling, Rep. Gloria Fox, former state Rep. Melvin H. King, and Roxbury activist Sadiki Kambon.

606 Peggy Hernandez, "Black Leaders Protest Job Picks, More Residents Urged at Work Site," *Boston Globe*, Dec. 16, 1990, 38.

607 Derrick Z. Jackson, "Fair-sharing in Roxbury," *Boston Globe*, Feb. 13, 1991 (no page cited).

608 Jackson, "Fair-sharing in Roxbury" (no page cited).

609 Diane E. Lewis, "A Shrinking Pie: Women, Minorities Press for More Construction Jobs; What Jobs, Ask Unions?" *Boston Globe*, June 5, 1991 (no page cited); Don Aucoin, "City, After Sit-In, Urges Project Hire More Minorities," *Boston Globe*, June 7, 1991 (no page cited).

610 Aucoin, "City, After Sit-In, Urges," (no page cited).

611 "Ship Firm Brings Jobs to Negroes," *Boston Globe*, July 11, 1965, 3.

612 "General Dynamics Recruiting Negroes," *Boston Globe*, Aug. 3, 1966, 48.

613 "Job Week Gets 309 Applicants," *Bay State Banner*, Sept. 3, 1966, 6.

614 Martin Gopen, "The Job Scene," *Bay State Banner*, Nov. 19, 1966, 6.

615 "NAACP Boycotts Three Local Baking Firms," *Bay State Banner*, Oct. 16, 1965, 1.

616 Janet Riddell, "Says City Denies Jobs to Negroes," *Boston Globe*, Aug. 18, 1966, 13.

617 "NAACP Presents Annual Awards," *Bay State Banner*, Dec. 10, 1966, 1.

618 In addition to job opportunities, the PPB was active in voter registration and education, educational counseling, youth programming, and black history and culture.

619 John A. Robinson, "NAACP Program Aids 1,000 Hub Jobless," *Boston Globe*, Nov. 15, 1968, 24.

620 "Guscott to Be Honored" *Bay State Banner*, Mar. 27, 1969, 2.

621 "Guscott Elected ABCD President," *Bay State Banner*, June 11, 1970, 9.

622 "Manpower," *Bay State Banner*, Oct. 8, 1970, 9A.

623 Tracy Dixon, "Family Business Has Roots in Rebuilding the Community," *Bay State Banner*, June 17, 1993, 2A.

624 Yawu Miller, "Ken Guscott, 91, Left Legacy in Hub," *Bay State Banner*, Thursday, Mar. 9, 2017, 1.

625 See, James Jennings, *Black Churches and Neighborhood Empowerment in Boston, Massachusetts 1960s and 1970s: Lessons for Today* (William Monroe Trotter Institute, University of Massachusetts Boston, 2012).

626 "O.I.C. Adds Four to Staff," *Bay State Banner*, Nov. 9, 1967, 11.

627 "Black Self-Help: List of Programs Initiated by Negroes to Improve Their Community," *Boston Globe*, Mar. 19, 1968, 30A.

628 "Manpower," *Bay State Banner*, Oct. 8, 1970, 9A.

629 Robert A. Jordan, "OIC Would Sever Federal Purse Strings: Hub Job Center Seeks Self Reliance," *Boston Globe*, May 26, 1968, 72; "Lee Names Execs," *Bay State Banner*, May 23, 1968, 13.

630 "Manpower," 9A.

631 "Employers Sign With Urban League Negro Jobs Program," *Boston Globe*, June 2, 1964, 4.

632 "Urban League Director Resigns," *Bay State Banner*, Jan. 14, 1967, 6.

633 John Daniels, *In Freedom's Birthplace: A Study of the Boston Negroes* (Boston, MA.: Houghton Mifflin, 1914), 6.

634 *Quock Walker v. Nathaniel Jennison.*

635 James Oliver Horton and Lois E. Horton, *Black Bostonians: Family Life and Community Struggle in the Antebellum North* (New York: Holmes & Meier, 1999), xvi.

636 William Cooper Nell, *The Colored Patriots of the American Revolution with Sketches of Several Distinguished Colored Persons: to Which is Added a Brief Survey of the Condition and Prospects of Colored Americans* (Boston: Robert F. Wallcut, 1855), 21.

637 Horton and Horton, *Black Bostonians: Family Life and Community Struggle in the Antebellum North*, xvi.

638 Nell, *The Colored Patriots*, 87–90.

639 Charles M. Wiltse, ed., *David Walker's Appeal, in Four Articles; Together with a Preamble to the Colored Citizens of the World* (New York: Hill and Wang, 1965), 4, 12, 43.

640 "Elections," *Boston Daily Evening Transcript*, Wednesday, Nov. 7, 1866, 4; "For Representative," *Boston Daily Advertiser*, Wednesday, Nov. 7, 1866, 4.

641 "Elections," 4; "For Representative," 4.

642 "The Council Meeting," *Boston Daily Advertiser*, Thursday, Sept. 13, 1883, 5.

643 Stephen Kantrowitz, *More than Freedom: Fighting for Black Citizenship in a White Republic, 1829–1888* (New York: Penguin, 2012), 326; *Massachusetts Home Journal*, Mar. 12–13, 1867, CMA.

644 "For Representatives," *Boston Daily Advertiser*, Nov. 3, 1869, 4; George Ruffin served two terms in the Statehouse, from 1870 through 1871. The third African American state representative, Republican John James Smith of Boston, was elected to the House on November 5, 1867, with 617 votes. He served two terms.

645 "Vote for Councilmen," *Boston Daily Globe*, Wednesday, Dec. 15, 1875, 1; "The Charlestown Judgeship: The Nomination of George L. Ruffin Confirmed by the Executive Council," *Boston Daily Advertiser*, Tuesday, Nov. 20, 1883, 4.

646 Chapelle was reelected on November 6, 1883, with 1,147 votes, on November 4, 1884, with 831 votes, and on November 3, 1885, with 670 votes.

647 St. 1885, c. 316.

648 "Vote for Representatives," *Boston Daily Globe*, Wednesday, Nov. 3, 1886, 1. Armstrong was reelected on November 8, 1887, with 679 votes. "Vote for Representatives," *Boston Daily Globe*, Wednesday, Nov. 9, 1887, 1.

649 "For Councilmen," *Boston Daily Globe*, Wednesday, Dec. 10, 1884, 5; "Vote for Councilman," *Boston Daily Globe*, Wednesday, Dec. 16, 1885, 2.

650 "Vote for Representatives," *Boston Daily Globe*, Wednesday, Nov. 8, 1893, 2.

651 St. 1895, c. 461; *Bryant v. Rich's Grill*, 216 Mass.344, 347, 103 N.E. 925, 926 (1914); Daniels, *In Freedom's Birthplace: A Study of Boston Negroes*, 95–96.

652 Gregory Bond, "The Strange Career of William Henry Lewis," in *Out of the Shadows: A Biographical History of African American Athletes*, ed. David Kenneth Wiggins (Fayetteville: University of Arkansas Press, 2006), 50. Lewis was also elected to represent the Fifth Ward as a Cambridge City Councilman on Dec. 12, 1899. See "Cambridge: Common Council," *Boston Daily Globe*, Wednesday, Dec. 13, 1899, 9.

653 "Cambridge," *Boston Daily Globe*, Wednesday, Nov. 5, 1902, 8.

654 "Mass. Elects First Negro," *Berkshire Evening Eagle*, Nov. 7, 1946, 1.

655 "Cambridge," *Boston Daily Globe*, Wednesday, Dec. 16, 1896, 3.

656 "Cambridge: Mayor Bancroft's Majority is 1655; City Again No License, Common Council," *Boston Daily Globe*, Wednesday, Dec. 12, 1894, 2.

657 "Gould in Chelsea: He Has 67 Plurality over Ex-Alderman Rowe," *Boston Post*, Wednesday, Dec. 12, 1900, 5. Williams also became the first African American to enter the volunteer army of the United States with a captain's commission on May 16, 1898. "First Colored Officers," *New York Times*, May 17, 1898.

658 "Plurality 971, Mayor Willard Gets it in Chelsea," *Boston Daily Globe*, Wednesday, Nov. 19, 1902, 2; "Willard Wins in Chelsea," *Boston Post*, Wednesday, Dec. 14, 1904, 12; "J. H. Malone Victor," *Boston Post*, Wednesday, Dec. 13, 1911, 16; "Many Surprises in the City Elections," *Boston Post*, Wednesday, Dec. 11, 1912, 14; "Malone Beats Willard," *Boston Post*, Wednesday, Dec. 15, 1915, 11; "Heavy Vote in Chelsea," *Boston Daily Globe*, Tuesday, Dec. 14, 1915, 5; "Bigger Margin for Wets," *Boston Post*, Wednesday, Dec. 12, 1917, 2.

659 During the nineteenth century it was called the Boston School Board.

660 "The City Election: Republican Ward Caucuses Last Night," *Boston Daily Advertiser*, Friday, Dec. 11, 1874, 1; "Republican Ward Caucuses," *Boston Post*, Friday, Dec. 11, 1874, 3; "The Vote for School Committee," *Boston Daily Globe*, Wednesday, Dec. 16, 1874, 1.

661 "School Committee," *Boston Daily Globe*, Wednesday, Dec. 16, 1896, 1; "Vote for School Committee," *Boston Daily Globe*, Wednesday, Dec. 22, 1897, 4–5.

662 "Boston Negro Gets Office: William H. Lewis Appointed Assistant United States District Attorney," *New York Times*, Jan. 13, 1903, 8.

663 "Colored Lawyer for High Office," *Lowell Sun*, Friday, Oct. 28, 1910, 12.

664 "Lewis is Confirmed," *Boston Transcript*, June 15, 1911; J. Clay Smith Jr., *Emancipation: The Making of the Black Lawyer, 1844–1944* (Philadelphia: University of Pennsylvania Press, 1999), 106.

665 "Negro Lawyer One of the First to Defend Ponzi," *Boston Daily Globe*, June 27, 1957, 11.

666 *Harvard University Directory* (Cambridge: Harvard University Press, 1914), 379; *General Alumni Catalogue of Boston University 1918*, 213; "First Colored Man to Get the Office: L. S. Hicks Made Assistant Corporation Counsel," *Boston Daily Globe*, Monday, Dec. 24, 1917, 2; "Hicks Named as Assistant: Joins Corporation Counsel of the City," *Boston Post*, Tuesday, Dec. 25, 1917, 11.

667 "Kaan and Bullock Appointed by Benton to Assist in Legal Work on 'Northern Artery,'" *Boston Daily Globe*, July 1, 1924, 17.

668 "Fuller Names Bullock to State Parole Board," *Boston Daily Globe*, Mar. 24, 1927, 19.

669 Bullock was replaced on the parole board by Dr. Silas "Shag" F. Taylor, a black pharmacist from Roxbury.

670 "Confirm Appointment of Worcester Doctor," *Fitchburg Sentinel*, Wednesday, Apr. 14, 1943, 5; "Governor Hints He May Drop Bullock from Parole Post," *Boston Daily Globe*, June 16, 1949, 1.

671 "Matthew Bullock, 91, Athlete, Parole Official," *Boston Daily Globe*, Dec. 19, 1972, 29; "Try Correction," *Boston Daily Globe*, Tuesday, Aug. 31, 1948, 16; "Use of Paroles to Cut Crime Urged by Expert," *Berkshire Evening Eagle*, Tuesday, Aug. 31, 1948, 4.

672 *Catalogue of Graduates of the Public Latin School in Boston, 1816–1917* (Boston, Mass: Boston Latin School Association, 1917), 75; *Quinquennial Catalogue of the Officers and Graduates of Harvard University, 1636–1915* (Cambridge, MA: Harvard University Press, 1915), 409, 1043; "Several Appointed to Posts in Boston Law Department," *Boston Daily Globe*, Feb. 1, 1930, 4; "Two Lawyers Lose City Jobs: Wolff Went to Harvard with Roosevelt," *Boston Daily Globe*, Mar. 7, 1934, 8; "Kelly Names 18 Assistants," *Lowell Sun*, Monday, Jan. 17, 1949, 7.

673 "Profile of Board," *Boston Daily Globe*, Wednesday, Nov. 13, 1963, 2.

674 "Lane Named Clerk of Juvenile Court," *Boston Daily Globe*, Thursday, Feb. 12, 1931, 25.

675 "Profile of Board," 2.

676 "Executive Council Okays Lane for the Parole Board," *Boston Daily Globe*, Friday, June 26, 1959, 33; "Legislature Heading for Adjournment?" *Boston Daily Globe*, Friday, June 12, 1964, 6.

677 William C. Nell, "Harvard Class Day Honors," *New York Age*, Saturday, June 28, 1890, issue 40, 1.

678 Stephen R. Fox, *The Guardian of Boston: William Monroe Trotter* (New York: Atheneum, 1970), 27–30; "Goodbye, Fair Harvard," *Boston Daily Globe*, Wednesday, June 24, 1896, 4–5.

679 *Boston Literary and Historical Association Program 1904–1905.*

680 "Negroes in New England: Richard Carroll Writes of Their Good Education and Poor Business Opportunities," 10.

681 *Boston Herald*, Feb. 20, 1907, (Social Column); Elizabeth McHenry, *Forgotten Readers: Recovering the Lost History of African American Literary Societies* (Durham, NC: Duke University Press, 2002), 360.

682 "The Sooty Trade: Chimney Sweeps and their History in Boston," *Boston Post*, Thursday, Oct. 8, 1885, 1.

683 Isaac S. Mullen, "A Brief History of Negro Business and Professional Men of Boston from 1846 to 1915 and Other Facts of the Race," in *Official Souvenir Program of Sixteenth Convention of the National Negro Business League* (Boston: A. W. Lavalle, Printer, 1915), 51.

684 "Sweep-Oh-Sweep!" *Boston Daily Globe*, Saturday, Jan. 9, 1892, 4.

685 "Richest Colored Man: Nathaniel Springfield Dead in Portsmouth, Va.," *Boston Daily Globe*, Thursday, Dec. 17, 1896, 4; Mullen, "A Brief History of Negro Business and Professional Men of Boston from 1846 to 1915 and Other Facts of the Race," 51; "Sets in Colored Society," 29.

686 "Three Churches Remembered: Will of the Late Nathaniel Springfield Filed in Probate Court," *Boston Daily Globe*, Monday, Dec. 28, 1896, 5.

687 William Newton Hartshorn, *An Era of Progress and Promise, 1863–1910* (Boston, MA: Priscilla Publishing, 1910), 416.

688 Gilbert & Co. advertisement, *The Women's Era*, vol. 3, no. 2, July 1896.

689 A'Lelia Bundles, *On Her Own Ground: The Life and Times of Madam C.J. Walker* (New York: Scribner, 2001), 213.

690 *Official Souvenir Program*, 42.

691 *Official Souvenir Program*, 42.

692 Bundles, *On Her Own Ground: The Life and Times of Madam C.J. Walker*, 69.

693 *The Boston Directory Containing the City Record, Directory of the Citizens, Business Directory and Street Directory with Maps for the Year Commencing July 1, 1908, No. CIV* (Boston: Sampson & Murdock, 1908), 2116; *The Boston Directory for the Year Commencing August 1, 1924, No. CXX* (Boston: Sampson & Murdock, 1924), 990.

694 "To Be Permanent: The National Negro Business League Organized," *Boston Daily Globe*, Saturday, Aug. 25, 1900, 2.

695 Phoebe Ann Glover's date of birth is a mystery. In the 1900 US census, she indicated that she was born in May 1850; however, in the earlier 1880 US census, she reported that she was thirty-five years old, making her year of birth about 1845. In the city of Boston's marriage registry for the year 1867—the year that she married William Glover—she listed her age as twenty-five, establishing her birth in about the year 1842. But in the earliest record available, the 1865 US census, Glover claimed she was twenty-four years old, making her year of birth 1841.

696 Adelaide M. Cromwell, *The Other Brahmins: Boston's Black Upper Class 1750–1950* (Fayetteville: University of Arkansas Press, 1994), 53.

697 *The Boston Directory Containing the City Record, Directory of the Citizens, Business Directory and Street Directory with Map for the Year Commencing July 1, 1907, No. CIII* (Boston: Sampson & Murdock, 1907), 719.

698 *The Boston Directory Containing the City Record, a Directory of the Citizens, Business Directory and Street Directory for the Year Commencing July 1, 1893, No. LXXXIX* (Boston: Sampson, Murdock, 1893), 616; *The Boston Directory Containing the City Record, a Directory of the Citizens, Business Directory and Street Directory for the Year Commencing July 1, 1895, No. XCI* (Boston: Sampson, Murdock, 1895), 649; *Boston 1904 City Business Directory*, p. 260; *Boston Register and Business Directory 1921, vol. 85* (Boston: Sampson & Murdock, 1921), 337.

699 "James R. Hamm: News Dealer Who Does a $10,000 Business in Periodicals Yearly," *New York Age*, Thursday, Oct. 17, 1907, 1.

700 *Official Souvenir Program*, back cover.

701 *Official Souvenir Program*, 18.

702 *1880 U.S. Federal Census*, Needham, Norfolk County, Massachusetts, Page No. 18, Lines 7–10. Therese, their third child, was born on August 25, 1881, in Wellesley, Massachusetts, and Narka, their last, was born on December 16, 1888, in Newton, Massachusetts. *1900 U.S. Federal Census*, Boston, Ward 12, Suffolk County, Massachusetts, Sheet No. 2, Lines 85–90; *Births Registered in the Town of Wellesley for the Year 1881*, Page No. 311; *Births Registered in the City of Newton for the Year 1888*, Page No. 248, Line 489.

703 *Directory of the City of Newton 1884–85* (Newton, MA: Press of the Newton Graphic, 1884),108; *The Newton Directory, Containing a General Directory of the Citizens, a Numerical House Directory of the Citizens and*

a *Business Directory, and the City Record, No. X* (Worcester: Drew, Allis, 1887), 204, 498; *The Newton Directory, Containing a General Directory of the Citizens, a Numerical House Directory of the Citizens and a Business Directory, and the City and County Register, No. XIV* (Worcester: Drew Allis, 1895), 383, 706.

704 "Newton's Rich Men," *Boston Daily Advertiser*, Friday, Sept. 10, 1886, 8.

705 "Some Vacation Rambles: Lawyer Stewart in New England," *New York Freeman*, Vol. II, No. 43, Saturday, Sept. 11, 1886, 1.

706 "President Harrison's Family: How They Will Be Lodged and Served During Their Stay at Newton," *Boston Daily Advertiser*, Friday, Sept. 11, 1891, 8; "Hotel Abbotsford" Advertisement, *Boston Evening Transcript*, Thursday, Sept. 17, 1891, 3; "Business Troubles," *Boston Daily Globe*, Saturday, Apr. 23, 1892, 10.

707 "Pres. Harrison's Family Eagerly Awaited," *Boston Daily Advertiser*, Monday, Sept. 14, 1891, 8.

708 "New Inn at Squantum Park," *Boston Daily Globe*, May 14, 1898, 7.

709 *Official Souvenir Program*, 53; *The Boston Directory Containing the City Record, a Directory of the Citizens Business Directory and Street Directory with Map for the Year Commencing July 1, 1916, No. CXII*, 1715.

710 He died in Natick, Massachusetts, on April 3, 1975.

711 *"Negroes Display Progress,"* Gazette and Courier (Greenfield, MA), Aug. 21, 1915, 7.

712 "Negroes in New England: Richard Carroll Writes of Their Good Education and Poor Business Opportunities," *State* (Columbia, S.C.), Nov. 22, 1911, issue 7344, 10.

713 "Edgar P. Benjamin Has Done Much for the Hub's Colored People," *Boston Daily Globe*, Aug. 4, 1927, 23.

714 "Nathaniel Julien Credit Union Founder 86," *Boston Daily Globe*, Aug. 10, 1967, 45.

715 "Church Honors Credit Union for High Standards," *Boston Daily Globe*, Monday, Apr. 27, 1953, 6.

716 "Bank Takes Over Credit Union," *Boston Daily Globe*, Dec. 25, 1980, 63.

717 "Real Estate Matters, *Boston Daily Globe*, Monday, Jan. 20, 1902, 4; "Transfers in Roxbury and Other Parts of the City," *Boston Daily Globe*, Wednesday, Mar. 11, 1903, 8; "South End Sales," *Boston Daily Globe*, Friday, Apr. 2, 1920, 9.

718 *New York Age*, Thursday, Oct. 17, 1907, 1.

719 *Sarah C. Roberts v. City of Boston*, 59 Mass. 198, 5 Cush. 198 (1849).

720 Mass. Laws 1855, Ch. 256, § 1.

721 "Eminent Colored Folks," *Boston Sunday Globe*, Sunday, July 29, 1894, 14.

722 J. Clay Smith Jr., *Emancipation: The Making of the Black Lawyer, 1844–1944* (Philadelphia: University of Pennsylvania Press, 1999), 103.

723 *The Boston Directory Containing the City Record, a Directory of the Citizens, Business Directory and Street Directory for the Year Commencing July 1, 1886, No. LXXXII* (Boston: Sampson, Murdock, 1886), 1329.

724 Edward Everett Brown, "Importance of Race Pride," in *Lift Every Voice: African American Oratory 1787–1900*, eds. Philip S. Foner and Robert James Branham (Tuscaloosa, AL: University of Alabama Press, 1998), 685.

725 "Claims of Colored Men: They Propose to Bolt the Republican Ticket Unless They Are Recognized," *Boston Daily Globe*, Monday, Aug. 24, 1891, 3.

726 "Wolff to Lead Bay State G. A. R.," *Boston Daily Globe*, Tuesday, Feb. 14, 1905, 14; "To Lead Great Parade: Commander Wolff Will Have Unique Honor at Denver," 3.

727 James H. Wolff, *The Building of the Republic: An Oration Delivered at Faneuil Hall, July 4, 1910* (Boston: Printing Department Document No. 94, 1910), 12.

728 "James Wolff Dies in Hospital," *Boston Herald*, Monday, May 5, 1913.

729 *General Alumni Catalogue of Boston University 1918* (Boston: W. J. Maxwell, 1918), 166; Wilson also attended Harvard Law School for one year in 1917.

730 "Boston's National League," *New York Age*, Saturday, Nov. 5, 1887, issue 4, 1; "Commending the Generous: Meeting of the Colored National League," *Boston Daily Globe*, Wednesday, Jan. 2, 1889, 2.

731 J. Gordon Street, "Boston Wakes the Echoes," *New York Freeman*, Saturday, Aug. 20, 1887, issue 40, 1.

732 "Will Not Be Moved Away: Meeting of the Corporation of the Home for Aged Colored Women," *Boston Daily Globe*, Wednesday, Jan. 10, 1900, 10.

733 *Thirty-sixth Annual Report of the State Board of Charity of Massachusetts for the Year Ending November 30, 1914, Part II* (Boston: Wright & Potter, 1915), 69.

734 They were initially admitted to the ABA in 1911, but immediately expelled by its executive committee when their races were revealed. "Men's League for Women's Suffrage Has Meeting and Outlines Some of Its Plans," *Boston Daily Globe*, Thursday, Mar. 11, 1915, 18.

735 *Boston Literary and Historical Association Program 1904–05.*

736 *The Crisis*, December 1939, 374; "Pythians Reelect Barco Chancellor: 3,500 Membership Reported by Colored Group," *Boston Daily Globe*, July 8, 1926, 4.

737 Reno, *Memoirs of the Judiciary and the Bar of New England for the Nineteenth Century*, 566.

738 Gatewood, *Aristocrats of Color: The Black Elite*, 325.

739 "Bar Plantation Songs from Boston Schools as Result of Protest By Leading Colored Citizens," *Lowell Sun*, Friday, Nov. 13, 1914, 4.

740 "Somerville" *Boston Daily Globe*, Tuesday, Feb. 14, 1922, 5.

741 "Much Still Remains to Be Done Actually to Emancipate Negroes," [*San Jose*] *Evening News*, Dec. 14, 1918, vol. 168, no. 578, 6; Mark R. Schneider, *Boston Confronts Jim Crow, 1890–1920* (Boston: Northeastern University Press, 1997), 136.

742 "Fr. Haas Declares America Responsible for Dictators," *Boston Daily Globe*, May 20, 1938, 16.

743 *The Crisis*, December 1939, 374.

744 "Race Line in Politics: Republicans Denounced for Not Keeping Promises," *Boston Daily Globe*, Wednesday, Jan. 14, 1891; "In Memory of Devens: the Colored National League Pass Resolutions of Regret," *Boston Daily Advertiser*, Wednesday, Jan. 14, 1891, No. 12, Column G; "They Remembered Gen. Butler," *Boston Daily Globe*, Wednesday, Jan. 18, 1893, 3.

745 "Commending the Generous: Meeting of the Colored National League," *Boston Daily Globe*, Wednesday, Jan. 2, 1889, 2; "Colored National League: Election of Officers and Reports on Matters of Particular Interests," *Boston Daily Globe*, Wednesday, Jan. 13, 1892, 3.

746 "Voted Not to Amalgamate," *Boston Daily Globe*, Thursday, July 8, 1897, 8; "Attucks Honored: Colored Speakers Join in Denouncing Expansion," *Boston Post*, Tuesday, Mar. 7, 1899, 8.

747 "Lawyer Brown Considered Good Wheel in Fitzgerald Machine," *Boston Post*, Feb. 14, 1907, 5.

748 "Observe 20 Years of Married Life," *Boston Sunday Post*, Sept. 22, 1912, 11.

749 "Colored Men for Gaston," 2.

750 In the February 1890 issue of the *New England Magazine*, for example, Grimké provided an absorbing historical account of "Colonel Robert G. Shaw and His Black Regiment," and in the December 1890 issue, he provided an interesting historical paper on "Anti-Slavery Boston." "Magazines of the Month," *Indianapolis Journal*, Thursday, Feb. 6, 1890, 7; "Magazines of the Month," *Indianapolis Journal*, Thursday, Dec. 11, 1890, 3; Wilson,

"The Selection of an Auditor," 1; "Hard Work Did It: Archibald H. Grimké is a Close Student, a Successful Lawyer and Literary Man, and is Liked by His Friends," *Boston Daily Globe*, Friday, July 27, 1894, 4.

751 Archibald Henry Grimké, *William Lloyd Garrison, the Abolitionist* (New York: Funk & Wagnalls, 1891); Archibald Henry Grimké, *The Life of Charles Sumner, the Scholar in Politics* (New York: Funk & Wagnalls, 1892); Archibald Henry Grimké, *Why Disfranchisement is Bad* (Philadelphia: Press of E. A. Wright, 1904).

752 *Boston Literary and Historical Association Program 1904–1905*.

753 "Annual Meeting of the National Association for the Advancement of Colored People, *The Appeal* (Saint Paul, MN), Saturday, Jan. 22, 1916.

754 "NAACP," *The Appeal* (Saint Paul, MN), Saturday, July 12, 1919, 2.

755 "Collector Gill Not Worried," *Boston Post*, Friday, June 24, 1898, 8.

756 "Young Grand Master: Head of Colored Free Masons in Massachusetts, William L. Reed of Boston Chosen by Prince Hall Grand Lodge," *Boston Daily Globe*, Friday, Dec. 22, 1899, 7.

757 "George U. Crocker for the Position of City Treasurer," *Boston Daily Globe*, Saturday, Aug. 10, 1901, 3; "William L. Reed, Council Executive Secretary, Dies," 10.

758 "Around the Town," *Boston Daily Globe*, Aug. 30, 1904, 6; "Gov. Cox Reappoints Reed Executive Secretary," 22.

759 "Reed Reelected Despite His Age: Curley Praises Veteran Executive Secretary," 16.

760 "William L. Reed, Council Executive Secretary Dies," 10.

761 Smith, *Emancipation: The Making of the Black Lawyer, 1844–1944*, 110.

762 "Several Appointed to Posts in Boston Law Department," *Boston Daily Globe*, Feb. 1, 1930, 4.

763 "Rainey to Be Highest Paid Colored Officer," *Boston Daily Globe*, Feb. 2, 1930, A29.

764 "Atty. Julian Rainey Served as Advisor to Pres. Roosevelt," *Boston Globe*, Mar. 31, 1961, 25.

765 "As Alternates Chairman McGrath Picks Representatives of Eight Racial Groups," *North Adams Transcript*, Saturday, Mar. 7, 1936, 6; "National Convention: Democratic Slate," *Boston Daily Globe*, Apr. 29, 1936, 14.

766 "Rainey Appointed Campaign Leader: Will Direct Democratic Negro Work in the East," *Boston Daily Globe*, July 30, 1936, 6.

767 "Bill No. 1751," *Boston Daily Globe*, Mar. 22, 1941, 10.

768 "Discrimination Cases Cited by U.S. Official at Legislative Hearing," *Boston Daily Globe*, Mar. 14, 1945, 4.

769 *General Alumni Catalogue of Boston University 1918* (Boston: W. J. Maxwell, 1918), 211.

770 "Four Women and 153 Men Pass Bar Examinations," *Boston Daily Globe,* July 21, 1908, 1.

771 "Three Men Selected to Supervise Coaching of Athletic Teams in Boston High Schools," *Boston Daily Globe,* Jan. 25, 1908, 4; "Appoints Athletic Teachers," *Boston Post,* May 19, 1908, 9; "Four Transferred: Shakeup in Boston High School Athletic Instructors," *Boston Daily Globe,* Sept. 16, 1910, 11; "Hub Instructors and Coaches Assigned," *Boston Post,* Thursday, Sept. 12, 1912. Although Matthews resigned from his position as athletic instructor and coach for the Boston Public Schools, he continued to coach the football and baseball teams at Mechanic Arts High School for a year. See "Somerville Starts Today," *Boston Post,* Tuesday, Sept. 9, 1913, 10.

772 "Matthews in U.S. Service," *Boston Post,* Wednesday, Apr. 24, 1912, 8; "W. C. Matthews Dies Suddenly in Capital," *Boston Daily Globe,* Apr. 11, 1928, 4.

773 "Matthews Named Special Assistant," *Boston Daily Globe,* Oct. 25, 1925, B7.

774 "John W. Schenck Named Asst. U.S. District Attorney," *Cambridge Chronicle,* Sept. 9, 1922, 18; "Schenck Now Assistant U.S. District Attorney," *Boston Daily Globe,* Sept. 10, 1922, 14.

775 "Taking Oath After Appointment: Governor Swears In Three Men," *Boston Daily Globe,* Jan. 7, 1937, 12; "John W. Schenck, Ex-U.S. Attorney, 93," *Boston Globe,* Feb. 6, 1962, 26.

776 "Judge Robinson Gives Testimonial as Juvenile Aide," *Boston Daily Globe,* Mar. 22, 1949, 3.

777 George Washington Williams, *History of the Negro Race in America, from 1619 to 1880, vol. 2* (New York: G. P. Putnam's Sons, 1883), 133–34; *General Catalogue of Bowdoin College and the Medical School of Maine, 1794–1902* (Brunswick, ME: Bowdoin College, 1902), 167. The first two black graduates of an American medical school graduated in 1847. David Jones Peck graduated from Rush Medical College in Chicago, and Henry Jenkins Roberts graduated from the Berkshire Medical Institute in Pittsfield, Massachusetts.

778 *The Liberator,* Friday, July 1, 1853, issue 26, 103.

779 "Summary of News," *Boston Investigator,* Wednesday, Sept. 20, 1854, 3.

780 Williams, *History of the Negro Race in America, from 1619 to 1880, vol. 2,* 133–34.

781 Herbert M. Morais, *The History of the Negro in Medicine* (New York: Publishers Company, 1967), 38.

782 Kantrowitz, *More than Freedom*, 229.

783 Smith, *Emancipation: The Making of the Black Lawyer*, 100; "Boston Post Court Record," *Boston Post*, Monday, Sept. 16, 1861, Column B.

784 *Marriages Solemnized in Charlestown, Middlesex County, Massachusetts, 1852; Marriages Registered in the Town of Charlestown for the years 1843 to 1873*, Vol. 9. Line No. 118.

785 *Eleventh Annual Report of the New England Female Medical College*, 4.

786 The other women were Mary Lockwood Allen of Williston, Vermont, and Elizabeth Kimball of South Reading, Massachusetts. "New England Female Medical College," *Boston Daily Advertiser*, Thursday, Mar. 3, 1864, issue 53, column F; "News Items," *The Congregationalist*, (Boston, MA) Friday, Mar. 11, 1864, 43; *Sixteenth Annual Catalogue and Report of the New England Female Medical College* (Boston: Published by the trustees, 1864), 4–5.

787 Rebecca Crumpler, MD, *A Book of Medical Discourses in Two Parts* (Boston: Cashman, Keating, 1883), 2–3.

788 Crumpler, *A Book of Medical Discourses.*

789 "Sets in Colored Society," *Boston Sunday Globe*, Sunday, July 22, 1894, 29.

790 "Sets in Colored Society," 29.

791 "Death of Dr. Still: Only Colored Man Ever Elected to Boston School Board," *Boston Daily Globe*, Saturday, June 22, 1895, 10.

792 That was also his residence. *The Boston Directory Embracing the City Record, a General Directory of the Citizens, and Business Directory for the Year Commencing July 1, 1876, No. LXXII* (Boston: Sampson, Davenport, 1876), 1065.

793 "Professor and Judge: Distinguished Colored Graduates of Harvard University," *Boston Daily Globe*, Saturday, Oct. 26, 1889, 6.

794 Nercessian, *Against All Odds*, 79.

795 See U.S., World War II Draft Registration Card of Augustus Riley. Sallie and Thomas had five children together: Carrie, John, Martha or "Mattie," Augustus, and Charles. *1880 U.S. Federal Census*, Monroe County, Alabama, page 6, lines 41–47.

796 He subsequently moved it to 536 Commonwealth Avenue, and then to 59 Bay State Road. *The Boston Directory Containing the City Record, Directory of the Citizens, Business Directory and Street Directory with Map for the Year Commencing July 1, 1916, No. CXII* (Boston: Sampson & Murdock, 1916), 2356.

797 "Harvard Lecturer 35 Years: Dr. Augustus Riley, 86, Retired Urology Expert," *Boston Daily Globe*, May 19, 1966, 40.

798 Robert C. Hayden and Jacqueline L. Harris, *Nine Black American Doctors* (Reading, MA: Addison-Wesley, 1976), 34; Nercessian, *Against All Odds*, 277.

799 Robert C. Hayden, *African-Americans in Boston: More Than 350 Years* (Boston: trustees of the Boston Public Library, 1992), 145.

800 *The Boston Directory ... for the Year Commencing July 1, 1916*, 2357.

801 *Journal of the National Medical Association* 46, no. 5, Sept. 1954, 370.

802 Richard R. Wright Jr., *Centennial Encyclopedia of the African Methodist Episcopal Church* (Philadelphia: Book of Concern of the A.M.E. Church, 1916), 294.

803 Hayden, *African-Americans in Boston*, 41.

804 "Councilmen Elected," *Boston Post*, Wednesday, Dec. 14, 1904, 4; "For Common Councilmen," *Boston Globe*, Wednesday, Dec. 14, 1904, 7; "Vote for Common Council, *Boston Globe*, Wednesday, Dec. 13, 1905, 4; "Common Council," *Boston Globe*, Wednesday, Dec. 13, 1905, 5; Vote for Common Council," *Boston Post*, Wednesday, Dec. 13, 1905, 8; "Vote for Common Council," *Boston Post*, Wednesday, Dec. 12, 1906, 9.

805 John T. Hilton served as most worshipful grand master from 1826 to 1827 and from 1837 to 1847. Prince Hall, the first most worshipful grand master, served from 1791 to 1807. Most Worshipful Prince Hall Grand Lodge, Free and Accepted Masons, Jurisdiction of Massachusetts, Past Most Worshipful Grand Masters <http:// www.princehall.org/pgm.html> (accessed Dec. 22, 2013).

806 John A. Kenney, *The Negro in Medicine* (Tuskegee, AL: Tuskegee Institute Press, 1912), 30.

807 "Colored Nurses' School: New Institution at 12 East Springfield St. Established through Efforts of Dr. C. N. Garland," *Boston Daily Globe*, Feb. 26, 1908, 3; John Daniels, *In Freedom's Birthplace: A Study of Boston Negroes* (Boston: Houghton Mifflin, 1914), 360; Nercessian, *Against All Odds*, 272.

808 Nercessian, *Against All Odds*, 270. Originally from North Carolina, Dr. Harrison graduated from Tufts College Medical School in 1906. He was a resident of 85 Chandler Street and maintained a practice at 35 Common Street.

809 "Colored Nurses' School," 3.

810 *Official Souvenir Program of the Sixteenth Convention of the National Negro Business League* (Boston: A. W. Lavalle, 1915), 53.

811 The School of Nursing at Boston City Hospital did not admit African American women until 1929. That year two black women were admitted, Frances Harris and Letitia Campfield.

812 "Colored Doctors Name Officers," *Boston Daily Globe*, Aug. 27, 1909, 7.

813 Kenney, *The Negro in Medicine*, 30.

814 Nercessian, *Against All Odds*, 273.

815 *The Boston Directory ... for the Year Commencing July 1, 1916*, 2354.

816 Mary Kaplan, *Solomon Carter Fuller: Where My Caravan Has Rested* (Lanham, MD: University Press of America, 2005), 18.

817 It was later known as the Westborough State Hospital.

818 Kaplan, *Solomon Carter Fuller*, 21; *First Annual Report of the Trustees of the Westborough Insane Hospital for the Year Ending September 30, 1885* (Boston: Wright and Potter, 1886), 3.

819 W. Montague Cobb, "Solomon Carter Fuller, 1872–1953," *Journal of the National Medical Association* 46, no. 5, Sept. 1954, 370.

820 "Homeopathy's Foothold," *Boston Globe*, Wednesday, Apr. 10, 1901, p. 7; "Four Cases of Pernicious Anemia Among Insane Subjects," *New England Medical Gazette*, 1901.

821 Among Fuller's other contributions to the medical literature in his field are: "A Study of the Neurofibrils in Dementia Paralytica, Dementia Senilis, Chronic Alcoholism, Cerebral Lues and Microcephalic Idiosy" (*American Journal of Insanity*, 1906); "An Analysis of 100 Cases of Dementia Praecox in Men" (*Proceedings of the Society of Neurology and Psychiatry*, 1908); "An Analysis of 3,140 Admissions to Westborough State Hospital, with Reference to the Diagnosis of Involutional Melancholia" (*Proceedings of the Society of Neurology and Psychiatry*, 1911); "A Study of the Miliary Plaques Found in Brains of the Aged" (*American Journal of Psychiatry*, 1911), and "Alzheimer's Disease: the Report of a Case and Review of Published Cases" (*Journal of Nervous and Mental Disease*, 1912). See Kenney, *The Negro in Medicine*, 14–15.

822 Orna Ophir, *Psychosis, Psychoanalysis and Psychiatry in Postwar USA: On the Borderland of Madness* (New York: Routledge, 2015), 10.

823 W. Scott Terry, "A Missed Opportunity for Psychology: The Story of Solomon Carter Fuller," *Association for Psychological Science Observer*, June/July 2008, 1. <http://psychologicalscience.org/observer/getArticle.cfm?id = 2357> (accessed Dec. 28, 2013).

824 Cobb, "Solomon Carter Fuller, 1872–1953," *Journal of the National Medical Association*, 371.

825 Cobb, "Solomon Carter Fuller," 370.

826 In 1940, Harvard Dental School was reorganized as Harvard School of Dental Medicine. The first African American to obtain a degree in dentistry was Robert Tanner Freeman, who had graduated from the same school a year earlier but elected to establish his practice in Washington, DC.

827 "Professor and Judge," 6.

828 George Grant—Black Inventor Online Museum http://www. blackinventor. com/pages/george-grant.html, Accessed Dec. 1, 2013.

829 Daniels, *In Freedom's Birthplace*, 360; "Professor and Judge," 6.

830 "Professor and Judge," 6; *The Boston Almanac and Business Directory 1880*, 257.

831 Nercessian, *Against All Odds*, 83.

832 *Quinquennial Catalogue of the Dental School of Harvard University 1869–1920* (Cambridge: Harvard Dental School, 1920), 91.

833 *Boston 1910 Directory*, 1578.

834 Nercessian, *Against All Odds*, 270.

835 "Graduation at Girls' High School: Diplomas Presented to 348 Seniors," *Boston Daily Globe*, Thursday, June 22, 1916, 9.

836 The *Boston Directory Containing the City Record, a Directory of the Citizens, Business Directory and Street Directory with Map for the Year Commencing July 1, 1921, No. CXVII* (Boston: Sampson & Murdock, 1921), 1851.

837 *The Boston Directory for the Year Commencing August 1, 1930, No. CXXVI* (Boston: Sampson & Murdock, 1930), 2660.

838 Robert C. Hayden, Jr., *Pills, Potions, Powders and Poisons: A Pioneering African American in Pharmacy: Robert H. Carter III (1847–1908).* (Littleton, Mass.: Tapestry Press, 2010). 9–10, 34.

839 , Hayden, *Pills, Potions, Powders and Poisons*, 39.

840 *The Boston Directory Containing the City Record, Directory of the Citizens, Business Directory and Street Directory with Map for the Year Commencing July 1, 1904, No. C* (Boston: Sampson & Murdock, 1904), 359.

841 Elmer Anderson Carter, "In the News Columns: Thomas William Patrick," in *Opportunity Journal of Negro Life* XV, no. 4, April 1937: 102.

842 Nercessian, *Against All Odds*, 269.

843 "Negro Business League: Annual Nation Convention in Nashville Next Week Will Have Many Boston Delegates," *Boston Daily Globe*, Thursday, Aug. 13, 1903, 6; "Colored Businessmen Meet at Nashville," *Boston Post*, Thursday, Aug. 20, 1903, 5.

844 Thomas William Patrick, *Patrick's Course in Pharmacy: Specially Designed for Preparing Drug Clerks to Pass the Board of Pharmacy ... in*

Twenty Lessons (Boston: Blanchard Printing, 1906); Carter, "In the News Columns: Thomas William Patrick," 102.

845 *The Boston Directory for the Year Commencing August 1, 1927, No. CXXIII* (Boston: Sampson & Murdock, 1927), 1892; *The Boston Directory for the Year Commencing August 1, 1928, No. CXXIV* (Boston: Sampson & Murdock, 1928), 1867.

846 Bay State Pharmacy placed an ad in the Alpha Phi Alpha Fraternity's 1948 Eastern Regional Convention Program. The convention took place in Boston from November 19 through November 21, 1948. At that time, the pharmacy was still located at 840 Tremont Street.

847 "Mary Eliza Mahoney," *Winston-Salem Chronicle*, Thursday, Jan. 26, 1989, C7; Edward T. James, ed., *Notable American Women 1607–1950: A Biographical Dictionary, Vol. I* (Cambridge, MA: Belknap Press of Harvard University Press, 1971), 486.

848 See *Annual Report of the School Committee of the City of Boston, 1864* (Boston: J. E. Farwell, 1864), 274; *Register and Circular of the State Normal School at Salem, Mass., Spring and Summer Term, 1868*, 4.

849 *Annual Report of the School Committee of the City of Boston, 1894* (Boston: Rockwell and Churchill, 1894), 164; *Annual Report of the School Committee of the City of Boston, 1899* (Boston: Municipal Printing, 1899), 241; "Local Summary," *Boston Post*, Thursday, Apr. 24, 1879, Column A; "Local Summary," *Boston Post*, Wednesday, Dec. 3, 1879, Column B.

850 "Woman's Realm: Something about Mrs. Ruffin, Colored Delegate that was Barred at Woman's Federation," *Duluth News-Tribune*, published as *Sunday News Tribune*, June 17, 1900, 21.

851 *Annual Report of the School Committee for the City of Boston, 1879* (Boston: Rockwell and Churchill, 1879), 58; "Graduation Time," *Boston Daily Advertiser*, Tuesday, June 29, 1880, issue 156, column H; *Annual Report of the School Committee of the City of Boston, 1880* (Boston: Rockwell and Churchill, 1881), 54; "The Public Schools: Appointments Confirmed," *Boston Daily Globe*, Supplement, Wednesday, Oct. 13, 1880, 1; "School Board Session," *Boston Daily Globe*, Wednesday, Oct. 26, 1881, 1; "The School Board," *Boston Daily Globe*, Wednesday, Jan. 24, 1883, 4.

852 *Annual Report of the School Committee for the City of Boston, 1882* (Boston: Rockwell and Churchill, 1883), 171; *Annual Report of the School Committee for the City of Boston, 1888* (Boston: Rockwell and Churchill, 1889), 183; *Annual Report of the School Committee for the City of Boston, 1889* (Boston: Rockwell and Churchill, 1890), 281. Florida Y. Ruffin married Ulysses A. Ridley on Oct. 13, 1888.

853 The other young black woman was Sarah E. Tynes. "Graduation Exercises: Cambridge High School," *Boston Post*, Thursday, July 2, 1874.

854 "Suburban Matters: Cambridge, School Board Meeting," *Boston Post*, Saturday, Nov. 18, 1882, 1.

855 *Blue Book of Cambridge for 1895: Containing a List of the Leading Residents, Societies, Etc.* (Boston: Edward A. Jones, 1894), 10.

856 "Brains, Not Color: Men of Negro Race Have Chance in Cambridge, Prominent in Politics and the Learned Professions," *Boston Daily Globe*, Aug. 16, 1903, 20.

857 Edward T. James, *Notable American Women 1607–1950: A Biographical Dictionary, Vol. 1* (Cambridge, MA.: Belknap Press of Harvard University Press, 2004), 87.

858 Among the women who founded the League of Women for Community Service were Maria Louise Baldwin, Josephine St. Pierre Ruffin, and her daughter, Florida Ruffin Ridley.

859 "Colored Women Open Clubhouse: Soup Kitchen Part of Its Community Service," *Boston Daily Globe*, Mar. 21, 1920, 48.

Index

Strodder, John 199
Strong, Lester 265
Stuart, Charles 118, 260
(Stuart), Matthew 118
Stull, Donald A. 143
Stull, Donald L. 143
Sullivan, Leon 93, 94, 320
Sullivan, Leon, Reverend 93
Sumner, Charles 8, 284, 287, 351
Suttle, Charles F. 271
Swift, Jane 129
Sykes, Kirk 175, 334

T

Taft, President 277
Taft, William Howard 275
Taney, Roger 10
Tarantino, Francis 108
Taylor, Frazier xix
Taylor, Nancy S., Reverend 268
Taylor, Thomas 124
Taylor, Walter O., Dr. 294
Teamoh, Robert 233
Teamoh, Robert Thomas 273
Terry, Lucy 232
Thernstrom, Stephan 203, 337
Thompson, Gilbert 115
Thornell, Consuela 192
Till, Emmett 248, 263
Timilty, Joseph 55
Tompkins, Steve 130
Toon, Thurman 266
Tosado, Jose 44
Tourse, Dennis 338
Tourse, Dennis R. 210
Trotter, James Monroe 276
Trotter, John 156
(Trotter), Maude 277

Trotter, Virginia Isaacs 276
Trotter, William Monroe xxi, xxiii,
    227, 234, 236, 276, 287, 294,
    342, 3346
Trump, Donald 64
Tsongas, Paul 35
Turner, Charles "Chuck" 71, 73, 75,
    83, 84, 85, 201, 215, 222, 317,
    339, 340
Turner, Chuck 71, 73, 75, 83, 84, 85,
    222, 317, 339, 340
Tutu, Desmond, Bishop 99

V

Van Der Meer, Tony 41
Vaughan, Harold 326
Vaughan, Harold J. 142
Vega, Aaron 44
Vest, George 109
Volpe, John 28, 30, 68, 81
Vrabel, Jim 66, 316

W

Walcott, Eugene xv
Walker, Adrian 266
Walker, David 6, 271, 272, 343
Walker, Edwin G. 285
Walker, Edwin Garrison 271, 272
Walker, Liz 257, 260, 262
Walker, Quock 269, 342
Walker, Richard xviii
Wall, Bruce, Reverend 108
Wall, Bruce 112
Wallace, George 15
Walsh, Martin 120, 122, 126
Walsh, Martin J. 57
Ward, Karen Holmes 261, 265
Warren, Joseph 191

Z

CPSIA information can be obtained
at www.ICGtesting.com
Printed in the USA
LVHW092132270720
661693LV00001B/17